Seasons They Change

Seasons They Change

THE STORY OF Acid AND Psychedelic Folk

Jeanette Leech

FOREWORD BY Greg Weeks

Vashti Bunyan and Devendra Banhart,
Glasgow, Scotland, 2005.

Seasons They Change

THE STORY OF ACID AND PSYCHEDELIC FOLK

JEANETTE LEECH

A GENUINE JAWBONE BOOK
First Edition 2010
Published in the UK and the USA by Jawbone Press
2a Union Court,
20–22 Union Road,
London SW4 6JP,
England

www.jawbonepress.com

ISBN 978-1-906002-32-9

DESIGN Paul Cooper Design
EDITOR Thomas Jerome Seabrook

Printed by Everbest Printing Co Ltd, China

1 2 3 4 5 14 13 12 11 10

Contents

CLOCKWISE FROM TOP LEFT: **Shirley and Dolly Collins at work on their 1966 LP** *The Sweet Primeroses*; **Robin Williamson (left) and Mike Heron of The Incredible String Band during sessions for** *Wee Tam And The Big Huge*; **a late-60s Elektra promo shot of The Holy Modal Rounders.**

CLOCKWISE FROM LEFT: **Tim Buckley in Copenhagen, Denmark, October 1969; an early promo shot of Vashti Bunyan, taken around the time of her 'Train Song' single; Tom Rapp on stage in 1972; Bonnie Dobson among the flowers in Ashdown Forest, East Sussex, during the summer of 1969.**

CLOCKWISE FROM TOP LEFT: **Dr Strangely Strange** take a tea break, 1970; Anne and Graham Hemingway of **The Sun Also Rises** during a rare television appearance; an early promo shot of **Comus** in a local woodland.

CLOCKWISE FROM ABOVE: **Mark Fry** outside a church near Carrara, Italy, 1971; Mellow Candle, pictured around the time of their *Swaddling Songs* LP, 1972; an intimate performance by Collie Ryan.

CLOCKWISE FROM LEFT: **Current 93**'s David Tibet, with Noddys, 1988; an early promo shot of Bobb Trimble, taken around the time of his debut LP, *Iron Curtain Innocence*; Sonja Kristina with Tim and Simon Whitaker, with whom she made *Songs From The Acid Folk*, 1991.

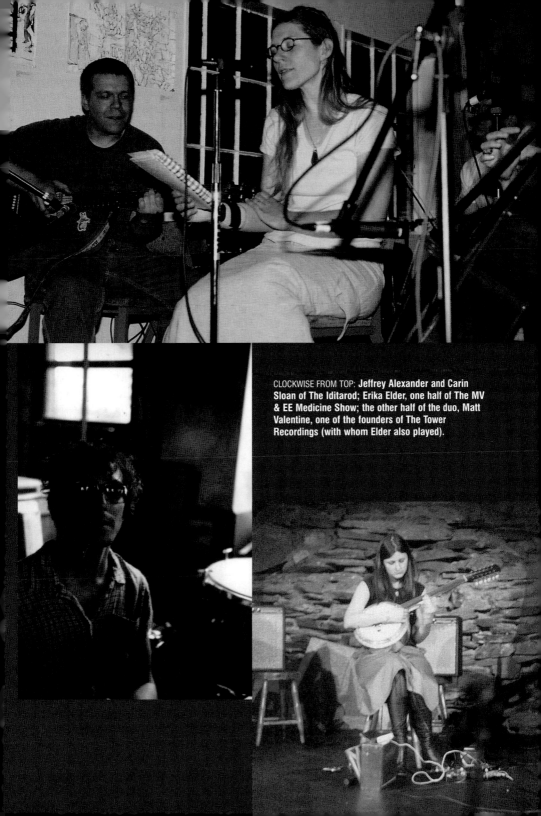

CLOCKWISE FROM TOP: **Jeffrey Alexander and Carin Sloan of The Iditarod; Erika Elder, one half of The MV & EE Medicine Show; the other half of the duo, Matt Valentine, one of the founders of The Tower Recordings (with whom Elder also played).**

CLOCKWISE FROM TOP LEFT: **Sharron Kraus**, pictured around the time of her 2002 LP *Beautiful Twisted*; Alasdair Roberts on stage at the Go Slow Café in Glasgow, Scotland, 2009; Marissa Nadler, 2009; an out-take from the shoot for Joanna Newsom's debut LP, *The Milk-Eyed Mender*, taken in her back yard in San Francisco, September 2003; Andy Cabic (left) and Devendra Banhart at work on the first Vetiver demo.

Espers at Big Sur, 2006.

Foreword

Tradition holds that cultural movements are on the wane once published materials about them hit the mainstream (or the microstream, within which most musical movements are framed). This is certainly the case concerning the psychedelic folk revival of the early 21st century, which peaked in the public eye long after it reached critical mass in terms of cult currency. Longevity has never been pop culture's strength, so it helps, when lamenting the relative obscurity of a critical artist or band – an act I am certainly guilty of – or when musing over the average three-to-five year lifespan of the psych-folk progenitors of the 60s and 70s, to be thankful that any artist that one loves is granted lodging in the semi-permanence of cultural memory.

It is unfortunate (and yet critical) that the inherent strengths of new musical movements lie within their generative qualities. Once we've figured out what's actually going on within the music – the stuff that makes it fresh or exciting – the initial vitality turns regenerative, a quality resulting in far less palatable versions of what initially was so exciting.

David Bowie understood this fact better than any modern rock artist and acted accordingly, shifting his musical focus and visual aesthetic to mirror the shifting tastes of the times. It takes a particular skill and disposition to carry out that brand of constant reinvention (not to mention a questionable desire to want to). Such attempts destroyed many a classic rock or folk artist's career as the 70s slipped into the 80s, illuminating the unforgiving nature of a fickle populace and the desperate moves artists are willing to make in order to maintain a viable career (one that keeps them eating and under a sound roof).

Ideally, musicianship and songwriting are crafts to be honed over decades. Folk music is largely about community. Music itself is about what came before. As your style of music falls out of favour the purity of your convictions are tested, which is an interesting thing. One of the nicest yet saddest aspects of the momentarily rejuvenated careers of psychedelic folk's initial heralds is the fact that they had to be rediscovered at all. Most of us who followed in their wake will be lucky to meet a similar fate.

My focus may seem dour, but accepting that folk and psychedelic music, once driving cultural forces, have now been relegated to the periphery is perhaps the best way to illuminate the significance of a tome dedicated to understanding the deep connections between the form's first and second wave artists. As technology continues to blur cultural boundaries, it is interesting to see an evocation of a musical movement that plucked inspiration from a largely forgotten form, built itself up through a true community of friends and artists, and was largely happy to remain under the shadow of obscurity from whence it originated. Perhaps obscurity is for the best.

Greg Weeks
August 2010

CHAPTER 1

Hares On The Mountain

IN THE WINTER OF 1953, when Shirley Elizabeth Collins arrived in London at the age of 18, she had one thing in mind: "to get to Cecil Sharp House and look at as many books as I possibly could".

After a false start at teacher training college in Tooting and a stint as a bus conductress in Hastings, it had become clear to Collins that she wanted to pursue what had been in her genes since her earliest memories: the singing of folk songs. "We sang at home a lot because there wasn't much else going on in those days," she recalls. "Singing was just part of everyday life. Three of my best songs came from home: 'Just As The Tide Is Flowing', which Aunt Grace taught us two verses of, a version of 'The Cuckoo' from my great granny, and 'The Bonny Labouring Boy', which granddad sang."

Collins's relocation to London was timely. She found herself at the tornado's eye of a folk revolution that began at Cecil Sharp House and took root in the cities and suburbs of Britain. It diversified and redefined exactly what folk music was, and what it could become. Collins herself would be instrumental in helping folk open out into this space of possibility.

During the mid 50s, however, these gatherings were largely centred on two places: around the cellar at Cecil Sharp House, at events run by Peter Kennedy, the director of the English Folk Dance And Song Society; and at University College London, where they were organised by John Hasted, a physics professor and folk musician who took banjo and guitar lessons with Pete Seeger. The same crowd of 20 or 30 people would attend both sets of events. "They were youthful gatherings," Collins recalls. "There we were, all milling around, not really knowing what we were doing, but being encouraged by these two blokes. We were all people who were really keen to sing."

This small scene began to change when Ewan MacColl came to prominence. Born in Lancashire to Scottish parents, MacColl had felt his interest in folk music growing since the early 50s, while his enthusiasm for his first chosen career – acting – began to wane. He too had come to London and found in these 'singarounds' an outlet for his fascination with traditional music; unlike Collins, however, he was keen to steer the shape and direction of the gatherings to his own particular interpretations of the folk tradition. With his partner, Peggy Seeger, he formed the Critics Group, dedicated to both the preservation of folk songs and the provision of an appropriate forum for the songs' serious exhibition.

In a 2002 editorial for *The Living Tradition* magazine, Seeger wrote that the intention of the Critics Group was to preserve songs within their original social and artistic parameters. The upshot of this was a policy that prohibited any singer from performing a song from a language or culture that he or she wasn't born into. There was an associated rule that the songs should be performed without accompaniment of any sort – again, unless a singer was born into doing so. The idea was not to tell singers what – or how – to sing, Seeger added, although she did admit: "If we became evangelical and sounded dictatorial, well – that's the way things go. The intentions were honourable."

MacColl and Seeger's prescriptive attitude annoyed Shirley Collins, following as it did the more intimate, democratic attitude of the earlier gatherings. "I didn't like his singing and I didn't like him," she says of MacColl. "He was a bit hectoring, and the Critics Group was ruled with a rod of iron." Collins felt that MacColl passed judgement both on the songs that were sung and the people who got up on stage. "It was like cloning people," she says. "And I didn't want to be part of that production line."

M

Born a few years later than Collins was someone else who resolutely refused to be boxed. The young Davy Graham (sometimes 'Davey') had come to London with his parents as a child and had grown up in Ladbroke Grove. He became fascinated with the guitar in his early teens, and at the age of 18 left London to busk in Greece, Tangiers, and Paris, where he was spotted by Elizabeth Taylor and ended up performing at one of her star-studded parties on the French Riviera. Whenever he returned to London, he came to the coffee shops of Soho, displaying ever more impressive techniques that he had picked up firsthand from the likes of Steve Benbow, whose interpretation of 'Miserlou' was a very early example of the incorporation of Eastern exoticism into British folk music.

Graham was never so intrinsic a part of the folk community as Collins. He had grown up with a fierce love of rock'n'roll, which in turn led to an involvement in jazz and the emerging British blues scene. His eclectic influences and huge talent were such that, when he was just 18, he was featured in Ken Russell's 1959 BBC documentary *Hound Dogs & Bach Addicts: The Guitar Craze*, in which he fingerpicks his way through an inventive and highly complex version of 'Cry Me A River'. Two years later, he recorded the EP *3/4* in collaboration with Alexis Korner, the pioneering instrumental 'Angi' at its centre. Around 1962 he began using the DADGAD guitar tuning, most notably in his arrangement of 'She Moves Through The Fair'. This intense, bushy-haired young man was forging acres of new ground during the early 60s; every other guitarist in Britain was watching him very closely indeed.

While both Collins and Graham were making their first records – Collins's *False True Lovers*, a haunting collection of British and American traditional songs, came out in 1959 – a network of folk clubs inspired by the singarounds had begun to spring up. Ewan MacColl's brusque attitude may have infuriated some, but he was a very good publicist, and his Critics Group a highly visible focal point and inspiration for others. This was a truly grassroots, locally driven phenomenon; the form and rules of the clubs – if there were any – differed from place to place, although many did follow MacColl and Seeger's lead. As the 60s dawned, they had become a visible and vital presence in even the smallest of towns.

The rise of these clubs took place in parallel with the sharper ascent (and quicker decline) of another largely youth-driven movement in Britain: skiffle. Invigorated by blues, jazz, and – eventually – rock'n'roll, energetic British teenagers had started to adapt furniture and bric-a-brac into primitive yet effectively noisy instruments, their enthusiasm often sustained by the live shows of US bluesmen like Big Bill Broonzy and Brownie McGhee. From 1955 onward, Lonnie Donegan gave skiffle its own hero, and when his version of Leadbelly's 'Rock Island Line' became a huge hit in 1956, the skiffle craze spread through the youth of the country. Significantly, skiffle groups would often include in their sets a few frenzied takes on folk songs from the British Isles, and with even Ewan MacColl and Peggy Seeger performing in Alan Lomax's skiffle group The Ramblers in the mid 50s, the new fad for skiffle and the revival of interest in traditional music became closely related, even if they didn't always agree with one another.

Like folk music, skiffle had its own public space. The British coffeehouses of the late 50s played host to teenagers motivated by nothing more complicated than a desire to escape their parents, down espressos, and crowd around the jukebox to enthuse over the latest American releases and gossip on who did what with whom. For some, whether blessed with precocious talent or brimming over with self-confidence, these coffeehouses were a platform. Among the budding young performers were the rambunctious Suzie & The Hula Hoops, formed in 1959 and featuring a young Mark Feld (later known as Marc Bolan) and Helen Shapiro, both of whom were clearly already developing a taste for the stage.

The vigour of performing traditional song – whether unaccompanied in folk clubs or with an impromptu cigar-box fiddle in a coffeehouse in Hackney – made folk music seem approachable and relevant again. Skiffle and folk clubs were a seedbed for a new, open approach to traditional song and expression. These twin developments were the foundations upon which British folk music of the 60s and 70s came to grow. A high proportion of the musicians who would go on to make eclectic folk records a decade or so later had their first youthful taste of creating music in skiffle bands.

Meanwhile, Shirley Collins and Davy Graham had both spent the early part of the 60s gathering a diverse set of experiences, and now, in their own way, projected a rebellious image that would occasionally set them at odds with the folk establishment. During this period, Collins released several EPs on Topic Records, as well as the album *Sweet England*, while concurrently gaining a formidable reputation for her performances throughout the folk clubs of Britain. "I'm not saying that I was being criticised all the time," she says. "Some people liked what I did, but quite a few people didn't. They didn't like the arrangements I was using and they didn't like the fact that I worked with Davy Graham."

If Collins attracted criticism, then Graham was either disapproved of or ignored entirely. He did not particularly see himself as a folk artist, and yet his 1963 LP *The Guitar Player* was – one original aside – a furious ride through inventive reinterpretations of American jazz and rhythm & blues into folk instrumentals, each track arranged with breathtaking originality. "I find I'm more happy arranging tunes," he told *Ptolemaic Terrascope* magazine in one of his final published interviews. "It's like setting a jewel in a ring."[1] The recurring Eastern motifs on *The Guitar Player* – most notably 'How Long,

How Long Blues' and a spacey 'Cry Me A River', here sounding radically different to the version performed on *The Guitar Craze* – brought a very new attitude to the acoustic guitar.

Shirley Collins and Davy Graham knew each other, and they knew each other's work. They had met a number of times during the early 60s, but the impetus to work together came at the suggestion of Collins's husband, 'Austin' John Marshall, a jazz enthusiast who greatly admired *The Guitar Player* and Graham's integration of Indian and Arabic influences into his work. Furthermore, Collins noted a similarity between the modes of Arabian music and the Appalachian folksong she had experienced firsthand while touring America with Alan Lomax in 1959. Graham in turn was impressed by Collins's voice and presence.

"I remember hearing Shirley sing 'I Rode To Church Last Sunday'," he later recalled. "That lovely blonde hair with a kind of high collar, floral long-sleeved blouse with sort of lace, and a banjo. And every time I'd get the goose pimples when I'd hear her sing 'Lord Gregory'."[2]

Graham joined Collins on stage at the Mercury Theatre in London in July 1964; shortly afterward, the pair took their newfound creative partnership into the recording studio. The resulting *Folk Roots, New Routes* bulldozed the barriers of folk music in Britain. Recorded in Decca's Studio 3 in West Hampstead during September 1964, it was produced by Ray Horricks and engineered by Gus Dudgeon.

Collins remembers the experience with fondness, the odd personality clash notwithstanding. "Musically, it was wonderful," she says. "It was extremely exhilarating, and [Graham] just had such a remarkably different approach." *Folk Roots, New Routes* contains fiery re-interpretations of 13 traditional songs, one Graham instrumental, and two jazz numbers. Graham's complex fingerpicking draws together and develops the diverse influences he explored on *The Guitar Player* while pulsating against Collins' nuanced, melancholy vocal interpretations.

Graham later claimed that, while Collins had learnt the modes of the tunes, he hadn't. It was this, coupled with their differing backgrounds and perspectives, that made *Folk Roots, New Routes* such a successful experiment. It *was* a folk album, since an album largely comprised of traditional material performed acoustically could not reasonably be called by any other name, but it was also something *else*.

Decca Records didn't know and probably didn't care what it had on its hands at the time, however. The label's interest in the record was likely grounded in a desire to cash in on the folk boom rather than seriously expecting – or even wanting – an album as experimental as this. *Folk Roots, New Routes* was sold as a 'folk-swinging' album. It usually shared advertising space with Graham's *Folk, Blues And Beyond*, which was released around the same time and pushed even further his fascination for and expertise in the instruments and styles of Eastern music.

Graham's influence lay not only in his technical proficiency and experimentation but his overall interest in counterculture and exotic philosophies. "He would always have some book on the go," Collins recalls. "Some Oriental or Indian mystic, or he'd lend you one." Although Collins's own interest in these belief systems was limited – as was her patience for the increasingly copious amounts of drugs that Graham was using – the pair's mutual respect endured to span a few concerts in 1964 and 1965 to support the album, most notably at Cecil Sharp House itself, where the performance was billed as A Folk Blues Happening. *Folk Roots, New Routes* unlocked what was possible in British folk, and most of the experimental folk that followed owes it a debt.

ᛝ

Collins and Graham weren't alone in adopting a progressive attitude to folk music as it began to rub up against the transformative society of the 60s. The emergence of *Folk Roots, New Routes* shone a hindsight light on those barely perceptible movements that had taken place beforehand. The live reputations of Martin Carthy, The Copper Family, The Watersons, and Hamish Imlach, among others, showed that sensitive preservation of folksong could be twinned with modernity, making centuries-old songs as relevant to the shape-shifting 60s as they had been to pre-industrial Britain. This was a more muted progress than that made by Collins and Graham, but it would prove influential in its own way.

The popularity of these British folk revival singers allowed a virtuous and increasing circle to develop between folk artists and collectors. Archivists like A.L. Lloyd and Peter Kennedy (as well as the record company Topic) were already aware that their work was valuable from a preservation point of view, but the anthologising and performance of folksong was now also starting to become commercially viable. It was becoming easier – in practical terms – for the public to acquire folksong anthologies and learn about traditional music of the British Isles without necessarily having grown up with it.

One revival singer tackled the tradition with a particularly modern, liberated mettle. Anne Briggs barely set foot in a recording studio during the 60s, but gained a strong reputation for her unusually pure voice and bucking-horse wildness. She could improvise like a jazz singer and drink anyone under the table.

In 1959, the 15-year-old Briggs hitched from Nottingham to Edinburgh, attracted to its folk scene; by 1962 she had relocated to London. She quickly and easily became a noticeable part of the still relatively small folk club scene, but playing the game of building a career was another thing entirely. She released an EP of her own on Topic, 1964's *The Hazards Of Love*, and contributed to two more EPs of unaccompanied traditional songs – *The Iron Muse* (1963) and *The Bird In The Bush* (1966) – but was generally unconcerned with leaving recorded footprints, or even performing for money. Instead, having seldom stayed in one place for very long, she spent most of her mid-60s summers in Ireland, playing the bouzouki and busking. "It was always much easier to do informal sessions in the Irish countryside with traditional musicians or busking in the street," she said.[3]

Briggs would not become widely known until she recorded an album for CBS in the early 70s, but her youthful, unruly attitude was inspirational to many on the 60s scene. She was driven by a desire to kick against convention and expectations, which she did regularly. "The role of women was very defined and restrictive," she later said, "but right through my teenage years, I'd just been shedding everything as I went. Why can't I do that if blokes can do it? In fact, I'm going to do it, so try and stop me and see what happens."[4]

The character of folk music in the UK was changing, and it was also subject to shocks coming from across the Atlantic. No one could ignore the phenomenal impact of Bob Dylan. He was a fixture in the music press, his songs were covered by a huge and diverse array of musicians, and the more cerebral teenagers couldn't get enough of him. "I realised that there was something going on," says David Costa, a North London teen during the early 60s and later a member of Trees. "I would look at album sleeves and see this name continually appearing: Dylan, Dylan, Dylan."

While Dylan's most visible effect was to usher in a school of wide-eyed young bucks anxious to share their own poetic observations and acoustic strumming, his influence worked in a more subtle way to make the singer-songwriter part of the popular definition of folk music in Britain. Those who wrote and performed their own material were by no means always accepted as 'folk artists', but the popular classification of 'folk' was undoubtedly starting to include American (and British) singer-songwriters.

25

The young Scottish guitarist Bert Jansch was a close friend of Anne Briggs and shared her wayward defiance. "I identified with his music, and somehow he identified with my very traditional approach to ballads," Briggs later recalled. "It was like we unlocked musical doors for each other."[5] During the winter of 1962–63, Briggs and Jansch shared a squat in Earl's Court and bounced off each other's considerable talent, writing songs and sharing ideas. The poignant 'Wishing Well', 'The Time Has Come', and 'Go Your Way My Love' are from this period. Briggs also taught Jansch the traditional 'Blackwater Side'.

In terms of guitar playing, Jansch was influenced both by the blues and by his peers, especially Davy Graham. (He received guitar lessons in the early 60s from Jill Doyle, Graham's sister.) By the time *Bert Jansch* emerged in April 1965 on the Transatlantic label, however, its 19-year-old author had mutated the Graham influence into his own distinctive style. Although it is technically an album of acoustic guitar and voice, recorded cheaply in Bill Leader's kitchen, straight to Revox, *Bert Jansch* seemed to recreate the backstage jams, late-night political debates, and heartbreaks of metropolitan jazz. 'Casbah' fuses Charles Mingus with Scottish open spaces to create a new brand of loneliness, while the stark 'Needle Of Death' pits the narrative intensity of the traditional ballad against the contemporary subject of heroin use. The deserted air of *Bert Jansch* summed up the artist's situation at the time. "From leaving school up until my first marriage I was a tramp on the streets," he later recalled. "When I made the first album, I had no home and no possessions, not even a guitar. I borrowed one from Martin Carthy for the recording."[6]

Bert Jansch is an early milestone in British singer-songwriter folk, both for its stylistic invention and its lyrical content – and indeed for not aping Bob Dylan. Jansch followed it with another intense, insular mediation, *It Don't Bother Me*, which solidified his reputation and stretched into new areas on the political 'Anti-Apartheid' and the banjo-led '900 Miles'. It was also the first of his albums to feature John Renbourn, who plays on the guitar duel 'Lucky Thirteen'.

Renbourn was another blues aficionado – a badge the Londoner wore on his sleeve for his self-titled 1966 debut. By the time of 'Lucky Thirteen', Jansch and Renbourn were among the most well-respected and inventive musicians in Britain. Their elaborate, Davy Graham-derived style was often tagged as 'folk-baroque'. They shared a flat and ran a club together at the Three Horseshoes on Tottenham Court Road, London, while their recorded collaborations flowed thick and fast. Jansch's *Jack Orion* (1966) features Renbourn heavily, and was a huge step forward from *It Don't Bother Me*. But it was on *Bert & John*, released around the same time, that folk-baroque reached its apex. The album is primarily instrumental, with Jansch and Renbourn's own compositions at its core, but also features Anne Briggs's 'The Time Has Come' and Charles Mingus's 'Goodbye Pork Pie Hat'. The importance of the album was in the approach. It is taut and youthful, yet permeated with an older wisdom so pregnant with possibility.

There were a number of US folk ex-pats in London, and one in particular was taken to the heart of the British community. Jackson C. Frank dated Sandy Denny for a while, and his generous nature helped several impoverished performers find their next meal. Bert Jansch would later make clear the influence of Frank's consummate song-craft on his fellow performers.

As Frank wrote on the back of his self-titled 1965 debut: "In the field of creative endeavour, anything that can confuse us totally is generally given over to rejection or abject praise." *Jackson C. Frank* fused the Greenwich Village and London folk scenes but with a haunting dejection all of its own, and contributed significantly to the forging of new ground in British folk.

Jackson Carey Frank's early life had been far from easy. In 1954, at the age of 11, he was involved in a horrific accident that killed 15 students at his newly built school in Cheektowaga, New York. "It had a wooden annexe that was used for music instruction," he recalled in 1995. "It was heated by a big furnace. One day during music lessons in the annexe the furnace blew up."[7] Jackson was rushed to hospital, and remained there for seven months. When he emerged he had extensive and noticeable physical scarring, as well as the obvious psychological trauma.

If such an incident could ever have a positive side, it was that it gave the young Jackson, already blessed with a high tenor voice, space to develop as a guitar player. Encouraged by hospital visits from his tutor, Charlie Casatelli, Jackson began to see the instrument as a vessel for expressing his emotions. He continued to play throughout his teens, and by the age of 17 had developed a particular passion for Civil War songs. "I would record the ones I could sing," he later recalled. "I remember going into the studio back then and cutting a side of tracks for seven dollars."[8]

By 1964, Frank had started to hang out at the Limelight, a coffeehouse in Buffalo, New York, where he enjoyed live performances by local folkies and travelling blues artists. Later that year, after finally receiving a $100,000 insurance settlement – ten years after the accident – Frank wound up in London. He had begun writing his own songs and joined up with fellow ex-pats Paul Simon and Art Garfunkel.

Beneath his open-handed exterior, Frank was desperately self-conscious about his abilities. According to Al Stewart, who was present at the recording session for Jackson's album: "Even when Paul [Simon, who produced the album] would say, 'OK, we're ready,' often this would be followed by two or three minutes of total silence while he [Frank] psyched himself into singing."[9] Frank literally screened himself from view. "I remember hiding behind a screen while I was singing and playing," he recalled. "I was just a little nervous and I didn't want anyone else to see me."[10]

Jackson C. Frank is full of rhythmically vibrant arrangements and throbs with a verve that belies its downbeat subject matter. 'Yellow Walls', which features second guitar by Al Stewart, is the most adventurous of all, echoing the outer limits of the Bert Jansch oeuvre, while the acerbic 'Milk And Honey' precipitated the new directions in folk so effectively that it would translate easily to a psychedelic interpretation by Bonnie Dobson in 1970.

Frank's friends dearly loved the album, as did the local folk community in London, and some of the wider public got to hear the music through the brief patronage of John Peel. For Frank himself, however, things were beginning to fall apart. The insecurity he displayed at the recording session became more prominent as the appreciative audiences diminished and writer's block started to hamper his songwriting. With his wealth dwindling, he returned to the USA in 1966. When he came back to Britain in 1968, he was a changed man. "He started doing things that were completely impenetrable," Al Stewart later recalled. "They were basically about psychological angst, played at full volume with lots of thrashing. I don't remember a single word of them; it just did not work."[11] Although Jackson C. Frank cut some increasingly fraught, desperate demos over the years, he never released another record.

The next key development in British folk took root in Scotland, and would ultimately lead the music in an incredible new direction. Robin Williamson was born in Edinburgh and had a twin fascination for folk and beat culture. "My big influence was Jack Kerouac," he says. "I wanted to try and write spontaneously, but I also liked traditional music. I liked things like Jeannie Robinson, Joe Heaney, those sort of traditional British forms, and was looking for some fusion between Jack Kerouac and Scots-Irish traditional music."

Another important influence was the American musician Tom Paley, who turned up in Edinburgh looking for a fiddle player in the early 60s. "I ended up doing a tour with him round about 1962, when I was about 19," Williamson continues. "He pretty much taught me how to play fiddle." Paley was a member of The New Lost City Ramblers, who specialised in old-timey music and had done much to spark revivals of interest in it Stateside.

When Williamson encountered the 20-year-old Londoner Clive Palmer in 1963 he found someone who had already been performing for more than half his life. Palmer had endured a bout of polio as a child, during which time he saw hospitals as "my second home", but despite this had also been a raging success as a child performer. He appeared on stage with a dance troupe at the age of eight and began playing solo shows shortly thereafter before finding local fame with his skiffle group.

Palmer had been playing banjo since the age of ten, and spent his teenage years hanging around the jazz clubs and coffee bars of London and Brighton. A stint at art college followed, as did a period of busking in Paris, sometimes with Wizz Jones, a young, innovative, and nomadic guitarist who was inspired in equal measure by American bluesmen, Davy Graham, and beat culture. "On and off, I did that for about three years," Palmer says. "You could make a lot of money then. In those days there weren't very many people doing it – it was a novelty." But although he was enjoying the atmosphere, and the financial rewards, he eventually got sick of the French police and moved back to London.

"I had a friend who was a Gordonstoun dropout," he recalls, Gordonstoun being the elite Scottish boarding school known for its links to the British royal family. "We decided we were going to go up to Scotland and do some hunting, because he was mad on hunting." Palmer bought a shotgun and a licence and the pair made their way north of the border. When they got to Edinburgh, in late 1962, Palmer was told about a folk club at the Crown Bar, run by Archie Fisher every Tuesday, and encouraged to get himself along there and play. He did. "They were amazed, because they'd never heard banjo like it," he says. "They were all bowled over. At the end, this bloke came up to me. He had a sort of reddish face and a white Arran jumper on. It was Robin Williamson."

Before long Palmer and Williamson had teamed up as Robin & Clive, playing a blend of traditional Scottish folksong and bluegrass. Fanning out from Archie Fisher's club, the duo gigged throughout Britain's folk clubs in 1963 and 1964 until Palmer – who, as time will show, found it hard to stick with one group for too long – made a suggestion. "I said to Robin one day: 'Do you think it might be a good idea to get another person in, because it would give us a bit more ... *thing*?'"

"I was hired as a strummer," the successful applicant, Mike Heron, recalls. Heron's musical background was very different: he was already a veteran of several rock bands but had recently become a regular punter at Fisher's club, where he saw Bert Jansch, John Martyn, and of course Robin & Clive.

Williamson was still not totally sold on the idea of bringing in a new band-member when Heron joined in 1965, and he wasn't the only one who needed a bit of convincing. "The people who were used to us and our traditional stuff got a bit miffy about it," Palmer recalls. "They said: 'Well, we want to book you but we don't really want that other bloke as well.'" Heron's songs and showmanship soon won over the audiences, however. "You could see it was starting to work," Palmer says.

After Palmer coined the name The Incredible String Band, the trio set up their own regular all-night event, Clive's Incredible Folk Club, in Glasgow's Sauchiehall Street. The club hosted John Martyn, Bert Jansch, and Davy Graham, among others, and lasted around a year before the police closed it down. (The ostensible justification was the health and safely concerns caused by the tiny, hazardous lift into the club, but in truth the police had never been too happy about the all-night aspect of the club.)

As Mike Heron recalls, there was a mixed clientele at Clive's, which might also have contributed to the police's concerns. "There were people who just wanted to smoke dope and listen to the music," he says, "but it was also full of people who wanted to be out all night, like various petty criminals, and some gang members with swords down their trouser legs."

One day in Glasgow, Palmer received a chicly dressed visitor: the American Joe Boyd, who was in town looking for talent as the new British scout for the US-based Elektra Records. In May 1965, Boyd had watched Robin & Clive perform what he describes in his memoir, *White Bicycles*, as "Scots traditional music as if it had taken a trip to the Appalachians and back via Morocco and Bulgaria". Now he wondered whether Palmer and co would be interested in making a recording. "Yeah, sure," Palmer replied.[12]

"We talked about money," Palmer recalls, "which was ridiculous now I think about it; we didn't know much about it then. So, anyway, all that ended up with us making our first record in London with Elektra." Elektra president Jac Holzman was impressed enough with the demo Boyd sent him, of Williamson's 'October Song', to hand over a small budget for Williamson,

Palmer, and Heron to go into Sound Techniques with Boyd to record their 16-song debut in May 1966.

Although it contains only three traditional songs, *The Incredible String Band* has a lineage with folk, yet there's no doubt the tradition is being nudged. There's a jerky raucousness that's not quite the same as the madcap American old-timey music of Williamson's heritage or the proletarian music-hall comedy that seeped into Palmer's banjo. Similarly, the music is not recast in the rock idiom of Heron's background. *The Incredible String Band* is the sum of all of them, plus more; it sounds long on the vine and newly picked, strummed and plucked with considerable flair.

Tucked deep within side one is 'The Tree', a Mike Heron composition that draws on striking but surreal natural imagery underpinned by Williamson's spacey, sparse mandolin. This would eventually be the song that pointed toward future directions, but for now it remained in a continuum with the jugular folk of 'How Happy I Am' and 'Dandelion Blues'.

"We hadn't got that much out of it, as often happens," Palmer recalls. Heron agrees. "It became obvious that the jug-band stuff, and bluesy American banjo playing, was not really wanted by an American record company," he says. "They wanted original songs. So it pushed me and Robin into the foreground a bit and Clive into the background, because he wasn't really writing much at that time: he was more wanting to do the traditional stuff." There are seven Heron originals on the album, and six songs by Williamson, but only one by Palmer.

Palmer was unimpressed with the lack of success of the first album and left for India and Afghanistan; Williamson travelled to Morocco. Only Mike Heron stayed in Scotland, gigging solo around nights promoted by Archie Fisher, playing mainly Dylan covers. The Incredible String Band fizzled out with little fanfare or mourning, while by the end of the year Joe Boyd had ended his association with Elektra.

In time, the impact of Mike Heron, Robin Williamson, Joe Boyd, and Clive Palmer would be colossal. But as 1966 drew to an end, the four men were dispersed in time and space; the casually attired, fresh-faced trio gazing from the muted cover of *The Incredible String Band* were already lost to a bygone era. The splintered String Band left behind a folk climate in Britain that was now primed for some serious disruption. When they eventually returned it would be they, first and foremost, who would blow it apart.

CHAPTER 2

Vibrations

"I SAW THIS HOT GIRL IN CLASS. She was married, but she said I should meet her, her husband, and her friend who play folk music." And that was enough for the young Peter Stampfel to become a convert to folk and to start on the road that led him to carefully conserve American tradition – and to regularly poke it in the ribs.

Folk music wasn't completely new to Stampfel when he saw that pretty girl in 1956. Like millions of teenagers, he had grown up during the USA's brief post-war love affair with folk. The 1949 Walt Disney film *So Dear To My Heart* had brought the 17th century English ballad 'Lavender Blue', sung by Burl Ives, straight into American lives. (Ives's radio show, *The Wayfaring Stranger*, had been showcasing traditional song since 1940.) A flurry of popular folk songs followed the scent of 'Lavender Blue', with one particular four-piece group rising to prominence. The Weavers were led by Peggy Seeger's half-brother, Pete, and had a huge hit with their sentimental, glossy take on the Leadbelly song 'Goodnight Irene'. The song ushered in a wave of similar folk tunes recast in saccharine fashion for Middle American ears that would continue until the early 50s and the McCarthy era crackdown on the known or suspected communist affiliations of this wave of folk musicians.

A period of blacklisting followed, with Burl Ives and The Weavers falling victim to it. Within three or four short years, folk music had gone from harmless sentimental pastime to political outsider, investigated by the FBI and the subject of popular disapproval. In 1953, Decca Records unceremoniously dumped the once phenomenally successful Weavers, deleting their back catalogue to boot. Folk music was just too much trouble.

Over the course of the next decade, folk music in America was becoming just as difficult to define as it was in Britain. Harry Smith's *Anthology Of American Folk Music*, first published in 1952, had become a touchstone for the new breed of folk artists, among them The Kingston Trio, Joan Baez, and Bob Dylan. The climate had changed considerably since Decca ousted The Weavers; the Kennedy era was in full swing, and folk music could be performed without the immediate assumption of card-carrying communism.

Another radical musical fibre was emerging, too: one that, in 1959, attracted very little notice. Takoma Records was founded that year by John Fahey, a steel-string guitarist from Takoma Park, Maryland, who had digested country-blues, rural tradition, and modern classical music in his youth and reformed them into a blistering, self-taught picking style. As he later explained, Fahey thought going to "commercial record companies" and making demos would be a waste of time. "Don't forget, I was doing what I was doing, and nobody understood what I was doing."[1]

The first Takoma release was Fahey's own debut, with one side credited to his alter ego, Blind Joe Death. "In the music I was composing I was trying to express my emotions, my so called negative emotions, which were depression, anger, and so forth," he later explained. "Everybody else was just trying to copy folk musicians. I wasn't trying to do that."[2] He pressed 100 copies of *John Fahey / Blind Joe Death*, and that was it: Fahey went off to university, and Takoma was put on hiatus until 1963.

Fahey was probably right: few, if any, record companies would have been interested in his music. While folk was popular in American homes once again, its polished, packaged signature style was the polar opposite of what Fahey was doing. Peter Paul & Mary dominated the US album charts in 1962 with their self-titled debut, which remained on the *Billboard* listings for two more years, while the *Hootenanny!* TV show offered folk musicians a fast route to nationwide exposure.

America did see a corresponding upsurge in grassroots folk activity, however. Coffeehouses and small-scale venues sympathetic to folk multiplied, and were no longer limited to big cities and university towns. These hangouts became forums for individual expression; going along to one outwardly denoted an allegiance to the bohemian lifestyle of drugs, poetry, and obscure literature. Tight, supportive communities were created in parallel with the now-bubbling Greenwich Village. Some in the mainstream were noticeably adopting a tougher attitude to folk music, with Richard and Mimi Fariña – he a beat-affiliated writer, she Joan Baez's sister – especially daring. Richard's dulcimer playing was strident, the duo's arrangements had perceptible Indian and Latin influences, and they adopted electric folk early on the tracks 'One-Way Ticket' and 'Reno Nevada' from their 1965 Vanguard album *Celebrations For A Grey Day*.

"There was an innocence about us all in the beginning," says Bonnie Dobson, a young Canadian folksinger who had landed in New York from Toronto in 1960 and signed a contract with Prestige. "It didn't really change until Dylan signed and got all that money upfront for his first album. Everybody started looking over their shoulder then." The attention that Dylan in particular brought to the Greenwich Village scene over the next few years changed the ground that folk music was built on. His finely wrought, poetic songs rubber-stamped the tendency for 'folk music' now to refer to original as well as traditional material – as long as it was performed in a folk *style*.

Meanwhile, back in Milwaukee, Peter Stampfel had been satisfying his whetted appetite for folk by learning to play the banjo, the instrument he had liked so much on those records by The Weavers. "I just realised that I had to play it," he says. "It wasn't even a realisation, it was like something I already had known. It was absolutely a piece of me that needed to be attached."

He was becoming a budding bohemian, too. "I read of all the beat stuff in the paper," he says, "and I went to San Francisco in May of '58 to see what was going on. Something interesting was happening." Ultimately, of course, Stampfel could only end up in one place: New York. He arrived in 1959, drawn in by the smell of the coffeehouses, the artistic fire at their centres, and the ability to have an exciting, carefree life with minimal financial resources. Stampfel found a $44-a-month four-room apartment in New York, which he shared with a friend, and quickly settled into a new circle.

Peter Stampfel's kismet came one day in November 1962. In the bathroom of the Blind Lemon coffeehouse, waitress Barbara Ann Goldblatt, now known simply as Antonia, had written the words 'You Are All God Accordingly'. "I had taken some mescaline," Stampfel recalls. "I saw that sign and I wrote underneath: 'Verified On Mescaline'." Before long they were dating, and the free-spirited Antonia had a profound influence on Stampfel's worldview. "Peter had it in his head that anything written after 1941 wasn't worth playing," Antonia recalled in 2006. "I taught him, showed him that any music should be played if done with abandon." Prior to meeting Stampfel, she had had a tempestuous two-and-a-half-year relationship with the equally fiery and unruly Steve Weber. "Steve was always barefoot," she explained, "and his guitar playing was amazing."[3] The relationship was peppered with amphetamine-fuelled fights, some of them physical. One ended with Antonia breaking Weber's own guitar over his head.

Weber came from Bucks County, Pennsylvania, and as a youth had enjoyed pranks like greasing railroad tracks so that the train overshot the station platform. Like Stampfel, he had been captivated by The Weavers, but he also knew Fred Ramsay, the folklorist whose field recordings were released by Folkways Records. Weber picked up the guitar and used it to express himself. He was drawn to the more hazardous and hedonistic aspects of the bohemian lifestyle.

"Antonia told me all these stories," Stampfel says. "He was 'Evil Weber the speed freak'." Mescaline, marijuana, barbiturates, and even heroin were used and widely accepted on the folk scene; amphetamines were, as Stampfel puts it, "the only really denigrated drug". There were all manner of urban myths about 'speed freaks' and 'meth monsters': that they used black magic to cast spells against each other; that they were constantly at war with rival splinter groups of users; that they would shoot themselves up in the throat and spray anyone within ten feet with their blood.

There was a reason why Antonia regaled Stampfel with tales of Weber's escapades. "Her idea was for us to get the idea to play together without her suggesting it because she didn't want to be pushy," he says. Antonia felt that "Peter was missing a piece of himself, and so was Steve".[4] When the two men met, in May 1963, Stampfel was fascinated; Weber wasn't what he expected. Instead of some demented meth monster, here was a supernaturally charming man whose sanguine abandon immediately drew Stampfel in. "I thought he was my long-lost brother, basically," Stampfel says. "The first time we played together it was perfect. It just miraculously fit together, as if we'd been doing it forever."

The two men got lost in amphetamines and music until, hours later, Stampfel realised he had a gig at a baskethouse. He asked Weber to come along, offering to split the proceeds, and with that began a three-day bender of performances in numerous venues around Greenwich Village. On the third day, Weber and Stampfel were on stage at Café Wha? when Stampfel suddenly felt overwhelmed. "They had this mirror in the corner," he recalls, "and the performers could see themselves in this mirror. I looked up and I saw the two of us playing there and I thought, holy fuck! This is absolutely one of the most uncanny things I've ever seen in my life and it would be beyond amazing if we could continue to do this."

Weber was reaching the end of his rope with the back-to-back performances, however, and threw a strop. "I hit a bad note and Weber sort of crumpled up as if he'd been hit in the belly," Stampfel recalls. "And then he played a really bad chord on the next beat, and then a worse chord after that. He played five dissonant chords, each one more dissonant than the last, and then he screamed and leapt from the stage and started running for the door."

The incident did not put Stampfel off Weber, however. Far from it. "I tilted my seat back, so I started falling backward," he recalls, "and at the same instance that he was going through the door screaming I was flat on my back on stage – this is less than five seconds after we'd been playing together perfectly. I remember thinking 'damn, this is *magical*'."

Stampfel and Weber worked so well together that they seemed destined to become a full-time duo. They played around with various group names for a few weeks before coming up with Total Modal Rounders. "Someone said Holy Modal Rounders instead of Total Modal Rounders," Stampfel recalls, "and I thought that's better yet. We'd always put our new name on a little card in front of us, and this time everyone started calling us The Holy Modal Rounders, so we knew this was the proper name."

The Holy Modal Rounders soon developed a signature style that was totally different to everyone else on the New York scene at the time. "A lot of [the other musicians] I really respected musically and personally," Stampfel says. "But almost everyone had this 'we're involved in a serious undertaking' attitude, which sort of had an edge of moral superiority, like we are in a position to dictate or preach proper attitudes. And I found that repellent." Stampfel took a different view of the folk traditions. "Those guys were goofy as shit!" he says. "The skillet lickers, the horsehair pullers, the goofiness was a massive part of the music, it was really crazy shit. And there just wasn't any crazy shit in the folk scene."

The early Holy Modal Rounders brought in a new brand of crazy shit. The band's performances mixed old-timey, harebrained songs with contemporary, drug-soaked recklessness and post-rock'n'roll clatter, balancing a respect for the songs with a healthy sense of humour.

By late 1963, The Holy Modal Rounders had signed a deal with Prestige Records and went into the studio on November 21 – the day before the assassination of John F. Kennedy – having first consumed a fair amount of speed and pot. The album that emerged in February 1964, *The Holy Modal Rounders*, was a very new type of folk record, and a fine reflection of their anarchic live shows. "Steve calls it rockabilly and I call it progressive old-timey," Stampfel wrote in the original liner notes. "No one has ever played music like us before."

Something else that no one had ever done before was use the word "psychedelic" in song. The term, coined in 1957 by psychiatrist Humphrey Osmond, was originally used to describe hallucinogenic drugs, but by 1963 – thanks largely to Timothy Leary and Aldous Huxley – it had come to refer to any experience that mimicked a hallucinogenic trip: kaleidoscopic colours, altered reality, expanded consciousness. In their rewrite of banjoist Charlie Poole's 'Hesitation Blues', The Holy Modal Rounders included the lines: "Got my psychedelic feet / In my psychedelic shoes / I believe, lordy mama / Got the psychedelic blues."

The Holy Modal Rounders was largely ignored on release. One of the very few reviews it received was in *Sing Out!* magazine, where it was dismissed as a parody. Meanwhile, Stampfel and Weber joined a new group away from folk but far deeper into the counterculture. The Fugs was the pet project of two New York poets, Ed Sanders and Tuli Kupferberg, who wanted to create a "dirty rock'n'roll group", and who sensed in The Holy Modal Rounders the same mix of flippancy and radicalism to which they themselves aspired. Weber and Stampfel joined the group in early 1965 and played on their first record, *The Village Fugs Sing Ballads Of Contemporary Protest, Point Of Views, And General Dissatisfaction* (also known as *The Fugs First Album*), which includes Weber's smut-classic 'Boobs A Lot'.

The Holy Modal Rounders continued to work as a duo, too, and recorded a second album for Prestige, *The Holy Modal Rounders 2*. This record was an extension of the first, the two together forming a definitive statement of The Holy Modal Rounders' folk lawlessness, but Stampfel knew the whole thing was coming to an end. "Weber realised that we had a possibility of some level of success, but he didn't even like to admit that we were working together," he says. "Like one evening I said: 'We're going to work' and he was: 'No! We're not going to work! We're just going to the Village because it's getting dark and since we're going to the Village I might as well take my guitar and maybe we'll stop at a coffee house.' He didn't want to be committed; he wanted to be a totally free spirit." Weber had stopped practicing, missed gigs, and was uninterested in working on new songs. Instead, he preferred to wander around New York trying to get himself arrested. Beyond exasperated, Stampfel ceased playing in both The Fugs and The Holy Modal Rounders in July 1965.

⋈

Nestling in between the traditional songs on *The Holy Modal Rounders* is the screwball original 'Euphoria', written by an old pal of Steve Weber's from Pennsylvania, fiddle player Robin Remaily. Another of their friends from back home was Michael Hurley, who had been playing the mandolin since the age of 13. "It was all out of tune, always," he recalled in 1965. "But I would take it and go into a dark room, and sit there for about four or five hours, sometimes, just strumming. This was an aberration to most people," he added – including his parents, who worried about his behaviour.[5]

Hurley soon moved on to the guitar, and during the early 60s set off hitchhiking across the USA with Remaily. They eventually wound up in Greenwich Village, where they both played extensively until Hurley ended up in Bellevue Hospital for six months of 1963 with a severe case of hepatitis. The hospital stay affected Hurley's budding songwriting. He developed a calmer and more measured approach to music – partly so he could practice without disturbing the other patients – but with an undimmed folk-undone spirit. Upon his discharge from Bellevue, Hurley wanted to do something with his body of work. Claiming to distrust the scouts and labels that sought him out, he instead approached Folkways, leading to the release of *First Songs* in 1965.

Credited to Mike Hurley, the album is an early landmark of American outsider (or loner) folk. Hurley wears his life on his sleeve, but the songs have a jerky, unusual tone, the wackiness of the Rounders supplanted by bleak, lonely minstrelsy. The tempos are slow, the lyrics bleak, and even the moments of surrealist humour tend to be undercut by a tragic coda. There's a tension throughout between the freewheeling, hitchhiking, anything-goes Hurley and his introspective, reflective counterpoint. Nowhere is this clearer than on 'Werewolf', a song whose genesis was as simple as its effect was strangely new. "We were sitting around, a bunch of people jamming, about six people in a little circle, playing all these songs," Hurley later recalled. "We had played for probably three or four hours and we didn't know any more songs. And we figured there should be more songs. We figured there should be a song about a werewolf. And I just rattled that one out."[6]

Michael Hurley would not make another album until 1971, but echoes of his bizarre troubadour persona would resonate long and hard in the intervening years. The folk singer-songwriter scene was taking a turn for the decidedly unusual, and two mavericks at Elektra Records, one of the major homes of American folk music, were about to twist it further – with one of them set to transform it beyond all recognition.

Founded by Jac Holzman back in 1950, Elektra had dipped its toes in blues, jazz, and non-Western music, but in its first decade had gained a particular reputation for its albums of traditional folksong, beginning with *Jean Ritchie Singing The Traditional Songs Of Her Kentucky Mountain Family* (1952). By the early 60s, however, the label had become known more for its popular folk signings, including Phil Ochs, Tom Paxton, and the very successful Judy Collins.

Four months after releasing the debut album by The Incredible String Band, Elektra put out an even more atypical folk album. Pat Kilroy was hardly well known, but his album *Light Of Day* (1966), with its melange of gossamer-folk poetry, early psych, Eastern spiritual infusions, and vocal gymnastics, was the sound of something new and strange. Released even a couple of years later, the album would not have sounded out of place; in 1966 there wasn't even a name for what Kilroy was doing.

"I joyously let this musical journey flow through the unknown regions of the next horizons," the mystical Kilroy wrote in the liner notes. "There can be no limits on the musical explorations through which I am destined to go." He put the diverse sound of the album down to his grounding in rock'n'roll and traditional folksong, alongside "the sturdy work chants of Hebrides Islanders, the lively moods of Spanish gypsies, the magnetic pulsations of Africa's hypnotic drums, the eerie wave of Middle Eastern dances". Mixed in with all of this was a fascination with Indian spirituality, Hermann Hesse, Aldous Huxley, and George Gurdjieff. He was also influenced by the Indian classical musician and composer Ali Akbar Khan.

Light Of Day makes great use of tabla player Bob Amacker, who had switched to the cheaper instrument after his drums were stolen, and flautist Susan Graubard, who had previously played with Kilroy in New York. There's also guitar by Stefan Grossman, a graduate of the early Fugs. The album was produced by one of Elektra's young guns, Peter K. Siegel, who had a strong interest in non-Western music and field recordings.

After recording *Light Of Day*, Kilroy and Graubard went off travelling together. "We usually slept in cow pastures along the road, in our sleeping bags, and sometimes under bridges," Graubard (now Susan Archuletta) later recalled. "It was mainly during our intense travel in Europe and Morocco that we began to merge more as a team."[7] On their return to America, Kilroy and Graubard settled in Berkeley, where they moved into an abandoned one-room hunting cabin on Bear Creek and formed The New Age with Jeffrey Stewart on congas. They were a regular fixture throughout late 1966 and 1967 in their local coffeehouse, the Jabberwock; they performed at the Human Be-In in Golden Gate Park on January 14 1967 and also appeared in the movie *The Love-Ins*, which walks a fine line between countercultural evocation and cash-in exploitation.

By the summer of 1967, Kilroy and Elektra had had a falling out, so The New Age signed instead to Warner Bros and started work on an album that goes much further than *Light Of Day*. 'Dance Around The Sun' and 'Bhairavi' go deep into raga territory, with the music's folk heartbeat fully surrounded by chanting, improvisation, and hard-line psychedelia. The checklist of instruments used includes Spanish cowbells, bell tree, silver and bamboo flutes, viola, tamboura, and congas. (The trio had vastly expanded their range through their studies of Indian music at the American Society For Eastern Arts, while Warner Bros was generous in providing the group with whichever instruments they wanted.)

Before The New Age could explore their hitherto untried folk fusions any further, however, Kilroy became ill. "It was quite a shock when we appeared at the recording studio and found out about Patrick's condition," Graubard later recalled. He had been diagnosed with Hodgkin's lymphoma. "It was very painful to see Patrick in this condition, and I did not have any preparation or guidance for how to deal with it." Kilroy went into the UC Medical Center in San Francisco and passed away on Christmas day 1967. The new American folk music had lost one of its first visionaries.

While Elektra's attitude toward Pat Kilroy was indifferent at best, the label had huge expectations for another of its new signings. By late 1966, Tim Buckley had become Elektra's great folk hope, his delicate cheekbones and profound dark eyes staring out from the cover of his debut album. He had the looks, the talent, the sensitivity, and the authenticity. Elektra sensed that Buckley could be the cleft-chinned Bob Dylan – hopefully without the motorbike accidents and disappearances. "I explained to Tim that Elektra was growing in a creative direction at that time," Jac Holzman gushed in a contemporary press release, "and that he was exactly the kind of artist with whom we wanted to grow – young and in the process of developing, extraordinary and uniquely gifted, and so 'untyped' that there existed no formula or pattern to which anyone would be committed."

Buckley had a vocal range of somewhere between four and five-and-a-half octaves, so it wasn't surprising that he wished to use this formidable asset as one might approach a piano or a guitar. He had grown up on Johnny Cash, Little Richard, and Ella Fitzgerald, and knew the power of both the finely honed voice and the primal yowl. He saw no separation between the voice and other instruments, and claimed to have accurately imitated the sound of Miles Davis's trumpet as a child.

Buckley learnt to play the banjo at 11 and soon started what was to be the first of many folk groups. These groups would usually play the folk hits of the day, by The Weavers or The Kingston Trio; in his early teens, Buckley would shake these up with guitar experiments, in particular his use of open tunings. He added Ravi Shankar and country-blues to his favourite music and performed acoustically at local high schools, accompanied by his friends Jim Fielder and Larry Beckett, under the name The Bohemians. He and Beckett also began a songwriting partnership.

At the same time as playing accessible folk and pop with The Bohemians, Buckley, Beckett, and Fielder had another group, The Harlequin Three. This was a far more outré and beat-influenced affair, mixing improvised singing, poetry reading, and atonal playing, with Buckley now using bowed strings and open tunings. The two groups would play at a makeshift club called the Two Tables in Bell Gardens, Anaheim, California, where Buckley would also sometimes perform solo. They also made regular journeys up to Los Angeles to hang out on Sunset Strip and gaze into the windows of the psychedelic club the Trip.

One night, while Buckley and his buddies were indulging in their usual moan about how everyone misunderstood their radical music, they caught the ear of someone who cared: Jimmy Carl Black, who had started playing alongside Frank Zappa in The Mothers. Through Black they met The Mothers' manager, Herb Cohen, who signed The Bohemians to a publishing contract. The 18-year-old Buckley was soon persuaded to ditch the band and recast himself as a solo performer, although he would continue to write songs with Beckett.

The buzz Tim Buckley created in the clubs under Cohen's tutelage led him to the offices of Elektra Records in New York. His first album, *Tim Buckley*, was recorded in August 1966 and released that December. Featuring contributions by Jack Nitzsche, who had honed his craft with Phil Spector, and Van Dyke Parks, who brought with him the rococo qualities of the harpsichord and celeste, the album unveiled a gentle folk-rock with a lush, baroque character. Yet for all that, *Tim Buckley* is a cautious affair, the psychedelic influence present but far less so than on what Pat Kilroy had been doing. There are flashes of the Harlequin Three spirit, particularly in the curious dance-band air of 'Strange Street Affair Under Blue', but overall the album is earnest and conventional, of its time and of Buckley's young age. It sold modestly – perhaps rather more modestly than Holzman had expected.

Interviewed in early 1967, Buckley sounded confident about the album, but was already beginning to display a sense of itchiness. "Dylan was the one who intrigued me," he said, "because he grew with each album. These other people stayed in the same thing, and that showed me that they didn't grow."[8]

Buckley grew. He bought a 12-string guitar, hung out with Nico, and added a young African-American conga player, Carter Crawford Christopher Collins, to his band. Then, with Beckett, he wrote 'Hallucinations'. The song, which features on Buckley's second album, has an unusual skittering rhythm, spaced-out lyrics, and an Eastern feel. The songwriting duo also came up with 'Knight-Errant', one of the most overtly psychedelic folk tracks that Buckley would ever commit to vinyl. They were also starting to grouse about Elektra's expectations for Buckley's next album.

"They weren't going to take any shit from Holzman," producer Jerry Yester later recalled. "They really wanted to record, but not if it meant bastardizing what they believed in."[9] The culmination of this was the eight-minute title track, a song-story documenting the rise of the new generation against the oppressions of the previous one. The imagery is a little naïve and over-explicit – as Buckley himself would later admit – but the challenging attitude Buckley took toward folk music's accepted musical structures foretold his later radical innovation.

Released in August 1967, *Goodbye And Hello* eked out a few more sales than its predecessor, but still didn't sell to the extent that Elektra had hoped. This may have been because Buckley didn't seem to care much about being a star, or money, or chart positions. The promotional tour in support of *Goodbye And Hello* was peppered with disastrous TV appearances. Buckley acted up in rehearsals, and live on air. He was bothered about making music, not selling it; he was already onto the next project and prone to digging his heels in whenever he thought he would have to undertake tedious unit-shifting tasks at the expense of his muse.

"It is very tricky sometimes, with a singer-songwriter," he said in 1974. "You just cannot be objective about what you're doing. Sometimes it's not commercial, what you're feeling. You overdo it for the general public's ear." He went on to reveal that he felt he'd exhausted the folk-rock format on *Goodbye And Hello*. "Most of the bases were touched. That was the end of my apprenticeship of writing songs. Whatever I wrote after that wasn't adolescent, which means it wasn't easy to write after that, because you can't repeat yourself." The fact that the industry – and his audiences – expected him to repeat himself was a major bugbear. "People like a certain thing, a certain period of time," he said. "It's really hard to progress them."[10]

As 1967 drew to a close, Buckley was about to enter his most prolific and experimental phase. Shortly after making *Goodbye And Hello* he added a jazz bassist, John Miller, to his group alongside Beckett and Collins. Together, they would stretch out even the very clipped songs from his first two albums – if they performed them at all – while Buckley himself took increasingly to piercing the affecting beauty of his voice with yelps and squalls. Elektra held meetings about the lack of commercial appeal in his work. The label was right to be concerned.

✕

Takoma Records had no such trouble with its roster, given that the label itself was one of the least conventional in the whole of the USA. John Fahey had brought in Eugene 'ED' Denson and Norman Pierce to help run the label, which he reactivated in 1963 with an album by the bluesman Bukka White and two new records of his own: *Death Chants, Break Downs And Military Waltzes* and *The Dance Of Death And Other Plantation Favorites*.

Fahey's distinctive steel-string guitar-soli fingerstyle technique – which he called 'American Primitivism' – soon started to attract interest. In 1964, Takoma put out the first Robbie Basho album, *The Seal Of The Blue Lotus*. Basho became another American Primitive master, embarking on a series of albums that took influence from psychedelic mysticism and obscure philosophies.

Another exciting practitioner of the guitar-soli technique was Sandy Bull, who released his debut, *Fantasies For Guitar And Banjo*, on Vanguard in 1963. The album features the side-long 'Blend' and fused American folk with non-Western styles. In the last interview conducted before his death in 2001, Bull revealed that 'Blend' came about as a result of "listening to Ravi Shankar and Ali Akbar Khan in New York, and playing on a guitar tuned to Indian drums. I'd been looking into a lot of Folkways albums, music from all over, and I loved it all, and tried to take pieces and put it together".[11]

American Primitivism was swelling in influence. Its uncompromising stance and mixture of complexity and harshness, as well as the enigmatic appeal of its practitioners, would prove to be a very hardy and influential thread through the decades.

As the Summer of Love was spreading its heat, folk music in America was starting to warp. Psychedelic influences were spreading fast, and at this stage still came about as a result of an artist's exploratory spirit rather than a cynical affectation to gain a shortcut to a record contract. The nascent psychedelic-folk music – especially that of The Holy Modal Rounders – brought with it a strong drive to reach back into the folk past, to pull out its entrails and dip them in a new 60s consciousness. Soon, one American label would bring together all these qualities and put out some of the greatest strange folk records of the decade. But, first, British folk had a bit of catching up to do.

CHAPTER 3

Waltz Of The New Moon

THE MOST INFLUENTIAL of all the folk clubs in London was unprepossessing to look at, housed as it was beneath a restaurant at 49 Greek Street, Soho. Les Cousins was owned by the same Greek couple, the Matheous, who ran the restaurant. It regularly reached its 150-person capacity, attracting youthful, bohemian audiences. Sessions lasted all night; there was an enormous wagon wheel on the wall and fisherman's netting on the ceiling, as well as a small stage, a piano, a single electrical socket, and a microphone. The club became a going concern in April 1965, with Bert Jansch its first resident performer, and soon gained a reputation for its laissez-faire attitude to folk music's wilder touches. (It seemed an appropriate changing of the guard that the same building had previously housed the Skiffle Cellar.)

Les Cousins wasn't the only place in town. There were dozens if not hundreds more clubs: the Troubadour in Earl's Court, Bunjies and the Phoenix near Leicester Square, the Student Prince in D'Arblay Street, Le Macabre on Wardour Street, with its coffin-shaped tables, and many more. Each had an ear open to folk music and provided performance spaces to the growing number of youngsters with guitars. "Folk clubs were the places where cool people would hang out," says Mike Heron, who continued to play in them as a solo performer after the first Incredible String Band line-up split in late 1966. "All kinds of music was acceptable to play, and there were very few barriers."

In a parallel existence were the underground clubs, a more electric breeding ground for British psychedelia. The most famous of them was UFO, the Friday-night club opened in 1966 by Joe Boyd and John 'Hoppy' Hopkins,

45

situated in the basement of an Irish dance hall in Tottenham Court Road with a sprung floor and a snow machine. There was the Electric Garden, which was quickly relaunched as Middle Earth, as well as Happening 44, Blaises, and the Speakeasy. "All of them *were* literally underground," says Judy Dyble, who played in most of them during the early days of Fairport Convention. "Cavernous places, very dark, dimly lit, with oily lightshows that used to catch fire if the operators weren't vigilant." These clubs were friendly to folk acts, even if they didn't seem to give the matter of genre much thought. "Compartmentalisation really didn't exist then," Fairport's Ashley Hutchings recalls. "You could play what you wanted, but they were short sets, so you learned fairly quickly what you could do in that time."

Folk musicians were certainly cutting their teeth in these new performance spaces of 60s London, but there was also another route they could take, too – one where they didn't have to queue up to enter. British folk had begun to grow another limb that brought it bang in line with 60s culture: the development of a post-Beatles, post-Dylan brand of folk-pop that would eventually feed directly into the development of psychedelic and amorphous folk music.

One man who had his ear to the ground was Andrew Loog Oldham, the manager of The Rolling Stones, who discovered the UK's premier folk-pop goddess of the period, Marianne Faithfull, in 1964, and cut a folk-hued single with Nico a year later. But the biggest – if also the slowest burning – impression on strange folk music came from another member of Oldham's stable: from an artist who would come to be revered as 'the godmother of freak folk' – but who, ironically, never wanted to be a folk artist, didn't like folk music much, and whose recordings with Oldham were far less folksy than those he made with Faithfull or Nico.

Vashti Bunyan had grown up, in London, with a receptivity to pop music that had wrapped its roots around her heart by the time she was a teenager. She mentions records by The Everly Brothers, Ricky Nelson, and Cliff Richard as examples of "those incredibly neat pop songs that said everything that needed to be said. First verse, middle-eight, verse, and that's it. I thought they were wonderful. When I first started writing songs, that was what I was writing, but I was trying to make it say a little bit more than the usual pop songs. Some of those early songs I wrote I'm really very proud of, because they were so simple and so concise".

Bunyan first started to write songs while attending Ruskin School of Art in Oxford, where she had literally walked into a fellow student and pop addict,

Jennifer Lewis. "We both had our big portfolios full of drawings, and we sort of bumped into each other trying to get through the door," Lewis recalls. "And Vashti dropped her portfolio, so all her drawings skidded out in this hushed museum. And then we just started laughing, and we laughed and laughed. We didn't even know each other's names then. But then we became very good friends." Lewis had been in a skiffle group in her youth, and had begun to play around with songwriting. While sharing a tiny flat, Bunyan picked up Lewis's guitar, which Lewis called 'Benji', and the two girls began to write together.

Before long, Bunyan's childhood friend Angela Strange came to visit and met Jenny Lewis for the first time. They decided to become a girl group, which they named The Three Of Us, and soon found a gig backing another local group, The Four Beats. Lewis and Bunyan continued to write songs together, including one called '17 Pink Sugar Elephants', while also developing their own succinct, touching brand of pop.

When Vashti Bunyan got kicked out of art school and returned to London, Jenny Lewis stayed in Oxford. Bunyan's time there had armed her with a body of songs and a burning desire to do something with them. "I was so not the right person to try and do all of that," she recalls. "I was horribly shy, and yet I had this huge ego about my songs: I thought they were really, really, really good and that I should be able to get them out there."

As luck would have it, Bunyan met Andrew Loog Oldham not long after Faithfull had left his roster. She knew this could be her big break, but her introverted nature hampered any efforts at self-promotion. "Being around The Rolling Stones and Andrew Oldham, I was just this little tiny figure, cowering in the corner, watching this amazing pantomime going on all around me," she recalls. "I didn't have the personality to be confident around those kinds of people. I doubt if they even noticed I was there, really."

Bunyan cut a version of the Rolling Stones song 'Some Things Just Stick In Your Mind' – "I was appalled," she says. "I thought I wrote better songs!" – but despite its sumptuous production, the single bombed. Disheartened, and sensing that another single with Oldham would not materialise, she left his stable to join up with Canadian producer Peter Snell. Together they recorded 'Train Song', the melody of which stemmed from '17 Pink Sugar Elephants', with lyrics by a bona fide folkie, Alastair Clayre. This was the true beginning of Bunyan's refracted relationship with folk music.

"I thought, I've done it all wrong," Bunyan says of 'Train Song'. "I don't need Andrew Oldham and his huge orchestra and his huge this and his huge that. I need to do just what I set out to do, to try to bring some kind of acoustic music into mainstream pop." But 'Train Song' didn't sell either, and from then on Bunyan's optimism began to ebb away. Singles lay unreleased, and the brief interest that the media had taken in her around the release of her first single evaporated. She grew apart from the London scene. "There were networks, but they were very insular," she says. "What I was doing was neither folk nor pop, and I found it very difficult to find my way at all."

Meanwhile, Jennifer Lewis and Angela Strange had embarked on a folk-pop career of their own. During Bunyan's first flurry of activity in London, she had introduced her friends, now performing together as a duo, to the agent Mervyn Conn. They released two outstanding singles, both written by Lewis: 'Bring It To Me' (1965) and 'I've Heard It All Before' (1966). Their sound hit the summit of mid-60s British folk-pop, with an embryonic post-beat, pre-psychedelia vibe; like 'Train Song', however, the singles sold poorly. Lewis and Strange loved making music, but before long they realised they were being pretty much left to flail as best they could within the industry.

"We were shuffled about a bit, and [manager] Mike Collier didn't take us very seriously," says Strange. Jenny Lewis agrees. "I think they thought a female singing duo was quite novel, that people would just take notice," she says. "But they didn't really give us enough time to develop." The crunch came when the album they had been promised was shelved in the middle of recording. Lewis and Strange laid down six tracks, with arrangements by Bunyan, before the whole thing fizzled out. (Despite efforts to recover them, the recordings appear to have been lost.) Fed up with swimming against the uninterested tide, Lewis and Strange gave up.

"It felt very much like unfinished business," Strange says. Sadly, the potential shown by Jennifer Lewis and Angela Strange's incredible folk-pop singles would remain unfulfilled. Vashti Bunyan's would not.

⋈

"I thought he was good, but very much like Bob Dylan," laughs Peter Eden, who first saw Donovan performing in a folk club called the Studio in Southend. "But then a lot of people were like Bob Dylan." By 1965, American performers were extensively covered in the British music press, so it was natural that Britain's most successful folk-pop proponent was – almost by rote – being compared to Dylan.

The curly-headed Donovan Leitch was a Scottish-born singer-songwriter who had lived in Hertfordshire since the age of ten. As a teenager with a chic, bohemian outlook, Donovan was a hit with the girls and started playing guitar at 14, learning to fingerpick a couple of years later via lessons from a kleptomaniac soap-dodger named Dirty Phil. Soon afterward he started to play at his local folk club. "The Cock pub was not overly fashionable," he later wrote, "just a wee boozer patronised by the local beatnik set."[1] Along with the Cock, there was the larger folk club at the Peacock, and a local R&B hangout to boot.

Accompanying Donovan on his field trip to Southend was a bluesy band from St Albans called Cops'n'Robbers, who were managed by Peter Eden. Cops'n'Robbers introduced Donovan to Eden, who in turn offered to manage the 18-year-old with the help of his songwriter friend, Geoff Stephens. Donovan then went to Stephens's publishers, Southern, in London to lay down some demo tracks. "We negotiated for him to be on *Ready Steady Go!*," Eden recalls. To Eden's surprise, Donovan was given a three-week run on the show. From his first appearance, in late January 1965, he was a hit.

"People liked him," Eden says. "He wrote some really good songs and then he took off." Donovan's first single, 'Catch The Wind', reached Number Four on the UK charts, while the album *What's Bin Did And What's Bin Hid* hit Number Three. There was a burst of Donovan mania as his tousled looks, doe eyes, and direct, affecting acoustic music caught the teenage imagination. Extensive media coverage, tours, and a cottage industry of 'Authentic Donovan Caps' followed.

In his first year of success, Donovan was constantly – and to a certain extent accurately – compared to Dylan. He didn't always help himself in this regard; his appearance in *Dont Look Back*, performing 'To Sing For You' to an impassive Dylan (who responded with a fiery rip through 'It's All Over Now Baby Blue'), left him looking like a tribute act. His appearance at the 1965 Newport Folk Festival had the same effect. Donovan performed 'Colours' as a duet with Joan Baez, in the manner of Dylan past; the man himself played his first electric set.

Donovan has always claimed that the likeness was coincidental. "I love Bob Dylan and his music," he later wrote, "but he was one of hundreds of influences on me, and most of those influences were in Dylan's music too."[2] To be fair, if Donovan did model himself on Dylan, that wasn't *all* he did. Three months before Dylan's electric performance at Newport, Donovan had appeared on British television during the *NME* Poll Winners Concert with a rock band, performing a meaty version of 'You're Going To Need Somebody On Your Bond'.

By the time of his second album, *Fairytale*, Donovan was moving away from ersatz Dylan toward something with far fewer precedents. The album brought a mystical lilt to his lyrics, more complex arrangements, and a softer guitar style, particularly on 'Sunny Goodge Street'. It was a transitional record. By the time of its release, in November 1965, Donovan's Breton fisherman's cap was conspicuous by its absence. The notable cover version on the album was British: Bert Jansch's 'Oh Deed I Do'. Donovan was emerging as a playful, whimsical folk poet, far less in thrall to America.

By then he had also parted company with Geoff Stephens and Peter Eden. Eden, as a freelancer, began to explore all sorts of directions, and got clever in pushing the right buttons with record companies. "You had to wander in and tell them it was something else," he says. "But you did get stuff recorded. There were people who worked for record companies who would back it up and do something with it." Eden was able to work freely with people he found interesting – which led to yet more significant records.

For Eden's ex-charge, however, the start of 1966 was the hangover following the whirlwind British media binge of 1965. Business wrangles and arguments with his UK label, Pye, resulted in the shelving of his new, distinctively different single, 'Sunshine Superman'.

Donovan was now working with the arranger John Cameron and the producer Mickie Most, whose past form was far more pop than folk. He and Most bounced off each other very well. "He played me this song, 'Sunshine Superman', and it had a very different colour to it from the way it is on record," Most later recalled. "We went into the studio at two o'clock on a Sunday afternoon, and by five o'clock it was finished. I was happy with it because it sounded different, and it sounded as though Donovan had got his own sound, which I was pleased about, because it was away from his acoustic folk guitar sound. A mysterious electronic sound."[3] (The planned B-side was another swirling folk-pop song, 'The Trip'.)

Unfortunately for Donovan's subsequent reputation, this psychedelic expedition of a single – recorded in January 1966 and due to be released later that same month – was shelved. To his dismay, Pye chose instead to put out a song from his first album, 'Josie', and released no new material until December, when 'Sunshine Superman' finally came out as a single. By then, Donovan once again looked like the follower. In a year when changes in musical style piled up to skyscraper heights, it was The Beatles who got the attention as psychedelic frontrunners. Cream and Pink Floyd were on the up, too. If 'Sunshine Superman' had been released when it was first recorded, it might have been seen as a breezy but significant folk-pop precursor to The Beatles' *Revolver*, but the delay meant it was cast as a watered-down imitator.

It was a different story in the USA, as Donovan moved from a small independent label, Hickory, to a major, Epic, for July's release of 'Sunshine Superman' and the subsequent *Sunshine Superman* LP. The album took the *Fairytale* experiments a step further, its packaging emblematic of early psychedelic imagery. The colours were bold and the fonts giddy art nouveau, with Donovan at the centre in an up-to-the-minute paisley shirt. But it was mainly in the songs that Donovan marked himself out from the crowd as he anticipated two significant inspirations for the psychedelic folk to come, first by exploring medieval imagery on 'Guinevere' and then by name-checking the acid-soaked Haight-Ashbury scene on 'The Fat Angel'. The songs are infused with sitars and harpsichords, although the electric howl of 'Season Of The Witch' would prove to be the album's most immediately noticeable track. Folk-pop had, rather unexpectedly, freaked out.

When Robin Williamson returned to the UK from Morocco, he had with him a gimbri, a sitar, a tamboura, an oud – and some new thoughts on music itself. "I brought back a number of instruments," he says, "and with them the idea of trying to put a number of different musical styles into one piece of music. The idea was naïve painting, painting without technique, and I thought the idea was to make music without technique: try instruments you couldn't play and break down the barriers between performer and audience."

Williamson's sometime band-mate, Mike Heron, had been keeping himself busy in the interim. In between gigs covering Dylan songs, he had been furiously writing some new material that owed far more to the haze of 'The Tree' than the pelt of 'Maybe Someday'. Joe Boyd, meanwhile, was back on the scene and free of his Elektra commitment. He wanted to bring The Incredible String Band back together under the aegis of his newly formed Witchseason Productions (named after Donovan's 'Season Of The Witch'). They agreed. Boyd thought that this new String Band would be completely in tune with the times and destined to be absolutely huge. Folk clubs were no longer their habitat; Boyd steered them into the UFO and other underground clubs. "I think Joe was very conscious of not promoting us as a folk band," Heron says. "He consciously took us out of that folk circuit, which I think was probably a good move."

According to Boyd, the band's new songs "had strange lyrics and rich melodies, and they kept coming up with off the wall ideas for harmonies and overdubs".[4] These songs would form an iconic record: *The 5000 Spirits Or The Layers Of The Onion*. The band cut some demos and works-in-progress at Sound Techniques (later released as *The Chelsea Sessions*); after that, these off-the-wall ideas gained legs and lyrics, ambiguous and graceful, that were deliberately intended to allow the listener to put his or her own thought processes onto the songs. The plethora of instruments and Williamson's concept of 'music without technique' brought the material to a state whereby there could be several changes within one song, or between different songs. This eclecticism and shiftlessness became the watermark of the album. Assisting Heron and Williamson on the album were: Licorice McKechnie, on percussion and vocals; Danny Thompson, on double bass; Nazir Jairazbhoy (credited as 'Soma'), on sitar; and John 'Hoppy' Hopkins, here credited with a few piano tinkles.

Although the psychedelic influence was the most initially striking feature of *5000 Spirits*, there were other, more important elements to what The Incredible String Band were doing. The instruments, the outlook, the fusions between folk and various other styles and sounds – in 1967, only the String Band (and, in America, The New Age) were doing this. And, as the product of Heron and Williamson's own journeys of discovery, these explorations sounded unmistakably authentic; according to a rave review in *Melody Maker*, the record had "almost everything".

As Williamson explained in 1979, the album's title "seemed to be a symbol of consciousness. You know, you either think of it of layers and layers and layers of onion, or thousands of voices".[5] The title is also an effective description of Heron and Williamson's cosmic and concentrated harmonising, the tapestry of sound, and the stream-of-consciousness movements unravelling and then re-layering with seemingly endless invention.

It was an extremely innovative album, and Joe Boyd knew it. He correctly surmised that it would slot in with the hippie movement currently in the process of going supernova, and claims to have deliberately targeted this audience in his marketing of the record. The first step was to have its hippie credentials writ large on the jacket, for which Boyd commissioned a lurid design by Dutch art collective The Fool. "Personally, I found their style auto-parodic," Boyd sniffs in *White Bicycles*. "But I knew it would send out the right signal." It did. John Peel played both sides, without interruption, on his *Perfumed Garden* radio show. The album started to really, really sell. "We melded into the 1967 culture and became very successful – entirely by accident, as far as I can see," Williamson recalled in 1999. "ISB played its first album in tiny folk clubs, its second in the Albert Hall."[6]

Although *5000 Spirits* provided the quantum leap between what the String Band once were and their new incarnation, some aspects of the album are indicative of birthing pains in the band's new approach. The saccharine whimsy and lack of restraint – both of which are apparent in more fanciful tracks like 'Little Cloud' – lead at times to a gilding of the psychedelic lily.

Hot on its heels, the band's next album would close that loophole by virtue of being an out-and-out masterpiece. *The Hangman's Beautiful Daughter* was recorded in late 1967 at Sound Techniques. It's ambitious, inventive, and has a fully ripe sound. Heron and Williamson both contributed outstanding songs, taking the expansive attitude of *5000 Spirits* to a higher plane. Nowhere is this clearer than on the 13-minute 'A Very Cellular Song'. "I had a little keyboard on the floor and I was listening to the radio," Heron recalls. "It was a Radio 4 programme, you know, like 'oh dear, mother, what shall I do' – that's a quote, probably from a play or something. They all became part of the experience. And I was listening to *The Music Of The Bahamas*, and that's the whole section from 'Lay down my dear sister', it's like a Bahaman spiritual. So I lifted that one from that. Everything else was kind of a description of the trip, I suppose. And it was a blessing at the end – 'May the long time sun shine', that kind of thing. It was just done through the night, just on a little tiny keyboard, then translated later into a slightly bigger landscape."

Another crucial difference was that the band was now recording on 16-track. Williamson later called this "a wonderful opening of the door" but admitted that "it was still done in a pretty slapdash, anarchic, have-a-go kind of way".[7] The album also features Dolly Collins on flute-organ. Heron and Williamson had recently got to know both Collins sisters; they both play on Shirley's *The Power Of The True Love Knot*, while Williamson later wrote 'God Dog' for her.

"I loved The Incredible String Band," says Shirley Collins. "You couldn't not love them. Some of their songs are so delightful and they themselves were so utterly delightful. But I do remember Dolly having almost a stand-up fight with Robin one day. Robin said to Dolly: 'You haven't seen a tree until you've taken LSD.' And she was so angry at this, she just erupted. That didn't suit me. I didn't like the drug aspect of it, the LSD and stuff." Nevertheless, the link between The Incredible String Band and the Collins sisters was an indication that, however far-out Heron and Williamson got, there was always a strong and recognisable thread of folk running throughout the music.

By now Heron and Williamson had added more instruments to their palate, from gimbri, oud, and chahannai to hammered dulcimer, water harp, and finger cymbals. *The Hangman's Beautiful Daughter* was a huge commercial success, reaching Number Five on the UK album chart. "I felt it was something special even as we were making it," Williamson later recalled.[8] The title itself was optimistic, the hangman referring to a bygone age of war and death and his 'beautiful daughter' representing the new, positive era. With two albums, and in less than a year, The Incredible String Band had smashed the definition of folk music in the UK and created a blueprint for others to follow.

⋈

While The Incredible String Band were basking in the glow of *The 5000 Spirits Or The Layers Of The Onion*, the summer of 1967 saw Joe Boyd cramming yet another act onto his roster when a band named Fairport Convention impressed him at the UFO. These six enthusiastic youngsters from Muswell Hill in North London had evolved out of numerous blues, skiffle, and jug bands but found most inspiration in psychedelic groups and American folk-rock.

The early core of Fairport Convention was formed by Ashley 'Tyger' Hutchings and Simon Nicol. Hutchings was a talented bass player and also the group's organiser – the one who planned the setlists and looked for opportunities to spread the word of the new band. Guitarist Nicol was his foil; equally gifted, musically, but a prankster. The line-up grew to incorporate guitarist Richard Thompson, a shy 17-year-old *wunderkind*, and an eccentric, sensitive drummer, Martin Lamble. None of the quartet felt at ease with their vocal abilities, so they recruited Judy Dyble. "I was part of the general heap of friends and I had long hair and played autoharp," she recalls. "Also, I was sort of going out with Richard, so I was there on the doorstep as it were. I was delighted, and so the fun began."

Another vocalist joined soon afterward. Ian Matthews (formerly Ian McDonald) already had experience in the music industry, having sung with the Deram group Pyramid. He and Dyble brought more than just their voices; she was a free-spirited beauty, and he had an aura of star quality. Together, they imbued Fairport Convention with a Haight-Ashbury inspired image to go alongside the current countercultural American sounds that the entire group appreciated. "We were different stylistically to all the other bands, because we had a wealth of contemporary American music constantly fed us by Joe," says

Matthews. "We played unusual covers, which in my opinion influenced the early writing in the band."

Little time passed before sessions for the debut album began at Sound Techniques. Matthews and Dyble recall these times with fondness, devoid of ego and boasting a collective bonhomie, encompassing friends and well-wishers who wandered in to jam and hang out. "It was the first time any of us had been into a studio," Dyble says, "and the thing that I remember most is the deadness of the sound. Very hushed and as though it was apart from the normal world outside."

Released in June 1968 on Polydor, *Fairport Convention* was a solid debut of US-inspired folk-rock with some *very* acidic touches, most notably on the strange, semi-improvised track, 'The Lobster', and Dyble's and Thompson's highlight, 'One Sure Thing'. Hutchings, however, says that the musicians were ultimately disappointed by the album's naïve sound. It certainly stands as both the most psychedelic and also the least overtly folky album they made, but whatever the band-members felt, it garnered support in influential quarters. "We found a lot of love from early on," Hutchings says, "including from John Peel, and it was great to have him on our side." Another prominent DJ, Tommy Vance, dubbed Fairport 'The English Jefferson Airplane' – a tag that stuck for longer than the band would have liked.

Despite critical success – or perhaps because of it – tensions grew within the young band. This resulted in the first of numerous personnel changes: the firing of Judy Dyble. In his memoir, *White Bicycles*, Joe Boyd says he didn't think that her vocals were suitable for the band; Dyble herself had little inkling of this at the time, and was taken aback when the axe fell just as the band was moving over to Island Records. She went on to work with Giles Giles & Fripp in an early incarnation of King Crimson, and would soon reappear in an artistic if not commercial psychedelic folk triumph as one half of Trader Horne. Fairport Convention, meanwhile, pressed on with a new female vocalist.

Sandy Denny seemed to have the perfect pedigree for Fairport's US-tinged electric folk-rock. She had attended Kingston Art College alongside John Renbourn, had been a member – briefly – of The Strawbs, and was dating Jackson C. Frank. It wasn't clear yet exactly how she would affect Fairport Convention, other than by the difference in voice, but from very early on in her tenure, one member realised that the group dynamic had shifted significantly. "Sandy arrived with all her folk baggage," Matthews recalls. "The band wanted to pursue that direction, and I was a fish completely out of water."

Even though Joe Boyd had steered his charges away from the folk clubs, those venues were still proving a breeding ground during this period for significant singer-songwriter developments. Bert Jansch continued on the roll started by his self-titled debut with *Nicola* (1967), which contained 'Go Your Way My Love', the song he co-wrote with Anne Briggs. Briggs herself still hadn't gone back in the studio since making her *The Bird In The Bush* EP.

Other names were gaining ground and attracting notice. Wizz Jones, a fixture of folk clubs and the busking trail in Europe, was in a duo with Pete Stanley; their *Sixteen Tons Of Bluegrass* (1966) provided a fine link between The Holy Modal Rounders' old-timey assault and a more pastoral, pensive Englishness.

Ralph McTell could be found on the streets of Europe with his guitar until 1966, when he relocated to Cornwall, Southwest England, to live in a caravan and play at a local club, the Folk Cottage. ("Its unique spirit got to me," he later said of the place, "a mix of swashbuckling seafarer bravado and Methodist rectitude."[9]) McTell formed a jug band featuring Mick Bennett on washboard, Henry Bartlett on jug, Bob Strawbridge on mandolin, Pete Berryman on guitar, and John The Fish on kazoo. The band enjoyed a significant local following until the end of summer 1967, when McTell went back to London.

Another maverick artist was Roy Harper, who gained a residency at Les Cousins in 1965. Like Jackson C. Frank and Michael Hurley, Harper was a man who poured his life into his songs, often couching his experiences in impenetrable lyrics. He had been brought up as a Jehovah's Witness and got away as soon as he could by joining the Air Force. He had started playing skiffle with his brother at the age of 13, and continued to do so in the Force, but his military experience was ultimately an unhappy one. He gained a discharge by feigning insanity, and was handed his freedom with a side order of electro-shock treatment and spells in a Surrey group-therapy centre and Lancaster Moor Mental Institution. He then vacillated between different hospitals and institutions (including jail) for a number of years. "All those situations hurled me headlong into desperate creativity," he later recalled. "It was just an urge, just to keep me head on and stay intact."[10]

Harper had begun composing poetry to cope with his situations, and by 1964 he was playing live. It was during his residency at Les Cousins that he came to the attention of the independent Strike record label, resulting in the release of his debut album, *Sophisticated Beggar* (1967). The lyrics might have been uncultivated, but the arrangements were considerably intricate. The album was recorded in one take to a Revox tape machine and features floating reverb, a full rock workout on 'Committed', and guest appearances by John Renbourn on two tracks. Harper would later bring his confessional, stream-of-consciousness style to a range of different media, but for now he was just about within the folk idiom.

This intense purple psychedelic patch in British folk music, led by The Incredible String Band in particular, would almost immediately spawn a whole crop of musicians. The possibilities offered by folk suddenly seemed limitless – and, crucially, were firmly in tune with the spirit of the times. More practically, the commercial success of the String Band persuaded British record companies that folk music twinned with hippie ideology could be a bankable proposition. What followed allowed the new psychedelic and outlandish folk music to be released on major labels in ways that they never had before and never would again. Meanwhile, back in America, the Technicolor dream was causing a riot of its own.

CHAPTER 4

Lepers And Roses

IN 1971, LESTER BANGS described ESP-Disk as "the most prototypically Underground record company in America". For once, this wasn't just Bangsian hyperbole: ESP-Disk was radical, it was diverse, and it was counter-cultural. It was also the first important enclave for psychedelic folk music in the USA.

The label was formed in 1960 by Bernard Stollman, a lawyer by training and a progressive by nature who for a number of years had offered legal counsel to African-American artists. He was particularly drawn to those who adopted an experimental approach, with improvisational jazz-based music a special passion. He applied this same ideology to the label's release schedule, trusting in the artistic vision of the acts who chose to make their records with him. It was enshrined in the motto for which the label would become famous: "The artists alone decide what you will hear on their ESP-Disk."

"I thought, give them a simple agreement and go your own way," he later recalled. "Ignore the industry and the 32 or 40-page contract. Every step of the way, everything I did just seemed logical and natural, and had no relation at all to what the industry was doing. I would not put my name on the record as producer – my sense of it was [that] the artists themselves were producers. Why should I move in on that or make any claims? So I didn't do it, I pointedly and purposely kept my name off of the credits."[1]

The name ESP-Disk – sometimes written as ESP-Disk' – came from Stollman's interest in Esperanto, the artificial hybrid language created in the late 1870s as a means of fostering cross-national communication and understanding. ESP-Disk's first release was the Esperanto-language *Ni Kantu En Esparantu*; for years, all of the label's releases carried mail-order information in English and Esperanto. As soon as Stollman got to grips with the simple mechanics of the record business, it became clear to him that he could use his label for all manner of niche interests. "You bring them the tape, cut the lacquers, plate it and press it, you do the artwork, they make the jacket," he later recalled. "You're dealing with a huge industrial plant, yet you can press as few as 500 records."[2]

ESP-Disk would become best known for its jazz output – despite Stollman's dislike for the word 'jazz', which he believed to be imprecise and racist – but also made significant moves into experimental rock with The Fugs and The Godz. Stollman also had an interest in folk. "I'd done some legal work with Moe Asch at Folkways," he later recalled. "I saw that Moe had arrived at a formula that was uncomplicated and inexpensive, and he was getting the music out. I was very taken with that."[3]

Just as psychedelia was starting to affect folk music in earnest, ESP-Disk was there to put out records that were folk-informed, psychedelic, and experimental. No one act fitted the bill better than Pearls Before Swine, the most successful and influential of the ESP-Disk folk groups. The band's founder and leader, Tom Rapp, was born in Bottineau, North Dakota, and started playing music at a very young age. "I wrote a song in 1954, when I was seven," he says. The song was called 'The End Of The Trail', and was about a dying cowboy. "Looking back, I realise I must have been this strange all my life."

Rapp's first instrument was the ukulele, which he learnt to play at the age of six; when he was nine, he was shown the basics of guitar by a local country & western performer. After the Rapp family moved to Minnesota, Tom's parents began to enter him in local talent shows, one of which pitted him against a young Bobby Zimmerman. "Both of us lost to a little girl in a red sequined dress who twirled baton," Rapp says. "I sure wish I could remember him playing, but I can't."

In 1966, shortly after graduating high school, Rapp was involved in a car accident. "I was thrown out of an Austin-Healey Sprite at 50 miles per hour," he recalls. "I remember lying there thinking the universe doesn't care at all, the only thing holding us up is us. And then I thought, there's a song there." He wrote the first Pearls Before Swine song, 'Another Time', about the experience.

Rapp would often hang out and play music with his friends Wayne Harley, Lane Lederer, and Roger Crissinger; when more songs began to flow, the four of them formed a band. Rapp took the name Pearls Before Swine from the biblical epithet about not giving precious artefacts to those who don't appreciate them, which he reinterpreted in a contemporary, countercultural way, with his generation the pearls cast before the swine of the establishment.

Rapp had recently become a fan of The Fugs and, sensing a shared mindset, sent some of his songs to their label. ESP-Disk sent a positive telegram straight back. Rapp was still scrawling down songs on the plane out to New York to record the first Pearls Before Swine album, but by the time the band hit the runway, everything was in place.

Rapp drew on a wide range of influences. "I was just writing songs and seeing where they went," he says. "Something by Dylan would push me in one direction, Tim Buckley in another, John Prine in another, Jefferson Airplane in another. I was constantly synthesizing everything around me." There's the personal experience of 'Another Time'; songs related to Rapp's anti-establishment and anti-war views, such as 'Uncle John' and 'Drop Out!'; and songs born of a fascination with history, like 'I Shall Not Care', which draws on a Sara Teasdale poem, an opera, and an epitaph from a Roman tomb. There's also a streak of Fugs-like insolence, most notably on 'Oh Dear (Miss Morse)', which spells out F-U-C-K in Morse Code. ("I looked up Morse code in a Boy Scout manual and tried L-O-V-E but that didn't work metrically," Rapp recalls. "God's will there, I think.")

One Nation Underground was recorded in four days at Impact Sound, New York, with engineer Richard Alderson, who also brought in the jazz drummer Warren Smith. The sessions gleefully incorporated multiple instruments that the band found hanging around the studio, including oud, tabla, and celeste. They also came prepared with a trick of their own. "We had brought along an oscilloscope to put 'I Shall Not Care' in the ascending higher and higher pitch," Rapp recalls. "We thought, boy, when people listen to this stoned …"

The album was released around May 1967, a Hieronymous Bosch painting on its front cover. "We always thought: 'Who wants to see four more white guys on a record cover?' We didn't care about being famous. Also, no photographs allowed for the creation of weird myths – that we were all in our sixties, we had a dwarf drummer, we were really well-known musicians doing experimental projects." Bosch's visions also suffused the album's 'Morning Song', while the artwork's nightmarish intensity proved an effective evocation of Rapp's fragile, mystic voice and the crooked acoustic apparitions within the grooves.

Perhaps surprisingly, given its idiosyncrasies, the album was a strong seller. The band's songs were printed in *Sing Out!* and *Broadside*, and even turned up on the radio. The LP also travelled: the German film director Rainer Werner Fassbinder incorporated 'Another Time' and 'Morning Song' into his 1971 film *Rio Das Mortes*. All in all, *One Nation Underground* sold somewhere between 100,000 and 250,000 copies – no mean feat for an unusual album on a small independent label. The band-members were largely ignorant of the music business, and unsure how much money they had earned, but presumed it would come to them somewhere down the line. When ESP-Disk asked them to do another album, Rapp readily agreed.

"*Balaklava* was always going to be an antiwar concept album," Rapp says of the second Pearls Before Swine record, which he named after a battle in the Crimean War and recorded during the Vietnam conflict. "I had recordings of the actual bugle sounded at the Charge Of The Light Brigade in the Battle Of Balaklava in 1854, and of Florence Nightingale, who treated soldiers as a nurse there. It was the last time that war could seriously be considered 'glorious'."

Whereas *One Nation Underground* had come to life in an impromptu manner, *Balaklava* took 18 months to get from concept to vinyl. "It took so long because all the time people were leaving the group, other people were joining, others were in college and couldn't get away," Rapp told the *New York Times*. "We recorded things, and a month later they sounded awful. Eventually it got done."[4]

Working again with engineer Richard Alderson at Impact Sound, the band – now also featuring Lee Crabtree – once more grazed at the buffet of instruments available to them at the studio. This time, however, Rapp remembers being more deliberate, and having more time and more awareness of both possibilities and limitations. The result was a more polished but no less effectively poetic sound filled with melancholic dissent. The scratchy samples of the bugler, Trumpeter Landfrey, and of Florence Nightingale (both take from *Voices Of History*) lend the album a subtle pathos and move it far away from the direct simplicity of most folk protest song. There are unpredictable dual vocals on 'Translucent Carriages' – one for the sorrowful narration, as inspired by the Greek historian Herodotus, and one for whispered, impressionistic emotion – and field recordings of animals embedded in 'Images Of April'. The final song, the Tolkien-inspired 'Ring Ring', ends with the sound of the master tape being rewound to the beginning, before Trumpeter Landfrey comes in again, the whole concept ever-spinning. *Balaklava* is the pity of war as lamented by the psychedelic 60s.

Once again, the band opted not to appear on the cover of the album. Instead they used a painting by Pieter Bruegel The Elder, *The Triumph Of Death*, a macabre panorama of skeletons slaughtering the living. For the reverse, Rapp chose to use the tortured cold-turkey drawings from Jean Cocteau's autobiography, *Opium*. "They seemed to express all the pain in the world," he recalls. "Perfect."

Balaklava proved to be the final ESP-Disk by Pearls Before Swine. Rapp appreciated the label's ethos, and was grateful for Stollman's adventurous philosophy, but there was one big problem: "We never got any money from ESP – not even like $100."[5] They ended up moving to Reprise, as did The Fugs. Although Reprise fell under the corporate wingspan of Warner Bros, the label had been set up with principles similar to Stollman's: Frank Sinatra, the founder, insisted that each artist have full creative freedom and ownership of their work. Pearls Before Swine would go on to make music that sounded just as beautiful and complicated as their work for ESP-Disk, if less obviously bizarre. Tom Rapp would soon be back.

Meanwhile, back in the heartland of bohemian New York, the rift between Steve Weber and Peter Stampfel that had brought the end of The Holy Modal Rounders during the summer of 1965 was still simmering. Weber's behaviour had become so chaotic that by the end of the year he had also been kicked out of The Fugs. Like Stampfel, vocalist Ed Sanders felt that the general bedlam surrounding Weber was sabotaging The Fugs' chances of success. As Sanders later recalled, the band had been booked to play with Pete Seeger at Carnegie Hall. "It was a glorious opportunity for us and he didn't show up," he said. "He would occasionally fall asleep in gigs, using his guitar as a pillow. He's the only human being I ever saw who, as a remedy for toothache, took LSD."[6]

Stampfel himself had started to write songs with his girlfriend, Antonia, and was keen to put together a band away from Weber. One such attempt was with Bill Barth and Nancy Jeffries, who came to stay with Stampfel and Antonia in New York but ended up forming a psychedelic pop group of their own, The Insect Trust. Stampfel had also met and begun to play with a budding playwright and drummer, Sam Shepard.

In early 1967, Stampfel received a call from Bernard Stollman, urging him to consider making a Holy Modal Rounders album for ESP-Disk. Stampfel recounted the problems with Weber: he wouldn't rehearse; he wouldn't commit; he couldn't be forced to do *anything*. Furthermore, he continued, they hadn't played together for a couple of years apart from at a one-off gig in Illinois in 1966.

Stollman was unconcerned, and eventually persuaded The Holy Modal Rounders – now Stampfel, Weber, Shepard, and keyboardist Lee Crabtree – to record a new album. According to Stampfel, however, he and Weber were speeding and completely unrehearsed. Stampfel dislikes the resulting *Indian War Whoop* intensely, feeling it to be a sloppy crystallisation of all of the problems he warned Stollman about. He also regrets not attending the mixing session. "If you're not [there]," he says, "things will happen that will make you very unhappy." One such thing was the decision to dispense with the gaps between songs for a more overtly psychedelic effect.

Indian War Whoop is certainly very, very different from the first two Holy Modal Rounders records, and also from the gentle surreal glide of label-mates Pearls Before Swine. The deranged old-timey feel is still in there, but is now encircled in a hoop of full-on psychedelia and spaced-out improvisation – which doesn't always work, and which means that the Rounders lose some of what originally made them special.

There are nevertheless some important moments on the album. The band deconstructs traditional folksong – represented here by 'Sweet Apple Cider', 'Soldier's Joy', and 'Bay Rum Blues' – to a kind of babble only hinted at before, while the spoken-word interludes and hallucinogenic tableaux move the warped folk of their first two albums decisively into the summer of 1967. And, if nothing else, the album did get the Rounders back together, even if the reunion lasted only as long as the studio time.

Indian War Whoop ended up being the Rounders' only album for ESP-Disk. The band received no royalties for it, although Stampfel notes that, in 1966, Stollman gave him $200 in royalties from the first Fugs album. Once work on the album had been completed, Stampfel vowed never to work with Weber again – a pledge that would not even last for as long as the one he made in 1965.

Although the riotous *Indian War Whoop* and the plaintive intensity of the two Pearls Before Swine albums are ESP-Disk's best-known experimental folk albums, the label also put out a number of other records linked to the genre. There were three albums by Greenwich Village regular Randy Burns, and three others issued by the label's shortlived 'pop' subsidiary, Oro: *Folksinger* by Tod Kelley, *Side One (Play The Other Side First)* by All That The Name

Implies, and a self-titled album by Bruce MacKay, later reissued as *Midnight Minstrel*, that features Lee Crabtree on keys amid a palate of flute, melodica, and electric harpsichord.

By 1968, if Bernard Stollman is to be believed, ESP-Disk had attracted the attention of the US government and the Mafia. Distribution deals in Japan and Europe mysteriously fell through, while the pressing plant was allegedly bootlegging various ESP-Disk albums, including those by the label's top sellers, Pearls Before Swine.

"It is a mystery," Stollman later recalled, "and whether the US government got involved, I can't even begin to guess. We had been effectively out of business since '68, but for six years we kept going on money we had in the bank, and I guess we were just disregarding the reality of the situation."[7] Stollman also claimed that he got a call from Jac Holzman at Elektra, encouraging him to sell up to Warner Bros, and that the departures of The Fugs and Pearls Before Swine were engineered by the government in an attempt to silence their anti-war stance.

Unsurprisingly, the bands themselves see things rather differently. As the official history on the band's website puts it: "The Fugs relationship with ESP records was, mildly to state it, turbulent. We were told, for instance, that the Mafia was illegally manufacturing Fugs records and selling them. We can be forgiven for not really believing that the Genovese crime family would bother with The Fugs, when there were The Beatles, the Stones, Mantovani, and Petula Clark to rip off."[8]

Tom Rapp is even more forthright. "My real sense is that [Stollman] was abducted by aliens," he later recalled, "and when he was probed it erased his memory of where all the money was. I think that probably makes as much sense as the Mafia and the CIA."[9] Nevertheless, the label soldiered on for a few more years. In the late 60s, it released two novel but poorly distributed records that, even by ESP-Disk standards, would languish in unfair obscurity for decades.

The first was by an artist that even Tom Rapp found outlandish, according to the man himself, who recalls hearing that Rapp found his record "really strange". Ed Askew had started performing at poetry events while studying art at Yale and had become known for his unusual choice of instrument: the tiple, a small instrument with superficial similarities to the ukulele and the lute that dates back to 16th century Colombia. Askew's was US-made by Martin, and had ten strings arranged between four courses. It was complex to play, and it sounds it.

The songs on Askew's debut come from the period after his graduation from Yale, when he taught at a private boarding school in Ridgefield, Connecticut. After moving to New York, he began to work the Greenwich Village circuit, taking his tiple and singing at basket houses to raise cash. An onlooker who was struck by Askew's unusual songs and playing style suggested he get in touch with Bernard Stollman.

Stollman wouldn't make a decision based on Askew's live performance, but eventually offered the singer an album deal after asking him to find a tape recorder and put down some songs. The resulting album, originally self-titled but soon reissued as *Ask The Unicorn*, was recorded in August 1968. It offers surface comparisons to Michael Hurley's *First Songs*, particularly in the way that its personal subjects are embedded in dreamlike verse. Askew's opaque, nuanced lyricism certainly betrays the time he had spent at poetry readings, and yet the album has a far more unusual sound than, say, *Bruce MacKay*. The tiple-playing, which gives the songs an echoic texture akin to hearing a symphony through a telescope, is offset by the harrowing quality of Askew's voice. He later claimed that he sounds so stressed because the tiple is so difficult to play; whatever the reason, his voice is the yin to the instrument's yang, helping to create a compelling combination like nothing ever heard before.

Without waiting for royalties or to see whether *Ask The Unicorn* would be a success, Askew almost immediately laid down the follow-up, *Little Eyes*. A more delicate affair, with slightly calmer vocals, it was recorded virtually as a live performance. By 1970, however, ESP-Disk was losing money hand over fist, and *Little Eyes* stayed in the vaults. Without ever having had a fair shot at the marketplace, *Ask The Unicorn* would soon join it in limbo.

The second of the later folk mavericks signed to ESP-Disk was a man named Jim Holberg. As a young man he was injured in a road accident when his motorcycle collided with a Chevy Corvette filled with drunken teenagers who had run a red light, resulting in a fractured skull, spinal meningitis, a hearing impairment, and an epiphany. "The thoughts I got from the whole thing were like: this is not my path, and the path I must take it different, and if I change this path something bad will happen to kick me back on my path," he says.

Holberg began to turn his whole outlook away from the regular world. He took to calling himself Mij (Jim backward) and thought more about music. "I was probably the most shy person in history," he says, "but I learned in the Navy that I can sing a song, and it somehow got the conversation started. So the guitar makes the crutch that lets me open myself up."

The insurance money from the accident allowed Mij to buy a better guitar and to travel, so he went to Boston. "I was in the park trying to see how high I could get my voice to go," he recalls, "when suddenly it cracked from a weak falsetto to another range that doesn't sound false and is strong and carries for blocks." This new voice opened his mind up to the possibility that, somehow, the music flowing through him came from a bigger force. "It was this continuous magic out of nowhere," he says. "And I guess that is also how this album got developed."

The album itself also came about by chance. Mij was singing in Washington Square one Sunday when, he says, Bernard Stollman – out walking seven blocks away – heard his voice carry across the distance. Stollman made the offer of an album for ESP-Disk there and then.

Mij went into the studio on January 12 1969. The music on his album, originally titled *Color Mij By The Number* but reissued as *Yodeling Astrologer*, streamed out in a suitably haphazard fashion. The most unusual track, 'Grok (Martian Love Call)', was largely the result of studio experimentation. "I didn't have a 'high voice' song written yet," he says, "so I took stuff out of my head and worked it into a song right there." The contents of his head that day included whistling, vocal pops and clicks, snatches of the spiritual 'Sinnerman', and an invented language – all delivered in high-pitched jabbers and hoots. Throughout the record, Mij makes marked use of echo and looping techniques. He claims in some instances to have been trying to write Dylanesque songs, like 'Door Keys' and 'Look Into The (K)night', but even these are exceptionally far out. "The whole thing was like a spiritual unknowing awareness between all involved without words that made all the right things happen."

He was unhappy that he was only given limited studio time by ESP-Disk, however. "I told them to write on the album that it was made in only three hours," he says, "because I didn't have a chance to fix any of my mistakes. It was a mess, really, from what I expected. But it was also a miracle how everything came out."

Color Mij By The Number and *Ask The Unicorn* were, in some ways, the logical extremes suggested by the earlier material of Pearls Before Swine and The Holy Modal Rounders. But they were also the products of singular visions, two unconventional folk artists who were unlikely to find an appropriate home anywhere else.

Tom Rapp too appreciates the pioneer spirit of ESP-Disk. "Despite all the problems I had about never getting paid," he later said, "[Stollman] did get these products out there, especially the jazz and the experimental stuff. And then what happened to the people who did it – that's another story. But he did provide a conduit where a lot of good things got released out into the world."[10]

ESP-Disk limped on until 1974, by which time, Stollman has since claimed, it had been irreparably damaged by bootleggers. He also alleged that the CIA had planted a staff member at the label to deliberately undermine the company from within. Whatever the truth, it was a sad, messy, inglorious finale to one of the most open-minded record labels ever to have existed.

Despite the corner-cutting, questionable financial policies, and at times fraught relationship with artists, ESP-Disk was one of the earliest focal points for the stranger end of folk music in the USA. These records are a microcosm of how far folk could stretch given full artistic control – of just how weird and beautiful it could be – and would prove both a touchstone for and an alternative narrative to the blooming of US psychedelic folk.

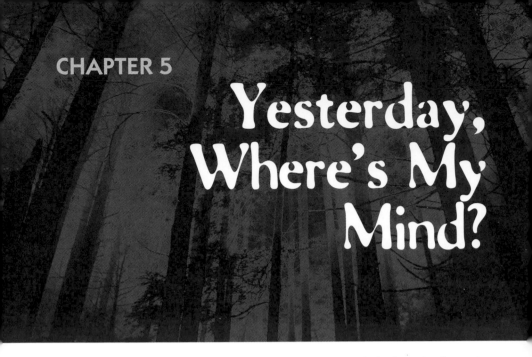

CHAPTER 5

Yesterday, Where's My Mind?

FOR AMERICAN MUSICIANS looking for a record deal in the late 60s, there was a sense of optimism bordering on entitlement. The channels to mainstream exposure suddenly seemed more open than ever before, even to the least commercial psychedelic folk artists. "You could walk down the street, see someone, and show them your wares," says folksinger Susan Christie. "You just took it for granted that somebody would listen."

Record labels were seemingly willing to welcome artists who prized integrity and who were enterprising and eclectic in their music. The relationship could be productive and supportive, often with one individual employee at a label acting as a champion for a particular kind of niche music. But there was a flipside. Once the initial euphoria over the signing died down, label and artist often struggled to understand one another. Forays into popular culture could prove confusing or downright disastrous; sales might fall far short of even a modest label estimate; artistic temperaments, drug use, political views, and a general unwillingness to 'play the game' proved an ongoing headache.

When a far from commercial record emerged out of costly recording sessions, the label was usually unhappy – much to the puzzlement or anger of the artist, who presumed musical exploration was the basis upon which he or she had been signed. There was often a reluctance on the part of the label to throw more money at these awkward albums, leading to meagre distribution or promotion (or both). The records were left to wither on the vine, much to the frustration of those who created them.

Elektra Records was certainly one of the more progressive majors, and had already proved itself willing to diversify into the experimental folk genre with Pat Kilroy – and, perhaps inadvertently, with Tim Buckley. This particular wayward charge was not about to reverse his game.

In 1969 Buckley delivered *Happy Sad*. Although the album maintained a straight folk aura in places, its author was edging ever further from familiar musical categories. He had now taken sole responsibility for songwriting, adding a large dollop of jazz to an already diverse sound arranged for 12-string guitar, congas, bass, piano, and, most startlingly, David Friedman's vibraphone.

"I really loved doing that album," Buckley later recalled. "It was really a breakout period of time for me musically. ... It took a long time for me to write that album, and then to teach the people in the band, but they were all great people, so it was really a labour of love."[1] He had become adept at borrowing from – and adding his own sheen to – the work of musicians he admired; 'Strange Feelin'', for example, is adapted from Miles Davis's 'All Blues'. He was also beginning to refigure his own innovations. 'Love From Room 109 At The Islander (On Pacific Coast Highway)' took the episodic structure of 'Goodbye And Hello' much further, adding dream-like vocals and pealing ocean sounds.

With *Happy Sad*, Buckley emerged at the head of his own class of new folk music. It was ultra-modern and experimental, and yet still seemed to be developing. But for all its innovation, the album was still fairly accessible, and the reviews were good. It reached Number 81 on the *Billboard* chart – making it the highest-placing Buckley album to date – and looked set to bury the receipts for the more familiar-sounding *Goodbye And Hello*. When sales began to stall after a few months, however, it became clear that Buckley's mainstream position was in peril. He was contracted to one more album with Elektra. Were he to deliver an album of heartfelt folk music, the label might keep him on the roster. Take a further excursion into the avant-garde, however, and Elektra was unlikely to keep him on any longer than it had to. In fact, he would end up making both records within the next year, but Elektra wouldn't get the one it wanted.

The bristles between Buckley and Elektra stemmed from the fact that, when he joined the label, there were few indications that he would veer so far (or so quickly) to the left. There would be no such illusions when The Holy Modal Rounders were brought back together – and onto Elektra – by in-house producer Frasier Mohawk, a long-time fan of the group, in late 1967. In an effort to extricate himself from the Rounders, Peter Stampfel had formed an electric rock group, The Moray Eels. Elektra, however, was more interested in the idea of a Rounders record. "I didn't want to make [another] album with [Steve] Weber," Stampfel says. Instead, he said he'd only make another Rounders record if his new band could play on it. "[But then], in a fit of amphetamine-fuelled exuberance, we said: 'Oh, we'll play with Weber again! We should call it The Holy Modal Rounders again.'"

As before, Stampfel warned the label that Weber wouldn't rehearse; Mohawk, like ESP-Disk's Bernard Stollman, batted his objections away. For Stampfel, the resulting sessions paralleled the experience of making *Indian War Whoop*. Weber wasn't at all prepared; the band went into the studio cold; vast amounts of speed were consumed. "I thought it was a very disappointing, flawed album," he says, although history suggests otherwise: *The Moray Eels Eat The Holy Modal Rounders* is now seen as a classic psychedelic-folk record.

"Everybody was so stoned in the making of that [album] that there isn't one tune that has an ending, or that is complete," Mohawk later recalled.[2] This ad hoc feel results in a disarming and original freshness that most other psychedelic bands were losing in their moves toward a more polished sound. Even Stampfel admits that the album stood apart. "Things changed in 1968," he says. "Before that, pop music was incredibly eclectic, and there really wasn't any artistic pretension until The Beatles made *Sgt Pepper*. And they took eight months to make an album. Before that album, all the first rate people would do two or three albums a year. But all of a sudden, making an album was a big artistic deal and pretentiousness basically reared its ugly head. Suddenly people were making *art*."

If other musicians were concerned with painting the ceiling of the Sistine chapel, The Holy Modal Rounders were working firmly in the tradition of naïve art. But that didn't mean the songs lacked structure or forethought. "All of those things that I thought in [Stampfel's] music were quirks, I [later] realised were in fact very well constructed and planned," Mohawk recalled. "There's very little randomness in his randomness."[3]

The Moray Eels Eat The Holy Modal Rounders is a journey through snippets of distorted rock psychedelics, kite-high elation, Mothers Of Invention-style cultural refraction, and the inimitable folk music of the earlier Rounders. From the untrammelled joy of 'Bird Song' to the hysterically troubled version of Michael Hurley's 'Werewolf', the album doesn't shy away from real emotions. It might sound like an album saturated with drugs, but to characterise it solely as that misses its wider haphazard and individual invention.

The Holy Modal Rounders' Elektra period saw the band brushing against the mainstream spotlight. There was a surreal appearance on *Rowan & Martin's Laugh-In* for a performance of 'Got The Right String, Baby, But The Wrong Yo-Yo' that was so riotous the show's producers wouldn't let the group finish the song. But that was a mere splash compared to the exposure the band received from the appearance of 'Bird Song' on the soundtrack to *Easy Rider*. The song can be heard when George Hanson (played by Jack Nicholson) is riding pillion behind Wyatt (Peter Fonda); Hanson's arms are outstretched, as if he is testing out his own wingspan. It's the perfect visual complement to the song's exhilaration. The *Easy Rider* soundtrack album made Number Six on *Billboard*, but neither the Rounders nor Antonia, who wrote the song, received royalties from it.

This time around, the Rounders hadn't split up as soon as the studio door closed, but the *Easy Rider* exposure brought about little discernible difference to them. They were simply unwilling – or unable – to capitalise on the moment. There were no further albums for Elektra, despite a couple of aborted attempts. The first was another session organised by Mohawk, which yielded little usable material; the second was an idea of Elektra's to capitalise on Sam Shepard's growing literary reputation by having him pen a comedy-musical piece for the Rounders to record. Stampfel rejected this idea, and the group's flirtation with both major labels and popular culture came to an end.

It took him a while to get there, but in 1968, Dino Valenti recorded a solo album. Known variously as Jackie Powers, Jesse Oris Farrow, and by his birth name, Chet Powers Jr, Valenti occupies an ambiguous place in the story of psychedelic folk. On one hand, he was a folk-pop pioneer, unafraid to experiment and profoundly influential on others; on the other, he was a narcissistic nightmare, a hustler with an eye always on the main chance. "You were either with it or you weren't," his friend and band-mate, Gary Duncan, later recalled. "If you were with it, that meant you were with the carnival, and everybody else was a mark. He was on the outside of society looking in, like a gypsy."[4]

Duncan wasn't being flippant: Chet Powers really did grow up with the carnival. His parents were both performers, and he and his sister helped out on stalls and sideshows from a young age. The Powers children were stigmatised at school but grew up savvy and self-sufficient. The young Chet started playing guitar after being ejected from the Air Force, and in 1960 wound up in Greenwich Village with a new name, Dino Valenti.

Valenti polarised opinion from the get-go. Some – Peter Stampfel among them – saw him as an arrogant egotist; others enjoyed his company. It was during his time in New York that Valenti wrote 'Get Together', a prescient slice of peace-and-love idealism that would later provide The Youngbloods with a US Top Five hit. In 1964, now based in San Francisco, he recorded another remarkable forerunner of future musical direction, the electric folk-rock single 'Birdses'. There was some talk of him forming a band with Roger McGuinn, but Valenti eventually hatched a plan with guitarist John Cipollina, whom he had met in 1965. The idea was for a high-concept psychedelic band to flaunt both musical virtuosity and flamboyant showmanship. That scheme was put on hold, however, when Valenti was arrested for possession of marijuana and amphetamines and sent to Folsom Prison.

Cipollina took the nucleus of the idea he and Valenti had discussed and formed Quicksilver Messenger Service with Jim Murray, David Freiberg, Gary Duncan, and Greg Elmore. The band eventually signed a deal with Capitol Records in 1967 and achieved considerable critical and popular success with their self-titled debut album the following year. Rumour has it that Quicksilver had delayed signing a major-label deal until then because they were waiting for Valenti's release from prison. If so, they would have been disappointed. Firstly, it took Valenti longer than expected to secure a release (and even then it came at significant future cost, as he was forced to sell the rights to 'Get Together' in order to raise his legal fees). Secondly, when Valenti did emerge from Folsom in 1967, he decided instead to sign a solo deal with Epic, a prominent subsidiary of Columbia.

Dino Valenti's relationship with Epic was fraught from the start. The label's first attempt at recording him ended in disaster when an album's worth of pop-oriented material produced by Jack Nitzsche was scrapped because Valenti felt it was not valid artistically. "Dino was notoriously hard to deal with," Gary Duncan later recalled. "He had a reputation of being a total fucking prick."[5]

For their next attempt at recording Valenti, Epic enlisted Bob Johnston, who had a reputation for getting the best from unpredictable artists and whose softly-softly methods had worked effectively with Johnny Cash and Bob Dylan. The unflappable Johnston knew that he would have to be subtle if he was to coax anything out of Valenti, who subsequently wasted studio time by spending days making paper planes, hanging out with his horde of female admirers, or calling up bagpipe players whose efforts wouldn't actually make it onto the album.

When the album was eventually completed, it introduced a new form of folk music imbued with San Franciscan psychedelia and embryonic country-rock. Pat Kilroy had trodden the same San Francisco circuit, but his *Light Of Day* was steeped in Asian, African, and European influences; Valenti's album, on the other hand, was soaked in his national heritage: cowboy hats, dusty roads, 12-string twang, and acid-flecked reverb. The lyrics – mostly geared toward constructing a kind of hippie Hugh Hefner persona – also found inspiration in the mind-bending rock of Haight-Ashbury. On the rockier tracks, Valenti's nasal twang is so heavily echoed it sounds like he's singing straight down a canyon; elsewhere, most obviously on the kaleidoscopic 'Test', his voice is an ethereal mutter, while the flute arrangement is as uncanny as anything on the ISB's *5000 Spirits*.

The album was released in 1968 with the curiously misspelt title *Dino Valente* – alleged by some to be a vindictive swipe by a label incensed by Valenti's poor attitude and the high cost of making the album. It was poorly distributed and largely ignored, but Valenti himself seemed undeterred. "With all this fucking renewed energy and the knowledge I've picked up in the studio," he said in 1969, "I can go in there and put down a fucking album that is just going to cream everybody."[6]

It didn't quite work like that. Epic didn't want another Valenti album; even if he was about to 'cream everybody', he wasn't worth the hassle. As Gary Duncan later recalled, the failure of *Dino Valente* really started to hit home when Valenti went to play in New York and only three or four people showed up. "Prior to that, he had been a lot nicer. He got really bitter after that event. And then he got mad at everybody."[7]

Valenti moved back to New York in 1969 and formed a shortlived band, The Outlaws, with Gary Duncan. With no record deal in prospect, however, he finally threw in his lot with Quicksilver Messenger Service – just as they had passed their peak. His prophet-like quality for anticipating musical trends seemed sadly to have passed, and he began to recede slowly from relevance.

In the confusion of the early Quicksilver Message Service, another member had come and gone before the band ever really got going: Alexander 'Skip' Spence. Like Valenti, Spence was blessed with a magnetic and singular personality; there was, as his one-time band-mate Peter Lewis put it, "a very messianic thing about Skip".[8]

Spence made a solo album, *Oar*, the same year Valenti recorded his. But whereas *Dino Valente* was psychedelic folk as peacock display, *Oar* represented an inner space. Spence's experience in Jefferson Airplane and Moby Grape – two of the most prominent San Franciscan bands of all – infused *Oar* with a high-quality psychedelic heritage; his own rapid personal unravelling, which had begun in earnest during the recording of Moby Grape's *Wow*, lent the album an air of fractured psychological examination. The folk elements come not from years of slogging around the Greenwich Village circuit, but from peeling back the layers of his troubles and exploring them away from the confines of rock music. Like Spence himself, *Oar* really was a one-off.

Spence was born in Canada, but his family had moved to San Jose in the late 50s. From the time of his discharge from the US Navy in 1965, he was a face on the San Francisco scene. After a chance meeting at a hip club, the Matrix, Marty Balin invited Spence – by then playing guitar with Quicksilver Messenger Service – to take over on drums in his band, Jefferson Airplane. Spence's intoxicatingly instinctive playing suited the Airplane well. He stayed with the group for their first album, *Jefferson Airplane Takes Off* (1966), for which he co-wrote two songs, but was fired shortly thereafter when he sauntered off to Mexico instead of playing a gig. Spence bounced straight back, forming Moby Grape with two other guitarists, Jerry Miller and Peter Lewis, drummer Don Stevenson, and bassist Bob Mosley.

The band's first year together was like a fairytale, but things began to come undone around the time of the release of their self-titled debut in June 1967. Columbia Records' strategy of releasing five simultaneous singles robbed the band of a hit, while the glitz of the label's Hollywood-style album launch proved unpopular with their local fans. Further problems ensued when the band came to record their second album, *Wow*.

"There were some people there that were into harder drugs and a harder lifestyle, and some very weird shit," Jerry Miller later recalled. "[Spence] kind of flew off with those people."[9] Spence was by now consuming vast quantities of LSD, his mental health was worsening, and he was developing a dangerous interest in the occult. "The aura of light was gone," Marty Balin recalled of a chance meeting with his former band-mate. "He didn't look anything like the guy I loved."[10]

Matters came to a head one night in New York, when Spence chopped through the door of *Wow* producer David Rubinson's hotel room with an axe and then went looking for the rest of Moby Grape. He didn't hurt anybody, but he ended up in the NYPD's holding facility, 'The Tombs', before being admitted to Bellevue Hospital for a six-month stay.

When he was discharged, Spence had nothing left but the prison uniform he was wearing when he entered the hospital – and reams and reams of lyrics. Columbia put Spence up in a hotel and gave him an advance, which he spent on a motorcycle before heading to Nashville to record his new songs away from New York, San Francisco, and Moby Grape.

The common assumption about *Oar* – that it offers a chaotic peek into an unstable mind – is vastly oversimplified. It is, in fact, an insightful and largely figurative exploration not just of Spence's despair but also the ongoing healing process. (The only song of his that could truly be described as a raw representation of mental disharmony is 'Skip's Song', which actually predates *Oar* but was subsequently recorded as 'Seeing', without Spence, by a later configuration of Moby Grape.)

Skip Spence did everything on *Oar* – all the instruments, production, and arrangement – and performed with honesty and artistic grace. His voice is powerful and yet carefully reflects the lyrics: he growls defensively on 'Cripple Creek' but is all impudent brashness on more humorous interludes like the warped, Disney-style sing-along, 'Lawrence Of Euphoria'. The most 'folk' tracks on the album are the pained, wheezing 'Diana' and the improvised bass-and-drums closer, 'Grey/Afro', which anticipates Tim Buckley's later free-folk explorations, and indeed those by subsequent generations of folk-influenced artists. Spence circled around psychedelia, bringing it back to an unvarnished country-blues state that reflects his experiences in the unvarnished areas of life itself.

Despite the claim in the liner notes that *Oar* was completed in a single day, it was actually recorded over four days in December 1968 on a near-obsolete three-track system by Columbia's Nashville engineer Mike Figlio. Figlio was a colleague of Bob Johnston, who had advised him to take the same gentle approach as had worked with Dino Valenti. In the original liner notes, David Rubinson described the album as "so guileless – so remarkably unselfconscious, that its integrity is its unity. It is the purest possible representation of that human being who was Spence at the time".

In his review for *Rolling Stone*, Greil Marcus hailed "the sort of haphazard folk music that might have been made around campfires after the California gold rush burned itself out – sad, clumsy tunes that seem to laugh at themselves". He encouraged readers to buy the album before it disappeared, but his advice fell on deaf ears. Soon after its May 1969 release, *Oar* did indeed vanish from the shelves. It is estimated to have been one of the poorest-selling records in Columbia's history.

Spence himself went back to California. He was only in his early twenties, but was in no position to negotiate another record deal even if one had been offered. His mental health had worsened again, and he would soon be beset by a series of physical problems. Aside from a few one-off appearances over the years, Alexander 'Skip' Spence had retired from music.

California was also home to another musician with a personal and highly evolved vision. Linda Perhacs knew from a young age that she was experiencing the world differently from other people. She saw and felt sound and thought as multi-dimensional phenomena. "I tried to learn from [these experiences] rather than be afraid of them," she says. "I now know they usually represent energy frequencies that are very normal and common in our universe, it's just that we've become too low in our vibration to see and hear them."

These concepts are explored in depth in Annie Besant and Charles Webster Leadbeater's *Thought-Forms*. "Every thought gives rise to a set of correlated vibrations in the matter of the body," they write, "accompanied with a marvellous play of colour, like that in the spray of a waterfall as the sunlight strikes it." For Perhacs, these visual phenomena occurred in music. "When a sound tone is generated, it has a specific wavelength in physics," she says. "Simultaneously there is a *colour* wavelength that goes with this sound wavelength. These wavelengths are very refined. They are present at all times, but to see them, we must rise to *their* level, not the other way around."

Perhacs had an early aptitude for music and physical movement. As a child, she generated songs and choreography in her home in Mill Valley, just north of the Golden Gate Bridge. Neither family nor school encouraged her musical and esoteric gifts, however, and so it wasn't until the age of 27 that she began to write songs that explored 'thought-forms' and visual music. She became a recording artist following a chance meeting with the film composer Leonard Rosenman, a patient at the Beverley Hills surgery at which Perhacs worked as a dental hygienist.

Rosenman invited Perhacs to his studio, where he brought a classical atonality and an early electronic sensibility to her delicate, acoustic songs. He had spent his career working with both sound and vision, and so well understood her concept of cross-sensory perception. He put a lot of time and resources into the project, bringing in skilled session players and working to develop the songs until they evoked the three dimensions Perhacs wanted.

The time and care was worthwhile. *Parallelograms* is a tessellated aural experience that comes as close as one might get to a synthesis of the senses with musical echoes, overlapping vocals, dissonance, and a minimalist sensibility that flits between pause and activity. When Perhacs sings about "silences between leaves" on 'Chimacum Rain', guitar and multiple voices tumble down and spring up around her words like rain bouncing off a rock pool. These effects find their most explicit expression in the title track. "There is a whole galaxy in the geometric shape and form of a parallelogram," Perhacs says. "I am glad I chose the word. It encompasses many levels of thought and creation."

Once the album was completed, Rosenman secured a release for it on the Kapp label in 1970. It was then that Linda Perhacs's musical vision was impaired. The poor vinyl pressing of *Parallelograms* muffled the iridescent spray created in the studio, and Kapp failed to promote the album, leaving it largely unheard and unseen. "I was terribly disappointed," she says. She resumed her dental career and never released another album.

One act that was able to enjoy a stable relationship with a big label – at least to begin with – was Tom Rapp's Pearls Before Swine. They were taken from ESP-Disk to Reprise by their manager, Peter Edmiston, who had a 'personal service' contract with Rapp, which meant he dealt with the business of selling Rapp's records to the label, and with all financial matters. For now, this worked well; Rapp's bills were paid, and at least some money was reaching him.

In the light of the continued crumbling of ESP-Disk – and the non-payment of royalties for Pearls Before Swine's two hit albums – the band's move to Reprise was understandable, but there were still some who saw Rapp as disloyal. To Lester Bangs, who had never been much of a fan anyway, "the fuckin' place [Reprise] was *made* for P.B. Swine, just find 'em a berth in the stable for snotnose minstrels, right between Arlo and the one reserved for James Taylor".[11]

If the band's first album for Reprise, *These Things Too* (1969), was more conventional, this was not down to any directive from his new label. Even before signing to Reprise, Rapp had been thinking of adopting a gentler sound. "It's more in the way of folk-rock, more optimistic," he had said. "The previous stuff has tended to be pessimistic. I take things less seriously on the next album."[12] Indeed, the only pressure from the label was "to use actual photos of me or the band" in the album artwork.

Rapp's literary leanings were also given more legroom. The album opens with 'Footnote', which sets W.H. Auden's 'Epitaph For A Tyrant' to glistening folk music. There are country leanings on 'If You Don't Want To', and the cheeky soul of 'Oh Dear (Miss Morse)' peeps through on 'Frog In The Window'.

These Things Too is different in other ways. Pearls Before Swine had ceased being a group in the traditional sense, and was now a name for Rapp and whichever musicians he chose to collaborate with. Wayne Harley from the original group was still present, but was joined by other musicians, including jazz drummer Grady Tate and Rapp's wife, Elisabeth, on vocals. Rapp was also reaching out in other areas. "No one believes this but I had never smoked marijuana until I was writing the third album," he later said. "Everyone around me was doing it, but ... I was very conservative in those days."[13]

Tom and Elisabeth Rapp spent some time in Holland during 1969, where he wrote the songs for the next Pearls Before Swine album, *The Use Of Ashes*. "It was a little semi-detached house, next to a misty lake, surrounded by rose bushes and swans," he later recalled. "There was a 15th century bridge on part of the lake. And across the field, about a hundred feet away, was a Nazi bunker, barbed wire, swastikas and all. The government, I guess, left it there as a reminder. So it was a place of strange, mixed emotions."[14]

The Use Of Ashes is more lyrically intimate than *These Things Too*. The best-known song, 'Rocket Man', was written while Rapp was watching the 1969 moon landing. When it was recorded, in Nashville, the musicians added a luxuriant medieval feel, with Rapp's trademark lisp complemented by a small orchestra.

The move to Reprise seemed to be working out. The anxious energy and fresh beauty of ESP-Disk-era Pearls Before Swine may no longer have been present, but this meant that Rapp was not treading over old ground. Instead, he was broadening his lyrical concerns, finding new subtleties in his words, and planting his feet down as the axis around which other musicians revolved. It was also during the early Reprise period that Rapp become more confident about playing live, allowing Pearls Before Swine to move from being a studio-based group into one that was equally happy on tour.

In late 1969, music journalist Lillian Roxon created a new genre especially for Rapp's project. "What the underground group called Pearls Before Swine sings is acid folk," she wrote in her seminal *Rock Encyclopaedia*, "that is folk music affected by the discoveries of an LSD-influenced generation." The term would not become widely used for some time, but offered a perfect summation of the sound of Pearls Before Swine and their peers. It wasn't folk music made under the influence of LSD per se but folk music profoundly affected by the attitudes of exploration that also prompted the use of hallucinogens. Furthermore, Roxon's term also held resonance for the other meanings of the word 'acid' in the sense of tartness or a corrosive, uncomfortable sensation.

⋈

"Acid folk as a label is fine," Rapp says, "in that it implies borderlessness." Indeed, this new folk music was seeping through borders everywhere. Its influence was felt in pop records, which would sometimes include one or two psychedelic or acid folk tracks, such as 'Flowers In The Air' from *Hair* actress Sally Eaton's *Farewell American Tour* (1970), while even jazz musicians were crossing over. Noted jazz pianist Keith Jarrett made an unexpected move in the direction of acid folk on *Restoration Ruin* (1968), on which he runs amok with flute, harmonica, and haphazard drumming, while Californian vocalist Kathy McCord's self-titled debut for CTI, a jazz label run by Creed Taylor, featured a deconstructed folk take on The Beatles' 'She's Leaving Home' (as 'I'm Leaving Home').

It might seem that the most natural crossover point would come when conventional folksingers added a psychedelic element to their sound, but in practice this rarely happened in any sustained fashion. Among the more notable exceptions was Carolyn Hester, whose recording career dated back to 1957 and possibly included a session with Buddy Holly, which would make her one of the very first folk/rock crossover artists. She was briefly married to Richard Fariña in the early 60s, and was instrumental in helping Bob Dylan come to the attention of Columbia Records. In the late 60s she formed an electric rock band, The Carolyn Hester Coalition. Both *The Carolyn Hester Coalition* (1969) and *Magazine* (1970) explore the direct collision between psychedelic guitar and Hester's high voice; they're interesting if patchy albums, a mosaic rather than a watercolour of sound.

More successful in creating a true fusion of pure folk and contemporary psychedelia was the Canadian folksinger Bonnie Dobson. She admits that "a lot of people weren't happy" about the change in direction she took in 1969, but says "a lot of people liked it a lot. It brought me to a new audience".

Folk music had been a "hobby" of Dobson's since her early adolescence in

50s Canada; it was also linked to her family's leftwing politics and her father's trade union activities. Anxious to strike out on her own during her teenage years, Dobson took a job as a camp counsellor in Quebec and soon found herself enjoying Saturday night performances by the likes of Pete Seeger, Leon Bibb, and Earl Robinson.

Dobson herself began to perform after her father bought her a guitar. She worked her way up through impromptu high school performances and the Toronto folk scene before moving to New York and securing a recording contract with Prestige in 1960. "You're learning, you're out there, and you're fresh," she says of her early recordings. She enjoyed researching folk songs and included both traditional material and contemporary covers on her albums. Her first self-composed song, 'Morning Dew', appeared on *Bonnie Dobson At Folk City* (1962). It was widely covered on the folk scene and beyond before becoming the subject of decades of litigation following Tim Rose's claim to have co-written the lyrics.

These Prestige LPs – along with Dobson's 1964 Mercury Records album, *For The Love Of Him* – are all solid contemporary folk records, reflective both of Dobson's interest in folksong and of the Greenwich Village community. At the time, Dobson was often compared to Joan Baez, to the point where Dobson became neurotic about it. "I have a letter that Joan Baez's mother sent to me after I'd released my first album," she recalls. "She said how much she liked it, and how she and Joannie listened to it a lot. So I can say that, actually, I don't sound like her, she sounds like me."

After leaving New York in 1965, Dobson took a five-year break from recording, during which time she changed as a person, artist, and experimenter. She moved back to Canada, where she continued to write songs and appeared regularly on a CBC radio show called *1967 And All That*. She also travelled extensively and co-hosted another radio show, *La Ronde*, which mixed jazz, blues, and folk, broadening her horizons and enriching her musical taste.

"One of the producers at CBC suggested we do this album," she recalls of the origins of what became *Bonnie Dobson*. "I was ready for a change. I can look at that album and see where I was at the time." The material, on which she worked with arranger Ben McPeek and producer Jack Richardson, was certainly a significant departure. As beautiful as Dobson's earlier records had been, they consisted of straight folk material and predated the opening out of the folk scene during the 60s; *Bonnie Dobson*, by contrast, is fully submerged in these new influences, which give the songs a tremulous, uncomfortable quality, particularly on Dobson's five self-composed songs and on McPeek's sitar-drenched 'Bird Of Space'. There's a heady mood throughout, the youngster of before replaced by a grown woman of thorny passion. The honeyed drone of the opener, 'I Got Stung', introduces a theme of sorrow and revenge that is further developed on 'I'm Your Woman' and a version of 'You Never Wanted Me' by Jackson C. Frank. But it's the final track that completes Dobson's transition toward psychedelic folk: 'Winter's Going', a "scary little song", as Dobson puts it, coated in sonorous Eastern strings.

Bonnie Dobson's evolution was rubber-stamped by the album's liner notes: "Bonnie's a puzzle. Her promise of a childhood dream shatters in the reality of her songs ... and the shockwaves twist in your mind." Dobson's Prestige albums had all featured conventional portraits on the cover; this one has a stylised painting of the artist surrounded by irises, looking the height of hippie-folk fashion. ("It wasn't a conscious image," she says, "it was just the way I looked.")

Although CBC had instigated the album, it was licensed to the Nimbus 9 and RCA labels for release. Then came a swift follow-up, *Good Morning Rain*, which sees her reunited with McPeek and Richardson and has a mellower country buzz to it. Psychedelia is not the main focus but its bubbling undercurrent occasionally spills out – most significantly on another tender Jackson C. Frank cover, 'Milk And Honey'.

Before the album even hit the shelves, Dobson had decided to up sticks once again, this time to England, where she toured solidly and found a place on the folk scene. She also released another significant album, *Bonnie Dobson* (1972), a subtle work that holds a diaphanous balance between her earlier folk material and newer singer-songwriter trends.

Like Bonnie Dobson, Susan Christie made an album in the late 60s that was radically different to her previous recorded output. Known until then for her pop records, she now created one of the heaviest and most haunting acid-folk albums to date.

Christie's musical and romantic partner was John Hill, whom she had met in high school. "I always swear that he only dated me because we had a piano in our house," she says. "We were in the junior play; we met, and we've been hanging out ever since." They both went on to study at the Berklee College of Music in Boston, Massachusetts, where they started to consider music seriously as a career.

The couple's first major excursion into the music business came about when Cameo-Parkway producer, arranger, songwriter, and A&R man Dave Appell was keen to find a suitable song for Hill and Christie to perform. The interest of such a prominent label gave them the confidence to develop their skills, but they soon decided to concentrate on folk music instead. "Our first act was called The Highlanders," Christie says. "We did a lot of folk festivals." They also cut two songs intended for a single in 1966: 'No-one Can Hear You Cry', a Bacharach-esque mini-symphony, and 'When Love Comes', a fine sunshine-folk number. After being turned down by several labels, however, they gave up on these tracks.

"John just said: 'I'm going to write a hit song,'" Christie recalls. The couple borrowed $700, roped in friends and relatives, and recorded 'I Love Onions'. They took the cutesy pop number to Columbia, who liked it: the song hit Number 63 on Billboard in 1966 and Christie became associated with a breathy, quirky pop-vocal style. Two more novelty singles followed, but neither charted. In any case, the duo had grown weary of playing to the crowd's expectations

"I was very tired of that style," Christie says. "And then this wonderful opportunity came for us to do things the way we would like to do them": an album offer from ABC-Paramount. The pair handpicked songs that they admired, mainly in a country-folk vein, although the versions they worked on were more than just straight covers. Hill created innovative new arrangements of songs that ranged from the phantasmal 'Ghost Riders In The Sky' to the unusually drum-heavy, slow funk of 'For The Love Of A Soldier'; Christie sang with her crystal-tipped voice.

The most jaw-dropping track is 'Yesterday, Where's My Mind?', a nine-minute psychedelic epic that Hill and Christie had uncovered in the form of a demo by singer-songwriter John Reid. "It was a mind-blowing demo," Hill says, "so we tried to make a mind-blowing single as well." Christie recited the lyric – a continuous narrative of smashed adventures in the side streets of the late 60s – with a range of euphoria, fear, anger, and passion over Hill's heady arrangement. "It really reflected the times," she recalls. "People were having these experiences, and it started coming out in the music."

Hill and Christie were convinced they had done something unique with the album, and were very proud of it. ABC-Paramount was not so pleased. "We're still not entirely sure why it wasn't released," Hill says with a sigh. "I guess the label didn't like it." An acetate was pressed up, and Hill retained the master tapes, but it took a while for the couple to lick their wounds. "Susan was always especially disappointed that 'Ghost Riders In The Sky' didn't get released," Hill says, "because she said for years and years that was the best thing she ever sang." Christie buried her disappointment and largely gave up on front-line singing. "I think I just dismissed it and said, that's it, I'll go back to making rhubarb pie," she says.

Released 30 years later as *Paint A Lady*, the album represents one of the most intense of all acid-folk records. In a genre that often leaned toward the gossamer, this was full, hearty music. "The stuff on the album, like most stuff of then, wasn't the result of a self-conscious choice to be part of the time," Hill says. "It was inevitably of the time."

Hill went on to work on another significant psychedelic folk number: 'Love', the closing track on Margo Guryan's 1969 album on Bell, *Take A Picture*. He had been drafted in to work on the album after the first producer, John Simon, left to work with Janis Joplin. "On 'Love', there was a big contribution from John [Hill]," Guryan later recalled. "He organised, wrote, and played on the long instrumental intro. We recorded sections in 7/4, 6/4, 5/4, and, at last, 4/4. John had the sections cross-faded until finally the vocal kicks in when 4/4 arrives."[15] 'Love' carries the spirit of the unreleased Susan Christie album, all compressed into five-and-a-half minutes.

The rejection of Christie's album by ABC-Paramount might simply have been a one-off business decision. It was, after all, at the extreme end not only of psychedelic folk but also of music's outlying districts in general, and was hardly something that would appeal to the same audience who had bought 'I Love Onions'. But it may also have been a sign that the era of US major labels taking on the new tripped-out directions in folk music had already passed. In the UK, during the same period, there was a similar open season for record companies to sign up acid and psych folk artists, and it too would provide a platform for some extraordinary and exploratory music.

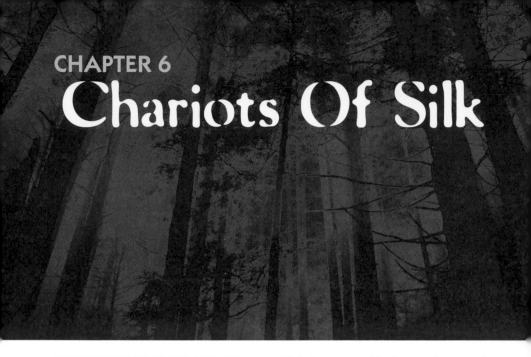

CHAPTER 6
Chariots Of Silk

IN BRITAIN IN THE LATE 60S, record labels were suddenly very interested in the newly minted genre of psychedelic folk, perhaps even more so than across the Atlantic. "Companies were falling over themselves to sign anyone they possibly could," says David Costa of Trees. "You'd go: 'great, we got signed' – and then you'd realise you were locked in forever for no money."

This enthusiasm for young underground folk acts coincided with the emergence of new imprints from the major labels explicitly designed to court the budding progressive-rock audience. Having an acoustic or folk-rock group with similar hippie ideals became the standard aim for major-label offshoots like Harvest, Dawn, and Decca Nova, which would usually have at least one staff member able to spot an adventurous and potentially successful new folk-oriented act. Even if an artist or group was signed to a major label itself rather than one of its specialist branches, there was often a supportive atmosphere to artistic endeavour – at least at the outset of the contract. Furthermore, brand new labels like John Peel's Dandelion and the independent Village Thing had a stated commitment to integrity and artist welfare.

A related phenomenon was the enormous and supportive university circuit, which freed groups from having to play solely at folk clubs or hip nightspots. The Ellis-Wright Agency began the trend for booking psychedelic rock acts for colleges in 1967, while similar organisations were quick to spring up in its wake. The travelling was unforgiving, the pay meagre, but there were ample opportunities for even the most obscure groups to play throughout the country as university entertainment budgets swelled.

"We travelled a lot," Barbara Gaskin of Spirogyra recalls. "Because we lived in Canterbury, any trip involved an extra hour and a half up and down the A2. We couldn't afford hotels and rarely stayed the night anywhere, regardless of distance. At the time I was still studying to finish my degree, so I read in the van."

The underground clubs sustained their influence in London, with some new ones sprouting up throughout the country, notably Mothers, which opened in Birmingham in summer 1968. For some, folk clubs were an appropriate and welcoming place for psychedelic or unusual folk music. Marianne Segal, who would soon form the group Jade, has fond recollections. "The atmosphere was always so warm, and they received you so well," she says. Singer-songwriter Michael Chapman concurs. "People on the folk scene would say: 'Oh, come and stay at our place, have a bottle of beer or a glass of wine or a cup of coffee.' The only problem was that there were sometimes a lot more people sitting in somebody's kitchen after the gig than would pay to go into the gig itself."

For record companies to sign these bands, and for promoters to stage them, there had to be a good few of them out there. By 1969 there certainly was, with The Incredible String Band having a particularly striking effect throughout Britain. "They practically invented the psych-folk genre," says Martin Welham of Forest. "*5000 Spirits* took acoustic music to new heights."

Like many other groups of the period, Forest also took inspiration from the folk revival singers; the more rock-oriented underground groups; American folk; and the adventurousness of mainstream groups like The Beatles, The Kinks, and The Moody Blues. It all led to what could convincingly be described as a scene. The groups usually knew one another, and kept a keen eye on what was going on. "There was a definite friendly competitiveness between the artists," Welham says. "'You thought that was good? Now listen to this!'"

The growth of folk-rock (or electric folk) in Britain was an important parallel development. Perhaps surprisingly, given the rock leanings of their first album, Fairport Convention were at the forefront of this decisively British-focused new fusion of traditional song with rock, blues, and jazz. The group's second album, *What We Did On Our Holidays*, is the first to feature Sandy Denny and contains their earliest recorded forays into traditional music: 'Nottamun Town' and 'She Moves Through The Fair'. With hindsight, the album can be seen a significant step on the path Fairport Convention would soon take in redefining the boundaries and possibilities of traditional folksong. At the time of its release, however, it seemed simply to be a diverse folk album.

In the year 1969, a decade's worth of changes took place within Fairport Convention. Shortly after *What We Did On Our Holidays* was released, in January, Ian Matthews left the group. "After the fact, I learned to love that music," he notes, wryly, of Fairport's forays into traditional folksong, "but at the time it grated on me, and this was apparent." Matthews was summarily dispatched by Joe Boyd before moving on to commercial and critical success in Matthews Southern Comfort.

The rest of the band got on with making their next album, *Unhalfbricking*, which contains their most ambitious song to date: an extraordinary 11-minute rendering of the traditional song 'A Sailor's Life'. Before the album was released, however, the band were involved in a horrific road accident that killed drummer Martin Lamble and Richard Thompson's girlfriend, Jeannie Franklyn. "In the aftermath, we thought a lot about what to do, whether to call it a day," Simon Nicol later recalled. "We all felt psychologically traumatised, as well as being damaged physically. But by the time Ashley's face was back together and Richard's bones were healing, we'd decided to rebuild the band and carry on."[1]

Following the release of – and positive response to – *Unhalfbricking*, the recovering band headed to a house in the country, just outside Winchester, to work on *Liege & Lief*. Dave Mattacks came in on drums, while Dave Swarbrick, who had played fiddle on 'A Sailor's Life', became a full-time member. "I can't emphasise enough what a remarkable few months it was," says bassist Ashley Hutchings. "It was a real voyage of discovery, and it was great to sit in the room and hear Sandy singing those songs, and to hear Swarbrick and Richard trading licks." Hutchings, like the rest of Fairport, had become familiar with traditional folksong during a youth spent in folk clubs, but his curiosity had since gained a more studious flavour. "Sandy helped to rekindle that interest in traditional music, and once it was rekindled, I was the first out there, rummaging around in libraries, talking to die-hard traditional people about music, and picking up songs."

Liege & Lief was a huge leap into new waters. It received mixed reviews at the time, but its influence – in creating a British template for folk-rock – was immense. Shortly after the album was completed, however, both Sandy Denny and Ashley Hutchings left the group. "I don't think it was down to the music," Hutchings says. "I think it was something that was in the air – a delayed reaction to the crash and the deaths." So, in 1970, the Fairport family tree gained two new branches: Fotheringay (Denny) and Steeleye Span (Hutchings).

Another big folk-rock act of the time was Pentangle. Although they didn't have a premeditated plan to form a group, Bert Jansch, John Renbourn, Jacqui McShee, Terry Cox, and Danny Thompson all knew one another, and began playing together in 1967 with a series of ramshackle and largely improvisational performances at their own Sunday club at the Horseshoe Hotel on London's Tottenham Court Road. The band moved beyond the folk club scene after acquiring a strident American manager, Jo Lustig, in 1968.

The group found mainstream success with their first three albums – *The Pentangle*, *Sweet Child* (both 1968), and *Basket Of Light* (1970) – which culminated in the use of their hit single 'Light Fight' as the theme to the BBC drama *Take Three Girls*. Pentangle differed from Fairport Convention in that, although they reconfigured traditional material into the contemporary folk-rock vernacular, they also incorporated influences from jazz and (thanks to Renbourn) early music. Renbourn had released a solo album, *Sir John A Lot Of Merrie Englande's Musyk Thyng And Ye Grene Knyghte*, almost simultaneously with *The Pentangle*, and integrated these medieval influences into the group's sound.

The commercial success of Fairport Convention and Pentangle was far less unexpected than that of The Incredible String Band, whose wide popularity and fiercely loyal fan base were particularly surprising given that, unlike Pentangle, they didn't have a well-oiled publicity machine behind them. Live, the String Band were a huge draw, despite refusing to compromise their sound. In *Melody Maker*, Karl Dallas praised their "anti-showmanship", noting that they seemed to approach a 1968 Royal Festival Hall show "as if it is a private party into which several thousand people have somehow strayed". (Support came from Tim Buckley, which for Dallas "amply illustrated the difference in approach between the British and American creative scenes".[2])

In November 1968, the String Band released another brilliant album, the double-disc *Wee Tam And The Big Huge*. "It was just an extension really of the previous one," Mike Heron says, "but we were beginning to have a *lot* of songs. It had got to the point where we were touring maybe six months of the year, and by that time we all lived together, in eight cottages joined together in this place called Glen Row. When we were not on the road we were either in the studio or playing each other songs that we'd written. So it came out of the experience of just being in each other's company all the time."

Wee Tam And The Big Huge is distended and ambitious, and set the bar even higher for possibilities in acoustic music. Perhaps inevitably, for a double album, it is looser in feel than *The 5000 Spirits Or The Layers Of The Onion* or *The Hangman's Beautiful Daughter*; where before the experimental sprawl was in perfect equilibrium with Williamson and Heron's underrated flair for hooks, now that balance had been tipped. Yet that barely mattered when the experimentation was of such high class, or as *Disc & Music Echo* put it, "so completely varied and poetically perfect that it's as easy to tire of as the sky or the sea or the wind". The album effortlessly cemented The Incredible String Band's place among the most influential groups in Britain.

M

Back in 1967, while The Incredible String Band were putting the finishing touches to *5000 Spirits*, a young musician by the name of Marc Bolan was growing increasingly frustrated with his current group, John's Children. His manager, Simon Napier-Bell, had installed him in the group after the failure of his first attempt at a solo career, but while Bolan had come to enjoy some of the band's wild performances, he was generally unhappy with the situation, particularly when plans to release his song 'Midsummer Night's Scene' as a single were cancelled.

In June 1967, Napier-Bell agreed to Bolan's request to form another group as an outlet for the songs he had been writing on tour. Bolan placed an advertisement in *Melody Maker* looking for a "freaky lead guitarist, bass guitarist, and drummer", plus "any other astral flyers like with cars, amplification, and that which never grew in window boxes". Bolan chose his new band-mates not on the basis of coherent musical talent but on their looks and their names: the more cosmic the better. He also decided to unveil his new (amplified) band to the public mere hours after auditioning the band-members. The resulting gig at the Electric Garden was, unsurprisingly, chaotic and poorly received. Shortly afterward, Bolan decided to go acoustic.

This wasn't Bolan's first attempt at folk music. In fact, the former teen model Mark Feld might never have become Marc Bolan at all had the folk-pop demo he recorded in 1964 as Toby Tyler contained anything stronger than an insipid cover of 'Blowin' In The Wind'. Shortly after that, as Bolan, he had signed to Decca and released the 'The Wizard', a significant antecedent of his later psychedelic folk complete with a Tolkien-inspired B-side, 'Beyond The Risin' Sun'. The beat-driven sound of 'The Wizard' chimed well with the British mod scene of the time, but the lyrics – full of golden eagles, silver sunlight, and Eastern skies – marked Bolan out as something different.

Despite some good reviews and an appearance on *Ready Steady Go!*, 'The Wizard' stayed firmly on the shelves. Bolan tried again, releasing 'The Third Degree' / 'San Francisco Poet' in June 1966. This was something of a mixture; the driving beat of 'The Wizard' mixed with the cut-price Greenwich Village feel of Toby Tyler. It was another flop. It was after a third single, 'Hippy Gumbo', again failed to chart that new manager Napier-Bell deposited Bolan in John's Children. Now he was getting another chance to do his own thing.

Bolan set his ambitions high. He called the band Tyrannosaurus Rex because he wanted them to be the biggest act in Britain. His only band-mate was Steve Peregrin Took, a long-haired bongo player whose name was derived from *The Lord Of The Rings*, and who had been part of the Electric Garden fiasco. The pair bonded by busking in London's Hyde Park, and Bolan began to grow out his John's Children feather cut. Napier-Bell was so irritated by Bolan's new hippie persona that he stopped managing him.

Tyrannosaurus Rex might not have progressed much further than 'Hippy Gumbo' were it not for two things: the trailblazing success of the Incredible String Band, and the priceless support of John Peel, who played a demo of 'Highways' on his *Perfumed Garden* show on Radio London in August 1967, and continued to champion the group following his move to BBC Radio 1. Peel helped Bolan in any way he could, even insisting that, whenever he was booked for live DJ work, Tyrannosaurus Rex should be invited along, too.

Also among those charmed by Tyrannosaurus Rex was Tony Visconti, a young American record producer who had recently relocated to London. "I met Marc in the UFO Club," he recalled in 1982. "He was sitting cross-legged on stage, playing his strange little songs with his voice wobbling, and Steve Peregrin Took was banging on his bongos, and I was just drawn in there with the rest of the crowd."[3] After the performance, Visconti asked if the duo had a recording contract. Undeterred by Bolan's claim that the great and the good – including John Lennon – were queuing up to work with Tyrannosaurus Rex, Visconti gave them his number, "in case everything falls through". Bolan called him the next morning.

The first Tyrannosaurus Rex single was 'Debora', released in April 1968 through EMI Regal Zonophone, followed in July by *My People Were Fair And Had Sky In Their Hair ... But Now They're Content To Wear Stars On Their Brows*. The album has a beautifully tumbledown sound, the pair's cheap equipment and Visconti's beginner's enthusiasm the perfect complement to Bolan's rambling, psychedelic lyrics and skiffle roguishness. Took's bongo playing is sensitive, his use of the Pixiphone (a kind of toy xylophone) stops just the right side of cloying, and his falsetto is a fine counterpoint to Bolan's scampering vocal style. John Peel also makes an appearance as the narrator of the fanciful 'Frowning Atahuallpa (My Inca Love)'.

A slightly harder-edged single, 'One Inch Rock', appeared in August, followed in October by a second album, *Prophets, Seers & Sages The Angels Of The Ages*. *Disc & Music Echo* noted: "It appears that you either cannot hear enough of Tyrannosaurus Rex, or else you hate them with a deep and deadly loathing." As the review implies, the differences between the two albums are subtle at best, although there are some darker lyrics on *Prophets* and a few more signs of more studio experimentation, like the backward effects on 'Deboraarobed'.

By the time of May 1969's *Unicorn*, however, the Tyrannosaurus Rex sound had changed significantly. The band had been playing live extensively, in ever-bigger venues, and their new material was noticeably chunkier. Visconti, meanwhile, had been learning about the possibilities of the studio and was interested in erecting a Spector-esque Wall Of Sound. Then came a drastic change of direction for the electric single 'King Of The Rumbling Spires'. Bolan had reportedly been jamming with Eric Clapton, and now felt that *this* was the way to take charge of an audience. Took moved over to drums rather than bongos, while Bolan appeared to have restrained the more fantastical ruminations of his earlier lyrics.

The single, released during the summer of 1969, marked Took's final recorded appearance with Tyrannosaurus Rex. His playing was intuitive and warm on the albums, and he was unquestionably an integral part of the sound, but he was becoming a liability for Bolan. His drug use was rampant and increasing, and so was his dissatisfaction that all the Tyrannosaurus Rex songs were by Bolan. (Took was also a budding songwriter, but couldn't persuade Bolan to record any of his material.) By some accounts, the pair had agreed to split following *Unicorn*, but were contractually obliged to tour the USA in June 1969. By then, Took was dropping acid on a daily basis, and on the New York date treated the crowd to a striptease and an attack on the band's equipment. Bolan waited no longer to disentangle himself. He returned from America alone.

Marc Bolan's new foil, Mickey Finn, proved that Bolan was still swayed by the idea of working with people who looked the part. Finn may not have been able to match Took's percussive complexities and glorious harmonies, but his cheekbones could sculpt ice. The two men headed off to Wales to begin work on the next album, *A Beard Of Stars*, wiping Took's existing contributions from the tapes. "It was fairly clear that the Tyrannosaurus *shtick* was at an end," said musician and journalist Mick Farren, who was a friend of Took's at the time. "The externals of it – the toy instruments, the sitting cross-legged – were getting tired. The moment Marc got Mickey Finn he wasn't sitting down anymore."[4]

⋈

If anybody was going to be an early adopter of psychedelic folk, it would surely be Marc Bolan. He was ambitious, already steeped in whimsical fantasy, and able to adapt his songs, within a blink, from the brutal mod stylings of John's Children to the fey acoustics of Tyrannosaurus Rex. Not far behind, however, were the Irish group Dr Strangely Strange.

Their story begins when Tim Booth, a folk guitarist with an interesting claw-hammer style, was asked to perform at a reception for new students at Trinity College in 1967. Booth invited a couple of local musicians to play with him, one of whom was his friend, bassist Ivan Pawle. Deciding to continue as a band following the success of their short, four-song set, Booth and Pawle teamed up with Brian Trench, who played keyboards among other instruments. When Trench left Dublin, they found Tim Goulding, who brought with him a harmonium and a slightly different outlook.

"Tim had learned cello at school, and came from a more classical line," Pawle recalls. "But like any young person he was listening to what was going on at the time as well." The three spent a lot of time together at a Dublin commune known as the Orphanage and started to write songs. "We each had our own songs which we would bring to the band, and then we would just orchestrate them as we could," Pawle adds. "We would suggest musical ideas to each other, but basically it was always just one of us who wrote a song and would say: 'what do you want to do on this?'" From early on, the songs had a humour to them, and carried something of the charming cheekiness of The Holy Modal Rounders.

The band named themselves Dr Strangely Strange after the Marvel superhero Dr Stephen Strange and a phrase their friend Jim Duncan would often use ("that's strangely strange but oddly normal"). The name certainly suited their developing musical style and use of unusual instruments, which included recorders, whistles, kazoos, and Japanese ping-pong bats. They began playing a wide selection of venues, carting Goulding's harmonium around behind them. "Tim said it was a bit like being a nocturnal furniture remover," Pawle laughs.

The band became friends with The Incredible String Band, and through this friendship came to the attention of Joe Boyd. According to Pawle, Robin Williamson told Boyd to check them out, so Boyd came over to Ireland. "We did a gig in Carlow supporting Skid Row. And I think Joe was most impressed by Brush, who was the leader of Skid Row, who's quite an Irish character." Nevertheless, Boyd offered Dr Strangely Strange an album deal, having apparently described them as "ISB-lite".

They went to London to record the album. "In Ireland, there were only a couple of folk clubs, really, around Dublin," Pawle recalls. "When we went over to England there were folk clubs and the university circuit had started up as well, so we did a lot of travelling around." While they were recording the album, *Kip Of The Serenes*, at Sound Techniques, they stayed on Boyd's floor. "We'd done very little recording before that, just home recording with an old Revox tape recorder, so this was just wonderful," Pawle says. "Joe was just a master at recording. He'd say: 'Oh, you know, if you just play that bit a bit slower, maybe that guitar is slightly out of tune.' He had plenty of other things he was trying to do at the same time, so we did the whole thing in a very short time. But it was great!"

Boyd's Witchseason Productions sold *Kip Of The Serenes* to Island Records, home of Fairport Convention. This in itself was unusual. As Tim Booth later recalled: "I think we got our deal with Island before Thin Lizzy got any sort of deal. It was very rare for an Irish band to have an English recording contract."[5]

Playing live had started to present a few practical problems. "We were always sleeping on floors and all that kind of stuff, because we were never commercially viable," Pawle says. "We wanted to be able to play in larger venues, and that was very difficult, playing acoustic. We also had to lug this harmonium around everywhere. We did a gig with Status Quo on Irish television. Tim [Goulding] was very impressed by their little Farfisa organ ... he said: 'I've got to get one of those' – and he did. It was very handy, and it was easier to move around. But it started to alter the dynamic then, from the harmonium sound into something more electrical."

A further change ensued when the band realised that Island wasn't over keen on releasing another album by the group, given the slow sales of *Kip Of The Serenes*. They moved instead to the Phonogram subsidiary Vertigo, which was leading the charge for heavy progressive rock but – with the exception of albumslike Tudor Lodge's 1971 self-titled LP – had less of an interest in underground folk than other similar imprints. Since Magna Carta was

Vertigo's flagship band, however, it seemed appropriate for the now more commercially conscious Dr Strangely Strange to find a home with the label. And so *Heavy Petting* was released in 1970, bringing the band's new electric sound to the foreground and featuring guest appearances by Fairport drummer Dave Mattacks and Skid Row guitarist Gary Moore. "We began to think maybe we can be a folk-rock band," Tim Booth later recalled. "We sort of became a pale imitation of Fairport ... and to some extent we lost our identity."[6] Goulding left shortly afterward.

"We went a bit adrift, in a way," Pawle says of the band's electric period. "We just thought we might be more mainstream and also become slightly more commercially successful." Dr Strangely Strange weren't alone in moving toward amplification: The Incredible String Band's 1969 album *Changing Horses* features electric guitar and bass alongside the acoustic instruments, with Pawle himself making a guest appearance. "That's when they were going through a transition," he says, adding that he turned down the offer of a full-time role in the group. "I think The Incredible String Band had really reached their apex at that stage and I don't think I would have brought anything. They got some great players to play with them over the next few years. But it had peaked, really."

So, too, had Dr Strangely Strange, whose own attempts at reinvigoration, with the addition of Gay and Terry Woods, were unsuccessful. The band split in May 1971. As for The Incredible String Band, Pawle was right: with *Changing Horses*, they were moving into ambiguous territory.

Back over at EMI, with underground groups like Pink Floyd, The Pretty Things, Deep Purple, and indeed Tyrannosaurus Rex becoming more and more prevalent, trainee manager Malcolm Jones suggested the label ought to create a consistent brand. The result was Harvest, launched in 1969 with Jones at its head and Deep Purple's *The Book Of Taliesyn* as its first release. Not all the groups switched over – Tyrannosaurus Rex stayed on the Regal Zonophone subsidiary – but enough did to make Harvest a recognisable and instantly credible label.

Harvest was launched at a gig at London's Roundhouse with a bill that included new signings Shirley and Dolly Collins. "Dolly and I got booed because we weren't the Edgar Broughton Band or Deep Purple or whatever," Shirley recalls. "They just thought we were wasting time until somebody that they knew better came on." After a shaky start, however, she found her steely side. "Somebody was heckling me in the audience. And I was always grateful to that bloke who heckled, because I put him down, but in a way that made everybody laugh, and then they were on our side after that."

The Collins sisters' *Anthems In Eden* was Harvest's first folk album. Shirley Collins had been watching the unfolding psychedelic folk scene with some bemusement. "I thought all the psychedelic stuff and the hippie stuff was dead silly," she says. "I'm too down-to-earth, really. I'm too sensible and I've got my feet in Sussex soil." Despite her reluctance to be bracketed within this new strain of folk music, however, the album's inclusion on the Harvest roster made perfect sense. The Incredible String Band loved the Collins sisters, as did John Peel.

Shirley Collins first began to assemble *Anthems In Eden* with the help of her husband, 'Austin' John Marshall. "I think we felt all these songs from Southern England could link into a simple story," she says. "We put together a sequence of songs that would tell this story, leading up to the culmination of the First World War and the loss of that generation." 'A Song-Story' offers an unsentimental, moving evocation of the changes to rural England and the dislocation of folk traditions and communities. The Collins sisters had also developed a strong interest in early-music instruments, becoming friends with David Munrow and attending rehearsals of the Musica Reservata, an ensemble of musicians who played a huge range of traditional instruments.

'A Song-Story' was originally broadcast on BBC Radio 1 in August 1968. It was too good to end with just one airing. "John was able to persuade Harvest to record it," Shirley recalls. "For some reason they just thought we would fit in. And it's just a stroke of luck that we were around at that time, as it could have just sunk without a trace." Instead, *Anthems In Eden* went on to become a landmark album by the Collins sisters, its use of early instruments broadening the parameters of what was possible in folk music while 'A Song-Story' provided a blueprint for a more conceptual approach to folk LPs.

The following year, Shirley and Dolly Collins released their second Harvest album, the bleak *Love, Death And The Lady*. "I was breaking up with John at the time," Shirley recalls. "It was at my instigation: I couldn't stay with him, he was impossible to live with, but it was a huge upheaval. The songs I sang on that album largely reflected the sadness of the time. I'm a very cheerful person on the whole, and yet I love melancholy as well, and that's partly because the English tradition is infused with melancholy." The album reunited the sisters with several musicians from *Anthems In Eden* but has a stripped, stark feel. The songs spill over from melancholic to sinister and downright violent on several occasions, while the gatefold cover shows the sisters black-clad and sombre.

The Harvest folk release that followed *Anthems In Eden* was in many ways its polar opposite. Northern Englishman Michael Chapman had grown up in skiffle and rock'n'roll bands with a gritty, no-nonsense attitude. "I played in rock'n'roll bands, but only for the money," he says. "Basically the guitar bought my education. I put myself through college by playing the guitar." After graduating, Chapman became a teacher, and music was largely sidelined until he clashed with the board of governors over his teaching methods.

"I left before I got the sack," he recalls, "without a clue as to what to do with the rest of my life. I went down to Cornwall for a week and ran out of money, like you do. It was raining one night and I went into a folk club and said: 'I can't afford to pay to come in, but I'll play.'" He ended up a resident performer there for the remainder of the summer.

Eventually, a talent scout for Essex Music spotted him. "They signed me up to do a guitar album, because I wasn't writing my own material at that point," he says. "I think they thought I was going to be the next Davy Graham or something. But in the meantime, before the album came around, I'd started writing songs. I had to pull up one night when I was driving home from a gig, because I was just too tired to go any further, and I realised I was going to kill myself. And I just pulled up in this transport café and wrote the first song I ever did, which was a song called 'Goodbye To Monday Night'. I thought Christ! I've written a song! That's where they come from, you just talk about your life."

Chapman's debut, *Rainmaker* (1969), was the first of four albums he made for Harvest. It is unlike any of his other records. His early style was infused with the spirits of American Primitive and Davy Graham, his tunings so open they made one acoustic guitar sound like a three-way battle, especially on the instrumentals 'Rainmaker' and 'Thank You P.K. 1944'. His songwriting and singing sat somewhere between Bert Jansch at his grainiest and Roy Harper at his rockiest.

Steeped in angst and overflowing with experimental guitar, *Rainmaker* was a shot in the arm for the genre of singer-songwriters. As Harvest's fifth release, it ensured the new label's place firmly at the edge of this particular cliff-face. And yet Chapman himself felt slightly ambivalent about it. "It's a bit scrappy," he says. "I didn't know what I could do in a studio, I didn't know what a studio could do for me, and I didn't know what Gus Dudgeon could do as a producer. I was just so pleased to be making a record."

With his next album, *Fully Qualified Survivor* (1970), Chapman crept away from the American Primitive guitar-style and the Bert Jansch troubadour effect. "I knew what I wanted by then," he says. "I knew who I wanted to be on it: I wanted Rick Kemp on bass and Mick Ronson on guitar, and I'd worked with Barry Morgan, the drummer." *Fully Qualified Survivor* was a strong seller for Harvest, and set Chapman on the road he would follow from here on: a fuller sound, with his intensely personal lyrics wedded to a larger and increasingly rockier blues base. "I don't consider myself a folk singer," he says. "I'm much more interested in songwriters than the generic term 'folk music'."

Harvest snipped the edges of experimental, acid, and psychedelic folk music on a number of its other releases. The Third Ear Band's debut, *Alchemy* (1969), was a minimal, beaty, freakish album, derived from Indian ragas, free jazz, modern classical, psychedelic folk, and early music; Syd Barrett's *The Madcap Laughs* (1969) and *Barrett* (1970) certainly have the acid half of the equation covered, with folk one of many musical forms on show. There was also Roy Harper.

Following *Sophisticated Beggar*, and prior to his stint at Harvest, Harper had made two albums, *Come Out Fighting Ghengis Smith* and the Eastern-flavoured *Folkjokeopus*. The second of these contains the 17-minute 'McGoohan's Blues', a psychedelic epic named after Patrick McGoohan, the creator of *The Prisoner*. Harper had built up a dedicated cult following by the time he made his first Harvest album, *Flat Baroque And Berserk*, which was also the first of his albums to be recorded in more than one take. He may have toned down the bizarre extremities of his previous work, but he still sounds as uproariously uncompromising as ever. On tour in the USA to promote the album (and raise the label's profile), he greeted his first audience, in Los Angeles, by saying: "I am now going to piss on the front row. I am very stoned and very tired and if you don't like me you can come back tomorrow night."

Harvest also signed two groups who were directly influenced by The Incredible String Band and slotted firmly into the psychedelic-folk genre. The first was Tea & Symphony, an acoustic trio from Birmingham who signed to the label in 1969 and promptly released their creepy, unhinged debut, *An Asylum For The Musically Insane*. The band decided to fill out their sound with bass and drums on their second album, *Jo Sago* (1970). It marks an ambitious leap forward, with side one consisting of a conceptual piece about the travails of an immigrant living near Birmingham, but sold just as poorly as its predecessor. In the light of increasing instability in the band's line-up, Tea & Symphony split up in late 1971.

Better known than Tea & Symphony was another Birmingham-based trio, Forest, who took a circuitous route toward underground folk. Martin Welham and his brother, Adrian, had grown up obsessed with The Beatles but had had their heads turned by their sister Barbara's folk records. Martin formed a trio with Lincolnshire school friends Dez Allenby and Rory Greig and set about playing standards, jigs, and reels in local clubs; when Greig left for university, Adrian Welham stepped in and The Foresters Of Walesby truly began. They soon landed a gig playing alongside The Young Tradition, who introduced them to the London folk scene, cannabis, and obscure folk, jazz, and blues records. There was even talk of the band recording an album for Topic or Transatlantic. But The Foresters Of Walesby were in a bit of a quandary, well aware that the folk club revolution was growing increasingly long in the tooth.

"There was a dearth of suitable material that hadn't already been sung by artists like Shirley Collins, Anne Briggs, The Young Tradition, and The Watersons, whose brilliant interpretations were so often definitive," Martin Welham says. After relocating to Birmingham in 1967, the trio began to write their own material and perform around the Midlands. By now they were starting to be influenced by psychedelia – particularly The Beatles' recent albums – but their biggest inspiration was The Incredible String Band. They also gleefully embraced the burgeoning drug culture, although Welham admits their experiments with acid were infrequent. "Like many others," he says, "we soon concluded that we'd learned as much about our minds, life, and the universe generally that we didn't feel it was worthwhile tripping out any more."

The three musicians lived communally, considered themselves to be hippies, and would play impromptu concerts to friends to thank them for bringing tins of food. By the summer of 1968, they had shortened their name to The Foresters. Their music was changing too. Allenby now played mandolin, with Adrian Welham on six-string guitar and his brother on 12-string, each of them chipping in with tin whistles, harmonicas, violins, and violas. The band continued to add more self-penned material to their repertoire, and soon had an album's worth of original material.

At an open-air festival in Canon Park Hill, Birmingham, the band met manager Mark Williams, who prompted them to further shorten their name to Forest. He also introduced them to John Peel. "We found him to be a kindred spirit," Martin Welham says. "We played him a few songs, which he enjoyed enough to immediately book us for a *Night Ride* session." Peel also wanted the group for his new label, Dandelion, which he was in the process of setting up with CBS, but the delays were such that he advised Forest to sign with Harvest instead. Then, in the spring of 1969, they cut their self-titled debut at Abbey Road. "It was evident that we were going to have to record quickly," Welham says, "as studio time was extremely costly, and this inevitably meant that takes which could have been played and sung better had to be accepted and overdubs added on the spot." The consolation was that Abbey Road was well equipped with instruments, which Forest had *carte blanche* to experiment with, and they ended up rather liking the hectic, impromptu nature of the sessions. The resulting album was released in October, preceded by the single 'Searching For Shadows' / 'Mirror Of Life', and featured liner notes by John Peel.

Forest didn't sell very well, but the band-members were unconcerned. "We had a small but loyal following and had never been particularly bothered about whether we were commercially successful or not," Welham says. "Our songs were principally written for each other. If anyone else liked them it was welcomed, but it was essentially a bonus." The record was housed in a pastoral, hippie-ish jacket painted by a local book illustrator, Joan Melville.

When they came to record their next album, *Full Circle*, the band plotted out the arrangements beforehand. The songs came from their live repertoire and stretched back far enough to include the traditional 'Famine Song'. *Full Circle* has a less layered production, but the band felt happy with it; they liked the clean sound and thought the songs had been done justice. Joan Melville produced another stunning piece of artwork, this time of a church with added sinister gallows, and the album was released at the end of 1970. John Peel once again offered his support both on air and off. Peel's widow, Sheila Ravenscroft, later noted that the band spent a lot of time at Peel's house, and that Peel had made mention in his diary of "the luckless Forest, whose second LP is beautiful and almost certain not to sell at all".[7]

Forest had always had lingering concerns that they were something of an afterthought to both Harvest and their management agency, Blackhill Enterprises, which also represented Syd Barrett and The Edgar Broughton Band. "This was understandable in retrospect," Martin Welham says, "but frustrating to us at the time." The acoustic Forest would often come off poorly when they had to share the stage with a loud rock band, and were generally unsuitable for stadium-sized gigs, but they couldn't go back to playing folk clubs either. The university circuit was their saviour, and – for now – where they found their audience.

⋈

Harvest was just one of several major-label subsidiaries that offered a home to musicians operating in the outer reaches of folk music. Pye Records launched its Dawn imprint at the very end of 1969 with early releases by Man and John Kongos. According to in-house producer Barry Murray, who had previously managed a range of progressive and folk bands through his Red Bus company, Pye "had no idea what to do" with Dawn. The label would, however, release two very important acid-folk albums.

The first of these albums came from a shortlived duo who, on paper, made for an unlikely combination. After her departure from Fairport Convention, Judy Dyble had spent a few months singing with the quirky group Giles Giles & Fripp, soon to become King Crimson. Jackie McAuley, meanwhile, had begun his musical career as the keyboardist in blues-rock hard-nuts Them before forming The Belfast Gypsies with his brother, Pat.

Dyble and McAuley met in 1969 and before long had formed a trio with McAuley's housemate, Pete Sears. When Sears took off for America, McAuley and Dyble decided to continue as a duo. McAuley had already started planning a children's album, and this became the core of the new band's material. They started gigging as Trader Horne – John Peel's nickname for his nanny – and soon came to the attention of Barry Murray's Dawn. Dawn, still only a few months old, was able to spend time and money on Trader Horne. "It was a bit like being let loose in a sweet shop," Dyble recalls. "The studios at Pye were enormous. Barry Murray must have persuaded the record label to let him hire whichever instruments were wanted, hence the array of organs, harpsichords, and so on. We had some string and horn players as well."

The duo recorded a number of McAuley's songs as well as the traditional 'Down And Out Blues', Dyble's 'Morning Way', and a song she co-wrote with Steamhammer's Martin Quittenton, 'Velvet To Atone', weaving them together as a loosely conceptual album. *Morning Way* fused a childlike simplicity with a hippie romanticism tinged with sadness that this time was coming to an end.

"I thought it might be a bit too fairy-ish when it was finished," Dyble says. "It is a pretty thing and Jack's songs are excellent. I find it interesting that it seems to have been called so many classifications in its life, wyrd folk, psych folk, acid folk, when it wasn't really folk-anything when it was made. I don't know what it set out to be!"

As soon as the album was completed, Red Bus sent the duo to Scotland, Ireland, and every corner of England. McAuley took on the lion's share of the driving. "How we didn't have any major accidents through tiredness I shall never know," Dyble says. They were also booked for television appearances, usually on local evening magazine shows. Unfortunately, none of this seemed to help *Morning Way* sell. Dyble felt physically and emotionally drained; Red Bus pushed even harder, booking the band to perform at its Hollywood Festival in Newcastle-under-Lyme on May 23–24 1970 alongside various homegrown acts and The Grateful Dead. "There was the expectation that it was going to be the making of us," Dyble recalls. "I felt I was being put under enormous pressure and I just ran away. My personal life was in a muddle, I had broken up with someone that I absolutely adored, and I guess I just wanted to hide. It was just sheer misery, and none of the band or the management had any idea what I was going through, so flight seemed to be my only option."

McAuley recruited a new vocalist, Saffron Summerfield, with whom he soldiered on as Trader Horne into 1971. He then recorded a vibrant self-titled solo album on which traces of folk can be heard, particularly on the track 'Cameramen, Wilson, And Homes'. Dyble, meanwhile, resurfaced briefly in the jazz-oriented band DC & The MBs.

Dawn had become a successful label, although hardly as a result of its progressive signings. The label scored a huge Number One hit in 1970 with Mungo Jerry's 'In The Summertime', but that didn't stop Murray signing up one of the most uncompromising acid-folk acts of all, Comus, whose *First Utterance* would soon stretch the skin of folk music so tight that veins, bones, and tendons would all be visible underneath.

Another key progressive imprint was Nova, founded by Decca in 1969. "Nova is new; a new album series devoted to new talent and new outlook," the label announced. To encourage buyers to take a chance on these records, they were given a lower retail price than regular Decca/Deram releases. Nova benefited from the A&R talents of teenage in-house producer David Hitchcock; Decca relied on his youth and contacts to provide them with credible underground talent for the label.

Two of the initial Nova releases were folk-oriented. The first was Sunforest, an American trio of Terry Tucker, Erika Eigen, and Freya Houge who were reportedly discovered by producer Vic Smith in a London greasy spoon café. *The Sound Of Sunforest* was recorded in 1969 at Olympic Studios; appropriately enough, it evokes a sunny woodland walk dressed in medieval tunics and a cowgirl's Stetson. Stanley Kubrick liked the album enough to include re-recorded versions of two tracks, 'Lighthouse Keeper' and 'Overture To The Sun', on the soundtrack to *A Clockwork Orange*.

Nova's second folk voyage was *Sorcerers* by Jan Dukes De Grey, the Yorkshire-bred duo of Derek Noy and Michael Bairstow. Noy had been playing in groups since the age of 13, and had learned to follow the money early on. In the mid 60s he had formed a soul band, the 11-piece Buster Somers Express, when he thought that was what people wanted to hear; now there was a new trend in town, and Noy anticipated record companies and audiences gravitating toward it.

"Basically, how I got into the folk thing was I saw Donovan with a flute player, I think it was on *Top Of The Pops*," he recalls. "It was obvious that contemporary folk music was taking off in quite a big way. I realised there were a lot of clubs and I thought there was something coming in that was going to be big. It *was* mercenary. I was a musician earning a living. But I did like the style." Eyeballing the success of The Incredible String Band and Fairport Convention, Noy broke up the soul band and spent a few months intently listening to new folk music. He recruited Bairstow to play flute and bongos, slung on a 12-string guitar, and began writing songs.

Although his initial impetus for Jan Dukes De Grey was commercially motivated, Noy took to his new venture with gusto. "I found there was a lot of freedom in it," he says. "You weren't constricted, because people weren't going to dance to it. I liked the freedom of being able to split time, and go off into suspended time. I liked the artistic element of that." The songs went down well at the folk clubs, Noy enjoying the intimacy of the atmosphere.

By 1969, Jan Dukes De Grey had signed with the Zenith management company, through which they gained a deal with Nova. With David Hitchcock producing, the duo went into Decca's West Hampstead studio in October 1969 to make an album. *Sorcerers* contains 18 vignette-style songs – a compromise, according to Noy. "We were playing all those songs live, but each one was much longer," he says. "Dave Hitchcock wanted the improvisational stuff taken out, because he wanted to fit as many tracks on it as possible, so they were stripped right down."

Despite Noy's reservations, the clipped pace of the songs gave *Sorcerers* a distinct identity. Perhaps as a result of his frustration, however, the band changed their sound almost as soon as the album was in the can. *Sorcerers* was released in January 1970; that same month he dismissed it, in an interview with the *Yorkshire Evening Post*, as "a record where people can sit at home and relax" – unlike the band's new sound, which was "something to play in the clubs – something heavier".[8] The new Jan Dukes De Grey would be unveiled in June 1971. Just as Noy promised, theirs would be folk of a very different hue.

M

Given the pivotal role John Peel played in the underground, it seemed only natural that he would set up a record label. In 1969, he founded Dandelion Records with business partner Clive Selwood. "The half-witted, idealistic notion behind Dandelion and our other violent, capitalist enterprise, Biscuit Music, is that any profits, if such there be, should go to the artists," Peel wrote in an advertisement for the label. The plan was for 50 per cent of the income from each record to go to the artist, with the rest ploughed back into the label. Selwood and Peel did not take salaries.

The very first Dandelion album was distinctly folk-hued: *Ask Me No Questions* by Bridget St John, a dark-voiced singer-songwriter with an intimate lyrical style. She had met Peel while recording a BBC session in August 1968. "John really liked what I did," she later recalled, "and the next day he rang up and had got me a television thing."[9] Peel also arranged gigs for her, and produced *Ask Me No Questions*. He put layers of birdsong and church bells on the title track, using sound effects culled from the BBC Sound Archive to elevate an already exquisitely pastoral song into the realms of the otherworldly.

Perhaps surprisingly, given Peel's support for bands like Tyrannosaurus Rex and Forest, Bridget St John proved to be the closest Dandelion got to a psychedelic or acid-folk act. Her two subsequent albums for the label contain flashes of avant-garde adventurousness, but are closer in spirit to Nick Drake or a post-Fotheringay Sandy Denny. Her music is refined, intelligent, and warm, but not overtly experimental or psychedelic.

Another label with a similar mindset to Dandelion – albeit with a more explicit intention to release folk music right from the outset – was the Bristol-based Village Thing, set up in December 1969 by singer-songwriter Ian A. Anderson and John Turner, manager of the Troubadour folk club and a member of the surreal musical-comedy group The Pigsty Hill Light Orchestra. "We were living above the Troubadour," Anderson recalls, "and there was an amazingly intense folk scene in Bristol at the time. And we thought: 'Why don't we go to Saydisc and say we want to start a contemporary folk label?'"

Saydisc was the local label through which Anderson and British bluesman Mike Cooper had organised the 1968 country-blues compilation *Blues Like Showers Of Rain*. Picked up by John Peel, the album brought exposure to a number of unsigned musicians. Many would shortly find deals – Anderson included. For Anderson, however, the major-label experience had been anything but happy. He had been booted off Island Records, which was due to release his *Stereo Death Breakdown*, after Jethro Tull's management complained about the 'confusion' that might be caused by having two Ian Andersons on the label. The album eventually came out on Liberty instead; the follow-up, *Book Of Changes*, was released by Philips, with whom Anderson clashed over the cover art.

Village Thing was therefore guided by the idea of doing things differently, and with a focus on the local area. Anderson himself, meanwhile, had begun to move away from hearty country-blues toward underground folk – a style that would have a strong presence on Village Thing.

Across the Severn Bridge, in Wales, could be found a similar bubbling discontent toward major labels and the London-centric industry. Meic Stevens, 'The Welsh Bob Dylan', had had an unhappy experience with Decca in the mid 60s. "Small artists like me can't ever prosper on a major label," he recalled.[10] After his first single performed poorly, the rest of his recordings remained unreleased.

Label frustrations and mental health difficulties led Stevens to quit the choppy London streets for the Welsh countryside in 1966, ushering in a rediscovery of the country and its language. He translated his existing songs and began to write in Welsh, recording three EPs of earthy primitivism and mineral beauty for the tiny label Wren. "Modern Welsh music was virtually non-existent at that time," he later said. "We had a lot of fun creating it, though it was a constant hassle to get into a decent studio."[11]

Wales itself was experiencing a surge of nationalism. The Welsh Language Society (Cymdeithas Yr Iaith Gymraeg) was founded in 1962; the direct action group Movement For The Defence Of Wales (Mudiad Amddiffyn Cymru) followed a year later in response to the flooding of the Afon Tryweryn valley to provide water for Liverpool. In 1969, two members of the first group, Dafydd Iwan and Huw Jones, set up a record label, Sain, with the explicit intention of promoting Welsh-language music. From the outset, Sain released unusual folk records at a prodigious rate, including the acidic folk-pop of girl group Sidan and the high, clear sparkle of Heather Jones. Meanwhile, on one of his regular trips back to London, Meic Stevens had come to the attention of Warner Bros. The result was an album, *Outlander* (1970), on which Stevens's folk fundamentals merge with mystical strings and rock volts.

Stevens chose not to stick around on the major label merry-go-round. He was soon back in Wales, armed with a renewed knowledge of the music industry and sound recording that enabled him to help Sain flourish, and also to release a particularly psychedelic EP on his own Newyddion Da imprint. In a rare but pleasing twist, it transpired that all of this, including the eccentric

1972 album *Gwymon*, was done at Warners's expense. "My contract stipulated they had no jurisdiction over my Welsh language recordings," he recalled. "They hated me doing them, and they thought I was wasting my time. But by then they'd given up on me anyway."[12]

⋈

As this brief flowering of acid folk came to a close, there were certain signs toward future directions for both individual artists and wider trends. One such notice flared in the career of Jade, led by the South London-based guitarist and singer Marianne Segal. She had long been entranced with American folk artists – Dylan, Buckley, Baez – but was also fascinated by the meticulous structure underpinning Phil Spector's powerhouse recordings. After a brief spell as a solo performer, she decided she wanted to develop a bigger sound.

"I found that I felt much more comfortable having somebody on stage with me, another guitarist, a band around me, or at least two musicians," she recalls. After meeting guitarist Dave Waite, Segal struck a deal first with booking agent Sandy Glennon and then with Jon Miller at Dick James Music. The duo went into the studio in March 1970 to record the sweet, iridescent *Fly On Strangewings*. Although there are suggestions of 60s folk-rock and glowing English pastorality in the songs, it's clear that Segal's pop intellect was already primed for the 70s, with elements of country-rock and power-pop on show alongside the more ethereal, hippie overhangs.

Segal and Waite had recorded *Fly On Strangewings* with session musicians; following its completion, Rod Edwards of the psychedelic pop group Piccadilly Line became the permanent keyboardist in a three-piece now trading as Jade (or Silver Jade in the USA). There seemed no reason why the group's commercial take on folk wouldn't do very well. "Jon Miller said: 'You need to go on the road now with this album,'" Segal recalls. "It all fell into place. We did a lot of work, we did TV; we were doing the colleges and universities, and were terribly well-received."

The album did well in the USA, and Jade had the honour of playing at many of the famous venues Segal had dreamed of performing in back when she was a young starry-eyed Dylan fan. When they returned to Britain, however, the band came to an abrupt halt. "I think certain members of Jade were influenced by the American tour, and the music in America," Segal says. "Certain people wanted to go this way and others wanted to go that way, and that included my management. We split apart; it was crazy. It shocked me. I just stood back and watched it happen."

Rod Edwards left in October 1970 to perform in another duo; Segal was left distraught. "Bearing in mind I was only 21 or 22, I was still a bit green," she says. "I didn't do anything about it. I watched it crumble." Her subsequent project, The Marianne Segal Band, reflected the influence of a rockier American sound.

As brief as their lifespan had been, Jade were very important in the sense of bringing a *new* American sound into British folk music. They had anticipated the new trends on the horizon and attempted to incorporate them into their sound. Their split, caused by arguments over direction, was another harbinger of what was to come. Not only were the genres starting to change, they were also beginning to stratify away from one another. Fusions of sound, taken for granted in the late 60s, would soon be far harder to achieve.

None of the acid and psychedelic-folk bands signed by record companies in the wake of The Incredible String Band sold many records. As 1970 ticked away, so did the record labels' patience. "Gone was the willingness of record companies to sign a wide range of underground artists and to stick with them," Forest's Martin Welham recalls, "and in came the accountants and financial advisers. At first, it didn't seem as though we would be dropped, as we'd begun discussions with Malcolm Jones for our third album."

Forest never saw the supportive Jones again. His replacement was much less enthusiastic about a third Forest album; when even he was substituted for a barefaced hatchet man, Forest decided to accept their fate and left the label.

The golden period of British record labels anxiously signing up underground folk groups had ground decisively to a halt. The innovative approaches to folk music these acts had displayed – and the success some of them had achieved on the live circuit – had not translated into sufficient sales. Record labels became increasingly reluctant to sign more new groups in the idiom – or even to stand by those acts they already had. In the case of Decca's Nova imprint, the plug was pulled on the whole specialist venture.

Many of the greatest British experimental folk albums were still to come. Some artists had snuck in at the tail end of the boom, found a lucky ear at a label, or would even release their records themselves. Some would take the opportunity and run with it to work in new subgenres, such as progressive folk, or use folk as a conduit for personal vision. Underground folk had shown that it wasn't going to be the next big commercial thing. But it was still maturing as a sound. Creatively, it was far, *far* from bankrupt.

CHAPTER 7
Spirit Of Love

ONCE THE NECESSARY infrastructure had been established on both sides of the Atlantic, the multiple nuanced hues of experimental folk offered musicians a wide palette. It could be gossamer-graceful and luminous; it could also explore the darkest sides of human nature. As acid and psychedelic folk moved beyond its first burst of youthful vigour toward adulthood, it became a vessel for numerous visions, discoveries, and songs of innocence and experience.

One of the first to do so was Donovan, who released the lavish double-album set *A Gift From A Flower To A Garden* in 1967, having recently become a father for the first time and begun to follow the teachings of the Mahareshi Mahesh Yogi. Like Donovan, Clive Palmer was among the original crop of innovators in psychedelic folk. Unlike Donovan, he was not exactly a household name.

"It's a bit convoluted," Palmer says of the period that followed his departure from The Incredible String Band. Since the release of *The Incredible String Band*, he had been travelling throughout Europe, the Middle East, and Asia; returning to the UK in late 1966, he found that Mike Heron and Robin Williamson had reformed the band, but professed indifference. Anyway, by December, he had more pressing concerns: "I got busted in Glasgow for LSD. It was the first case ever in Scotland, so they didn't really know what to do about it. I got a £100 fine in the end, and six weeks at Barlinnie." (Barlinnie was a Glaswegian prison with a particularly hard-knock reputation; Palmer passed his time there crafting a chess set out of soap.)

On his release, Palmer headed for London, where he began playing traditional songs on the banjo at clubs like Les Cousins, sometimes in partnership with Wizz Jones. It was around this time that he met Peter Eden, who produced Palmer's *Banjoland* at the end of 1967. "A lot of my influences are popular songs from the 50s and the 40s, because that's what I sang on stage as a child," Palmer says. "So that leaks in to my music." Wizz Jones plays guitar on several of the *Banjoland* tracks, while the touching 'Stories Of Jesus' features a string quartet.

Eden made the record without a label contract and then tried in vain to sell it. "I used to take it to record companies," he recalls, "and nobody would even listen to it – or if they did they'd go: 'blimey, not likely!'" Even if Eden mentioned that Palmer used to be in the now-hot Incredible String Band, this album of Edwardian banjo music was so far removed from what Heron and Williamson were now doing that it wouldn't have made a jot of difference. The defiantly uncommercial LP remained unreleased for nearly 40 years.

By late 1968 Palmer was feeling a familiar itch to move on. "I went down to Cornwall," he says. "I stayed with some friends in Helston, and they said there was a folk club at Mitchell. There was this thing they called the Folk Cottage. It belonged to a farmer, and his son ran a club there. So I started playing there."

Martin Val Baker ran The Mask Club in St Ives. "Talent is taken for granted in London," he recalls. "In Cornwall, there is time and space for it to be nurtured and developed. There were half a dozen clubs in West Cornwall alone, and a terrific outpouring of new music." At the Folk Cottage, enthusiasm and talent were in abundance, and there was an anarchic edge to the all-night sessions. "It was a fantastic experience," says Pete Berryman, who had also recently relocated to Cornwall. "There were all ages of people there. It was quite sparky – you were sitting on benches and things, and there wasn't a bar."

Berryman had been playing guitar since his teens and was now working in a hotel where, he says, he met "a very eccentric character" named Barney Potter. "He said: 'I play banjo, I hear you play guitar.' And he took me out to the Folk Cottage." Berryman soon found himself in Potter's band alongside 'Whispering' Mick Bennett, so named because of his loud voice, Ralph McTell, Bob Strawbridge, and 'Henry' Bartlett, whose real name was Michael (Henry came from his resemblance to Henry VIII).

It was a very loose arrangement. "People would join in on harmonies, and John The Fish would play along with the kazoo," Berryman recalls. "It could be three people or it could be seven people." When McTell returned to London in 1967, Berryman, Bennett, and Bartlett evolved into The Great Western Jug Band. Bartlett took over the organisation of the Folk Cottage in 1968 and things became even more eclectic. "Ron Geesin used to do this performance act," Berryman says. "He would do crazy things and spout poetry or recite or play things."

It was into this atmosphere that Clive Palmer alighted in 1968. "Clive was a bit of a catalyst," Val Baker recalls. "His early bands were all pretty original in completely different ways. I think they inspired a lot of local musicians to have a go at producing new music."

As Berryman recalls, Bartlett soon suggested that the two of them form a band with Palmer. The new trio went to Wadebridge Folk Club, where they saw The Jayfolk perform; they were so struck by the gleaming voice of singer Jill Johnson that they recruited her, too, and The Famous Jug Band was born. "Clive had quite a big repertoire of stuff, he had things he wanted to do, and he had written some songs as well," Berryman says. "I had quite a wide range too, as did Henry. I'd been a songwriter before, but I started to write appropriately for what I was doing with them."

Interest came quickly from Liberty Records, with the resulting *Sunshine Possibilities* released in July 1969. The album mixed traditional material with group originals, notably Palmer's stunning 'A Leaf Must Fall'. But Palmer was getting restless again, growing away from his band-mates and gravitating instead toward a new crowd: Mick Bennett, guitarist Tim Wellard, and Martin Val Baker's drumming sister, Genevieve. "They were more involved in the hippie, free-living lifestyle," Berryman says. "We were all friends, and we all played together, but they were more into that aspect than myself or Henry, and certainly Jill. Jill came straight out of school. It was quite traumatic for her to be on the road with us. It would be snowing and freezing up north, and we'd be sleeping on floors. Once, in Sheffield, Clive said: 'I know a nice place we can go for lunch' – and he took us into the Salvation Army shelter. For her, all that, it was quite a shock."

The Famous Jug Band carried on without Palmer, recording the intellectual, charismatic *Chameleon* (1970) as a trio. "I really went into overdrive with the writing myself," Berryman says. "I was interested in doing something that was a bit more jazzy. And Henry always was a frustrated jazzer." Shortly thereafter, however, the band ended. "The travelling and everything else began to take its toll on Jill's health," Berryman adds. "She'd had enough, basically. And it was great to play with a jug player, but it has its limits."

Palmer, meanwhile, had formed the four-piece Stockroom Five with Mick Bennett, John Bidwell, and Tim Wellard. Bidwell was a multi-instrumentalist, originally from a village near Newquay; he and Wellard had played together as teenagers. Stockroom Five was largely an outlet for Palmer's traditional repertoire and lasted from about May to September 1969. Bennett and Palmer then went off to spend the winter in London while Bidwell, Wellard, and Martin Val Baker's sister, Demelza, formed The Novelty Band. When Bennett and Palmer returned in the spring of 1970, they joined up with The Novelty Band, which then mutated into the more experimental Temple Creatures. "They started getting more far out with that, more Eastern-influenced," Berryman recalls.

"I used to play a lovely Homer C. Ledford Appalachian dulcimer in The Novelty Band and Temple Creatures," Bidwell recalls. "After a gig in Penzance, the dulcimer was put on the roof of the van during packing of instruments, and we drove off to a gig without it." This dulcimer inevitably didn't survive its high-velocity meeting with tarmac, leaving the band with a problem for their next gig. So they went rummaging around. "Clive and I found a really old and well-seasoned shelf liner of Parana pine," he says. "We basically designed the optimum instrument out of a rectangle of wood. It was fretted in the same way as the dulcimer, except we used chicken wire. We positioned the frets mainly using harmonics." The bridge was widened, increasing the area of vibration for the strings, giving a sitar-like drone. The instrument was named the dulcitar, and its pensive buzz was a singular sound.

Temple Creatures proved popular on the local circuit before limping out of existence toward the end of 1970. After a brief period in Scotland, Clive Palmer returned once again to Cornwall, where he lived with Mick Bennett in an outwardly ragged, inwardly cosy caravan they had found abandoned in the woods near Mylor.

The idea for the next – and most important – of these Cornish bands came from Jo Lustig, the manager of their old mucker Ralph McTell. In 1971, slightly later than most other labels, CBS Records expressed an interest in adding progressive folk artists to its roster. Lustig was all over the opportunity – partly, Palmer suggests, because it would give McTell production experience. With a deal in the works, McTell contacted his friends in Cornwall. Palmer and Bennett were already working on songs together in the caravan; they called up John Bidwell and, after a short period of rehearsals, the three of them travelled to London. Lustig was happy enough with their sound and suggested the name Clive's Original Band to cash in on Palmer's past with The Incredible String Band. Palmer was never the band's 'leader', however, and the name was always shortened to COB.

The songs that would make up the band's first album, *Spirit Of Love*, had very different origins. Two were traditionals (including a resurrection of 'Banjo Land' from Palmer's unreleased 1967 album); some dated back to Temple Creatures; others were newer compositions that sprang from the caravan. Mick Bennett had an endearing habit of going for long walks, shaking the Cornish countryside with his huge voice, and dreaming up new songs as he wandered around. "Mick would have a poem or a song, and he knew the sort of tune he wanted, and John and I would come up with them," Palmer says.

After only a few gigs as COB, the band went into the studio during the summer of 1971 with McTell producing, as planned. "I can safely say they were the most difficult sessions I have been involved with," he later recalled. "COB were loose and undisciplined, totally unaware of recording techniques."[1] John Bidwell disagrees. "Naïve is a better word," he says.

McTell has since said that constant improvisation, tuning disparities, and a general laissez-faire attitude made it difficult to achieve a consistency of sound – not that it's ever audible to the listener. *Spirit Of Love* sounds like a natural outgrowth of the harmony between the members of COB and McTell. There's an Eastern air from the Temple Creatures days and a blister of Stockroom Five tradition, but overall COB was more than the sum of the band-members' various previous permutations. The arcane 'Serpent's Kiss' is perhaps the most palpable sign of the presence of something visionary in COB, but there's an ethereal, rarefied air throughout.

Spirit Of Love came out in December 1971 to almost universal critical praise but very few sales. Lustig nonetheless kept COB busy with gigs and also suggested they make a radio-friendly single, the result of which was the reggae-groove misfire of 'Blue Morning' / 'Bones'. Despite Lustig's ploy of including a miniature bottle of whisky with each of the copies he sent out to DJs, the single didn't catch on. COB had inadvertently proven that being commercial was not what they excelled at.

"I've always been of the opinion that you should educate the audience," Palmer says. "The music should take you somewhere else and it should open a door for you, or try to." There's a greater unity of approach on COB's next record, *Moyshe McStiff And The Tartan Lancers Of The Sacred Heart*. According to Mick Bennett, it was written "as an album, rather than just being our live act". It's lyrically and instrumentally focused, invisibly knitting together complex rhythms and fine-spun poetry and giving the sense of a band at the peak of both sophistication and originality.

Moyshe was and is much more than something to stand back and admire, however. It has a profound emotional resonance and continues to inspire utter devotion. Numerous fan theories have been developed as to the meaning of the album, the most popular being that it is a song-cycle of a Crusader Knight's inner reflections – an idea that's likely influenced by the artwork and title as much as the contents, despite the band-members insisting that neither contains any deep meaning. Regarding the cover art, Palmer insists: "It was just farmed out, that." As for the title, he says that 'Moyshe McStiff' was a nickname for Bennett, derived from his Jewish-Scottish heritage; Bidwell and Palmer were 'The Tartan Lancers'; and 'The Sacred Heart' was, according to Ralph McTell, just another throwaway addition.

The songs are a different matter, however. Dense with imagery and saturated with an ancient, sacred aura, they have a singular essence running through them, although Mick Bennett has since said that the ideas came from a range of sources. 'Lion Of Judah', for example, was inspired by Haile Selassie; 'Pretty Kerry' was a simulated folk ballad, based on an overheard conversation; 'Martha And Mary' evolved from an earlier Bennett poem about the sisters of Lazarus in the Christian gospels. "Life's a spiritual journey," says Palmer, "and as you get older it becomes more important. That was our idea, that we could make it so it becomes an experience."

COB recorded *Moyshe* in the summer of 1972 before spending the autumn on tour with Pentangle. Although it was lucrative for the support act, the tour was a complete debacle for the headliners. Pentangle were at the point of implosion, fuelled by personality clashes, quarrels with their record label, heavy drinking, and an increasingly embattled attitude toward the music critics who had latterly turned on the band. When Danny Thompson fell ill, the final tour dates were cancelled and Pentangle effectively came to an end.

COB too split up shortly after the tour. In early 1973 they had a spell as the resident performers at the Half Moon pub in Putney, but when it had become clear that *Moyshe* wasn't going to sell much more than *Spirit Of Love*, a sense of ennui set in and arguments between the three musicians increased. A bust-up on stage in March provided the final full stop. "I fancied a rest," Palmer says. "It had been quite a long haul with COB, and it hadn't really got anywhere." John Bidwell agrees that the time was right to call it a day. "It was inevitable," he says. "We were getting virtually no support in the industry, we were nearly broke, and I for one was relieved when it finished."

Moyshe McStiff And The Tartan Lancers Of The Sacred Heart was released on a bespoke and ludicrously shortlived new label series, Polydor Folk Mill. Announced in August 1972, Folk Mill launched in October and released its fourth and final album in November. They had all been deleted by the following summer.

Having recently inked a production deal with Polydor, Jo Lustig was a key player in Folk Mill, just as he had been in CBS's push for progressive folk. A *Billboard* announcement in August 1972 indicated that the label's first two releases would be by COB and Wizz Jones. The Wizz Jones album never materialised, but in its place came another Lustig-related project: the debut solo album by Barry Dransfield.

Dransfield had recently broken away from performing in a distinctive and popular duo with his elder brother, Robin. The brothers played energetic and accomplished takes on traditional material, while their heartthrob looks and long hair didn't hurt their appeal. By 1971, with two albums under their belts and Lustig on board, the Dransfields were knocking on the door of breakthrough success. Lustig had set up a three-album US deal with Warner Bros, but none of this was making Barry Dransfield happy. He hated the second album and was decidedly ambivalent about the fame that everything seemed geared toward. "For some reason I let Robin go ahead with the idea, in spite of my lack of enthusiasm for it," he later recalled. "I was not at all enthusiastic about the idea of trying to make what we did truly commercial."[2]

An angry Jo Lustig initially told Barry that he'd "never work again", but he must have been fond of him. Lustig soon took him on again, negotiating a generous advance from Polydor for an album that would prove to be far more personal than the two he had recorded with his brother. *Barry Dransfield* contains a maverick's selection of material. There's a theme of rebellion running throughout – perhaps against those commercial pressures he disliked so much. In the liner notes, he mentions that he was keen on the way one of the album's best tracks, 'Robin Hood And The Peddlar', "shows the defiance of one man against the belligerence of two". Among the other highlights are the opening track – perhaps the most wretched version yet recorded of Michael Hurley's 'Werewolf' – and the *a cappella* brilliance of 'She's Like A Swallow'.

Barry Dransfield was the clearest statement Dransfield could make as to why his vision would not fit with aggressive marketing. It stood on its own, without asking for an audience. Although it would take decades, that audience eventually found it.

A similar break with the recent past came in 1971 from a group who had made many other transitions since the middle of the 60s: Mighty Baby. "What was happening musically and socially at the time shaped what happened to us as a group and individually," band-member Mike Evans recalled. "Everything was changing rapidly, and we realised it was not enough to just try and be yourself." Mighty Baby first emerged when Evans, Alan 'Bam' King, and Roger Powell decided to move on from the sound of their current band, mod firebrands The Action.

"As The Action, you could say we were a rhythm section with singers," Evans said. "As Mighty Baby we were free to explore. I remember playing at Middle Earth with The Byrds around the time of *Sweetheart Of The Rodeo*. We were very impressed by what they were achieving and consequently we started to think in a more 'stoned country' way." The band gained two new members – the intense, bluesy guitarist Martin Stone and multi-instrumentalist Ian Whiteman – and changed their name to Mighty Baby, releasing their self-titled psychedelic hard-rock debut in 1969.

The experience of making and touring *Mighty Baby* brought about yet more re-evaluation. "During this time a change occurred with the way bands set up their equipment for live gigs," Evans said. "Small amps on stage miked up to our own PA system gave us more control over the sound produced on stage. We could hear each other better and it made for a more consistent experience all round." Mighty Baby were on the road a lot and began to listen to their music differently. They also gained new concerns when all of the band-members – with the exception of King – became adherents of Sufism, the mystical branch of Islam characterised by a belief in becoming closer to God in this life rather than after death. "It was very much a Sufi album," Martin Stone later said of the group's second album, *A Jug Of Love*. "We lost the psychedelia and became more rootsy. Drink and drugs were out of the window."[3]

Although the songs came together on the road, only a few were tested out live. "A lot of the lyrics were influenced by books that we were reading at the time," Evans recalled. "'Tasting The Life' is about gigging around the country, and 'Keep On Jugging' is about a roadie. 'Happiest Man At The Carnival', 'A Jug Of Love', and 'Slipstreams' were all more studio-based, and more spiritually inclined." These songs were largely acoustic, personal, and emblematic of the band's religious convictions, offering a blissful exploration of the peace Sufism had brought. The West Coast influence is still prominent, but the overall sound is slower and more deliberate.

Released on producer Mike Vernon's Blue Horizon label in October 1971, *A Jug Of Love* failed to match the sales of its predecessor. Perhaps it was just too different from the loud Mighty Baby live experience; perhaps its religiosity was too off-putting for a rock audience; perhaps Blue Horizon, a label better known for heavy blues records, was an inappropriate home for this serene, folkish work. The album's release coincided with the band's splintering, although Whiteman and Powell continued to record together as The Habibiyya, signing to Island for the 1973 album *If Man But Knew*. The Habibiyya continued to delve into Sufism, and in doing so moved much further away from recognisable rock structures toward an early 'world music' ambience.

⋈

Somebody else who made music of the air and of the earth was Bill Fay. "The big influence on the songs lyrically was the outside world itself, with all its life and anti-life," he says. "I always remember a couplet from Ray Russell who, as well as being a great innovative guitarist, wrote poetry and prose. 'I opened my eyes wide and the world flew inside.' It's simple, but it kind of sums things up, influence-wise, for me."

Fay signed to Decca as a young singer-songwriter in 1967 and released the single 'Some Good Advice' / 'Scream In The Ears'. Like Clive Palmer, Fay was an unorthodox talent who had caught the ear of Peter Eden. Eden worked sensitively with Fay on the 1967 single. "I owe a lot to Peter," Fay says. "I think he had some ideas for the songs, but the big service he did me that day was to leave me to it."

Fay had been developing his self-taught piano-playing style and worked out his parts on the studio's Mellotron. He recorded the single with The Fingers, a solid, tight band whom Eden looked after. It was, Fay says, "a great day in the studio, then over all too soon. Can't be sure if it was picking tomatoes or cucumbers, or working at the metal foundry the following day".

Fay continued to work temporary jobs while under contract to Decca. The single didn't sell enough to earn royalties, and because Fay rarely played live at this point there were no proceeds from the university or club circuits. His contract with Decca was curiously ambiguous: it said the label wanted four *titles* from Bill Fay, but did not specify whether these were to be albums or singles. He recorded several more songs for Decca over the next 18 months, some of them augmented by banjo, harp, and brass, arranged by Pete Dello, and featuring the backing of Dello's group, Honeybus. At the time, Fay was frustrated that these songs weren't released but, with hindsight, he is grateful that they weren't – a single would have counted as a 'title' in his contract, and may have prevented him from making his two albums.

"By 1969, the songs had changed a lot," he says. Since recording his first single, Fay had engaged in several weighty discussions with his friend, Bob. The pair would speculate and philosophise on a raft of topics, from the meaning of life to the nature of communication and access to deeper consciousness. "The outcome for me was that there was something to find out, but more importantly, that you could find it out," he says. His new quest for meaning and discovery filtered into – and soon became the foundation of – his music. 'Garden Song' was the first example of this. "The outside world and my relationship to it entered the song in a seeking kind of way," he says. "The opening line is the beginning of a search for spiritual meaning. I wasn't trying to go within: I was trying to get outside my head, to connect with something that existed in its own right."

Fay had become aware of the work of Pierre Teilhard de Chardin, a Jesuit priest and palaeontologist who supported evolution in defiance of Catholic doctrine on creationism and posited the idea of the Omega Point, a phenomenon that existed in the future, toward which everything was drawn. "They [were] very optimistic concepts," Fay says. "He believed strongly that we were heading somewhere in a very purposeful way." When he received a letter from Bob about the Spirit Of Infinite Life And Power, from which all in the universe is derived, Fay came to feel "something very hard to put into words". Bob had chosen to refer to this Spirit as God, and included with his letter text from the Books of Revelation and Luke. Fay gained a heightened sense of the wonder, and of the new way the world was speaking to him.

Over at Decca, the decision had been taken to ask Bill Fay for an album. Fay's new songs reflected his spiritual development. Peter Eden was asked to produce and brought with him the jazz composer Mike Gibbs, who had not worked on arrangements before. Fay trusted Eden's judgement. He went to Gibbs's house and sang his songs into a cassette recorder. "On the morning of the session I arrived slightly late, and did turn to go, having opened what I thought was the wrong studio door," he says. "I thought it must have been Decca's Classical studio, but I spotted a nervous Mike in the middle of this giant assembly, who said he'd added this and added that, and had been awake, pacing up and down all night, worrying if it was going to work. It was so moving, to sing along, not knowing what you were going to hear next."

The arrangements were elaborate, complex, and clever – and all recorded in one day. *Bill Fay* was released in February 1970, on Nova, with the cover image apparently showing Fay walking on water. "That was an accident," he says. "We went to Hyde Park and took a shot by the lake, where there is a promontory upon which I stood. Some water had lapped onto it, and unknowingly it gave that impression."

The album went down well with the critics. *Record Mirror* invented a genre for it, "improved folk"; *Zig Zag*'s Jeff Cloves praised the album while lambasting Decca's pitiful promotional strategy. Peter Eden took the article to the label, using it to secure a re-release of the album. Decca also asked for a follow-up.

Meanwhile, Fay struck up a friendship with guitarist Ray Russell, who had played on *Bill Fay*, and Russell's friend Alan Rushton. The three men shared a similar seeking spirit, with Russell and Rushton particularly focused on investigating UFOs as a portent of the Second Coming of Christ. Fay travelled with Russell down to Warminster, an English town near Stonehenge with a history of sightings.

"It was looking away from ourselves at the world in a wider way with an open mind," Fay says. "It led to me waking up the next morning and looking at the tree outside the window. I felt deeply that it had been put there, formed by a Creator, a Being of all Beings." Shortly afterward, Fay found a collection of commentaries by 19th-century ministers on the Books of Daniel and Revelation at a jumble sale. "Many truths jumped out of the pages of that book and became the basis of the second album," he says. "'Time Of The Last Persecution' was a phrase used in one of the minister's commentaries."

While Fay continued to formulate his worldview, and did so increasingly around Biblical structures, the routines of everyday life and the political ferment of the time also fed into his songwriting. He spent time with homeless people while working as a traffic survey checker, and wrote 'Time Of The Last Persecution' after attending an anti-apartheid demonstration during which mounted police charged into the crowd. He felt a profound sadness that the edifice of society only seemed to deliver the same corruption and oppression.

Where *Bill Fay* felt optimistic, *Time Of The Last Persecution* is less formless in its idealism. "I needed to know that these things would have an end, that they couldn't just go on and on in perpetuity," Fay says. Eschewing Teilherd's optimistic Omega Point concept, he looked instead to an Omega Day of intervention. "How that was to come about, according to what is written, from Moses and the prophets through to the Gospels and the Book of Revelation was what I would be trying to understand from then on in."

Ray Russell produced *Time Of The Last Persecution*, with work once again completed in a single day. While Fay's lyrics reflect the extreme times he felt humanity was living through, Russell's revolving rays of cacophony and quiet do the same. The cover image, of a bearded, brooding Bill Fay, marked quite a change from the angelic portrait of the first album. It led to speculation over the years that Fay was in the midst of a drug burnout or breakdown, neither of which was true. "We were recording a serious song, probably the title track, so I looked serious," he says. "A lot of people back then let their hair and beard grow and you can look a bit more intense as a result. I wasn't involved in the drug culture aspect of those times."

The album was released in early 1971. Although Decca opted not to renew his contract, Fay felt no animosity toward the label. "In that three years I went from playing piano on my own, to playing with other musicians, and everything that all those different players brought to the songs," he says. "Also, the Decca contract ran parallel with my personal changes – and as far as I know, no one at Decca sought to oversee or influence what was recorded. That in itself was a big thing."

Fay continued to record sporadically, but would be unable to find another home for his music for many, many years. In the meantime, *Time Of The Last Persecution* slowly but very definitely amassed a following. Listeners pored over Fay's liner notes, tried to unpack his vivid but inscrutable worldview, and looked at the cover, wondering about the story behind its author.

Back in 1967, the most celebrated voyager of all was about to begin her journey. Vashti Bunyan was without a record deal and without a clue what to do next. Her brother, keen to help, organised a meeting with Ewan MacColl and Peggy Seeger. "My brother's friend was their agent, I think," she recalls. "So I took my little guitar and my little songs and I went over there, to the house, and I sat there. And I sang my songs, and they were both very solemn. It became obvious that I was going to have to go, and as I got up, Peggy Seeger said: 'All I can say is, beware of the ephemeral.' I didn't have the faintest idea of what she meant. I looked it up when I got home. Oh. That's exactly what I *want*."

Under parental pressure to work, Bunyan took on a job at a veterinary practice. "That was a disaster as well," she says, "because I just ended up with stray dogs in the house, and I think we had a monkey at one point. I was fed up and upset, my mother was in hospital, my father asked me to leave with my dog, so I went to see Robert, who was living in a wood behind the art school."

This was Robert Lewis, a penniless bohemian student at Ravensbourne College of Art in South East London. "He knew people with horses and wagons, these very young romantic children of aristocratic families who had got the idea of reopening lay lines," she says. "They were amazing, and they looked incredible, they had these wonderful clothes, gypsy crossed with Indian." Bunyan moved into Lewis's shelter in the woods. "We had the same kind of ideas, that life was intolerable really. We just couldn't make sense of it at all and didn't think that anyone else in authority was making any sense of it, and that what we had to do was make our own world away from it all." They lived on sparse food, augmenting their diet with nettles when needed; Bunyan fashioned curtains for the home out of butter muslin, and they sat on seats made from fallen trees.

The idyll was shortlived: Bunyan and Lewis were evicted by representatives from the Bank of England, who told them they were living on the land illegally. Spotting a horse-drawn wagon through a gap in a fence, the couple decided a house on wheels would be perfect for them and ended up buying it with money lent to them by Lewis's friend, Donovan, who told them about an artist's community he was setting up on the Isle of Skye, off to the west of Scotland. Donovan and the first batch of residents set off in a Land Rover; the wagon, drawn by a horse named Bess, followed in the summer of 1968. "We probably thought it would take us a few weeks," Bunyan says. "We soon learnt."

They tried to keep moving every day. On some days they would encounter generosity, on others slammed doors and police hassle. Their lifestyle was austere, with most of their money spent on shoeing Bess every 80 miles or so. "I remember looking in a sweet shop window and it was like a psychedelic experience," Bunyan says. "They were so forbidden. We lived on brown rice and brown bread."

It wasn't a straight line from London to Scotland. Arriving in the Lake District at the end of the year, Bunyan and Lewis met the unconventional Mac and Iris Macfarlane; within 20 minutes, the Macfarlanes had offered them their house for the winter. The Macfarlanes were also heading for the outposts of Scotland, to renovate a ruined house in North Uist. "I don't think people like that are made any more. They had no cynicism about them at all, total generosity," Bunyan says. "She was an amazing woman, Iris Macfarlane. She wrote one of the songs on *Diamond Day*."

Bunyan and Lewis also made a brief journey to the lowlands of Europe that winter, where Bunyan played a serious of disastrous youth-club gigs in Holland. At a low ebb, she met the US folk musician Derroll Adams by chance in a pub in Ghent. Lewis asked Adams to play his banjo; he said he would if Bunyan sang for him in return. "I told Derroll I'd given up on music, that I was never going to record again, that's it," she recalls. "And he said: 'You've got this light, you mustn't hide it.'"

Despite her ill feelings about the music business, Bunyan had not stopped writing songs. She had written 'Glow Worms' while living in the wood. "That was probably the last love song I wrote," she says. "Robert said: 'Why don't you stop writing all these miserable little love songs and write about the world around you, and all these wonderful things that we're finding?'" So that's what she did. She wrote 'Timothy Grub' first, about the eviction and finding the horse and wagon. Lewis wrote too, composing lyrics for 'Window Over The Bay', 'Hebridean Sun', and 'Trawlerman's Song'.

"That's not often acknowledged, that it was his idea to get on the road with the horse," Bunyan says. "Although we came to it together and we found it together, it was definitely his vision. But I think in the end I probably took it more seriously than he did, the dreaming." The songs kept them going when things were tough. Bunyan wrote 'Diamond Day' on the journey back from the ill-starred tour of Holland, while Lewis wrote the idyllic lyrics to 'Hebridean Sun' on the way through dour industrial landscapes.

"'Jog Along Bess' was written in one of the most bleak places I've ever been in my entire life," Bunyan recalls. "It was a glen up in the Highlands on the way to Skye, with no trees in it at all and this winding road through it. It was raining, and there were midges. Scottish midges are worse than mosquitoes. They're very tiny and they bite and they hurt and they itch. I was sitting against a wall, we had an American friend with us who was completely dumbfounded as to why anyone would want to live in this country, and she was listening to me as the verses came and she was getting more and more tearful as more came out, I suppose because it was so awful, this grey sky, the midges, and not knowing what was around the next corner. It seemed that the more lightweight songs came from a time when it was really horrible." The final part of the journey was especially hard for Bunyan. It was then that her mother, who had been ill for some time, passed away.

"We were about five miles short of the place when this Land Rover pulled up, and it was Donovan," she continues. It transpired that Donovan's idea of settling down in Skye had not unfolded as he imagined it; his fame and particularly his success in America had seen to it that he was always busy. The imagined community was largely self-managed by the now established residents who had allotted the houses and divided up the land. "I remember Robert and I just looking at each other," Bunyan continues. "We knew almost straight away that there wasn't going to be a place for us." The couple realised that they had become travellers; they didn't even ask if they could settle. Bunyan played one of her new songs, 'Rainbow River', to Donovan and then got back in the wagon, wondering what to do next.

On their way back from Holland, Bunyan and Lewis had passed through London, where they met Joe Boyd. Boyd knew of Bunyan's work with Andrew Loog Oldham, and had expressed a wish to work with her a few years earlier. She played her new songs to him, and he liked them; he gave her a five-pound note and a copy of *Wee Tam And The Big Huge* and promised to make an album with her when the journey was finished. He also invited the couple to dine that evening with The Incredible String Band. "There they were, in their finery," Bunyan recalls. "It was probably just about at the height of their success, and they were in these beautiful velvet clothes, beads and bangles, and *gorgeous* patchwork leather boots. And I was still probably wearing my sister's grandmother's dress and welly boots."

After spending some time up in North Uist and Berneray, Bunyan and Lewis returned to London in November 1969. True to his word, Boyd organised recording sessions for the following month. "I hadn't heard any other music, hardly, throughout that whole journey, apart from my own," Bunyan says. "I hadn't heard any of Nick Drake's stuff, and I didn't know who Robert Kirby was. I knew who Fairport Convention were but I didn't know their music." (A few years earlier, Bunyan had been handed a piece of paper with the telephone number of a band in need of a singer. It was Fairport Convention. She never called.)

The first night of recording comprised an improvisational exploration of the songs. Among those present were John James, who had been on some of the journey with Bunyan and co-wrote 'Where I Like To Stand', and Robin Williamson. Robert Kirby entered the frame on the second night. Bunyan was in awe of his artistic touch – "the way he had written the arrangements was kind of what was in my head for this album" – but wasn't afraid of speaking up if she didn't feel it was right for her song.

"He had written beautiful arrangements for the recorder for 'Rainbow River' but in the third verse he'd done some key changes to it and I didn't like it," she says. "So the *hippie* who knows nothing about music at all said: 'Don't like that one, can you repeat what you've done in the second verse for the third verse.' That's what he did. And then on 'Swallow Song' he'd written this beautiful bit for a solo violin. I know nothing about music theory, nothing at all, but I'd been listening to Hebridean fiddle players, and there was this extraordinary violin player with a Stradivarius. I said: 'Do you think you could do it without vibrato?' I don't think he'd played without vibrato since he was three. He was absolutely horrified! But he did it."

On the third night, Dave Swarbrick and Simon Nicol came in, adding fiddle, mandolin, and banjo to three tracks, most conspicuously 'Come Wind Come Rain'. The overt folkishness made Bunyan uncertain; she had similar reservations about Robin Williamson's fiddle on 'Jog Along Bess'.

Once the sessions were complete, Joe Boyd took the tapes back to America; Bunyan, now pregnant, went back to the Hebrides with Lewis. Eventually, Boyd sent her an acetate of *Just Another Diamond Day*. "I was thunderstruck," she says. "Having come from the Andrew Oldham days, where everything was very produced ... there were lots of bum notes that didn't need to be there, the strumming at the beginning of the *a cappella* bit in 'Window Over The Bay' was where I'd played myself some guitar notes to start off. They weren't meant to be in there, but he'd kept them in. They were very rough. There were lots of things in there that I couldn't bear, and the whole folksy nature of it: it felt like it had been recorded round a campfire. Which was obviously what Joe had the idea of, but I didn't. I didn't want it to sound handmade."

Bunyan couldn't bond with the album, and when it was released, in December 1970, she felt even worse about it. As well as being unheralded and under-promoted, it sounded exceptionally fragile for a world that was now moving away from the hippie dream. Sales barely reached three figures; Bunyan herself crammed it – metaphorically and physically – into a drawer.

And yet *Just Another Diamond Day*, like *Moyshe McStiff* and *Time Of The Last Persecution*, would eventually go on to attract the most ardent of followings. The music these records contain is so saturated with the souls of the artists that both the sounds and the philosophies feel entirely tangible to the listener. But visions are not always the stuff of dreams. There were darker creatures lurking in the shadows, too, and they were ready to bite.

CHAPTER 8

Bitten

IT SEEMS CURIOUSLY FITTING that the 1973 film *The Wicker Man* should have had so similar a fate as many of the acid and psychedelic-folk albums of the period. This tale of paganism, Christianity, human manipulation, and apples on a remote Scottish island was a creative triumph, but was never given a fair shot at box office success. From unsympathetic editing to poor distribution, the treatment of the film was so careless that it bordered on contemptuous.

Folk music was considered integral to *The Wicker Man* from the outset. Anthony Shaffer's script contained spaces for folksong to be used as subtle exposition of the beliefs and practices of the inhabitants of the fictional Summerisle. Shaffer's original plan to use traditional material changed when the American composer Paul Giovanni was recruited to the project.

Giovanni reconfigured older songs in places – notably 'Corn Rigs', based on a poem by Robert Burns – but worked mostly with original pieces, instructing his musicians (a six-piece band working under the name Magnet) to make the music sound as if it had been generated, with amateur zeal, by the islanders themselves. For once, *The Wicker Man* was inadvertently helped rather than hindered by the chaos at Shepperton Studios. According to Giovanni, the music played by Magnet "sounded too good for the band that was supposed to be playing it on screen … The bad recording process worked to our favour".[1]

The deeply uncomfortable *Wicker Man* soundtrack is a striking example of how folk music had in it the capacity to explore experiences that were sinister, desolate, and sometimes even sadistic and murderous. Some of the fates and emotions evoked in this music make even Sergeant Howie's appointment with The Wicker Man seem bearable.

Music such as this can truly be classed as acid folk. Here 'acid' refers not to the drug, or to a general psychedelic ambience, but to music that brings a searing, burning shock to the ear. It is not only the lyrics that are extreme, but also the sounds underpinning them. Much of this music is brutally uncompromising and, while it might have grown up in folk clubs and coffee houses, it is far removed even from those scenes' 'anything goes' atmosphere.

It all seemed to start innocently enough, with the husband and wife duo of Graham and Anne Hemingway, who operated under the upbeat name The Sun Also Rises and had met while he was performing as a solo guitarist in a Cardiff folk club. Graham had an ear-catching technique that channelled both classical training and self-taught flamenco panache, not to mention an attractive brooding personality. "That was always his mystery," Anne recalls. "He's somebody you have to draw out, and I think that's certainly quite attractive."

The Hemingways were married in 1968 and soon began performing together. "The only singing I'd done was in my school choir," Anne recalls, but she thought she'd have a go anyway. They became The Sun Also Rises – also the name of the first major novel by their namesake, Ernest Hemingway – and began to play a mix of traditional material and covers around Cardiff.

As Anne recalls, they were "just doing the standard things you do when you first go into folk clubs". But Graham was not a standard person. He was highly literary and well read; for him, the music was secondary to the words. "He had always really been into thinking a bit more deeply," Anne says. "I think he'd have liked to have been a poet, really." He began to write elegiac original songs about dark subjects that combined his poetic skill with both Hemingways' admiration for The Incredible String Band. "I don't think we ever tried to copy them as such, but they were so influential and so different. It was the rawness, the simplicity, and the experimental nature of it all."

The Hemingways got to know Ian A. Anderson, who liked them a great deal and invited them to record an album for his fledgling Village Thing label. "The thought that it wasn't one of the big players in the business was lovely," Anne recalls. "Everybody was so relaxed, and we just did our thing, and then wandered out into the garden." Anderson produced the album, giving it a simple gleam. But amid the fantastical worlds, the kazoos, and the thick, rhythmic guitar is a graphic dejection rare among the more whimsical trends in psychedelic folk of the time. Particularly desolate are 'Part Of The Room', 'Tales Of Jasmine And Suicide', and 'Death', all of which detail the miseries of everyday existence.

Released in 1970, *The Sun Also Rises* sold 2,000 copies, delighting all concerned and starting an early roll for Village Thing. "We got incredible press," Anderson says of the label's early releases, which also included the folk-comedy LP *Phlop!* by The Pigsty Hill Light Orchestra, *The Legendary Me* by Wizz Jones, and Anderson's own *Royal York Crescent*. "It was like we were doing the right thing in the right place at the right time. It's amazing what not having any money can do to make you come up with creative ways around it."

The Sun Also Rises went off on the university circuit but soon grew irritated with the travelling and the nights away from home. Graham was a reluctant driver; he hated the long journeys through unfamiliar territory, particularly the winter's icy hills and dark country lanes. Anne wanted to keep going, but ultimately the band's end came as a slow withdrawal. The Hemingways continued to perform as The Sun Also Rises until about 1974, albeit sporadically and usually only in Cardiff's folk clubs. They later demoed some more material, but the tapes were lost many years ago.

The Sun Also Rises served as an early partial eclipse of psychedelic folk – a portent that hippie idealism was being affected by the shadows of the encroaching 70s. Its authors may have been rare in their disquiet, but they were not alone. The very early 70s saw the release of three particularly dark albums in Britain. The first came from someone barely out of his teens.

"In truth, most of my friends didn't really care for *Pass The Distance*," Simon Finn recalls. "I think the best that can be said is that the people who did like it, really liked it." Finn had started playing guitar at 12, having been particularly drawn to Roy Orbison and Ray Davies, and started playing the folk clubs in 1967, at 16. "People were, in the main, very kind to me, perhaps because of my age and naïveté," Finn recalls. "There was a man called Diz Disley, who was a fine jazz guitarist. He was very helpful and generous to those less gifted and starting out." Finn was in dire financial straights at the time, but Disley "gave up an hour a week of his time to teach me how to improve my guitar ... he was cynical of pop, but extraordinarily kind. I used to polish off most of his biscuits".

In 1968, Finn went to Spain for a holiday and ended up staying there for months. "There seemed to be a totally unafraid emotional integrity that I'd only heard previously in some old blues records," he says of the Spanish atmosphere. "I was learning not to be afraid of saying and expressing what I felt in any manner I felt like." Finn wrote songs under the Spanish sun, developing a style all of his own that added a wincingly raw, intelligent fury to the emotional candour of Orbison and Davies. He is convinced that these songs would never have been recorded had it not been for the support of Vic Keary, whom he had first met in 1967, and who had, in the spring of 1969, recently set up Chalk Farm Studios. "Vic listened to 'Jerusalem' and a couple of others and smiled," Finn recalls. "He said: 'It's quite a change from your old stuff, Simon. They're kind of weird, but I like them.'"

Pass The Distance was recorded at Chalk Farm Studios and then released on Keary's own Mushroom Records. It's a strange, stark album but also fascinating and multi-layered, its subject matter opening out into apocalyptic vehemence while also narrowing into private headspace. With the skin-peeling 'Jerusalem' as its centrepiece, *Pass The Distance* feels like it's at the precipice of psychosis, but there's a lucid and lyrical focus to it. Its depth of insight is both tortured and torturing, almost intrusive, as reflected in Finn's anguished vocals.

Strangely enough, the album's musical content was not the most controversial element of the whole enterprise. "When Vic asked me what I fancied for the cover I dragged him outside the studio and pointed to a large billboard for children's shoes," Finn recalls. Hornsey Art School student David Toop, who also contributed musically to the album, then came up with an eyeball-searing version of the Start-Rite twins for the front cover and a grotesque, bad-trip adaptation of the same image for the back. The shoe manufacturer objected, and the album was pulled; it hadn't sold well enough to justify the expense of a new cover.

In a strange coda to *Pass The Distance*, the *Daily Mirror* covered the Start-Rite story, which in turn led to a meeting between Finn and Shel Talmy, the producer of records by The Kinks and The Who. "I played him about ten of my songs," Finn recalls. "After the first four, Shel stopped me and asked if I had anything 'more regular'. I played him some older songs. He said: 'We'll work with those.' Which kind of killed my excitement." Nothing came from the Talmy connection, and Finn would not make another record for years.

Like Simon Finn, Derek Noy had been disappointed with the compromises forced upon him when making the Jan Dukes De Grey album *Sorcerers* in 1970. He decided to change tack, bringing in a drummer, Dennis Conlon – "I wanted things a bit heavier," he explains – and turning his lyrical attention away from hippie mysticism toward Mayan and Aztec culture, including evocations of ritual and blood sacrifice. The band also developed a more theatrical presence on stage, exploring menace and death in performances that incorporated clanking bells of doom and torture-chamber sound effects.

This did not always go down well. "We hold the record for emptying Southampton University," Noy says. "We emptied it in five minutes." The group also faced flying bottles and even physical violence, including one incident when a girl bit Noy's ankle while screaming "I hate you!"

"You get the lot," he says. "But you also get the brilliant nights where they love it." The evening after the Southampton debacle, Jan Dukes De Grey played a far bigger outdoor event at the Cardiff Stadium and watched the exits with a nervous twitch. "But they went nuts, they really loved it, and the rest of the tour went really well after that," Noy says. "You've just got to believe you're right, and keep going."

Since the release of *Sorcerers*, Decca's Nova imprint had disintegrated, and Jan Dukes De Grey were not welcome under the company's mainstream umbrella. The band signed a new deal with Transatlantic in early 1971 and quickly started work on a second album with producer Stuart Taylor.

Like *Sorcerers*, *Mice And Rats In The Loft* was recorded quickly, but this time with less constraints on song length and improvisation. Whereas the first album comprised 18 short tracks, this one consists only of three: the epic, rhythmic 'Sun Symphonica'; the shuddering 'Call Of The Wild'; and the darkest track of all, 'Mice And Rats In The Loft'. "They are probably about 40 per cent written," Noy says. "The rest is purely improvised. And it's all live. We played off each other."

'Mice And Rats In The Loft' had gained a bizarre parallel existence when the choreographer Fergus Early approached the band after a performance at the Marquee club in London and told Noy that the track could make for a successful soundtrack to contemporary ballet. Noy ran with the idea: "That's why all the strings are on there," he says. Nat Joseph, the head of Transatlantic, was sceptical; it took some time for Noy to persuade him to fund the string section.

Mice And Rats In The Loft was released to little fanfare by the band's new label. Nat Joseph was famously careful with money, and kept promotion costs and effort to a minimum. With the band's line-up increasingly shaky, Jan Dukes De Grey eventually morphed into the more rock-oriented Noy's Band.

In 1974, Noy's Band released a strange, Beefheart-esque version of 'Love Potion No. 9', a song originally recorded by The Clovers, on Dawn Records.

By then, Dawn was a rare survivor in the specialist-label world, but the cost of that longevity had, ironically, been to dilute its underground intent. The label had taken increasingly to splicing its progressive rock output with shots at the mainstream by the likes of Brotherhood Of Man and The Casuals. And yet the indisputable fact remains: Dawn Records released the most radical acid-folk album of them all, *First Utterance* by Comus.

The origins of Comus may sound familiar, but this was one particular tree that definitely grew away from the sunlight. The young guitarist Roger Wootton lived just outside London and attended Ravensbourne College of Art. He had been a fan of John Renbourn, Bert Jansch, and The Incredible String Band since the mid 60s, but found himself in a group that played frenzied rhythm & blues.

At some point, fellow Ravensbourne student Glenn Goring asked to join the band but was knocked back. "They said I wasn't good enough," he recalls. Wootton changed his mind a few months later when he heard Goring's intense fingerpicking. The two students started jamming, and before long were performing at local folk clubs. "We mainly did Velvet Underground numbers," Goring says. "Roger used to play this six-string guitar which was literally held together with Sellotape. Our performances went down badly."

The duo soon expanded to include Roger Kite on drums and recorders and began to work on original material (since dismissed by Goring as "hippie, airy-fairy stuff"). Kite didn't last very long, but Wootton and Goring would soon be joined by several other musicians who not only played in the band but also came to live with them in their shared house in Beckenham: Colin Pearson, a classically trained violinist and Ravensbourne film student; Andy Hellaby, a bassist headhunted from another local band; Bobbie Watson, who already lived in the communal house, and who Goring happened to hear singing one day; and multi-instrumentalist Rob Young. The band also gained a manager, Chris Youle. "It was organic," Watson says. "When you're younger you have a huge circle of friends, and that's the way things happen."

The chemistry between the six musicians seemed to result in songs of an unusually dark nature. Youle suggested the band take a name to match these sinister sounds: Comus, which he took from a 1634 poem by John Milton about a depraved wood-dweller. The band's loose jam sessions started to gain definition, and songs such as 'In The Lost Queen's Eyes', 'The Prisoner', and the murderous 'Drip Drip' began to emerge. "The love and peace thing, it was very weak," Wootton says of the lyrics, for which he was primarily responsible. "It didn't have any teeth, and you wanted to give it a kick."

By 1969, the small Kent town of Beckenham was developing a reputation as a centre for musical experimentation. A young David Bowie had recently co-founded the Beckenham Arts Lab (also known as Growth) at the Three Tuns pub, while Comus's shared house became a meeting point for other local musicians and scene-setters. Rico, the Jamaican trombonist who would go on to record for Island and Two-Tone, played with Comus on Sundays; sometimes a cache of Rastas from Brixton would come along to share vibes, joints, and jamming sessions. Comus soon became regulars at Growth and supported Bowie at the Purcell Rooms toward the end of 1969. Chris Youle investigated a record deal for the band, landing a promising offer from RCA.

The fledgling band was paired with producer Sandy Roberton, who would go on to work with both Steeleye Span and Shirley Collins, and promptly sent away to work on their material for another six months. "We weren't ready to record, basically," Andy Hellaby says. During that time they honed their live show and appeared in Lindsay Shonteff's countercultural film *Permissive*. When they returned to RCA, however, there was no longer a place for them, but it didn't matter too much. Circumstances were still favourable for progressive and folk musicians, and Comus went to Dawn.

Although they were pleased to have a record deal, Comus soon suspected that they'd been signed simply on the cusp of a fashion wave, and that the new imprint had little real understanding of their sound. "It was terrible," Wootton says of dealing with the label, adding that producer Barry Murray had never seen the band play before they entered the studio together in October 1970. "The first thing he said was: 'Right, put the bass and drums down, put the rhythm tracks down.' We didn't have a drummer. And from then on he was lost."

Lack of interest in or knowledge of a band's sound from an in-house producer may not have been unusual, but it was still a problem, particularly for an act as complex as Comus. Murray often left Comus and the engineer Jeff Calver to their own devices. "We *were* a very difficult band to record in those days, we couldn't track anything and we had to basically play live, in the studio," Colin Pearson says. "We had a certain amount of separation that Jeff Calver could give us – but basically there's massive spill on everything."

All of this led to a sense of deflation about *First Utterance*, which the band felt was at odds with the full and pulsating sound they were able to generate live. "It wasn't as good as it could have been," Wootton says, while Watson adds: "I always thought it was an incredibly thin sound, practically no bass on it at all. It sounded kind of tinny. When we played, it seemed to me to be a big meaty sound, for an acoustic band. So, yes, I was disappointed."

The band's first release was a three-track maxi-single issued at the beginning of February 1971. While there was certainly something undeniably askance about the medieval-flavoured 'In The Lost Queen's Eyes' and the pastoral 'Winter Is A Coloured Bird', it was the adventurous 'Diana' that provided the real introduction to Comus. Written by Colin Pearson, it begins with an unnerving skitter and a memorable opening line – "Lust he follows virtue close / Through the steaming woodlands" – sung in a voice that seemingly manages to achieve a guttural snarl and a screeching falsetto within the space of a single note. This explicit and predatory cornucopia of sexualised violence pushed hard against the boundaries in acoustic music.

First Utterance followed two weeks later. The songs cover themes of rape, butchery, stalking, torture, and mental illness, but there's also an epic beauty to them. The opening 'Diana' is followed by 12 minutes of relative calm in the form of 'The Herald', a rural idyll in which the night is withdrawing. Bobbie Watson's pure, choral vocals and Glenn Goring's sensitive, fingerpicked guitar are soothing, but the relief is only temporary. 'Drip Drip', a story of prolonged slaughter, is underpinned by Rob Young's pounding bongos and Goring's unsettling slide guitar. 'Song To Comus', in which a virgin is taunted and tortured before being raped, was one of the last songs written for the album, but is perhaps its defining moment. It is followed by 'The Bite', about the goading of a Christian who has wandered into the woods, and a shuddering, atonal instrumental, 'Bitten'. The final blow comes with 'The Prisoner', a song narrated by an in-patient at a "hospital for the mentally sick" that ends with a chant of "INSANE! INSANE! INSANE! INSANE!"

First Utterance was housed in a gatefold cover with a memorably intricate band logo designed by Tony Kite. The inner sleeve, a painting by Goring, depicts a verdant landscape of deceptive tranquillity, the natural glory of 'The Herald', but the outward appearance of *First Utterance* is writ large in the form of Roger Wootton's drawing of an emaciated, hideous creature, ready to torment others while also shivering and suffering himself.

Already unhappy with the recorded sound, Comus were further disappointed by the reviews of the album. Critics saw and heard a spiteful, horrific, and explicit album and condemned it as unlistenable, incomprehensible, or merely a schlocky shock-value artefact. For *Record Mirror* there was "too much variation on weak themes"; for *Melody Maker*, it was all "very undistinguished".

While the band's live performances continued to draw in crowds, the critical response to the album killed any chance it had of selling well. Comus had their suspicions as to whether the record was even properly distributed, having received frustrated missives from fans who complained that they couldn't find it. It all had a destabilising effect, causing tension to mount between band and label, and between the band-members themselves. Rob Young, who had provided all the distinctive flutes and bongos on the album, was the first to leave. Comus would never again produce an acid-folk record. The sound of the British folk underground had reached a logical conclusion on *First Utterance*, and the music industry – while initially welcoming to the idea – did not provide the infrastructure to support it.

ᛗ

In America, one of the gloomiest visions of acid-folk came in the form of a lone single by a young girl. Nora Guthrie, the daughter of Woody and sister of Arlo, recorded 'Emily's Illness' for Mercury in 1967. At the time, Guthrie was dating a songwriter, Eric Eisner, but didn't consider herself a singer; she was training to be a dancer instead. Guthrie and Eric Eisner both had a wide, cheerful taste in music. They loved the harmonies of doo-wop, the sincerity of girl groups, and the flair of João and Astrud Gilberto. Eisner had studied classical guitar and played in a rhythm & blues / soul band, The Strangers, as a young teenager; his three brothers were all jazz saxophonists. The one type of music neither Guthrie nor Eisner was particularly interested in was folk. "I had grown up with Leadbelly hanging around the house," Guthrie later recalled, "so when it came to folk music I was kind of like, 'OK.'"[2]

'Emily's Illness' is a first-person account of a dying young girl whose one source of sustenance is the music she composes; Eisner wrote it on a nylon-string guitar, in dusky half-light, in a heightened emotional state. "At some point in childhood development you become aware of the concept of mortality, of the reality of life," he says. "I think that's what was going on with me at the time." Guthrie, then 17, was inspired to sing the song despite her lack of experience and previous indifference to recording.

Shortly thereafter, a friend of the Guthrie family, jazz and pop producer Jack Lewis, became aware of 'Emily's Illness'. A year earlier, he had persuaded a reluctant Nora Guthrie to attend an ultimately unsuccessful audition for Columbia Records. Now, with Eisner's song to sing, she was more willing to enter a studio. With Mercury Records offering a spot on their release schedule, Lewis produced the single and its B-side, 'Home After Dark'.

'Emily's Illness' is *grand guignol* squeezed into a perfectly realised folk-pop single. "It was hardly a performance," Guthrie later said. "I think of it more like a photograph."[3] Nevertheless, with her almost-spoken delivery, Guthrie splashes appropriate Gothic splendour over Eisner's words. "When my blood is let," she states, blankly, "my friend will play it on the clarinet."

Despite being a radio hit in San Francisco, 'Emily's Illness' was ultimately a commercially unsuccessful one-off. Guthrie went to NYU to continue her dance training, while Eisner studied to be a lawyer at Columbia. Their perfect gloomy melodrama cast a slim shadow over the Summer of Love.

The very polar opposite of Guthrie's concise nightmare of a single was the latest release by Tim Buckley, *Lorca*, an exercise in drawn-out anguish. "I can see where I'm really headed," Buckley said in 1969, following the release of *Happy Sad*, "and it will probably get farther and farther from what people expect of me."[4] And so it did.

Dropping his existing band, Buckley recruited John Balkin, a bass player with a strong background in jazz and modern classical music. Even Balkin was unused to the methods Buckley was now pursuing, however. He turned up to the sessions for what was to become *Lorca* having received no preparation from his new boss. Instead, Buckley insisted on improvisation using whatever instruments he could find in the studio; most of the songs were recorded in one take. Buckley's screaming, buzzing, grating, sonorous voice takes centre stage, spreading and whooping across the rhythmic stasis of the tracks. It's the sound of a long soul in torment.

Lorca is also the sound of a frame splintering – the frame of folk. 'I Had A Talk With My Woman' is the most obvious example of what remained of the folk influence, its plodding, bluesy rhythm aching with country-folk sting, but even the least folk-derived tracks retain elements of psychedelic tilt and folk narrative. For all its iconoclasm, *Lorca* is never merely destructive. Instead, it birthed a new type of folk — what would come to be known as free folk – although Buckley's lead would not be taken up with any great gusto for decades.

Elektra released *Lorca* in 1970 without the fanfare that accompanied Buckley's previous albums. The label's president, Jac Holzman, recognised that *Lorca* was "something he wanted to do and something he had to get out, but I just wasn't happy with the record".[5] After *Lorca*, Buckley and Elektra parted company, probably with a mutual sigh of relief. Buckley moved over to Straight, a far smaller label set up by Herb Cohen and Frank Zappa. This in itself was significant. Only a few years earlier, American major labels had

131

offered a playground to experimental folk musicians; now, in 1970, Buckley found himself an early casualty of the slamming of doors on the genre.

Lorca marked the end of an era for Buckley, and not simply because it finished his association with Elektra. A direct experimental line, at a keen upward slant, can be traced through each of the four albums he made for the label. From now on, however, his work would become far more erratic, both in quality and intent. This inconsistency started out with a delicious irony. His first album for Straight was *Blue Afternoon*, recorded after *Lorca* but released before it, and an almost wholesale retreat from *Lorca*'s outer limits. *Blue Afternoon* was the result of Buckley rooting through his archives, and consists of previously unrecorded songs that he had abandoned in the tyre-tracks of his race to extremism. The songs are shorter, the performances snappier, and – with the exception of the closing track, 'The Train' – the vocal acrobatics that dominated *Lorca* are kept in check. Had Buckley delivered *Blue Afternoon* to Elektra instead of lumbering them with *Lorca*, he may have retained his contract with the label. *Blue Afternoon* sold in reasonable numbers for a Straight record; *Lorca* tanked by any standards.

Records such as *First Utterance* and *Lorca* might have been stunning achievements in themselves, but by pushing folk to its very perimeters they served ironically to amplify warning bells that underground folk was now on borrowed time. In its vocals, music, and subject matter, this type of folk was unafraid to pick at lesions on the human psyche. It offered artistic fulfilment, high levels of musical sophistication, and a wide poetic licence. But it also demonstrated that the critics did not like acid-folk records, and that these works now served a shrinking niche market.

Underground folk music still had one further major direction in which to travel, and that would be along a progressive road. In general, however, the trend was now toward artists being dropped, finding themselves unable to get a record contract, self-releasing their records, or perhaps taking a sojourn into mainland Europe, where music such as this still found supportive pockets and diversified into whole new territories.

CHAPTER 9

Oeuvres

IN THE EARLY 70S, mainland Europe, like the USA and the UK, was dappled with light refracted by broken folk mirrors. While individual countries didn't experience quite the same flood of acid and psychedelic folk as had Britain, the diversity of the albums that did appear was staggering. Indigenous folk traditions, local rock and underground scenes, influences from abroad, and, as always, errant genius all combined to produce chaotic, beautiful, and unexpected music. From the electric simulacra of medieval France to a Norwegian talent contest, all flavours of folk were here. There were even a few *émigrés* thrown into the mix.

Given that France was the busking destination of choice for the UK's folk innovators, one might have expected the country to pick up on acid and psychedelic folk music relatively early. Indeed, when folk music migrated to Paris in the early 60s, the clubs were based on the British model, and the repertoires were heavily derived from British and American material. But the fertile French soils held immense power, as was soon recognised by a small group of French and foreign artists based at the Centre Américain. Their passion sparked off a search for the traditions of rural French folk, taking in early instruments and source singers. *Le mouvement folk* was comparable to the earlier British folk revival. It had its own clubs, like Le Bourdon and Le TMS in Paris and La Chanterelle in Lyons, and laid the groundwork for experimentation.

At the forefront of *le mouvement folk* was Alan Stivell, who came from Brittany, spoke the Breton language (which at the time was still widely belittled as a backward patois), and played two instruments distinct to the region: the Breton harp, which he learnt from the age of nine, and the bombarde (a kind of oboe). Stivell's enthusiasm spread to a study of Celtic culture as a whole, but he retained a particularly encyclopaedic knowledge of Brittany's traditions. He began his recording career in the late 50s, but it was in 1971, with *Renaissance Of The Celtic Harp*, that he recorded his *mouvement folk* milestone, recasting the overwhelming beauty of the ancient Breton harp in a challenging new soundscape.

French regional traditions were now proudly reanimated, and Stivell's work was a strong indication of folk's relevance to the present day. He was a magnet for talented musicians, one of whom was Gabriel Yacoub, who had come to French music by way of Bob Dylan and Woody Guthrie. In 1973, following his stint with Stivell, Yacoub recorded *Pierre De Grenoble* with a cache of excellent musicians that included his wife, Marie. This stunning, largely acoustic record captures the feel of vibrant oral tradition and ancient *joie de vivre* but is also couched in the modernity of post-60s musical literacy in which traditional instruments – the psaltery, the hurdy-gurdy, the crumhorn – jostle with Yacoub's buzzing guitar.

After making *Pierre De Grenoble*, the Yacoubs formed Malicorne. The group's self-titled debut, released in 1974, is an imaginatively arranged set of traditional French folk songs with a heavy early-instrument presence. They followed it with another album in 1975, offering more carefully reconstructed medieval atmosphere flecked with subtle electrics. "We had no limits," Yacoub recalled in 2000. "While trying to be respectful to this repertoire, we also tried to make it a bit more lively."[1] Malicorne released two more albums in 1976, both of which continue the *basse danse* in ever more complicated steps, before moving away from the folk style.

While Malicorne found commercial success and were central to the renovation of French folk, several other acts took the experimental edge of Stivell's *Renaissance* much further. Like Gabriel Yacoub, Emmanuelle Parrenin emerged from *le mouvement folk*. She grew up in a classical household – her father a violinist, her mother a harpist – and studied ballet before taking up the harp. Attending Le Bourdon regularly, she met Christian Gour'han, who played hurdy-gurdy on *Pierre De Grenoble*; early music specialist René Zosso; and of course Stivell. Parrenin too played the hurdy-gurdy and, from the time of her 1974 album *La Maumariee*, which she recorded in collaboration with Phil Fromont, she built a reputation for stark and intelligent interpretations of traditional music.

Parrenin soon incorporated a progressive approach on her albums. In 1976, she recorded *Chateau Dans Les Nuages* with Fromont and Claude Lefebvre, bringing in Eastern elements and general strangeness. But her masterpiece was 1977's *Maison Rose*. Translating as 'The Pink House', the title refers to her childhood home and the diet of musical ideas it served her. The album mixes partially improvised instrumentals with diaphanous songs, taking the revived instruments of *le mouvement folk* out into new territory. Parrenin adapted and created instruments, developing the spinet-like tulcivinâ and a wah-wah-enabled hurdy-gurdy, resulting in an embroidered complexity that's similar in its spaciness to that of Linda Perhacs's *Parallelograms*.

Parallel to Parrenin in her cutting-edge approach – but far outside the confines of any genre – was Brigitte Fontaine. Although she had cut her teeth on the mid-60s *chanson* scene, she subsequently embarked on an experimental path to rival that of Tim Buckley. Her decade-long purple patch began in 1968 with the avant-pop *Brigitte Fontaine Est … Folle?* and saw her flit between tender caresses, monotone chanting, and abrasive howls. Musically, she and partner Areski Belkacem drew on the freest of free jazz and generally swung between impulsive art and detailed musical autopsies. The only album that sustains a significant folk influence throughout is 1974's *L'Incendie*, one of her career highs.

If *L'Incendie* is high-church experimental folk, Catharsis offered an exuberant worship around a hastily constructed cross. The group's first album, *Masq*, was recorded in 1971 and gaily incorporated vaudevillian bombast alongside spontaneous free-folk digressions and wordless hippie vocals. Catharsis went on to release a series of bizarro-rock albums with a rotating cast of players, never surrendering their infectious charm.

Similar in approach were Mormos, a group of Paris-based Americans described by Pete Berryman as being "like an American Incredible String Band, but they were more jazzy, and [had] more musical theatre in their roots". Indeed, Mormos had originally been shipped to Paris with New York's La MaMa Experimental Theatre Club. Multi-instrumentalist James Cuomo had been in a psychedelic-rock group, Spoils Of War, but turned his focus toward folkier sounds on the first Mormos album, 1971's *Great Wall Of China*. The album's cacophonous undercurrent is unsurprising, given that Cuomo had studied under John Cage. This agitating edge is even more apparent on the follow-up, the jazz-inflected *Magic Spell Of Mother's Wrath* (1972).

After making these two albums, Mormos made their way to Cornwall, where they met Berryman. "Suddenly, from Paris, they were in a cottage in

Bodmin Moor," he recalls. "The whole house was wired up, and put through a PA system, and so you had this soundtrack everywhere in the house, a bit like The Electric Kool-Aid Acid Test." Berryman joined the group and toured with them in Africa, but they split soon after.

Before joining Mormos, Berryman himself had also led an itinerant life on the continent for a time. In Holland, he and Mick Bennett met flautist Ad Van Der Horst, with whom they formed a trio, Skeleton. They also met another pair of buskers, German violinist Theo Busch and Canadian guitarist Ron Tomasso, and formed the four-piece Noah's Roadshow. The group toured West Germany, recruiting cellist Sandy Spencer (who went on to play in Mormos) and two French musicians on mandolin and bass. "It was this fantastic, and I mean *fantastic*, acoustic big-band," Berryman says, "with string-quartet possibilities. Very short-lasting, but one of the great bands never to see the light of day."

⋈

Had Noah's Roadshow made a record, West Germany might have been receptive toward it. Of all of Europe, it was here where folk grew weirdest. This was hardly surprising: Germany had a febrile native history of experimental music, crowned by the colossal figure of Karlheinz Stockhausen. Furthermore, the country had been pop-literate for a decade, scarfing down everything from Dylan to The Fugs. German rock ingested all these flavours and expelled a new style known to those outside Germany as Krautrock and to those within it as *kosmische musik*. From the outset, *kosmische musik* was characterised by structural breakdown, extreme sonic experimentation, insurrectionary intent, and hardcore freakiness. With this Hydra of possibility, it didn't take long for new heads to sprout, one of which was Krautfolk.

Krautfolk was utterly unique: as far as experimentation went, it could make *Lorca* sound like Burl Ives. At its outermost point – which was certainly where many of these artists congregated – its radicalism stood alone until the emergence of the American free-folk artists of the early 21st century.

It all began in Munich, in 1967. "There was lots of music happening every single day," John Weinzierl, a member of the original Amon Düül commune, later recalled. "It was fun playing, and it was possible to express things through music that you could not express in any other way."[2] For Amon Düül, everyone in the commune was a musician, regardless of actual ability. They would play live at protest events, often handing out instruments to the crowd. Despite the shared ideals of social and artistic experimentation, however, priorities within the large collective soon began to differ. Just as they were about to perform at the 1968 Essener Sonntag Festival, Amon Düül split. Literally. They became Amon Düül and Amon Düül II.

For the leaderless Amon Düül, the priority was ideology; for Amon Düül II, led by Chris Karrer, the priority was music. The coherent musicians gravitated toward II; the nominal players remained with the original group. While Amon Düül II grew into an experimental rock band, careful and conscious of their musical expression, Amon Düül jammed for 48 hours straight before pulling three albums worth of material from this one intoxicated session.

And yet it was Amon Düül who ended up releasing an epic Krautfolk venture. While the three 'jam sessions' albums are only sporadically inspiring, the group's fourth LP, *Paradieswärts Düül*, was different. It was actually *planned* as an album, for one thing, and consists of three acoustic-based pieces. The 17-minute free-folk opener, 'Love Is Peace', retains the ad-libbed freedom of the earlier records but adds an episodic and consistently engaging pulse.

Paradieswärts Düül was recorded in the dying months of 1970. The Amon Düül commune ended soon afterward; the musicians had been forced out of their sizeable Munich house into a two-room apartment, which predictably brought tensions to the surface. The album came out on Ohr Records, an influential label set up that year by Rolf-Ulrich Kaiser, a former journalist with a long-time love of folk. Kaiser's next label project was Pilz, a subsidiary of BASF. Pilz put out a number of records that fell under the Krautfolk banner, by groups such as Flute & Voice, Hölderlin, Wallenstein, and four other acts who would prove themselves to be particularly noteworthy.

The first, Bröselmaschine, formed in 1968 with parallels to Amon Düül. "We all lived together in a commune," the group's founder, Peter Bursch, recalls. "We were a political band. We organised a lot of demonstrations and whatever we thought was necessary. We had to do something. We had a lot of police coming in our house, a lot of troubles, but it was a great time."

Full of youthful exuberance as well as political earnestness, Bröselmaschine soon became a popular live act. "For me, the most important thing in music is that you, as a player, have fun and the audience has fun," Bursch says. Spreading their wings, the group came to the UK in 1968 and met Pentangle and The Incredible String Band. "We came back home to Germany and did our first recording, which has some English backgrounds," Bursch continues. "There's a song called '(I Once Loved) Lassie', an old song we learnt in England. We had a big influence from these bands from England that we liked."

The resulting *Bröselmaschine* (1971) mixes acoustic stringed instruments, muted ragas, traditional folksong, and floating psychedelia, its six tracks produced by Dieter Dierks, who had previously worked with the *kosmische* groups Tangerine Dream and Ash Ra Tempel. "He had the first eight-track recording machine in Germany," Bursch recalls. This first iteration of Bröselmaschine stayed together until 1974, when vocalist Jenni Schucker went to India and the bass player Lutz Ringer left to become a farmer. Bursch recorded the more rock-oriented *Bröselmaschine 2* with a new line-up in 1975.

Another key Pilz signing was the delicate folk duo Emtidi. Bavarian Maik Hirschfeldt and Canadian Dolly Holmes (who guests on *The Hangman's Beautiful Daughter*) were based in Berlin but had first met in London. They recorded their first album, *Emtidi*, in a church in Darmstadt in July 1970; it was released in a run of only a few hundred copies by the tiny Thorofon label.

Seeking more clout in terms both of artistic scope and commercial reach, Emtidi signed a two-album deal with Pilz and set to work on an album with Dierks. The result was *Saat*, a furiously dense *meisterwerk* that compresses the acoustic simplicity of *Emtidi* into concentrated spoonfuls and extends into acid guitars, polyphonic organ, and sailing trance. While its predecessor was rooted in the 60s, the heavy groove of *Saat* is very definitely a child of the new decade. Emtidi were denied a second Pilz album by the label's demise in 1973. Holmes quit the group shortly afterward, and while Hirschfeldt carried on as Emtidi with different musicians, he left behind the Krautfolk sound of *Saat*.

Like Emtidi, Witthüser & Westrupp (whose first names were Bernd and Walter) had already begun their recording career before signing to Pilz. They made their dark folk debut, *Lieder Von Vampiren, Nonnen Und Toten*, for Ohr Records in 1970; despite profound contributions from Westrupp, however, it was credited only to Witthüser. The follow-up, *Trips Und Träume*, marked out Witthüser & Westrupp as the perfect psychedelic Krautfolk act. As anarchic as *The Moray Eels Eat The Holy Modal Rounders*, it contains humour and frenzy in equal measure alongside persistent rhythm and deranged strings. The album really has no forebears in German rock or folk, and its cover – a screaming, bespectacled head on a blazing orange background – is warning enough for the unadventurous to stay away.

By the time Witthüser & Westrupp signed to Pilz they had calmed their sound if not their imaginations. In 1972 they made *Der Jesuspilz*, a concept album about Christianity as a hallucinogenic experience that sounds as trippy as the premise suggests. The wheels began to fall off with their next album, *Bauer Path*, which – like many British records of the time – remained in the folk idiom but was heavier, rockier, and generally less distinctive. One retrospective live album aside, it would prove to be Witthüser & Westrupp's final record together.

The last ever Pilz album was also the label's most beautiful release. Founded by the intellectual heavyweight Florian Fricke, Popol Vuh had already made one album, *Affenstunde* (1971), by the time they signed to Pilz. The follow-up, *In Den Garten Pharaos* (1972), was broodier and more psychedelic. *Hosianna Mantra* (1973) was different again.

"I started to get into the theoretical physics of vibration," Fricke said at the time, "and it was there that I encountered religion."[3] He considered himself both Christian and Hindu – the album's title deliberately merged both – and aimed to create a devotional music that transcended earthly schism. Every moment of the six months Fricke spent on the album proved worthwhile. *Hosianna Mantra* soars toward a spirit of pure holiness, unmatched in its compassion, peerless in its liturgical effect, particularly on those tracks that feature vocals by Djong Yun.

Popol Vuh would go on to make numerous acclaimed albums over the years but *Hosianna Mantra* was the last one they – or indeed anyone – would make for Pilz. Having shut down the label, an increasingly drug-addled and alienated Rolf-Ulrich Kaiser entered an unhappy period that culminated in his subsequent withdrawal from the world in 1975.

Pilz was the primary home for German acid folk in the early 70s, but there were also a few rebels around. One of them was Franz De Byl, who hailed from Bottrop in the Ruhr valley and formed his first band, The Goons, at the age of 15. He received his first offer of a recording contract a year later, but his mother vetoed it until he had finished school and passed his exams. As soon as he had done so, he says, he "immediately escaped to Western Berlin. I submerged and disappeared. My parents and the police searched for me". De Byl felt at home in the city. "I met lots of crazy, crazy people, took several LSD pills and smoked some joints and played in all those clubs. Nearly each and every pub presented a chance for musicians to play there."

It was in one of these clubs that he met Heiner Hohenhaus, a violinist and protégé of the Berlin College of Arts. The pair began a popular partnership and soon received an offer to make an LP for Metronome. "We recorded in the famous Audio-Tonstudio and Heiner made a two-by-two-metre artwork for the LP," De Byl says. The experience quickly turned sour, however.

According to De Byl, *Franz De Byl And Heiner Hohnhaus* (1971) was released with unauthorised artwork and incorrect credits – even down to the misspelling of Hohenhaus's name. The artists protested but had few funds to fight the release. After the first run of 2,000 copies was pressed, the master tapes and artwork were destroyed; the album was then declared illegal, according to De Byl, who prefers to draw a veil across this period.

"After this very, very bad experience I met Heike Gottlieb," De Byl recalls. "We toured around; I was playing solo and later on Heike accompanied me as a dancer." Soon after that, Helmut König of Thorofon approached De Byl about making a solo record. "Helmut König was a high-school teacher," De Byl says. "He had a very good tape machine and a few Neumann mics. We made the record during summer vacation in his school, and Helmut gave me all possibilities to decide what is on the record and how it will look."

The resulting *Und*, a collection of rhythmic and compelling blues-folk infused equally with surrealist theatre and street-level grit, was released in 1972. By then, however, Krautfolk was already beginning to withdraw from its brief period of admittedly limited mainstream exposure. *Kosmische musik* itself had a few more years left before it too started to peter out, becoming increasingly self-indulgent and allying itself to conventional rock.

France and Germany may have been Europe's primary outposts for acid folk, but they weren't the only countries to offer up their own take on the music. Italy's folk music, like that of France, differs substantially from region to region. Alan Lomax had spent time there in the mid 50s, attempting to classify its hearty traditions, but the folk revival didn't really get going until the emergence a decade later of new performance spaces, record labels, and artists. Italy even gained its own centre dedicated to oral history and traditional music, the Istituto Ernesto de Martino in Milan, while the street singer Matteo Salvatore achieved widespread popular success.

In the early 70s, Italy became justly renowned for its cinematic, booming take on prog, or *rock progressivio Italio*, but movement in the opposite direction – toward a quieter, folk-influenced style – was far less common. One notable exception was Claudio Rocchi, the former bassist in prog-psychedelia group Stormy Six, who calmed the rock impulse on his 1970 debut, *Viaggio*. The album airs his interest in Eastern philosophies, his acoustic flair, and his experimental urges; it opens with arrhythmic percussion and a prolonged bout of panting. Rocchi was a considerable innovator. After making *Viaggio* he cut a series of challenging albums that, by the time of *Suoni Di Frontiera* (1975), took in abstraction, field recordings, and analogue synthesizers. His work stands proud as a foil to the greatest and strangest of all *kosmische musik*.

The greatest acid-folk album to emerge from Italy, however, was the work of a British teenager, Mark Fry. "It was 1970 when I got to Florence," he recalls. "I was very much doing my own thing at that time, and I was never a part of any English psychedelic scene." Fry found himself in the nucleus of a tumultuous time in the country. Wildcat strikes were immobilising industry, services, and education, while street-level discontent had taken aim at a government system riddled with vested interests. The early 70s also represented an amazingly hot phase for the Italian arts – something that Fry witnessed firsthand.

"It was a little like being in a film by Visconti," he says of the rich visual imagery that surrounded him at the Palazzo Caponi, where he lived at the time. "It was this great rambling, faded glory of a place. The family who lived there held court to these amazing artists like Dario Fo and Carmelo Bene."

Fry had arrived in Italy to study art at the Accademia Delle Belle Arti and was unusual in his cultural interests and influences. He had made his first guitar during carpentry lessons at boarding school in Dartington, Devon, and soon picked up the Alan Lomax songbook. By the time he reached Florence he had a small cache of original songs. He continued to write songs in Italy until one day his friend, Laura Papi, set up a meeting with the RCA subsidiary IT Dischi.

"I got an interview at RCA and played this man lots of songs while I was sitting on the edge of a chair," he recalls. "He surprisingly offered me a contract – a ten-year contract! It really did feel like I was signing away my life." Fry nevertheless accepted and began to re-imagine his songs as an album, *Dreaming With Alice*. He laid down some demos in Rome but says he "wasn't used to being in a studio" and found that the engineer was "not very sympathetic". Then, by chance, he met some Scottish musicians who had "a little basement studio on the outskirts of Rome". Fry ended up recording the album on their four-track Revox machine. The poky surroundings can be sensed at times – sometimes as cramped creepiness, sometimes as nose-touching intimacy. The vocals, sitar, and flute seem to bounce off each other and the sweaty studio walls.

The influences on *Dreaming With Alice* were legion: Jonathan Miller's 1966 BBC television adaptation of *Alice In Wonderland*; Eastern spirituality by way of Alan Watts and *The Tibetan Book Of The Dead*; the renegade psychoanalyst R.D. Laing; C.S. Lewis's *The Lion, The Witch And The Wardrobe*; Pre-Raphaelite painting; and the equally otherworldly experience of LSD. "It was getting in a rocket and going to another planet," he says. "We didn't just *drop acid*. It was all taken very seriously at the time."

One thing that made *Alice* even more distinctive was the splitting up of the title track into episodes throughout the album – a decision that was taken after the song was recorded. "I remember when it came through, the edits were pretty rough, but it worked," Fry says. "It was a brilliant, brilliant idea."

Once the basement sessions were in the can, Fry went on tour with the Italian singer-songwriter Lucio Dalla. The popular ferment Fry had experienced in Florence and Rome was nothing compared to that of Italy's hinterlands. "The further south you went, the more communist it became," he recalls. "The concerts were quite something. Highly charged, politically, and everyone throwing their fists in the air. They were big outdoor concerts, in piazzas, with people up in trees and hanging out of balconies."

After the tour, but before the album had even come out, Mark Fry returned to England. *Dreaming With Alice* arrived in the mail about six months later, by which time he had almost given up on it. "I remember thinking it was incredibly rough," he says. "I had thought that they might pull the plug on it. I listened to it, and I put it away. I was moving on and I didn't really listen to it again until ages and ages later. I almost forgot I'd made it." For now, Fry's extraordinary experience was at an end, with only a handful of Italians having heard *Dreaming With Alice*'s knotty, naïve radiance.

The American musician Tucker Zimmerman arrived in Italy in the late 60s for very different reasons. "I got drafted by the army and I escaped to Italy," he recalls. He studied composition in Rome and started performing live "to see what I would do and what my songs would do to an audience." In 1968, he left Italy for England and recorded *Ten Songs By Tucker Zimmerman* with Tyrannosaurus Rex producer Tony Visconti. His time in the UK was generally unhappy, however: he was refused a work permit, and found himself stuck in a three-year contract with EMI's Regal Zonophone imprint, which had barely released *Ten Songs* and had no interest in doing anything further with him.

In 1970 a frustrated Zimmerman returned to the continent. "It was in Belgium and Germany that I was welcomed," he says. "I liked not being understood, language-wise. These faithful audiences who came back to hear me, gig after gig, gave me a great gift – a new perspective about communication. I was encouraged to improve my craft and define what I wanted to say." Zimmerman recorded his new songs in his two-room apartment on the top floor of an old brick building in Liege's *quartier folklorique* with equipment and instruments that were either borrowed or broken. "I hated the tapes when I was finished," he says. "I wanted to throw them away." Fortunately, he didn't. The underrated, dislocated *Tucker Zimmerman* was issued in Germany by Autogram and licensed by Ian A. Anderson's Village Thing in the UK.

Meanwhile in Barcelona, Spain, a group called Musica Dispersa took as its primary influence the sound of *música laietana*, a mix of jazz, folk, psychedelia, and world music. The four-piece group was formed in 1969 by José Manuel Bravo, Jaume Sisa, Albert Batiste, and a young hippie known only as Selene. Their sole album is a work of tranquil poetry, circular strings, and ethereal vocals. *Musica Dispersa* was released on the Diabolo label in 1970; the band barely lasted long enough to see the vinyl pressed. Jaume Sisa went on to develop a cult following in Catalonian progressive music, beginning with 1971's *Orgia,* which sounds like a Dylan record emerging from a malfunctioning blender.

In the really obscure depths of acid folk can be found album curios that emerged from personal, mystical journeys, almost by accident, and bear little relation to whatever else existed around them. Such is the case with the music made by two young students, Juan Arkotxa and Leslie Mackenzie, who met in the less than otherworldly atmosphere of Edinburgh University's ski racing team in the early 70s.

The pair grew fascinated by non-Western religions and non-canonical Christianity. They were swept away, as Arkotxa puts it, "by the new wave of new ideas, and mind expanding drugs, as they were called then", and began to develop the concept of 'AM' – the root sound of the human chakras. Their physical journey, meanwhile, began in India in 1972 and in January 1974 took them to the Buddhist festival of Bodh Gaya. "Everyone was there, all our truest inspirers," Arkotxa says. "We had never seen such wild, spiritual people in our lives."

In 1975, Arkotxa and Mackenzie arrived in Ibiza, Spain, where they worked on a sumptuously engraved and illustrated book project, *The Garland Of Visions Of The Absolute.* It sold well, so they planned another: *The Book Of AM,* an exploration of world cultures and cosmology, which would also have a musical twin. "When we started playing together, we were amazed at our rapid progress," Arkotxa says of their improvisations with guitar and flute. "It was the energy and desire to communicate which helped us to advance."

The couple then moved on to Deià, where they met Daevid Allen and Gilli Smyth, former members of Soft Machine and Gong who now ran a recording studio called Banana Moon. They recorded what would become *The Book Of AM* there during a single 48-hour session with the help of Allen, Smyth, Pat Meadows, Stephanie Shepard, and Jerry Hart. Some of the songs were fully formed beforehand, otherwise were improvised. "For us, our music was a vehicle through which we could approach a timeless state and hence reach a state of meditation, contemplation, and, dare I say it, enlightenment," Arkotxa says. Not all of the other musicians shared their perspective, however, and sought to place the songs in the 'real world' context of contemporary styles such as reggae.

The record's appealingly 'undone' finish came as a result, in part, of the presence of Arkotxa and Mackenzie's disinterested young children. "We had to work fast with hardly any retakes," Arkotxa recalls. "It was almost impossible to tell what we had recorded, as far as levels and distortions were concerned, and there was no chance of listening to even a rough mix."

After completing the album, the couple decided to name their 'group' Can AM Des Puig, which translates as 'House Of AM On The Hill' in Catalan. They found the administration required to bring out the album wearing; despite initially planning a four volume series of records, none of the other albums were released. The accompanying book project was also shelved. Arkotxa and Mackenzie returned to Ibiza, leaving *The Book Of AM* to find its own audience in the Catalan hills.

М

Over in Holland, the psychedelic folk torch blazed in the form of Elly & Rikkert, a married couple who made a series of fanciful fairytale albums with an acid glow. They recorded *De Draad Van Ariadne* shortly after moving to the countryside in 1970. *Parsifal* (1971) has an even sunnier vibe, reflecting their joy at the birth of their first child, while *Der Oinkbeest* (1972) offers a microcosm of the couple's world of forests, faeries, and daydreams. *Maarten En Het Witte Paard* (1973) is their last truly psychedelic folk album; after that, they leave acid folk behind to focus on simpler, cleaner songs for children.

Turkey, too, had a thriving music scene in the 70s. Heavy drums, cheap fuzz, sprawling vocals, and an East-West folk fusion characterised the best work of Arif Sag, Edip Akbayram, Ersen, Mazhat & Fuat, and especially Selda Bagcan, whose politically charged psychedelic folk landed her unwelcome attention from the Turkish authorities. Bülent Ortaçgil's 1974 debut, *Benimle*

Oynar Misin, was influenced by Dylan, The Beatles, and Cat Stevens; most stunning of all, however, was the way he channelled the spirit of Donovan at his *Flower To A Garden* peak. *Benimle Oynar Misin* features a simple, fingerpicked guitar style, a voice choked with feeling, and a cast of well-regarded Turkish musicians including Onno Tunç and Atilla Özdemiroglu. Ortaçgil found a wide audience in Turkey but decided to give it all up shortly afterward. He married and became a chemical engineer before returning to music in the late 80s.

In Sweden, Radiomöbel erred on the side of folk on their darkly progressive debut *Trämsebox,* recorded in a basement and released on their own label in 1975. The band's second album, *Gudang Garam, Radiomöbel* (1978), was voiced by the spacey, shamanic Carin Bohlin, who helped the group toward a style deliciously and accurately termed *träskosymf,* which translates as 'wooden shoe symphonic'.

Finally, and in one of the least likely meetings of acid folk and pop culture, Norway produced the stunning Oriental Sunshine. The group was formed by Rune Walle and Nina Johansen, who found themselves catapulted to overnight fame after being encouraged by friends to appear on the popular television show *Talent 69.* To their surprise, they won. A brief period of national scrutiny followed, as did a deal with Philips. It was all whirlwind, heat, and flash. Neither Johansen nor Walle had given much thought to recording prior to – or even during – *Talent 69,* so they recruited a mutual friend, Satnam Singh, who was skilled in flute and tabla and had a profound knowledge of Indian classical music. After brief rehearsals, sessions for the group's only album, *Dedicated To The Bird We Love,* took place over a long weekend in early 1970.

"It seemed natural to sing in English, because no one was singing our sort of music in Norwegian and we were listening to a lot of other records in English," Johansen later recalled. "We were more or less left on our own, and I was able to direct the musicians without interference. It was pretty amazing."[4]

The songs on *Dedicated* range from the poppy 'Mother Nature', which Johansen and Walle had first performed on *Talent 69,* to the Brazilian-flavoured 'Let It Be My Birth'. The album as a whole is a tranquil psychedelic expedition with very heavy sitar. It got good reviews but little promotion. Talk of a UK release on Vertigo came to nothing, while any further progress was halted by the death of Johansen's father. "I just fell to pieces, and was unable to continue singing," she said. "Each time I opened my mouth I just started crying, so we had to give up."[5]

CHAPTER 10
The Furthest Point

THE SUN SHONE on those groups that landed a deal in the post-*5000 Spirits* scramble. The instruments, the fusions, the all-night clubs, the confidence, the buoyancy: fresh albums were grown in clement weather. The next broad trend was to supersede naïveté with knowledge. The genre became engorged with luscious sounds, unusual time signatures, classical-inspired suites, and elaborate imagery; concept albums increased in number; different artistic branches entwined in what could broadly be termed 'progressive folk'.

The first hints of this new direction began to appear as early as 1968; once again, Donovan proved to be a reliable weather vane. His US-only album, *The Hurdy-Gurdy Man*, was something of a jumble, yet between its psychedelic pop flummery, biting underground rock, and raga-influenced folk could be found the highly unusual jazz-folk evolution of 'Get Thy Bearings'. (The song's progressive credentials were confirmed when King Crimson included a vastly extended version of the song in their live set.)

Among the earliest groups to make the shift from rawness toward sophistication was Trees. They had been signed in the initial flurry of record company interest in experimental folk and would go on to precipitate folk's new direction with their layered, sophisticated second album.

Guitarist David Costa grew up in North London and learnt to play fingerstyle by slowing down a Martin Carthy record. After studying fine art at the University of East Anglia and playing on a privately pressed album by his friend Jeremy Harmer, *Idiosyncratics And Swallows' Wings* (1967), he had a fortuitous encounter with another guitarist, Barry Clarke. "We met on the steps of St Paul's, and that was that," Costa recalls. Within weeks they had formed a band with Clarke's housemate, Tobias 'Bias' Boshell, on bass, Unwin Brown on drums, and Celia Humphris on vocals.

"My sister, who worked at Philips records, took me along to the audition," Humphris (now Drummond) recalls. "They gave me all these folk songs to sing, and I hadn't a clue as to what any of them were. The only one I knew was 'Summertime', so I sang that and left." She found the experience enjoyable enough, however, that she quit college the next day to join the group.

Things continued to move at a pace. "We made quite a sweet sound together, and we all got on like a house on fire," Costa recalls. "And within a month we had a recording contract." Even before they had started playing live, Trees received offers from Dandelion and Liberty Records. They eventually decided to sign with one of the recording industry's big guns: CBS.

Thus far, CBS's only real connection to the psychedelic folk revolution had been through Marc Brierley, whose two albums, *Welcome To The Citadel* and *Hello* (both 1969), fell somewhere between Roy Harper and Donovan. Brierley had not caught the public's imagination, but Trees seemed like they might be a more commercially successful prospect. CBS offered Trees a contract that was weighted heavily toward the label in terms of money and ownership, but the young group cared little and signed anyway.

Immediately afterward, Trees demoed the majority of what would become their debut album. As Humphris recalls: "We put down everything we had at the time, to see what it would sound like." The band's repertoire mixed up acoustic and electric folk and included glacial originals by Boshell alongside traditional material. Costa was developing a historian's nose for folksong through research trips to Cecil Sharp House. "Tentacles would just spread out," he says. He was also inspired by other contemporary covers of traditional material, such as Buffy Sainte-Marie's version of 'Lady Margaret' and The Jim Sullivan Sound's sitar-heavy interpretation of 'She Moves Through The Fair'.

The Garden Of Jane Delawney was recorded in a blink, with little reliance on studio technology. "It sounded very naïve," Costa admits. "We were very poorly and sketchily recorded. But it was done and we moved on." (For Humphris, the result was "absolutely wonderful. It seemed terribly naïve, but it seemed to work".) Next came the challenge of playing the songs live. The band had trouble matching the volume between their acoustic and electric guitars, with feedback a constant problem, and took time simply to get to know one another on stage. "We would start a song, and we would get Celia over and done with, and then we would just *go*," Costa recalls. "There would always be a point at which Barry would step forward and all four of us would go: 'Oh Christ, where are we going now?'"

By October 1970, Trees were back in the studio. "We had grown up in that six months," Costa says. "Life had become significantly harder. We were piling into our blue transit every night, we were crashing on people's floors, we were living on oats. But we were actually beginning to listen to ourselves, and listen to what our strengths were." Humphris agrees that they had all become more aware of themselves. "By the second one, we'd smoothed off a lot of edges and added in a lot more different sounds," she says, citing the influence of Curved Air and Renaissance. "It did influence us a bit away from the solid folk into slightly more dreamy things. And Bias, who wrote most of the songs, became fascinated by the rhythms of ragas." Boshell also switched to keyboards, removing one of the problems Trees had faced on their first album: having three guitarists.

"Everything started to be a little bit more necessarily and productively constrained," Costa recalls. Some of the songs on the group's second album, *On The Shore*, date back to the *Jane Delawney* period, if not earlier; now they just felt right, even though several hadn't been tested out live before the recording. This is true even of the album's centrepiece, a version of the seminal British folk-rock tune 'Sally Free And Easy'. Accounts differ as to whether the group had even played the song in its entirety before recording it; Costa says that they had "started to rehearse" it before recording it in one take.

This ten-minute epic became the signature sound of *On The Shore*. It is moist and mottled, speckled with sunshine filtered through London's drizzle, taking folk-rock on a trip fuelled by power and invention and steered with poise and grace toward somewhere wholly new. "There is a particular sound to it, and that sound goes through all these different emotive iterations [of] tempo [and] mood," Costa says. For Humphris, the album was "a lot more sophisticated than the first one. It was a move in a different direction".

On The Shore might sound different to what came before, but some things hadn't changed. The sessions were marked by what Costa calls "the same kind of clock-watching and cheapskate approach", while the band again faced technical problems: they found it difficult to combine electric and acoustic instruments to their satisfaction and had a significant problem with leakage. But there was little will from the label to devote time and money to finding ways around these hitches, so Trees had to live with it.

On The Shore was released in February 1971 – complete with artwork by

Storm Thorgerson showing a spectral child in Victorian dress flinging an ellipsis of water over Hampstead Heath – to good reviews but sluggish sales. CBS decided it was time to give Trees a push. The label assigned the band a heavyweight American manager, gave them access to new equipment, and put them on tour with The Byrds. When the support slot was cancelled, however, the disenchantment grew; sales remained low and money was a constant struggle.

"It had an effect on us of rather stopping us being able to produce anything else," Humphris says. "I'm fairly sure that, had [the album] been more successful, had we been more successful on the road, it would have made a heck of a difference." For Costa, Trees were at a crossroads: they could either put in a huge energy to continue or else bow out gracefully. It wasn't just the "inordinate amount of effort" required to make *On The Shore* work in a live setting. Costa had recently married, and felt a pressing need for a steady income. In the end he decided to leave, as did Unwin and Bias. Humphris recalls feeling "quite bereft". She and Barry Clarke carried on for a while, but in the truth knew that "the guts left when David and Bias and Unwin left". For all intents and purposes, Trees ended in 1972, just as psychedelic folk itself was winding up.

Like Trees, Bread Love And Dreams began their recording career in the late 60s and matured in a very short space of time. The group formed when the duo of Angie Rew and Carolyn Davis met solo performer David McNiven in an Edinburgh folk club. "We decided to record some demos together," McNiven recalls. "We thought it sound[ed] quite good, and we kept going."

Rew describes the early days of the band as "very intense. We just rehearsed all the time, and played all the time. Every pub, club, community centre – wherever there was a gig, we played it". This included a fortnight-long trip to Cologne where they played a staggering *eight* shows per night in two clubs and in heavy snow. "In the first club, there was a Turkish bouncer, and he decided he was going to adopt us," Rew adds. "Carolyn and I would be carrying guitars and a speaker each, and he would pick one of us up under one arm, and the other one up under another arm, and jog down the road to the next club with us. Poor David had to struggle along in the snow behind!"

The group soon met Decca producer Ray Horricks, who heard their demo tape on one of his annual trips to Scotland and signed them up straightaway. "The first album we did in Edinburgh," McNiven recalls, "but then he took it down [to London] and added all these strange things onto it, like orchestras, and tried to link up the tracks and make it into a concept album, which it wasn't at all." "He only managed to link up the first three songs," Rew adds. "And then he ran out of ideas."

Bread Love And Dreams consists mainly of songs from the days when McNiven played solo and Rew and Davis were performing as a duo. "We hadn't thought it through properly with how we *really* wanted to present it," Rew says. "We were just overwhelmed at getting a record contract." Davis soon left the group to pursue a solo career; Decca tried to extricate itself, too, but Horricks persuaded the label to give the group another chance.

For Bread Love And Dreams mk II, Rew and McNiven retained their habit of writing alone but channelled their efforts more toward each other. Their new songs were more intimate, with a stronger sense of landscape and character-driven lyrics. They recorded this new batch of material over a week in Hampstead during the summer of 1970, with help from Danny Thompson and Terry Cox of Pentangle and a moonlighting singer-songwriter, Alan Trajan. They wanted to release the results of these sessions as a double album, but Decca soon put a damper on that idea. Instead, two separate releases were assembled.

The first of the two albums, *The Strange Tale Of Captain Shannon And The Hunchback From Gigha*, was released in November 1970. "The title track was based on a real person I met when I was about 18 months old," McNiven recalls. The real Captain Shannon used to regale McNiven with tales of sea monsters; the Hunchback of Gigha was a character created and performed by McNiven's uncle. "I think they're very pictorial," Rew says of the songs featured on the album. "I think there's a tremendous amount of imagery in the lyrics. You can see the places, see the people very clearly."

The second album plucked from the Hampstead sessions was a real treasure. "We really felt that was the direction that we were wanting to head in," Rew says. "In many ways it is quite mystical. The words and the lyrics are very visual and quite emotive." The first half of *Amaryllis* consists of the three-part, stream-of-consciousness title track; the second is made up of self-contained songs. "They were about things that happened to us," McNiven says. "They lean toward the first side, but they are individuals." Of the shorter songs, Rew's 'Brother John' is a mesmerising piece with its roots, like the previous album's 'Butterflyland', in Mexico. "There was a very, very old grave near a tumbledown chapel," she says. "It was completely in ruins and overgrown. And the name of the person, who had been a priest or was *Padre* something, I can't remember what his actual name was, but I called him John."

Amaryllis is a complete and satisfying work; Rew and McNiven were very pleased with it. The album was ostensibly released in July 1971, but Decca barely nudged it into the shops. "They decided that we were going to be a tax loss," McNiven recalls. Rew concurs. "They sent a huge consignment of our albums out to Sri Lanka, or Ceylon as it was then, despite the fact that very few people there had record players," she recalls. "The records were eventually returned unsold and we had to pay the freighting costs, a sum of money that mysteriously totalled £19,999 19s 11p – set against our first and only royalty statement of £20,000."

Rew and McNiven were left angered and disappointed by the way Decca had treated them. By the time their contract with the label expired, however, they had found a new outlet that better suited their unusual music: the Traverse Theatre Workshop Company, which was based in Edinburgh and led by Max Stafford-Clark. Initially, Bread Love And Dreams served as the resident band for Traverse, but they soon started to write and act for the company as well. One such piece was *Mother Earth*. "We used 'Amaryllis' as the basis for that workshop, an actual theatre piece around it, and that toured quite extensively all over the place," Rew recalls. "It was a really good time."

Rew and McNiven's association with Traverse highlighted an important tendency in progressive folk. "You would just meet and interlink and join up with other art forms that normally would have been quite separate," Rew says. "Suddenly, in that whole period of time, we all started to interlock."

The most high profile example of this came with The Incredible String Band's *U*. Robin Williamson in particular was fascinated by the possibilities of theatre; audience participation had long been a part of the Incredible String Band live experience anyway. "We had a huge amount of wooden pennywhistles with all the holes taped up but one," Mike Heron recalls, "and we got 20 people just taken from the audience up on the stage to play them. Robin conducted like it was a keyboard."

Robin Williamson described *U* at the time as "a surreal parable in song and dance". It was created in partnership with the dance and mime troupe Stone Monkey and performed in April 1970 at London's Roundhouse and New York's Fillmore East. It was, as Williamson wrote in the liner notes for the 2003 reissue of the soundtrack, "rapturously received by the crowds but absolutely panned by the critics". It was also financially disastrous, but the accompanying album was the String Band's best since *Wee Tam And The Big Huge*. *U* is spread over four sides and runs to nearly two hours, but took only

48 hours to record. It contains recognisable elements of the group's past alongside new and highly progressive elements, particularly in Heron's 'Rainbow' suite. Despite this, it failed to revive the String Band's fortunes, and they continued to bob ever further away from their 1968 godhead status.

Folk-rock, too, was evolving. The group that took it furthest – and earliest – was the five-piece 'supergroup' Steeleye Span. As Ashley Hutchings recalls, the idea for the group first emerged in the summer of 1969, a couple of months before he made *Liege & Lief* with Fairport Convention, when he met two couples at a music festival: Bob and Carole Pegg, and Tim Hart and Maddy Prior.

Hutchings, Hart, and Prior formed the first line-up of Steeleye Span with another couple, Gay and Terry Woods, releasing an album of careful, electrified folk, *Hark! The Village Wait*, in June 1970. "We were a lot more traditional," Hutchings says when comparing Steeleye to Fairport. "We didn't have a drummer. We thought there was a lot of difference between the two groups." Gay and Terry Woods soon left, replaced by Martin Carthy on electric guitar and Peter Knight on fiddle for *Please To See The King* (1971), an isolating, spartan, and sorrowful trailblazer for progressive folk-rock.

Meanwhile, Bob and Carole Pegg formed a six-piece group, Mr Fox, and would soon be marked out by *Melody Maker*'s Karl Dallas for their promising blend of classical arrangements and electric folk. The Peggs were very careful with their use of tradition. They had been directly involved in song collection in Yorkshire and now paid homage to the village bands of the Yorkshire Dales with their new group's combination of fiddle, melodeon, harmonium, clarinet, and cello, which closely paralleled those traditional outfits.

There were differences, too, of course. Mr Fox had bass and drums, and largely performed original songs. On *Mr Fox* (1970), they sing of the soil, peeling back any notion of rural idyll to expose simmering violence in 'The Hanged Man' and 'The Gay Goshawk'. *The Gypsy* (1971) is far more elaborate in ambition but less tethered to earthy sympathy. There's evidence of significant progression on the 13-minute title track and the fuzz-drenched 'Mendle'. Mr Fox foundered shortly after the album's release, however. The group's poor performance at the Loughborough Folk Festival was heavily slated and sparked a personnel merry-go-round that ended definitively when Carole Pegg left the group in 1972.

Of the various groups operating under the broad umbrella of folk-rock, one of the more interesting was Dando Shaft. The five-piece group first appeared on the Coventry circuit in 1968 and brought unusual influences, such as that of Bulgarian music, into a sound that also contained echoes of American country-rock. Their debut, *An Evening With Dando Shaft* (1970), is a solid and intricate folk-rock record. It was produced by former would-be pop star Miki Dallon, who released it on his Youngblood label.

Shortly thereafter, Dando Shaft moved to London, where they shared a large house in Ealing and brought in zoology student Polly Bolton on vocals. Bolton's untrained voice worked well with the increasingly progressive strangeness in the band's sound. They signed a deal with the newly (and somewhat belatedly) launched RCA Neon imprint in time for *Dando Shaft*, a melange of haunting vocals and swirling psychedelia. Bolton left the group shortly after making *Lantaloon* (1972), by which time Neon had gone the way of Decca's similar Nova imprint. Then, after a few more line-up changes and a final tour, Dando Shaft split up.

RCA Neon also snapped up another folk-rock group from the Midlands (Nuneaton, this time): Fresh Maggots, a duo formed by two 19-year-olds, Mick Burgoyne and Leigh Dolphin, in 1970. "We never thought we'd get anywhere," Burgoyne later recalled. "Then we were spotted and signed up and things started to happen very quickly."[1]

Fresh Maggots recorded a demo with producer Mike Berry, who shopped it around. The RCA representatives who had watched them perform in Coventry were impressed by the teenagers' Blitz spirit during a power cut; it was this, as well as their strangely tough folk songs, that persuaded the label that the duo would fit in with the Neon ethos.

Recorded at Radio Luxembourg's studios at the end of 1970, *Fresh Maggots* is more prone to pure rock thrills than many other albums of the genre, but nevertheless remains folk-centred; the heartfelt 'Rosemary Hill' and politicised 'Dole Song' are evidence enough of that. The album was subject to much delay, eventually limping out in October 1971. RCA procrastinated over various details, so much so that Neon no longer existed by the time of the album's release. Producer Mike Berry also lost interest. "After the initial excitement, things moved pretty slowly," Burgoyne recalled. "There were delays with string arrangements and even the cover."[2] The album received good reviews but by then the momentum had been lost. Fresh Maggots split up two short months later.

"It was an incredible era," says Ian A. Anderson, "because when you have the complete freedom to do whatever you want to do, it's interesting what it produces." Anderson's Village Thing label was going from strength to strength. *An Acoustic Confusion* (1971) by Steve Tilston garnered a lot of sales and press coverage and led to a manufacturing and distribution deal with Transatlantic. Other 'heavy folk' albums followed, including Anderson's own *A Vulture Is Not A Bird You Can Trust*; *The Words In Between* by Dave Evans; *Feelin' Fine* by a resurgent Derroll Adams; and a self-titled gem by New Zealander Chris Thompson.

Progressive music should, by definition, look further than its own genre backyard. One striking example of this came from the three-piece group Synanthesia, who explored the implications of jazz-folk fusion in the heartland of the emerging progressive rock scene. "We very rarely performed alongside other acoustic acts," founder Dennis Homes recalls. Instead, they shared the stage with The Edgar Broughton Band, Pink Floyd, Caravan, and King Crimson. "It was sometimes a little worrying when we'd set up our small PA and miked-up instruments alongside the masses of speakers that these other bands had," Homes says, "but it seemed to work."

In 1968, Homes had recorded a single with his rhythm & blues band, The Inhibition, for Island Records, not that anyone would know: the A-side, 'Tonopah', was not by the band at all, but by session musicians, and was credited to Henri & His Hobo Amigos. Homes, who had already begun to drift away from straight rhythm & blues, was appalled at the subterfuge and left the band.

"I was writing lots of songs on acoustic guitar and thought that it would be interesting to find a couple of like-minded musicians and form an acoustic trio," he recalls. He had been particularly taken by Harold McNair's flute on Donovan's *A Gift From A Flower To A Garden*, so he placed an advertisement in *Melody Maker* for a flautist and an acoustic guitarist.

The two successful respondents were Jim Fraser and Leslie Cook. Fraser had a solid jazz background and could play alto and soprano sax, flute, and oboe; Cook, just 18, had no previous band experience but was a superb guitarist and could also play mandolin, violin, and bongos. The three musicians clicked immediately. "It was obvious that this trio was going to be totally different from what I had envisaged, but it felt good," Homes says. "We could get a whole range of tone colours to our music." They called themselves Synanthesia at Fraser's suggestion, after a track by Yuseef Lateef, and started to rehearse at a community centre in London's Bethnal Green.

"Ideas came fast and furiously," Homes says. "When we used to meet up for rehearsals, either Leslie or myself would play a song, and then we would all just throw in ideas. Jim didn't write any songs but he was invariably the first to come up with ideas for arrangements and what instruments should be used." In one particular starburst of creativity, Homes wrote a song cycle about the Greek gods over a weekend. His songs benefited from Fraser's improvisational gusto; he and Cook soon had enough material for a live set. They found a spot at an East End folk club, Peanuts, and played their jazzy, progressive folk to a somewhat mystified audience.

Before long Synanthesia had recorded a demo and started performing on the university circuit with representation by the prestigious Ellis-Wright agency. When Sandy Roberton saw the group perform he immediately offered them a deal with his production company, September Productions, and arranged for a session at Sound Techniques in February 1969.

"It was recorded in two days flat," Homes says of the resulting *Synanthesia*. "There was hardly any overdubbing. It was almost done as a live recording." The band – still only six months old – felt the album was a rush-job. "I wish that we had taken more time over it and given it a lot more polish, but it represents where we were at that time," Homes says. They sound comfortable fluxing between numerous styles, with nothing appearing to have been shoehorned in for effect. The music is fleshy and free; the lyrics, too, are progressive, with Homes's classical imagery offset by Cook's abstract surrealism.

Synanthesia was released by RCA in November 1969. Soon afterward, the group recorded 'Shifting Sands', which was intended as a single but ended up on the *49 Greek Street* compilation instead. "We spent a lot more time on that number," Homes says, "and we were augmented by a string section that was arranged by David Palmer, who later became the keyboard player in Jethro Tull. The bowed string bass played a continuous D and my guitar had the bottom string tuned down to a D. It gave an Eastern drone effect that was quite hypnotic."

Synanthesia were ahead of their time but had little chance to consolidate their invention. Leslie Cook, who was also training to be a journalist, found the punishing live work too much. He left just two months after *Synanthesia* was released. Homes and Fraser carried on for another four months, bringing in a bass guitarist and drummer, but they knew they were playing a losing game. "The original idea of Synanthesia was no longer there," Homes says. "We were just turning into a mediocre rock group with a jazzy twinge. Enough was enough."

Another key band was Spirogyra. "I was a typical hippie," says Martin

Cockerham of his teenage years in Bolton, Lancashire. "In my school I was probably the first hippie. But I used to get high grades so, because of that, I didn't get into trouble."

Cockerham formed the first version of Spirogyra while still at school with his friend, Mark Francis, who had similarly long hair and shared with him an interest in politics and The Incredible String Band. After Cockerham moved to Canterbury to attend university, however, opportunities to play together were rare. In order to keep Spirogyra breathing, Cockerham began scouting around for new musicians. First came violinist Julian Cusack; by the end of his first term, Cockerham had added fellow students Steve Borrill (bass) and Barbara Gaskin (vocals) to the line-up.

The four-piece Spirogyra found themselves right in the middle of the burgeoning Canterbury scene. Although groups like Soft Machine and Caravan were outside of Spirogyra's immediate circle, Steve Hillage was a fellow student and friend; it was he who introduced Cockerham and Gaskin to one another. (There was some talk of Hillage joining Spirogyra at one point, but he was too busy with his own projects.)

Spirogyra found a manager, Max Hole, who used his position as Student Union Entertainment Secretary to set up gigs at universities throughout the country. Then, while the group tightened their sound through live work, he pressed on with finding them a record deal. They eventually signed a three-album deal with B&C, a small production company. Cockerham now feels that this was a mistake. "They didn't have the resources to promote us," he says, "and if you don't get promoted, you just disappear." (He would later suspect that B&C had taken on the group as a tax-loss exercise.)

In the summer of 1970, Spirogyra went into the revered Sound Techniques studio to record their first album, *St Radigunds*, which they named after the Canterbury street on which they all lived. Sandy Roberton produced the album; Robert Kirby provided the arrangements.

"We were a little bit too psyched up, a bit nervous, doing the first album," Cockerham recalls. "Robert Kirby did some beautiful arrangements but he didn't know the band very well. And we were still learning about how to use the studio." Gaskin agrees that there was some anxiety within the group but still remembers the wonder of entering the studio. "I loved the way the music sounded in enormous studio monitors," she says. "We enjoyed being able to experiment, accepting or rejecting ideas as we went along."

St Radigunds is effectively a document of Spirogyra's well-honed live set, featuring songs that address the group's political concerns. "We were preoccupied with political change, climate change, diminishing oil reserves, green issues," Gaskin says. "We were fervently anti-capitalist and anti-materialism. We rejected the status quo, and we believed in the power of music to influence ideas." Cockerham had studied politics at university but struggled with the direction of the course. "I thought, this is studying the Devil, and I dropped out," he says. "I thought there was more to it, so I studied alternative politics [and] the ancient traditions of India and China."

The next Spirogyra album, *Old Boot Wine*, represents an important shift. The band felt more at ease in the studio this time, particularly with Max Hole producing. Paradoxically, having lost the experience of Roberton and Kirby, they ended up with a more polished and coherent album. There are still plenty of psychedelic workouts, like 'Van Allen's Belt', but there are also catchier, more accessible kicks to be found.

It is the group's third album, however, that really marks them out as a beacon of progressive folk. Although Spirogyra had officially shrunk back to become a duo of Cockerham and Gaskin, Cusack and Borrill both play on the album. Constant touring may have heightened the tension between the four, yet they still enjoyed being in the studio together. But the land had shifted in one important respect. "Martin took complete artistic control, hiring in Dolly Collins to write arrangements," Gaskin recalls. "With freedom comes responsibility though, and I think he found that onerous after a while." *Bells, Boots And Shambles* bends away from the rockier elements of their first two albums toward weeping classicism and Eno-esque art-house soundtracks. The psychedelic current is still there, but it has evolved.

With the three-album deal with B&C now complete, however, that was effectively it for Spirogyra. "It was depressing," Cockerham says. "This was a very good little band, and artistically I was very happy with how it was going." He left for Ireland, embarking on a journey with a horse and cart and becoming more deeply involved with spirituality and self-sufficiency, living the life he had explored in his songs. Gaskin, too, felt restless. "I think we all needed to do something different," she says. "I decided to travel myself, as I found it impossible to settle down to conventional life."

⋈

Someone else who found the conventional life rather impossible was Alisha Sufit. From her childhood, when she first saw Jean Renoir's *The River*, she had found herself engulfed by Indian music. "When I was young I used to have the notion I had been Indian in a previous life," she says. "I discovered Ravi

Shankar when I was 16. My parents couldn't understand how I could like his music. I couldn't understand how my parents could not."

In 1968, Sufit had just left Chelsea School of Art when she met an Irish guitarist, who encouraged her to sing. It was just the release she needed; her mother had died when Sufit was 18, and it had been a difficult few years. "There was a lot of change in the air, a lot of positive energy and creativity," she says. "I had a reawakening and everything came alive again." She borrowed her father's Spanish guitar and went busking on Portobello Road. "I collected a surprising amount of money. I busked regularly after that. Dave Brock from Hawkwind and Geoff Leigh from Henry Cow were doing the same thing to make ends meet."

Sufit sang regularly at folk clubs and on the college circuit, eventually replacing her father's nylon-string guitar with her first steel-string. "I remember a friend asking me in 1971 if I'd like to be in a band," she says. "I said yes, but it would have to have a sitar player and a tabla player in it." By coincidence, Sufit was contacted three months later by the guitarist Jim Moyes, an old colleague from the art school now playing in a trio called Sargam with Clem Alford on sitar and Keshav Sathe on tabla. Sargam had already released one album, *Pop Explosion Sitar Style*, but it had been a disaster. The band's name was misspelled 'Sagram' on the cover, and they had had nothing to do with either the hyped-up title or the cheesy artwork, which featured a moustachioed lothario and a phallic candlestick.

Sargam had since signed to Mushroom Records, run by Vic Keary, who had already shown his bravery by releasing Simon Finn's *Pass The Distance*. Keary asked Sargam to find a singer. "So they found me," Sufit says. "Because I was writing a lot of my songs in open modal tunings, they were instantly compatible with sitar tunings. It all happened relatively easily."

With Sufit now on board, the band became Magic Carpet and headed into Keary's Chalk Farm Studios at the end of 1971. Not since *5000 Spirits* had there been such a successful partnership of English and Indian music as emerged on *Magic Carpet*. Sufit's songwriting and operatic vocals, and the band's obvious passion for and exhaustive knowledge of Indian music, brought forth a melodious chime; a true fusion of styles is evident on tracks like 'The Phoenix' and the beaty 'Do You Hear The Words'.

Unlike the String Band, however, Magic Carpet were unable to build on their twin foundations of skill and experimentation. They had little guidance from producers or management; when problems arose, they were left to blossom. "Magic Carpet came to an end basically because of interpersonal tensions," Sufit says. "There were certain elements that were not working well, and I was too unselfconfident to say bye-bye to those elements and get a replacement element." *Magic Carpet* was also one of the final releases on Mushroom – another small sign that the psychedelic-folk era was in its twilight zone.

A further sign came with the demise of Comus. The group sought to bring the influences of opera and classical music to the fore on what they intended as a follow-up to *First Utterance*, a project entitled *The Malgaard Suite*. They played the first part of it live a few times, but the second remained unfinished. "It didn't go down well live and people wondered what was going on," Andy Hellaby recalls. "It was too introspective, too complex, like a lot of progressive music was."

The group's label, Dawn, was similarly unimpressed. "Our manager, Chris Youle, played the first part to them," Bobbie Watson recalls. "Their response was: 'If they can come up with a three-minute version, we'll go with it.'" Comus began to unravel. First they left Dawn, then Youle stopped managing them. Then, after embarking on one final, poorly attended tour in 1972, they split up.

One of the most atypical and dramatic stories of the whole progressive folk genre has been preserved in the memories of two women. "I got together with Clodagh [Simonds] very early, at the age of ten," says Alison O'Donnell (formerly Alison Bools). "We started playing a couple of things like 'Da Do Ron Ron' and Helen Shapiro's songs. And then we started doing our own material, and playing those songs at school concerts. That was very unusual."

O'Donnell, Simonds, and Maria White attended the Holy Child Convent School in Killiney, Ireland, during the early 60s. They formed a group called The Gatecrashers and staked out the school's rehearsal space at lunchtimes. "We practiced nearly every day," O'Donnell says. "We were *incredibly* serious from that age. We were probably very annoying, because we were chirpy little girls."

The three girls were always looking to publicise their music and wouldn't be dissuaded in their ambition. "I thought we should make a record, [but] I had absolutely no idea about the music business," Simonds recalls with a laugh. "I thought what you had to do was send tapes to disc jockeys. And so we made a tape of just some of my songs."

Simonds sent the tape out to Radio Luxemburg; DJ Colin Nicol liked what he heard and arranged for the girls to meet producer Simon Napier-Bell, who had recently founded his own record label, SNB. The group, now calling themselves Mellow Candle, went to London to record the single 'Feeling High' / 'Tea In The Sun'. The A-side is a psychedelic girl-group song, the flip a surreal retro wedge; it wasn't folk, and it wasn't a hit, but it did give Mellow Candle a small bit of press.

It wasn't *quite* enough, however, to warrant a huge amount of hope for a future as teenage pop stars. Maria White, who was a year older than Simonds and O'Donnell, left Mellow Candle when she finished school. She had never been as committed to the group as the other two. "We were very intense from a very early age," O'Donnell says, "and she wasn't. So there was a difference very early on." White's departure was just the first step in the disintegration of Mellow Candle's initial incarnation. At her mother's request, Simonds left Ireland for a spell in Italy; O'Donnell stayed in Killiney, enrolling on a secretarial course before signing up for art college.

Shortly before leaving for Italy, Simonds had met guitarist Dave Williams at a party. She introduced him to O'Donnell, and while Simonds was away, O'Donnell began singing in Williams's covers band, Blue Tint. They also started to date. O'Donnell wrote to Simonds in Italy, saying she didn't want to perform as Mellow Candle anymore. According to Simonds, there was no acrimony. "She just said: 'This is what I want to do, I want to be in a band.'"

Simonds had avenues of her own to explore, having been encouraged by the DJ, Nicol, to become a solo singer-songwriter – something she admits she felt "a bit diffident about". Nevertheless, she played along for a time. "When I came back to Ireland, the first thing that happened was going into the studio with Colin and recording a few tracks."

Simonds, still unsure of her future, met up with Williams again. "He was keen to hear some of my material," she says. "I think he must have heard the old tapes, but he wanted to hear some of the more recent cuts, and he really liked it, and said let's all work together. It was really his idea to form the next step of Mellow Candle. Dave was *much* more musically literate than I was, and his influence was enormous on the band."

O'Donnell and Simonds were pleased to be working together again. "I didn't think my friendship with Alison had been damaged or anything," Simonds says of their brief split. "I'd met Dave and I really liked him, so I completely understood. I had no career plan, so I totally understood why it appealed to her to join a band with a guy who was very together." Simonds abandoned her potential solo career and Mellow Candle found their second flame.

Dave Williams was older than O'Donnell and Simonds. He was a gifted guitarist, a songwriter, and had a penchant for progressive music. Above all, he was methodical and driven; he knew that if Mellow Candle were going to have a shot at success they would need a manager. He found Ted Carroll (who also took care of Thin Lizzy) and recruited a fourth band-member, bassist Pat Morris. There followed an intense period of creativity, during which Simonds and Williams's existing songs were fine-tuned and O'Donnell too began to develop her writing style.

"Our pieces quite quickly became complex rhythmically," Simonds says. "I discovered I had an aptitude for quite complicated time signatures. Dave was always very keen on that, as was Pat. And Alison and I had been singing together for some years, so we had an intuitive understanding of each other's voice, and both of us were very interested in harmonies."

The demos the four-piece group recorded – with the help of Caravan drummer Richard Coughlan – were pared-down and fragile, and far more folk-influenced than the 'Feeling High' single. They represent a key seeding of the new Mellow Candle ground and form an abbreviation between the luscious pop of that first girl-group single and the intricacy of the new line-up's eventual album.

Pat Morris was particularly important in giving the songs a frame. "He was a huge Jethro Tull fan," O'Donnell says. "He used to slap the bass in that same, very percussive way." Morris soon began to feel the strain, however: according to O'Donnell, he stormed out of an Andy Warhol movie about "gay cowboys" during the trip to London and suffered generally with "the whole cultural shock thing". In the end he decided to return to his life in Ireland. "Pat was just not interested in drugs, basically," Simonds adds with a grin. "And you can probably imagine what kind of a chasm that represented for us." He was replaced by Frank Boylan, who *was* interested in drugs and the counter-culture, and had been in the beat group The Creatures since the 50s.

By late 1970, Mellow Candle were starting to attract notice from record labels. "A couple of people came over from England to see us," O'Donnell recalls. "We were doing a gig at the RDS, a big venue in Dublin. The guy who was doing the sound was tripping, and he just screwed the whole thing up, basically, because he was so out of his brain. We couldn't hear any of the monitors and the record company guys were not impressed at all. We were really annoyed when we got off the stage, and the sound guy was just smiling at us, saying: 'Wow, the lights were fantastic.' What can you say?"

In the end, Ted Carroll brokered a deal with the Decca offshoot Deram which, since disbanding Nova, was once again the settling ground for the label's progressive signings. At Decca's insistence, Mellow Candle added a full-time drummer, William Murray, who had recently enjoyed a stint in Kevin Ayers's Whole World group alongside Mike Oldfield. "Willy's influence was massive," Simonds says. "He introduced us to lots of music we hadn't known before."

Mellow Candle moved to London's Belsize Park and recorded their debut album, *Swaddling Songs*, in December 1971 with Decca's in-house producer, David Hitchcock. "The lighting was turned down, the studio was really nice, it was semi-lit, wonderful atmosphere," O'Donnell recalls. "We were smoking lots of dope, of course, and it was really a very conducive atmosphere to recording." There were also time pressures, however, and long singing sessions that O'Donnell says put a strain on her voice and caused other flaws in the recording.

Yet whether by accident or design, *Swaddling Songs* has that rare combination of youthful naïveté and Byzantine complexity. It's chipped and imperfect in one breath and highly developed in the next. The remnants of the girl-group days can still be heard – particularly on 'Lonely Man', which Simonds wrote at the age of 12 – but so can the newer sound of folk-rock, which reaches its peak here on 'Messenger Birds'. It's a truly indefinable album, with folk only one of many strands.

The progressive nature of *Swaddling Songs* is exemplified by its signature track, 'Reverend Sisters', which dates back to Simonds's time in Italy. "I wrote 'Reverend Sisters' when I thought I wasn't going to be working with Alison anymore, when I thought I was going to be on my own," she says. "It was written for solo voice, but when we came to record it, we thought it wouldn't really be on for me to take a lead vocal, so we both sang it in unison." The pair's circling, beguiling vocals give 'Reverend Sisters' both tension and intensity, while Simonds's piano seems ghostly, as if playing by itself in an empty room while the two women levitate around it.

Swaddling Songs is never only about Simonds and O'Donnell. The interweaving guitar and bass is restrained and appropriate, and Willy Murray's drumming is a sensitive keystone throughout. Simonds feels strongly that the group dynamic is what made the album work so well. "It was a band of five very talented people," she says, "not me and Alison and a backing band. I always feel it's very inaccurate and oversimplified when we're portrayed that way."

Like the work of Bread Love And Dreams, *Swaddling Songs* suffered from evasive promotion by Decca. "They were marvellous to record with but their follow-up process, in terms of PR, was woefully inadequate," O'Donnell says, although she and Simonds both accept that there were other reasons for the album's failure. "Ted Carroll said, later on, we were too rocky for the folk clubs and we were too folky for the rock clubs," she continues. "We just fell between two stools."

Simonds also feels that Mellow Candle were too eager to move beyond the 'paying dues' stage. "We should have built up more of a fan base, and should have been more experienced live," she says. "We weren't particularly engaging to watch, and we weren't brilliantly polished musically either. Apparently, we had been absolutely nagging Ted to get out of Ireland and go to London." Against his better judgement, Carroll yielded to the request. The local fan base the band was building lost momentum, and they became small fish in the big London pond.

"We had been signed by a major label, and we were treated well by them at the time," O'Donnell says. "We expected that [to] carry on to some degree." But Deram was not interested in another album, there were no bookings for live shows, and Ted Carroll ceased managing the group. The combination of factors that had given *Swaddling Songs* its unique sound started to work loose. Then Frank Boylan left, having become increasingly unsettled within the group as the others began to experiment with Scientology. (Willy Murray was first, and Simonds followed. "I was a huge Incredible String Band fan," she sighs, "so I was pretty easy to convert.")

Boylan's replacement was Steve Borrill, formerly of Spirogyra, who brought about another extremely significant shift in the group's dynamic. "He was listening to people like Hatfield & The North, much more jazzy and experimental," Simonds says. This seemed compatible with Murray's penchant for the more outré end of progressive rock, while Simonds, too, had been further developing her interest in challenging time signatures. To reflect their new direction, Mellow Candle became Grace Before Space.

As stimulating as Borrill's input might have been, it ushered in a difficult period. "The balance got lost at that point," Simonds says. "That's when everything changed." Two camps formed: Borrill, Murray, and Simonds in one, Williams in the other, and O'Donnell caught in the middle. The waters were muddied further by Simonds and Murray's decision to leave Scientology; for the time being, O'Donnell and Williams stuck with it, although they would both end up leaving shortly after the band's demise.

A huge practical problem had also barged its way into their lives. Their new manager, Pete Harmon, had disastrously entrusted the band's remaining money with an agent who promised Grace Before Space a tour of Holland that never materialised. "Everything else dried up after that," O'Donnell says. Harmon also departed, and the band was left on the point of destitution.

"Dave and Alison were married," Simonds recalls. "I was still a raging hippie at that time, so I thought we all loved each other." In the end she decided things couldn't continue as they were. "I thought the best thing to do would be for Dave and Alison to go off and form a separate group. Alison was writing by then, they were writing together. And it never even crossed my mind that she would have a problem with that."

O'Donnell was devastated. "What I thought was going to be a slightly difficult [conversation] turned into something like a horror movie," Simonds continues. "An arctic silence descended, which ended up lasting 16 years, during which time Willy and I had zero contact with Dave and Alison. I was so upset by what had happened that I just decided I never wanted to be in a band again. I literally couldn't believe things had come to such a messy end."

"I was broken-hearted, actually," O'Donnell says of the split, which occurred in 1973. "It was a really, really tough experience. It scattered us to the corners of the globe, practically. Dave and I went to Johannesburg and spent at least three years paying off a band debt, leaving us with practically no money. That made our time in a new country very, very difficult. We never talked about Mellow Candle."

"It was an incredibly delicate balance of five gifted people that sustained something very briefly," Simonds concludes. "We were all quite exploratory, experimental people, and there was just this brief window where we were all on track together. But then the whole thing toppled."

◩

Mellow Candle had started out in Ireland, but there was always a sense that they were separate from their environment, nurtured and eventually imploding within their own hothouse. The wider scene would be only sporadically inspiring, as Brian O'Reilly of Loudest Whisper remembers. "In Ireland at the time, there were lots of bands but they weren't beat groups or folk groups," he says. "There was what they call the show bands. There were hundreds of them. They would play whatever was in the Top 20."

There were, of course, exceptions, and indeed more of them as the 60s wore on. Sweeney's Men provided a crucial plank in the development of folk-rock in the British Isles on their second album, *The Tracks Of Sweeney* (1969), which offers intriguing psychedelic elements on 'Brain Jam' and 'Hall Of Mirrors'. After their short, combustible stint in Steeleye Span and a happier spell with Dr Strangely Strange, Gay and Terry Woods formed The Woods Band, releasing a hardwired self-titled folk album in 1971. Tír Na NÓg released three albums in the early 70s. The first two are full of warm acoustics; the third is a melange of pop, rock, and folk; all three contain sprinkles of strangeness. Meanwhile, a new genre, Celtic rock, had begun to drive up on the outside of folk, with Horslips forming in 1970.

Elements of all these sounds can be found in Loudest Whisper, who evolved from a beat group, The Wizard, and comprised Brian O'Reilly, his brother Paud, Brendan 'Bunny' Neligan, and John Aherne. Each had different tastes, from The Beach Boys to Black Sabbath. The band's new name seemed to represent both sides of their music: the folky and the heavy.

From 1970 onward, Loudest Whisper gained a reputation as a loud, intense blues-rock band. Alongside this, however, Brian O'Reilly had another idea. "I started looking around and thought it would be nice to do a musical, but in a folk music style," he recalls. By coincidence, a local priest asked him if he would engage in musical work with teenagers. With a prospective cast now at his disposal, O'Reilly found a rich seam of inspiration in Irish mythology. "It just kind of jumped out at me," he says of what became *The Children Of Lir*. "The children were turned into swans. The only request of the wicked stepmother was that they could retain their human voices. And then they would sing with beautiful voices that would enchant people."

By the summer of 1972, O'Reilly had completed his progressive-folk musical and was preparing to perform it. The local Youth Choir was on board, as were all the members of Loudest Whisper, but this ambitious project still required yet more recruits. "Anyone who played acoustic guitar, I went up to them and said: 'I want you to be in the orchestra,'" O'Reilly recalls. "We had a big acoustic sound and no one was miked up." Ron Kavanagh, a recent recruit to Loudest Whisper, was given the lead role in the production. *The Children Of Lir* had its debut in January 1973 in Fermoy.

Contrary to the low expectations of some of the early audiences, *The Children Of Lir* was a highly accomplished work. "It blew them away, and the word got out very fast," O'Reilly says. The musical was featured on RTÉ's national arts programme before hitting the road, at which point Polydor approached the band about a tie-in LP.

"We kind of said no," O'Reilly recalls. "We didn't really want to, because it's not a band project." Brian had considered *The Children Of Lir* to be separate from Loudest Whisper, even though the band's members were playing on it, because of its fundamental difference to their heavy rock reputation. These concerns aside, however, they decided to accept Polydor's offer and were delighted when the label assigned Leo O'Kelly of Tír Na NÓg to produce and brought in a string quartet. (The Youth Choir also came along: "We just took a busload of them up with us," O'Reilly says.)

The resulting supernatural, thoughtful concept album was released in Ireland in 1975 and enjoyed an initial burst of interest, spurring O'Reilly on to write further folk musicals. It also led to Geraldine Dorgan, whose exquisite voice peppered *The Children Of Lir*, becoming a full-time band member. For Bunny Neligan, however, the axis of Loudest Whisper had spun too far. "Bunny didn't like that transition to going that little more folksy," O'Reilly says. "So he left the band." Neligan's departure was just the first of many personnel changes for Loudest Whisper. Despite Brian O'Reilly's continued interest in stage musicals, Loudest Whisper's subsequent albums saw them return to hard rock.

Tellingly, Polydor had the opportunity to release *The Children Of Lir* in the UK, but declined. By 1975, psychedelic, progressive, and acid folk were of no interest in the marketplace. The sound's last outlet came from artists who grasped the means of production and put their records out themselves. It led to some of the strangest records of all.

CHAPTER 11
Sanctuary Stone

OVER THE YEARS, folk music has attracted professional players, semi-professional dilettantes, and rank amateurs alike, but the particular conditions of the early 70s were optimal for even bedroom musicians to thrive. The sound was widely liked, there were outlets for performance, and the start-up costs – often just the price of an acoustic guitar – were minimal. In folk clubs and coffeehouses, garages and living rooms, in the USA, the UK, and beyond, folk hummed in the atmosphere as thousands upon thousands of people tried their hand at it. By the law of averages, most of these earnest outpourings were probably not very good, while even if they were paradigm-shifting sensations, in the final analysis, it didn't matter: they all disappeared into the unreliable space of memory after their last notes were struck.

In a minority of cases, folk musicians or groups would release their music under their own steam. Many of these vinyl outings – described as 'private' or, less charitably, 'vanity' pressings – were not particularly great. Sometimes record labels are not interested for a reason. And yet the exceptions prove the rule. Occasionally, these tiny, tiny projects yielded fascinating, innovative, and excellent music. Creative solutions would be found to low budgets and short timescales; given that those who made these records assumed their music was only for a local market (sometimes only their acquaintances), there was a freewheeling liberty to them, too.

It is therefore astonishing that one of *the* key experimental-folk records was a self-released album of 300 copies, most of which were given away to strangers on a street corner in Philadelphia. "I felt empowered," says Perry

Leopold, the artist behind both the recording and unusual distribution of *Experiment In Metaphysics* (1970). "It was my way of sticking it to the establishment."

Perry Leopold was a curious and musical child. At the age of three, he would press his ear against the side of the family's piano while his older brother played. "It was mostly very intense piano concertos," Leopold says, "and I literally got lost in a world of tonality and overtones. It was my first experience of getting high off of music." By the age of five, Leopold had pestered his parents to buy him a guitar. He was proficient at it by eight, started writing songs around the same time, and joined his first band at ten.

As a teenager during the 60s, Leopold became involved not only in music but also in anti-establishment philosophy and direct action. He turned over political thoughts carefully, questioning not only the institutions of society but also the sloganeering of the counter-culture. "Do you die in a revolution because you are unwilling to die in an unjust war?" he asked himself. "Flower power began to lose its way, and Altamont made Woodstock seem like a distant memory." With the draft snatching his friends away to Vietnam, Leopold himself, having forfeited a place in college, was reclassified 1-A: available for military service.

Timothy Leary and Carlos Castaneda had a profound influence. Leopold fused hallucinogenic drug use with songwriting and saw a natural affinity between the two experiences. "Music has an uncanny magical aspect," he says. "It doesn't really exist except in some other dimension that is opened up when you hear it and it causes you to *feel*. It has the potential to open a door to a new consciousness." For Leopold, this was precisely the point of using drugs, too: "LSD and mescaline were not for 'getting high' or partying, but for exploring the mind and expanding its potential. LSD and black hashish became tools of my trade. I would drop acid, light a candle, smoke a bowl of hash, pick up my guitar, and just start playing. I was a vessel."

Writing in this way, Leopold thought of himself as a test subject. Songs flowed through him. Some came to him as mystical and impenetrable; some were pointed, such as 'Cold In Philadelphia', which he wrote amid the ominous draft. He titled his body of work *Experiment In Metaphysics*, he says, because that's what he believed it to be. But he also saw these songs within the context of the American folk tradition. "I called my music acid-folk," he says. "It was simply a statement of the obvious."

In June 1970, Leopold recorded *Experiment In Metaphysics* in the basement of a shoe-repair shop. The whole session took around five hours, including breaks to smoke a few bowls of hash; the owner of the store moonlighted as the engineer. "It was like a live gig," Leopold says, "except that I was able to re-do a song if I thought I could do better." The resulting recording is brutally raw, but suits the intuitive way that Leopold wrote the songs and approached his instrument. "All of my guitar tunings were studies in overtones, and the constant attempts to blend sounds in such a way so that one could faintly hear the echoes of flutes, violins, and other instruments in the background."

The rough and ready approach to recording *Experiment In Metaphysics* was matched by its packaging. Deciding to fund the release of the album himself rather than attempt to chase down a record company, Leopold arranged for 300 copies to be pressed at a local facility. "When I went to drop off the masters, the owner of the pressing plant asked when I would be delivering the artwork," he recalls. "I said there was no artwork, as I couldn't afford to get covers printed. I told him to just give me the records and I'll put them in paper bags or something. He looked at me like I was from Mars."

From the corner of his eye, Leopold saw a stack of plain gold covers, which the pressing plant let him have for ten cents apiece. "Afterward, I had an ink stamp made for two dollars with the title of the album, bought a box of Avery mailing labels, stamped them, and stuck them on to the gold cover. Voila."

That same summer, Leopold went to half a dozen local shops and put the records in the racks, agreeing to be paid only after the discs had been sold. Within a few weeks, he realised that his album was indeed selling, although no local retailers had passed on the proceeds. In no mood to be swindled, he confronted the stores about the records they had sold. "They made it seem like they had no idea what I was talking about," he says, "and it became apparent that I was getting ripped off. So I demanded to have all the albums back."

Leopold trudged around Philadelphia to each of the record stores and picked up his stock, on foot, in the blistering August heat. "By this point, I was exhausted," he recalls. "I just stood on the corner of 16th and Chestnut and started giving them away," Leopold says. Most passers-by tried to avoid the long-haired, bearded man and his bounty, but he would literally step in their path and force a copy of *Experiment In Metaphysics* into their hands. He even accosted drivers stopped at a red light. "The amazing thing is, I don't remember anyone saying a word to me, except: 'What is it?' I would reply: 'It's me.'"

Within an hour, Leopold had given away all of the albums bar the 25 copies he decided to keep. "As far as I was concerned it was over," he says. "I assumed most, if not all, people tossed it in the trash without bothering to listen to it. It was tantamount to putting a message in 300 bottles and throwing them all in the ocean."

Leopold moved on. He approached his second record, *Christian Lucifer*, from a more personal religious viewpoint, having written 'Everything Goes' after Christ appeared to him as an image, surrounded by light. "As my eyes were fixed on his, I saw the light behind him begin to darken, and a shadow came up behind the Christ image," he recalls. "Then, very slowly, as the shadow merged with Christ and the two became one, it became clear that the shadow was in fact the devil. I could see his face and his eyes as clearly as I could Christ's as they came together. But what completely took me by surprise was that the eyes of each remained the same."

Leopold was drawn to the idea of a 'Christian Lucifer' as a metaphor for the oxymoronic heart of the world. "The singularity of duality, a Judeo-Christian expression of Yin-Yang," he explains. He would start concerts during this period by telling the audience that Christian Lucifer was not *his* name but the name of his music. "It was not unusual to finish a song and look up to see the audience with their eyes closed, and totally silent," he recalls.

Leopold knew that the jagged, impromptu feel of *Experiment In Metaphysics* would not work for the *Christian Lucifer* material. "Instead of recording it live, and solo, it involved around two dozen people and took hundreds, maybe over a thousand hours," he says. He decided he wanted an orchestra for these songs. "Without having any experience in orchestrating, I did it myself. I wrote every note of every instrument." He found musicians who believed in his project enough to perform for free, while Doug Fearn agreed to engineer and produce the record for nothing.

The resulting album has a far more elaborate and ornate sound than *Experiment In Metaphysics* but still holds on to its strange folk heart. "Psychedelic references were frowned on by then," Leopold says. "My music was categorised as 'Metaphysical Baroque Folque'." *Christian Lucifer* was unable to match even the miniscule audience level of *Experiment In Metaphysics*. It remained unreleased, and then the master tapes were lost. With the acid-folk scene dying around him, Leopold found it hard to carry on. "Willingness on the part of audiences to experience new things seemed to be a thing of the past," he says of the mid 70s. After making a few scattered demos and playing on the college circuit, Perry Leopold retired from music with the belief that both of his albums had disappeared.

M

Unbuckled by fashions or creative restrictions, albums born of unmediated self-expression and pressed outside of conventional popular music careerism can weather the decades very well. This is certainly how Collie Ryan sees her music. "These songs grow out of the spirit of nature," she says. "The songs have never been a commercial venture, which is one reason why they're different."

As a child, Ryan loved to sing, both in the school choirs and along to the opera records played in her family home in the Bay Area of San Francisco. "When I was about 14 I took piano lessons," she recalls. "I didn't really enjoy them, but they were valuable lessons. Then I picked up the guitar, because I loved to sing, and one simply doesn't haul a piano around." Along with the guitar came a new abundance of folk; between the ages of 14 and 19, she learnt hundreds of traditional songs from America and the British Isles.

Ryan was also exploring different spiritual paths and philosophies. She was particularly drawn toward theosophy, which she describes as "traditional spiritual knowledge", and which draws together different religious systems and metaphysical ideas. One day, Ryan and a friend were arguing about philosophy and life; he suggested that she should write a song to prove her point. "He said: 'Do you want help?' and I said: 'No!'" she recalls with a laugh. Ryan's friend quickly became her creative foil, however. The pair would argue, and then she would write songs in an attempt to get her position across. "My friend loved the songs," she says. "He understood them completely, and said: 'Yes! That's what I was trying to tell you!'"

Like Perry Leopold, Collie Ryan felt almost as if she was a conduit for her music, such was the free, expressive way in which it came to life. She likens her approach to songwriting to the ancient traditions of oration and declaiming, whereby poetry and performing arts would be used to debate philosophical ideas. "I was never going to sing them for money," she says, "because spiritual ideas cannot be sold."

Fortunately, Ryan did not have to rely on using her music to make a living. Instead, she performed the songs privately for friends, and saw them wholly outside commercial concerns as a vehicle to explore her own beliefs and inspire others. She began to realise that her songs were unusual; that she wrote in a way that was not common among other musicians or contemporary styles. "The more different the music got, the less backup I was capable of having, so the music took its own way," she says. The songs became a virtuous cycle of self-expression and experimentation. "The whole rhythm of my music is completely different to most Western music. I called them magical songs – they were not songs you could sing in a bar."

In 1973, with funding from her friends at the nearby New Age Farms company, Ryan recorded a selection of her songs. She pressed them onto three LPs: *The Giving Tree, Indian Harvest,* and *Takin' Your Turn 'Round The Corner Of Day.* "My way of recording would be to concentrate my attention like an Olympic athlete," she says, "and then just sit down and run through them. I rarely had to redo anything." The songs on the albums sound intimate and unfettered, with Ryan's voice at the core and her graceful, nylon-stringed guitar surrounding it.

Ryan's songs were organic and grounded, reflecting the lifestyle she had chosen for herself. "For most of my life I have lived a certain kind of life, close to nature," she says. "I grow as much food as I can. I don't have electricity, none of that stuff. And by forgoing all that the modern world holds dear, I have time to live a spiritual life as best I can, and keep this sort of art alive."

Ryan's records were distributed at her cosy performances for friends; some went on sale at the Sun & Earth Health Food Store & Restaurant in Santa Barbara. Soon, however, Ryan's situation changed. "Life happened," she shrugs. "The whole union of us – there were a bunch of us together, we broke up, and the records got put in storage."

Ryan continued to write songs and poems, but did so further away from society, deep within the Texan desert. Visual art became her source of income, and she continues to paint mandalas – "the original design of nature" – on discarded hubcaps. The mandala, she says, has "always been with us in many forms, and people intuitively respond to it". And so it is with her unique, delicate songs.

⋈

Collie Ryan was not alone in using her albums as a spiritual outlet. Religious conviction underpinned dozens – if not hundreds – of privately pressed folk albums in the USA. Some touched on the psychedelic, such as Rising Hope's floral Christian folk and the Alaskan seven-piece group Windflower's explorations of the Bahá'í faith. One record stands alone in its brilliance, however: *The Christ Tree* by The Trees Community.

Katheryn Ruetenik and William 'Shipen' Lebzeltzer met in the autumn of 1969. She was a teenage student at Leelanau, a Christian Science school in Lake Michigan; he was a dapper, mesmeric man in his twenties who had gone to Leelanau to meet the students and discuss his belief system. Ruetenik was immediately struck by Lebzeltzer; he looked to her like "James Dean mixed with Timothy Leary and a generous dose of Jesus Christ".

Lebzeltzer's theory concerned 'Clear Children' and the idea that, as one moves toward the seven mindsets of faith, hope, charity, mercy, grace, peace, and love, one becomes 'clear'. The ultimate implication was that humans could become divine. With shades of Perry Leopold, Lebzeltzer had come up with the concept after a heavy LSD session and considered it to be a piece of automatic writing: he had written it, from beginning to end, in perfect order. Clear Children sparked interest in the unsettled, rebellious Ruetenik, who attended Lebzeltzer's informal sessions until Leelanau closed them down.

Lebzeltzer's impact on Ruetenik's life was profound. She started exploring a range of religious beliefs, reading *The I Ching*, *The Tibetan Book Of The Dead*, and Kahlil Gibran's *The Prophet* along with Timothy Leary and esoteric poetry. She also became more involved in anti-war demonstrations and progressive causes. When she graduated in 1970, Ruetenik went to New York and sought out Lebzeltzer in the hope that he would help her find direction for her spiritual journey.

Lebzeltzer's New York base was known as the Loft. He and a friend, Phillip 'Ariel' Dross, had moved into a condemned factory and turned it into both a space for exploring spiritual concerns and a hangout for local artists, theatre troupes, and musicians. The Loft's live-in residents camped in tents around a central, communal space. Over that first summer, Ruetenik – now calling herself Shishonee – developed her suite of religious interests to encompass Buddhism, Taoism, Judaism, Scientology, and Christianity.

The Loft too was expanding, its community attracting new members who would pitch their tents on the uncarpeted floor and bring their different artistic talents and spiritual concerns to the commune. The new arrivals included David Karasek, David Lynch, Stephen Gambill, and Stephanie Arje. It was then, as Ruetenik recalls, that "God took our rag-tag, mixed-up, dysfunctional band of gypsies and nurtured something very special within us – the gift of music".

The community had been listening to The Incredible String Band, Philip Glass, The Beatles, Bob Dylan, Joni Mitchell, Judy Collins, Buffalo Springfield, and Ravi Shankar; with each new member, new instruments and talents were added: sitars, harps, Tibetan gongs, silver flutes, wood blocks, and a Shenai horn alongside found objects like old telephone bells, pot lids, and used silverware. Together, they experimented with sounds, plucking and beating at their collection, communing through the shared experiences.

"The early music was strikingly beautiful," Ruetenik recalls. "It was haunting, and a gift given to us, much like speaking in tongues is a gift from the Holy Spirit." Sometimes they would feel as if they were travelling to a specific time or place with the music: a dusty road in Egypt in Old Testament times; an ancient wooden boat buffeted by a swelling sea. "At other times it seemed ethereal, like a small window into heaven had opened up and we could hear the incredible sounds of thousands of angels singing, overtones and light, all blended into one, reaching us in waves of sound," Ruetenik says. The gatherings eventually become more structured, and the community named its musical project The New York Tent City Symphony Of Souls.

Throughout 1970, the community as a whole became less eclectically countercultural and more fixed on spirituality. By the end of the year, they had become explicitly Christian. The residents of the Loft ended their association with Eastern religions and formed a union with the Cathedral Church Of St John The Divine. They also gained a Christian mentor, Canon Edward Nason West. "Throughout those days, our music and creativity flourished, and I was filled with a sense of wonder," Ruetenik says. "During the nightly music and prayer sessions, I honestly believe God sent His angels to sing through our voices."

This joyous period proved to be shortlived once the community got word that the Loft was to be torn down. They went on the road, converting an old school bus into a liveable camper van and embellishing it with Christian slogans. Possessions were given away, financial resources were pooled. As they travelled, stopping off at different Christian communities throughout North America, they still dedicated their evenings to music, which now floated across the landscapes. In September 1971 the troupe, now known as The Trees Group, was invited to sing at their first church concert. The audience was moved by the musicians' blend of uncomplicated melodies and more intricate jams; Ruetenik was inspired to pursue music in a more focused fashion. "I sensed the power in this type of ministry," she says. "I realised I loved performing."

Songs gained structure and performances increased in intensity, with costumes and theatricality as a part of the Trees experience. They would recite scripture as they made their entrance and end their performances with the hymn 'Glory Be To Jesus', clanging bells in front of a huge image of the crucified Christ. The response varied from place to place. The more conservative churches were "cold, and almost hostile", as Ruetenik puts it, while others were "initially shocked and sullen before warming up and then giving us standing ovations". Some of the more liberal churches joined in the performances wholeheartedly, singing and clapping in unison.

The Trees might have remained just another travelling performance community were it not for the decision to release the cassette album *A Portrait Of Christ In Music* (1974) and a vinyl follow-up, *The Christ Tree* (1975). The latter is a startlingly beautiful kaleidoscope of instruments that takes in Christian rock, monastic plainsong, American hymns, and a variety of Asian musical forms: Balinese monkey chants, Buddhist split-singing, Japanese koto and flute music, and Indian ragas.

"Usually either myself or David would write the core of a song then share it with the group," Ruetenik recalls. "Then everyone embellished it, changed it; added instruments, added raga sections." The songs are not dogmatic about the band-members' faith but instead reflect their diverse backgrounds and their liberal, hippie origins – not to mention the day-to-day struggle of living as Christians within cramped and sometimes fractious conditions. There's also a strong earthy sediment rubbing alongside the spirituality of the songs.

The Trees continued as a musical community for another three years. Their return to New York precipitated the crumbling of the group under economic stress, dwindling numbers, and the departure of their leader, Shipen Lebzeltzer. "It was a very sad time for me when the group gradually disintegrated," Ruetenik recalls, "since I was there from the beginning and was there at the very end." By January 1977, she was the sole remaining member. "I did not want it to end. It did not seem like it should have ended when it did. We broke up because one by one people in the group lost the vision or felt they wanted to pursue an education, marriage, raise a family or start a career. I experienced it in many ways like a death and grieved it for some time."

Nevertheless, Ruetenik believes The Trees touched lives. "Because we lived together, and our vocation was our music, our music was living, breathing," she says. "Some will find God in it, others might just enjoy the music on its own, some might be offended or only like some of it. It was and is, I think, a gift from the Lord."

M

If *The Christ Tree* was a halo of light, the albums *Apache* and *Inca*, released between 1970 and 1972 by Satya Sai Maitreya Kali, were hooded darkness. Satya Sai Maitreya Kali was a pseudonym for the rather less exotically named Craig Smith, a musician who had found himself right on the fringes of success for years as the real breaks seemed to just elude him.

Smith had first tried to make it as an actor. He starred in a 1965 pilot about the fictitious adventures of a group called The Happeners; it wasn't commissioned, but it did result in Smith meeting fellow folk-rock hopeful Chris Ducey. The two men recorded together as Chris & Craig, putting out a jolly psych-pop single in 1966 that went nowhere.

Sticking with breezy folk-rock, Smith and Ducey formed The Penny Arkade in Los Angeles, their home at the time. They soon gained the support of The Monkees' Mike Nesmith, who helped find additional band-members, provided them with equipment and a rehearsal space, and produced some recordings, which he then hawked around various record companies. But The Penny Arkade never took off. "We probably weren't good enough to break through," Ducey later recalled. "We were just another bunch of kids trying to break with some average tunes."[1] Nesmith withdrew his support, Smith left, and the group split in 1968.

Mike Nesmith's involvement did leave one important legacy. Penny Arkade songs were recorded by famous names – Glen Campbell, Andy Williams, and The Monkees themselves – and Smith picked up songwriting royalties. He used the proceeds to explore exotic locations, fringe religions, and radical philosophies in Asia and Central and South America.

When he eventually put his roots back down in California, Smith insisted that his name was Maitreya Kali. He had also moved away from folk-rock toward something far stranger: spoken-word sketches and barely-structured loner folk songs that reverberate with torment and distorted reality. He released this new material on two self-released albums, *Apache* and *Inca*. (Smith also had a practical streak, and had few qualms about padding out the material with Penny Arkade songs.)

The Satya Sai Maitreya Kali albums are sometimes compared to the Charles Manson recordings. While *Apache* and *Inca* are far more interesting and innovative, there are echoes of Manson in the crazy-eyed lyrics and the edgy discomfort of Smith's guitar. Furthermore, Smith's liner notes are jumbled and incoherent, giving credence to the woozy and occasionally threatening aura of the albums. Hearing a track as peculiar as the fragile, scratched 'Sam Pan Boat' alongside the sunshine folk-rock of The Penny Arkade's 'Country Girl' only adds to the listener's sense of queasiness.

Smith pressed approximately 300 copies of each album before dropping out of view. His former friends had found him difficult to be around since his return from travelling, and few liked his new musical direction. "It was a sad thing to hear his talent and originally good nature devolve into the loneliness of an echo chamber," Ducey recalled.[2] Although he was collecting royalties until the 90s, Smith's current whereabouts are unknown.

Most of the other privately pressed American LPs of the period were straight singer-songwriter fare or of only intermittent interest, their cachet coming from their hyper-rarity status rather than any intrinsic musical value. (There were a few exceptions: the self-titled, filmy album by the Hawaiian group These Trails; *The Wizard Am I* by the Tolkien-obsessed Gandalf The Grey; and the psychedelic folk-blues of *Ted Lucas*.)

Britain too spawned a number of these obscure recordings. As with their American equivalents, most don't make the grade in terms of quality, but a select few provide listening encounters unlike anything released on a major label at the time: John Fernando and Peter Howell's *Alice Through The Looking Glass*; Shide & Acorn's gothic *Under The Tree*; *Standing Stone* by Oliver (Chaplin); the Steeleye Span-esque self-titled album by Folkal Point; the skin-crawling *True Hearts And Sound Bottoms* by the husband-and-wife duo Vulcan's Hammer.

The best and most consistent privately pressed acid-folk album by a British group came from Norfolk, a county rich in folklore and eccentric history. Ken Saul grew up near the Norfolk coast and picked up a sense of local identity from a young age. "Both my grandmothers and one of my great aunts were great storytellers," he says. "They related tales partly from their own experience but also folky tales, local legends like Black Shuck."

Saul played in a beat group in his early teens but by the time he had turned 17 his interests lay squarely with folk and psychedelic rock. "There were two folk clubs in Yarmouth at that time, and I started going along to them," he recalls. He became infatuated with Fairport Convention, Steeleye Span, and Pentangle, bought two acoustic guitars (one six-string and one 12-string), and started playing the odd floor-spot. He also started working as a session musician at City Music studio in nearby Scratby, and used up slack tape and studio time to record what he now calls "twee singer-songwriter ditties". City Music paid for the release of one single, while Saul himself put out an album of the remaining tracks in 1971.

When the two Yarmouth clubs folded, Saul and his friends began to stage nights in each other's houses before formalising the idea with a new local club. "Paul Corrick and I had this Christmas party night at the club," he recalls. "We played this guitar duet version of 'God Rest Ye Merry Gentlemen', and [then] thought: 'Perhaps we need to do something more than this.'"

In December 1972, Corrick and Saul joined forces with singer Jill Child to become Midwinter. Child's voice was spooky and lilting – perfect for the songs Saul was now writing, which by now were beginning to reflect his fascination with local folklore. 'The Skater', based on the sorrowful tale of The Skater Of Hickling Broad, was one of the first. Legend had it that a soldier, in love with a young woman from a wealthy family, would skate over after dark to rendezvous with her. One night, the ice cracked, and he skated no more. Saul based 'Sanctuary Stone' on a story his aunt used to tell of children running around a local stone seven times and then putting their ear to the ground in order to hear the devil, while another of his songs drew on the Caister Lifeboat Disaster of 1901, which took the lives of two of his uncles. "My ancestry was directly involved," he says. "That was a flavour of things I was getting, rather than traditional songs *per se*."

"I felt we were very Pentangle influenced, two guitarists and a girl singer," Saul says of Midwinter. The group gigged throughout Norfolk and Suffolk, playing Pentangle songs in their live sets, and recorded a demo tape in 1973. This document of the Midwinter years, psychedelic folk at its most tender, was intended simply to gain more gigs rather than to be sent to record companies, but has subsequently been released as a standalone CD, *The Waters Of Sweet Sorrow*.

When Jill Child left for college in 1974, Midwinter came to an end. Saul and Corrick had thoroughly enjoyed the Midwinter experience, however, and looked to form a new band. By this time, Saul was dating Joan Bartle, a classically trained musician who had also studied early music. "She came on the scene being able to play crumhorns and things like that, which added the medieval part," he says.

Another new recruit was Dave Lambert who, like Saul, enjoyed Steeleye Span and modern folk-rock but also loved traditional jigs and reels. Mick Burroughes, who had provided percussion on the Midwinter demos, was a friend of Corrick's; the pair had played in electric and progressive bands. And so, with all the vigour of a new project, Stone Angel began a hectic schedule of gigs throughout East Anglia.

"I think we were oblivious that we were doing anything different," Saul says, "but it did enter our minds at the time that we didn't come across anybody else in Norfolk and Suffolk who had quite the same instrumental line-up as we did." (In fact, there was no other group in the whole country with quite the same range of influences and perspectives as Stone Angel. Although the band Gryphon used crumhorns, they did so largely to enhance their take on progressive rock, while Pentangle's early-music element, which had so inspired Ken Saul, was merely one thread of their overall eclecticism. Crucially, although there were dozens of acts that sang traditional folk from their local area, few if any actually *created* that body of work by reinterpreting local folk legends through original songs.)

Stone Angel began playing in earnest in February 1975 but knew that, by the end of the year, Saul and Corrick would be going to university. "We *were* attracting a lot of attention, at least from local audiences," Saul says. "We were young and naïve, and we thought: 'We'll make a record.' No record company or anything had approached us; probably no one had even heard of us outside of Norfolk and Suffolk. So it was a completely self-financed thing."

Unable to afford a commercial studio, the group roped in their friends to help make *Stone Angel*. They persuaded Eddy Green, a former member of Vulcan's Hammer, to record it on a two-track, and made use of the music studio at Keswick Hall, where Joan had studied. "It ended up as a live recording really, we didn't do any overdubs or anything," Saul says. "We were hoping that the thing was going to be mixed a bit more professionally." After a failed attempt to get a local studio to mix the albums, the songs remained as they were. The band asked another friend, Mel Harris, to provide the cover art, and pressed up 300 copies of the album, eventually shifting around two thirds of them.

As predicted, Saul and Corrick left the local area to follow their studies, although Saul and Joan Bartle (to whom he was now married) continued to play as a trio with Dave Lambert. Stone Angel spent the summer of 1976 playing at a local Country Club, where they were billed as a long-lost village band purportedly discovered by the venue's manager in the wilds of the Norfolk Broads.

After Lambert left the group, the Sauls continued to play semi-professionally as an acoustic duo, sometimes billed as Stone Angel, sometimes not. One night in 1976, they recorded some more songs direct to a cassette recorder in the All Saints Church, Filby. This tape, along with the Midwinter session and the 90 remaining copies of *Stone Angel*, would languish under the couple's bed for years; Joan Saul would occasionally threaten to throw away the box of unsold LPs.

Almost as obscure as Stone Angel is the Holy Grail of British Christian acid-folk: the eponymous 1978 album by Caedmon. The group was formed at Edinburgh University in 1973 by three young musicians and veterinary students, Ken Patterson, Angela Naylor, and Andy Love. "I wasn't from a church background at all, but I was caught by the Christian Union at the age of 14," Patterson recalls. He was also a budding guitarist, inspired equally by Pentangle's folk-rock and the Jesus Music movement of groups who played within contemporary rock forms but explored explicitly Christian content in their lyrics.

In 1974, Caedmon expanded to include Simon Jaquet and Sam Wilson, while Jim Bisset replaced Love. "I was attending Christian meetings and I always fell asleep in them," says Bisset, a rock guitarist and the son of a minister. "Somebody was lecturing away at the front and then there was an announcement that the Christian band Caedmon were looking for a guitarist. I went, thinking 'a folk band? What am I going to do in a folk band?' But the thing was, we got together as Christians rather than because of musical similarity." Indeed, the band-members' tastes included everything from Led Zeppelin and Steely Dan to the disco-funk of Rufus.

Caedmon's creative torrents would spill out on the weekends they spent working on their songs and jamming together as a group. The material that emerged was lilting, inspirational, and sometimes earnest but underpinned by heavy fuzz. The group did not take their lyrics lightly. "There was always a debate about whether we were evangelists trying to give out a message, or whether we were songwriters who happened to be Christians," Patterson recalls. The members' different Christian backgrounds led to a feeling that Caedmon should not seek to create 'message music'.

"I was a bit embarrassed by the happy-clappy chorus type stuff," Patterson says. "It seemed to be important to most Christian bands to be seen to be very overt." Bisset too felt that the band's songs shouldn't just be about conversion. "For me, the music was as much an articulation of what we felt as were the lyrics," he says. "And the music could be seen as Christian or non-Christian standing up in its own right."

In the end, there was a sense that Caedmon served a Christian audience and wanted to express their own beliefs, but that's not all they wanted. They played at secular venues too. "Christians talked through it just as enthusiastically as somebody in a pub when you were playing on a Friday night, though," Bisset recalls.

Aware that their time together was coming to an end, Caedmon planned a farewell concert and an album that they hoped would offer a permanent memento of their time together. No one can quite remember how the money was raised, but they amassed enough to book the local studio, Barclay Towers, for two concurrent Sundays. The first was spent recording the songs, the second tidying them up. "It was the amount of time and money we could afford to give," Patterson says. "There was a common feel in the excitement of the moment."

Indeed, *Caedmon* is a fine album, its devotional content enhanced by Naylor's vocals, the band's dexterous playing, and the serrated, unfinished edges. They pressed up 500 copies and sold pretty much all of them at the farewell gig.

Bisset is sanguine about the group's demise. "The obvious reason is we were all finishing university," he says, "but musically, we were late. In 1978, punk was already mainstream. I can remember buying *Melody Maker* and reading about punk and thinking: 'That's fine, but it's of no interest to us whatsoever.' But it meant, in a sense, we were identified with the dinosaurs. We were getting very, very clever about arrangements, and about song structure, while the rest of the world was saying we've had enough of that, we want to get back to two minutes."

CHAPTER 12

My Rose Has Left Me

"THE BEAUTIFUL DREAM OF THE 60S ... well, we began to realise that it wasn't going to come out as easy as that. It was like a false dawn, if you like," says Ivan Pawle of Dr Strangely Strange. "And it didn't just happen overnight on the stroke of midnight. The 70s were a great time for music, but especially rock I think, really."

An awful lot had happened since *The Holy Modal Rounders*, 'Sunshine Superman', *The 5000 Spirits And The Layers Of The Onion*, *Balaklava*, and *Just Another Diamond Day*. So much glorious, wild innovation took place in folk music that it still seems incomprehensible that it all happened in such a short space of time. These new strains of folk fused with virtually every genre possible and became conduits for the complete human and spiritual experience. There were even a few records sold in the process. So what went wrong?

From about 1972, interest in acid, psychedelic, and progressive folk began to fall. By 1973, this trend had become obvious even to casual observers. As the mid 70s took hold, artists couldn't get record deals, gig attendances dropped to sometimes pitiful levels, and, when such records as these did emerge, they often sounded flat and lifeless. There were exceptions, of course. Many of the best privately pressed records didn't appear until after the glory days, while acid and psychedelic folk continued to enjoy considerable support in mainland Europe. But in the USA and Britain – the two birthplaces of the sound – few seemed to care anymore.

In the UK, three obvious developments shot down the credibility and confidence of the genre: glam rock, the revival of traditional music, and a general lack of great records. It's a truism that perceptible shifts can sometimes highlight imperceptible changes that have already taken place. Here, that first shift – meaningless in terms of any wider trend at the time – can be dated back to 1970.

"Bolan goes electric!" the *Melody Maker* screamed with its review of that year's Tyrannosaurus Rex album, *A Beard Of Stars*. "Never before has T. Rex sounded so heavy or exciting. With the presence of new bongo and percussion man Mickey Finn, and a Clapton influence on Marc's electric guitar wailing, the two-man group achieve a whole new variety of effects while retaining their jolly, poetic appeal."[1]

Although they were still a duo, Tyrannosaurus Rex sounded like a full band on *A Beard Of Stars*. Producer Tony Visconti had made a leap forward in terms of self-assurance and general adventurousness, and the result was a more accessible sound than ever before. There was layering, effects, bass, organ, and a bona fide rock epic in the form of the closing track, 'Elemental Child'. There was less whimsy. There were fewer warbles. There was more *strut*.

"I always seem to have ideas long before I can carry them out," Bolan revealed around the time of the album's release. "I mean, T. Rex has sounded like *Beard Of Stars* to me for two years. I was *always* going to do it ... even when we did 'Debora', it was always 'next week I'll plug my Stratocaster in'."[2]

In private, Bolan was still sulking about his lack of success. His wife, June, was getting sick of hearing how he was going to jack it all in to become a poet; in early July, she snapped at him to put up or shut up. That same day, Bolan came up with 'Ride A White Swan'. He knew he had something, and phoned Visconti straight away. Visconti worked the pop song as he had done 'King Of The Rumbling Spires' and Tyrannosaurus Rex's other electric single, 'By The Light Of The Magical Moon', although this time he gilded more, adding Spector-esque strings and (at Bolan's insistence) a 50s-style tape-echo on the guitar.

'Ride A White Swan' was released in October 1970, the first record to come out under the newly shortened name T. Rex. It was brilliant, and it gave the British public something they didn't know they wanted: glam rock. The single soared to Number Two on the UK charts, helped by preening, pouting performances on *Top Of The Pops*. When Bolan sang about druids from "the old days", he might as well have been referring to his own recent past.

Not everyone made the jump with Bolan: a few loyal flower children voted with their feet and walked out of *Beard Of Stars*-era gigs. Boos and catcalls were heard in 1971, when T. Rex played the Weeley Festival. And when John

Peel played one of the band's biggest hits that year, he announced: "That was called 'Get It On', but I couldn't wait to get it off." (According to his diary, Peel hadn't been in touch with his once close friend, Bolan, since earlier in the year.)

Bolan was unconcerned by these comments from former friends and hippies. "I always wanted to be a rock'n'roll star," he said. "I went through the flowers and peace period, but I don't feel that way anymore."[3] He wasn't alone. "You just couldn't get anybody interested," says Peter Eden, who was working as an independent producer at the start of the 70s. "A few of the labels did some obscure things, but people moved onto smaller labels, or their own labels."

Glam became the UK's undisputed musical monarch. Record companies loved it: it sold and sold and sold. Acid and psychedelic folk, on the other hand, was tied to the 60s and smothered under a glitter bomb. "Before we knew it, the acoustic boom was over, and everyone was going electric and cranking up for big shoulder pads and silver jumpsuits," Alisha Sufit of Magic Carpet recalls. Bill Fay had recently made one of the most personal and complex albums of the period, but now felt the powerful effect of glam on the music scene. "All of a sudden – or it seemed that way – platform shoes came in and the conscious song went out of the window," he says.

There was no route back to the folk clubs, either. While artists like Forest and Jan Dukes De Grey busied themselves in underground clubs and on the university circuit, conservatism spread among the grassroots. Marianne Segal was one of the performers who fell victim to this new traditionalism. "I can remember walking in one day and someone said: 'Good god, here comes Led Zeppelin,'" she says of performing with The Marianne Segal Band during 1972–73. "Those were the sorts of comments we were getting."

"All the folk clubs became boring, middle-class," says Clive Palmer. "You got these long, dragged-out songs that don't have any good tunes to them, and it doesn't really work. You got these endless guitar singers, millions of them – Fred Smith, Joe Something, people you've never heard of. And they all sat there and listened to this rubbish because it was done in the right way."

Mike Heron also noticed the change. "The folk scene became very hand on the ear, very traditional," he says, adding that The Incredible String Band were squeezed out in a different way. "The kind of gigs we were being offered were not really any good for us. People wanted to go and see huge stadium concerts, where it would be an act that they knew really well. It was singing *at* the audience, rather than involving the audience, which is what we were all about."

Folk music was being ghettoised; acts like the String Band, who had benefited in the late 60s from having a mix of folk roots and experimental rock literacy, now found that they no longer appealed to a wide audience. This was further reflected by changes in the British music press. *Melody Maker*, the market leader, had already veered toward progressive rock when the *New Musical Express*, lagging behind, underwent a radical change in an attempt to catch its rival's coattails. Out went the pop coverage and the bland writing; in came a focus on rock, often written in the gonzo journalistic style. This much-needed makeover saved the *New Musical Express* from closure, but there was collateral damage. Gonzo journalism could be incredibly exciting, but it could also be arrogant and tactless, and tended toward a scorched earth principle. Music with the stench of yesterday was at best treated with suspicion; at worst it was mercilessly derided. Psychedelic folk carried just such a stench.

The success of The Incredible String Band had, to a large extent, been responsible for ushering in the great surge of the late 60s. Now, the group's decline was a definite harbinger that the surge was over. There have been many theories put forward as to why the String Band lost their edge: Scientology, personal differences, Joe Boyd's return to America, the move from Elektra to Island. Whatever the reason, by 1971 it was obvious that the glory days would not be relived.

"I think the main reason the band fell to bits was that [our] kind of music was not fashionable any more," Mike Heron recalls. He also felt that the switch to Island, as part of a package deal arranged by Boyd, was not quite right for the band. Their final albums, *Liquid Acrobat Regards The Air* (1971) and *Earthspan* (1972) were actively disappointing; for *Rolling Stone*, the latter was "a slick, precious, thoroughly pretentious mess" and "the lowest point the Incredibles have reached".

The Incredible String Band officially disbanded in October 1974. "There were no hassles, no big emotional scenes, no financial or legal complications," a press statement read. "So, with just a little nostalgia and a great deal of affection for each other and our public, we are all getting our new directions together."

It was inevitable that the weakening of the big players' hands would have knock-on effects further down the commercial scale. Transatlantic Records made a huge error of judgement by pressing up vast quantities of Pentangle's 1970 album *Cruel Sister*, expecting it to sell as well as its predecessor, *Basket*

Of Light. Instead, the album was an unmitigated commercial failure, leaving Transatlantic with thousands upon thousands of unsold copies. The label tried to make up for its losses in a variety of ways; skimping on a distribution deal with the independent Village Thing imprint was one of them.

"The whole company [Transatlantic] seemed to be going into meltdown," Village Thing founder Ian A. Anderson recalls. "And we were small fry. They just started making it more and more difficult. Me and my then wife, Maggie Holland, had to bear the brunt of making excuses to the artists of why records weren't in shops, why they weren't coming out when they were supposed to, why advertising that was supposed to be done wasn't being done. We were getting really, really depressed."

Village Thing had had a concurrent – and more commercially successful – line in putting out comedy albums by local performers, such as Fred Wedlock. "The very final Village Thing release was a guy called Noel Murphy, who was a really popular Irish performer around the folk clubs," Anderson recalls. "Now *that* should have sold shit-loads, but it vanished without trace." No longer able to maintain the artist-centred approach upon which the label had been founded, Anderson pulled the plug on Village Thing in 1973.

Events such as these highlighted the fragile foundations on which the boom years had been built. Record companies' poor distribution and promotion strategies had proved frustrating to artists and fans alike, but there had been an upside. The sheer volume of releases in the style meant there was *general* coverage of the sound, even if individual acts felt that their own records were sidelined. There had also been the lifeline of the university circuit, but that too was now in decline following the emergence of purpose-built, rock-oriented venues.

"These venues were our main livelihood," Martin Welham of Forest recalls, "[so] we and many of our fellow musicians would struggle to find work as the promoters increasingly booked only the bigger acts into the bigger venues. From comparing notes with other bands, we found that this was the norm for most acoustic acts."

Like The Incredible String Band, many of the acts that had once blazed the psychedelic folk trail were now dabbling in new directions and making indifferent if not poor records. Donovan's fatigued, vaguely rock-edged *Cosmic Wheels* (1973) felt forced and self-conscious, as if trying far too hard to prove its significance to the modern scene. Comus regrouped at Virgin Records' request to make *To Keep From Crying* (1974), a reasonable Sparks-esque album that nonetheless falls well short of the startling mania of *First*

Utterance. Marianne Segal cut a synth-heavy disco single, 'Love Amnesia', as Marianne Chase; Derek Noy recorded an unreleased Pink Floyd-style album, *Strange Terrain*, before reinventing himself as Rip Snorter for the punk send-up 'Standing In A Little 'Ole'. The have-a-go spirit might still have been there, but none of these records led to sustainable second careers.

Of all the UK psychedelic folk artists of the first era, the most artistically successful was Robin Williamson. His new project, The Merry Band, contained links to his past but was not tied to it. "The Merry Band was something that grew very much out of being in America," he says. "I moved to America after the String Band in 1975, and The Merry Band was from 1976 to 1979. The idea was to write new songs in a Celtic format, with a Chieftains-style line-up of harp, flute, mandocello, and that sort of thing."

The Merry Band played predominantly on the West Coast of America and only came to Britain rarely. They released three albums: *Journey's Edge* (1976), *American Stonehenge* (1978), and the bardic strangeness of *A Glint At The Kindling* (1979), an autobiographical work about Williamson's childhood in Scotland. By the mid 70s, however, most others had either given up on music or resigned themselves to recording without a deal, and could only watch on as Steeleye Span had a Number Five smash with 'All Around My Hat'. This was no freak hit: it was rousing, simplistic 'rock-folk' music aimed squarely at a mass market.

"The way we are interpreting what we are doing is lighter, not so intellectually bogged down musically and more fun," Bob Johnson, who replaced Martin Carthy in the group, told *Melody Maker* in 1975. "I would agree that it is becoming a little more commercialised. To me, commercial means getting as many people as possible to listen to what you're doing, which is what we want."[4] Thanks in part to 'All Around My Hat', folk as inane knees-up was the prevailing popular image in the later 70s. A small-scale progressive project like The Merry Band stood no chance.

There was also another, more sinister undertone to folk's image during this period. "We were, if you like, flying the flag for the history of England in the 70s," Ashley Hutchings says of his group The Albion Band, a behemoth of electric folk throughout the following decades. "[But] it became a very difficult position, our wish to celebrate this country's past, because we'd been hijacked to a certain extent by the British National Party." This potential association with Far Right, blood-and-soil nationalism – a tragic irony, given folk's longstanding involvement with social justice and leftwing politics – gave younger people yet another reason to stay away.

As the 80s began, the negative connotations were legion: folk music was conservative, old-fashioned, irrelevant, and riddled with bad clothes. Malcolm Taylor, who has worked at the Vaughan Williams Memorial Library at Cecil Sharp House since 1979, felt this keenly. "The media painted it in a particular way, with the stereotypical images they put forward," he says. "It was devalued a lot. And it couldn't get a place on the airwaves. It was really at a low ebb."

Much the same brickbats were hurled at hippies, who were now seen as naively idealistic, old-fashioned, irrelevant, and riddled with bad clothes. Perhaps unsurprisingly, psychedelic folk music became a target for satire. Neil Pye, the long-haired, pacifist, vegetarian character from the BBC comedy series *The Young Ones*, proved so popular that he released a single in 1984: a cover of Traffic's 'Hole In My Shoe' backed with an Incredible String Band caricature, 'Hurdy Gurdy Mushroom Man'. The follow-up LP, *Neil's Heavy Concept Album*, listed contributors either as 'Horrible Electric Musicians' or 'Beautiful Acoustic Musicians'; Spirogyra's Barbara Gaskin made a guest appearance as Pye's mother on 'Bad Karma In The UK'.

More palpable still in its lampooning of the hippie folk era was The Singing Corner, a series of sketches on the BBC Saturday morning show *Going Live!* in which two mild-mannered hippies, played by Trevor Neal and Simon Hickson, would get the hapless pop star of the day to "swing their pants" to a sing-along folk ditty. Like Neil Pye, The Singing Corner also released a single, this time a version of Donovan's 'Jennifer Juniper'. (Donovan himself appreciated the joke enough to appear as a guest vocalist.)

The parodies continued into the 90s with Vic Reeves and Bob Mortimer's Mulligan & O'Hare, a pair of folk singers bordering on middle age. Although they tended to target the more easy-listening end of folk, there was a definite hint of the String Band in their use of "ancient and mystical instruments" on their reinterpretation of Phil Collins's 'In The Air Tonight'.

All of these characters were aimed at an audience too young to remember psychedelic folk music firsthand. But the success of these creations depended not only on the talented writers and performers who brought them to life; it rested on the widely held view of folk performers (and folkish hippies in particular) as toothless, outmoded, and faintly ludicrous – a tenacious image that would last into the early 21st century.

M

Although there were significant parallels between the US and UK acid and psychedelic folk scenes, there were differences, too. They were siblings, not twins. Most of the American acts were solo performers, rather than bands, while there was no commercial breakthrough of the kind seen in the UK during 1967–68. Donovan was the most successful of these artists in the USA, and his music always retained its footing in more accessible sounds. There was no genuinely out-there yet successful flag-bearer to compare with The Incredible String Band – even Tim Buckley never really rose above cult status.

The decline in interest happened at roughly the same time, however. Although glam didn't take hold in the USA, there was still a musical and cultural shift that made psychedelic folk look like it was stuck in the 60s. There was also an ebbing away of musical innovation, although the later albums by America's leading lights were generally more consistent than those by their British counterparts, even if they lacked some of the earlier sparkle. Psychedelic folk left the American consciousness not with a slammed door but with a quiet goodbye.

The new trend at the start of the 70s was a move toward *adult* and *serious* music. The baby boomers were settled and mellowing, and taste had shifted away from pop, loud rock, and experimentation toward singer-songwriters who peddled introspection and endless unpicking of relationships. Lester Bangs, for one, hated it. In a 1971 article for *Who Put The Bomp*, he termed this music 'I-Rock' "because most of it is so relentlessly, involutedly egocentric that you finally actually stop hating the punk and just want to take the poor bastard out and get him a drink, and then kick his ass, preferably off a high cliff into the nearest ocean".[5] (To make his feelings plain, Bangs titled his piece 'James Taylor Marked For Death'.)

The carrier pigeon for this new music was FM radio, which had emerged in earnest in the late 60s as a freer, more challenging counterpoint to the pop-dominated AM radio. Album tracks, not singles, were FM's daily bread, and lent themselves well to a smaller, more knowledgeable, discerning audience. Yet that audience didn't stay small for long, and with the growth of FM radio's reach came commercial pressures. The loose genre in which FM radio specialised – album-oriented rock, or AOR – did not allow for 20-minute flute and bongo workouts. It connoted a *lack* of strangeness. The idea was to create a sustained mood – something that placid singer-songwriters did perfectly.

Those early records by James Taylor, Jackson Browne, Kris Kristofferson, and Carole King might have dealt with emotionally painful subjects, but this was not reflected in the music itself in the way that it was on, say, Skip Spence's *Oar*. Instead, the music has a sedentary feel, with arrangements designed to tastefully show off lyrics but not to interact with them.

There were a few exceptions, particularly early on in the singer-songwriter surge. Dino Valenti's old friend Karen Dalton combined deep blues and slanted folk on *It's So Hard To Tell Who's Going To Love You The Best*; Lottie Golden fused light psychedelia, tragic girl-group pop, and folk on *Motor-Cycle*; and Van Dyke Parks produced a joyous mêlée of the Tim Buckley kind on *Song Cycle*. All of these albums – and more besides – owed something to the openness of psychedelic folk.

Fortunes were mixed for psychedelic folk's original leaders, but none recaptured even the small levels of success they had achieved in the 60s. In the light of the new 'I-Rock', one might have expected Tim Buckley to continue down the path of *Blue Afternoon*; instead he made *Starsailor* (1970), which still stands as one of the most extreme singer-songwriter albums of all time.

If *Lorca* freed Buckley's music of folk's structure and restraint, *Starsailor* marks the point where be shook himself free of folk itself. Buckley now cited the esoteric modern-classic composers Olivier Messiaen and Krzysztof Penderecki as influences alongside John Coltrane and Albert Ayler; the album's title track forms an *a cappella* suite of his voice, with 16 overdubbed tracks of differing timbre, pitch, and volume. After this, Buckley retreated from the avant-garde. He made three mediocre albums before his tragically early death in 1975. His free-folk sound simmered, waiting for an opportunity to be rediscovered by equally unconventional storytellers decades later.

Meanwhile, The Holy Modal Rounders had become what Peter Stampfel calls "a seven-piece jam band" following the departure of Sam Shepard, whose career as a playwright was now very much in the ascendant. Stampfel's frayed relationship with Steve Weber held together long enough for the group to make the countrified *Good Taste Is Timeless* (1971), but "artistic differences" and a general dissatisfaction at playing the toilet circuit soon set in. When the rest of the group decided to relocate to Oregon, Stampfel stayed in New York. The Rounders continued in a number of different guises over the next few years, most notably when Stampfel returned for the 1976 album *Have Moicy!*, billed as a collaboration between Michael Hurley, The Unholy Modal Rounders, and Jeffrey Frederick & The Clamtones. Hurley himself returned to recording with two early-70s albums, *Armchair Boogie* and *Hi-Fi Snook Uptown*, which were issued by Warner Bros' tiny Raccoon offshoot. Both retain the strange grace of his only previous album, *First Songs* (1965), and are always warm and inviting, as if assuming the listener is a friend.

Those few new psychedelic-folk artists to emerge in the 70s did so without the backing of a major label. When Geoffrey De Mers made the Witchseason-like *Geoffrey* in 1972, for example, it was issued not by Elektra or RCA but by Concert Arts, a tiny Maryland label better known for its classical output. Similarly, Gary Higgins's countrified acid-folk album, *Red Hash* (1973), was released by his friends and supporters on the specially created Nufusmoon label while the artist himself was in prison.

In February 1972, *Rolling Stone* magazine described Tom Rapp as someone who "continues to write poetry that has balls, which, amidst all the whining indulgence we are getting these days, is enough of a virtue".[6] It was true: his music was never less than interesting. The lyrics were always thoughtful and original, the elegiac songs garlanded by sensitive yet innovative music.

Rapp delivered five albums in total to Reprise, but by the time of the fourth, *Beautiful Lies You Could Live In* (1971), he had begun to question the level of care the label actually took over his music, especially when his name was misspelled as 'Top Rapp' on the back cover. The label didn't even bother to tell him of its plans to release *Familiar Songs*, a collection of demos, the following year. After that, Rapp signed instead with the much smaller Blue Thumb.

Rapp says that the subsequent *Stardancer* (1972) marked the first time since the ESP-Disk days that he had felt in control of a record. The album features more electrical currents, notably on the science-fiction-themed title track and 'For The Dead In Space', and contains, in 'Fourth Day In July', his most biting anti-war song since *Balaklava*. It was issued under the name Tom Rapp, rather than Pearls Before Swine, and received almost universal critical praise.

The follow-up, *Sunforest*, was mostly recorded at the same time as *Stardancer*. Released in 1973, it marked the end – for 25 years – of Rapp's musical career. Deciding he had achieved all he wanted, he retired while still at the top of his game to forge a second life as a successful civil rights lawyer. His disappearance from the scene was perhaps *the* hammer blow to the survival of psychedelic folk in America. Rapp had released at least one album every year since 1967; now, without his consistency, there was no scene or genre to speak of. Once the ink dried on *Sunforest*'s reviews, records would no longer be classed as psychedelic or acid folk, and the terms themselves would be forgotten.

For now, it was over. Most of the records slowly drifted out of print, having never been strong enough sellers to warrant repressing. During the latter part of the 70s, glam and singer-songwriters were superseded – and to some extent actively slain – by punk and disco. Yet as curious as it may seem, it was punk that laid foundations for a new wave of experimental folk music. It would be a long road back, and there would be much still to overcome, but there *would* be a next generation. The genre was at rest. But it was not dead.

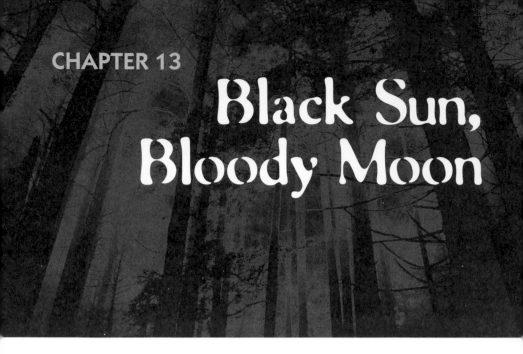

CHAPTER 13

Black Sun, Bloody Moon

ONE OF THE HARDIEST myths in popular music is that punk razed all that came before it. Over the years, punk has become synonymous with iconoclasm, and it's true that much did change when punk seized its day. But sometimes, the most telling trends are not what changes during a revolution, but what remains. The more thoughtful punk artists and commentators always knew that they were part of a lineage, and that this lineage included folk.

Those performers who were perhaps a little older, or whose own music predated the punk supernova (and helped to lay the foundations for it), were more likely to exhibit at least an implicit relationship to folk. Although The Modern Lovers would not release an album until 1976, Jonathan Richman had formed the group in 1970 with an eccentric conviviality with parallels to the untreated style of Michael Hurley. Patti Smith's work drew directly from the same beat and bohemian culture that had inspired Peter Stampfel ten years earlier. Lenny Kaye, Smith's guitarist and collaborator from 1971 onward, orchestrated the *Nuggets* compilation, the first-ever attempt to compile US garage bands of the 60s. Some garage bands – The Soup Greens, The Gregorians, Gypsy Trips – could be termed garage-folk; the most obviously folk-edged *Nuggets* track is 'A Public Execution' by Mouse, whose vocalist, Ronny Weiss, sounds like a punk-folk dime-store Dylan.

British punks shouted louder about severing the umbilical cord of musical history, but even in the UK, the influence of folk was sometimes acknowledged. As Don Letts later recalled: "I stupidly got rid of a lot of great music I was listening to before the ground zero of punk rock. Beatles, Dylan, folk music, which for me is originally punk rock anyway."[1] Poly Styrene of X-Ray Spex also had an unfashionable hippie past. "When I was doing the old hippie trail in Devon and Somerset we were living on the land," she later said. "After that, coming back to London, there was a lot of tacky things that hit me."[2] These sentiments could have come from the mouths of any number of psychedelic folk artists; Poly Styrene channelled her despair at the visual and moral ugliness of consumerism into the X-Ray Spex album *Germ Free Adolescents* (1978).

The parallels between folk and punk are there in the intimate club atmospheres, the involvement of performers of all abilities, the outspokenness of artists, and the tight-knit, regionalised communities. Yet punk took what folk only hinted at – a DIY attitude toward putting out music – and made it one of the movement's most durable legacies, emblematic of a principled anti-corporate stance.

In the USA, this tradition began with Patti Smith's first single, 'Hey Joe' / 'Piss Factory', which she released on her own Mer label in 1974; in the UK, self-releasing became symptomatic of true punk spirit. It all started up in Manchester, when Buzzcocks raised money from friends and family to put out the *Spiral Scratch* EP in January 1977. Recorded in three hours, the EP twinned the dynamic brilliance of the music with an autonomous spirit in getting it heard. But what made it different to virtually every other privately pressed record was the size of its audience: Buzzcocks hit the zeitgeist face on, and sales of *Spiral Scratch* topped 16,000. With Buzzcocks as their inspiration, hundreds of young bands went on to self-release their own raw punk salvos.

The now dormant acid and psychedelic folk music did not feel any immediate benefit from punk; if anything, artists who were still attempting to get a record deal felt only a thickening of the glass ceiling. Martin Cockerham of Spirogyra and Marianne Segal both recall being told by record company executives that, as much as they liked their music, it just didn't fit in anymore. For a select few, however, the switch from psychedelic folk to punk made sense.

"Punk changed everything for me," says Dan Ireton, who had grown up in Boston entranced by Tim Buckley and The Incredible String Band, as well as jazz and experimental rock, but now felt the electrifying vigour of punk. "Everything became exciting again ... for a while, I thought that everything that came before didn't matter anymore, and this was it. Punk also made me realise that I could be a musician: I'd been a lead singer in rock bands in high school, but I had never learned to play an instrument. I just assumed that I couldn't. But now, the whole world was at my feet."

Ireton became Dredd Foole; his band The Din, which featured members of the formidable Mission Of Burma, became a central part of the Boston punk scene. Throughout the 80s, Dredd Foole & The Din were known for their ear-splitting sound; *The Hangman's Beautiful Daughter* was not an audible influence.

Over in Marlborough, Massachusetts, 30 miles inland from Boston, was Bobb Trimble. As an enthusiastic 13-year-old Beatles fan, Trimble had received a guitar from his parents, but music suddenly seemed a lot less thrilling after he began to take lessons. "I was learning chord structures and everything," he recalls, "but it was very theory-based, it was very methodical, and I got nothing out of it. When you're forced to learn how to play, you really don't want to."

Trimble tossed the guitar aside. He would not pick it up again until several years later, when he started to learn anew from friends at the Worcester Academy. Calling themselves Bond, Trimble and his friends began performing around the local area in 1976; they were, he says, "the first rock'n'roll band" ever to play at the conservative Academy. Even now, however, music seemed to him a safe, authorised outlet. It was fun but certainly not rebellious. This was reflected in his earliest songs, mellow ballads inspired by the insular life on the Worcester Academy campus.

Things changed dramatically when Trimble heard *Wormtown '78*, a compilation of local punk bands including four from Worcester: The Towel, Crazy Jack & The Heart Attax, Blue Moon Band, and Hooker. In the issue of the *Wormtown Punk Press* that accompanied the album, local DJ L.B. Worm gave voice to a sense of small-town frustration and the idea of kicking against it with the sheer force of punk rock. "Wormtown," he wrote. "Who would ever think so much could happen in such a short time. Especially here."

"It was really very creative, fast-paced, and furious," Trimble says of *Wormtown '78*. "It was almost like an epiphany." He took another look at his existing songs and, realising that they fell short next to the sonic shots of the Wormtown scene, gave himself a year to come up with something more innovative, consciously changing his patterns of composition in order to challenge himself.

"I take different models of different aspects of life and kind of put them together," he says. "It starts from a certain model and then builds from other viewpoints, with all manner of opinions and interpretations, depending on your perspective. It's like a paint-by-numbers thing." Trimble's creative experiment led him away from straightforward mellow ballads toward something altogether more disconsolate. While punk was certainly the catalyst for his new songs, among them the intensely spooky 'Glass Menagerie Fantasies' and 'When The Raven Calls', they retain aspects of his previous efforts. "They're basically punk ballads," he says, "and I can actually say that without fear of contradiction."

Having assembled a batch of songs, including some rewritten from his high school days, Trimble decided to record them himself. When he pitched up at the local Country Thunder Sound, however, his plans were curtailed by the studio's facilities. "There's a lot of layering process in the sound and different instrumentation going on," he says. "Four-track wasn't enough. You can bounce stuff around but it's limited to how much you can add."

The Country Thunder Sound session was followed by a stint at an eight-track studio in Marlborough, Object Sound, although for Trimble, eight tracks "still didn't seem to be enough". And yet the low-budget studio layering gave the resulting album, *Iron Curtain Innocence* (1980), a truly otherworldly feel. Trimble's tremulous singing voice – sometimes deformed almost to the point of incomprehension – gives the songs an impact that is both directly emotional and distinctly surreal. These are, indeed, 'punk ballads'.

Bobb Trimble funded both the recording and release of the album. "The album sounded good, that was the main thing," he says. "It was recorded well and pressed well, so I was happy with that." Nevertheless, the recording, mastering, and pressing costs took up all of Trimble's budget, so by the time the vinyl was actually in his hands, corners had to be cut with the packaging. The album's cover was originally intended to be full colour, but Trimble ended up having to print it in black and white – a happy accident in that it gave the photograph of Trimble holding a guitar and a machine gun an extra level of roadside-punk grittiness.

Trimble also handled the promotion of the album himself, embarking on epic drives to New York, Philadelphia, and Connecticut to persuade radio stations to play the album. When it came to attracting interest from further afield, Trimble thought outside the box. "I had this stamp collection that my grandfather had given me and I just used all his old stamps to mail out the records," he says. "I really wasn't into stamp collecting."

One song recorded at Country Thunder Sound but not included on *Iron Curtain Innocence* was 'If Words Were All I Had'. "It was for my first boyfriend, Ronnie, who was killed in a car crash," Trimble recalls. The song hadn't come out the way he wanted, but he didn't want to abandon it completely. When he returned to the studio the following year, he used the song as his starting point.

"Maybe it's just as well we started on a tough note, because it just seemed to get better as we went along," Trimble recalls of the *Harvest Of Dreams* sessions. One song, 'Take Me Home Vienna', features his backing band of 12 and 13-year-olds, The Kidds, although their existence proved shortlived as they were forced to disband by parents suspicious of their leader's intentions. "It was a lot of hassle," he says with a sigh.

Conscious of the extent to which technology had curtailed his ambitions for *Iron Curtain Innocence*, Trimble headed straight for a 16-track studio this time. "But there still never seemed to be enough," he says, "with all the different sounds and stuff. We ended up eventually at 32 and even then ... yeah, there was enough by then!"

Harvest Of Dreams retains the outsider despondency and acoustic psychedelia of *Iron Curtain Innocence* but is more elaborate. The album is peppered with samples of telephone answering services, overheard conversations, static and silence. 'Armour Of The Shroud', with its glockenspiel tinkles and anguished, doubled-tracked vocals, is the centrepiece.

As with his previous album, Trimble funded *Harvest Of Dreams* himself. It made only the smallest of splashes when he released it in 1982, with the ripples largely confined to Wormtown. Trimble formed a new band, The Crippled Dog Band, but found it hard to play some of his songs live; the more tranquil among them, such as 'Premonitions' and 'One Mile From Heaven', were either adapted or dropped completely from his live sets. Trimble continued to perform live – and occasionally made recordings – up until the early 90s, but no further albums emerged.

ᛝ

Iron Curtain Innocence and *Harvest Of Dreams* were the first albums to show how the punk ethos could intermingle with folk music. "The first album, especially, was kind of folky," Trimble says. "I thought to myself, I really don't want to be a folk artist. I'm in a rock'n'roll band. I can't really say I'm not a folkie, but I can say that I'm not *only* a folkie. I tend to get put under the umbrella of folk artist, and it's so far away from the reality of who I am. I'm actually a rock'n'roller who wrote a few folk tunes."

While much of the value of these two albums stems from the very character of their author, their fusion of the spirit – if not the obvious stylistic hallmarks

– of folk and punk offered a completely new development. Yet one thing had not changed: the lack of commercial success. Bobb Trimble's albums ran completely under the radar.

Meanwhile, as punk became post-punk, the snotty kid at the back of the class grew into an overconfident, sharp-minded adolescent. Few groups epitomised this transition more perfectly – or with more speed – than Wire, who within a few short years had accelerated beyond the 28-second 'Field Day For The Sundays' to the punk-prog 'Map Ref. 41°N 93°W', which they 'promoted' by putting on a piece of performance art involving a procession of people pouring water into a glass.

Although there was no overt folk influence in Wire's music, the group's swift evolution from rudimentary minimalism to elongated ingenuity – and the eclecticism of post-punk generally – would have a clear impact on future folk. More immediately, when Wire disintegrated in 1980, band-members Bruce Gilbert and Graham Lewis founded the experimental music label Dome and brought out an exceptional album by an outsider folk artist who otherwise would probably have gone unrecorded.

Michael O'Shea was born in Northern Ireland but grew up across the border, in Eire. He was an itinerant and a dilettante; he claimed, in the liner notes to his only album, to have been a soldier, a labourer, a social worker, a psychonaut, a transvestite, a sculptor, a musician, and an instrument maker. That last occupation referred primarily to the Mo Cara (Gaelic for 'my friend'), an electric-sitar-like instrument fixed to what O'Shea called the Black Hole Space Echo Box that he developed and refined over a number of years. The Mo Cara emitted an unnerving and sometimes threatening drone – much like COB's dulcitar – and was certainly ear-catching. In 1980, while busking in London, O'Shea was invited to take up a residency at Ronnie Scott's, which then led him to a support slot for Ravi Shankar at the Royal Festival Hall.

O'Shea was not particularly affected by punk. He had been making music for years, and punk caused no discernible stylistic shift; rather, he found that his awkward folk now resonated strongly with the cerebral post-punk community. Returning to busking after his residency at Ronnie Scott's ended, O'Shea attracted the attention of Tom Johnston of The The, who introduced him to Gilbert and Lewis.

O'Shea was initially unresponsive to Gilbert and Lewis's offer for him to record for Dome. He had not been especially happy at Ronnie Scott's, and was now convinced that his music sounded better in the street. A year later, however, he changed his mind and turned up at the studio Gilbert and Lewis had told him about. The pair must have been surprised, but they honoured their original offer, and *Michael O'Shea* was born. It was one of the last of only a handful of Dome releases.

Michael O'Shea mixes the humming modernity of the Mo Cara with a folk-club floor-spot ambience, Eastern rhythms, traditional Irish music, and its author's vagabond humanity. It's as if Brian Eno had performed at Les Cousins. O'Shea then appeared on the former punk musician Stano's album *Content To Write In I Dine Weathercraft* (1983) but generally favoured performance over recording. In the late 80s, he aligned himself with the rave scene, but sadly passed away in 1991 following a road traffic accident.

In among the plethora of post-punk narratives was a particular grouping of experimental musicians whose work was tagged as 'industrial' and commonly characterised by a heaviness and harshness, disquieting imagery, tape loops, machine-like noise, dislocated vocals, and challenging live performances. The term is widely disliked by those who were branded with it. To David Tibet, the founder and leader of Current 93, it means only "one group and one record label". Tibet is referring to Throbbing Gristle, the highly charged and confrontational group led by Genesis P-Orridge, and their label, Industrial Records. Throbbing Gristle split up, after five tumultuous years, in 1981. Out of the debris came Psychic TV, or PTV, whose debut album, *Force The Hand Of Chance* (1982), opens, uncharacteristically, with the gentle, acoustic 'Just Drifting'.

Born David Michael Bunting, Tibet played briefly with Psychic TV during 1982–83 before recording a 12-inch EP of his own, *LAShTAL*, with PTV's John Balance and Fritz Häaman of 23 Skidoo. "I remember describing it later as 'pseudo-shamanic'," he says of this early work. "It was fine, but it was just 19, 20-year-old kids being weird. I think we were playing thigh bones on it." Tibet's recordings were immediately tagged as industrial, but were always more personal than that. "It's just lazy categorisation," he says, "which I really despise."

As far as Tibet is concerned, Current 93 didn't truly begin until *Nature Unveiled* (1984). By then, he had temporarily fallen out with Balance and struck up a creative partnership with Nurse With Wound's Steven Stapleton. From here on in, Tibet marked himself out as an absolute individual with a particular worldview. "It's got the apocalypse, it's got Christianity, it's got Antichrist," he says of *Nature Unveiled*, "and they're things that still drive me."

David Tibet describes his belief system as "93 per cent Catholic and seven per cent Thelemite" – Thelemite being the order of occultist Aleister Crowley's followers – and has a vast range of intellectual and theological concerns. His lyrics and delivery often seem menacing and uncompromising. "What I have to do is be as honest as I can to myself, even if that attempt at absolute honesty [is] incomprehensible to anyone else," he explains. "It's not incomprehensible to me. Perhaps God also finds it incomprehensible. But I've got great faith in His mercy and His patience."

For the first few years of Current 93, the conduit for Tibet's text was the chanting malevolence exemplified by 'Falling Back In Fields Of Rape' (1984), an astonishing piece that evokes bright yellow and blood red in whirring, looping blades of sounds. By the time of *Dawn* (1987), however, he had reached an artistic fork. "It was OK," he says, "but I could churn things like that out in my sleep. I could keep on doing this forever, and it's just not what interests me." *Dawn* would be the last Current 93 release of its type. "Of course there are some people who say that everything I did after *Dawn* was a complete sell-out because I started using acoustic guitars, and obviously wasn't *truly* darkness," Tibet says. "I gave up darkness for *Tales Of The Riverbank*, or something like that."

The first album on which Tibet really explored folk music was *Swastikas For Noddy* (1988). The vocals are direct and vulnerable, sometimes unaccompanied, and feel truly related to oral folk tradition, while the crinkled acoustic guitars are reminiscent of the difficult end of the post-String Band British folk boom. The album's preoccupations, however, are as individualist as ever. "I was on top of a roof and I'd been taking acid, and I was obsessed with Noddy," Tibet says. He believed Enid Blyton's creation to be a Gnostic icon and saw an image of the character being crucified. "I then thought: 'What's the most unsuitable Christmas present we could give to Noddy?'"

The album's title was sometimes misunderstood, provoking unfounded rumours of far-right leanings. But for those Current 93 followers who had followed Tibet since the PTV association, the idea of Tibet invoking Nazi symbolism was not entirely unexpected. Ironically, his departure from the *sound* of *Dawn* provided a much bigger shock. "It's such an odd record," Tibet says now. "People were going: 'You've destroyed yourself; people are going to hate this record.' They said it sounded like Simon & Garfunkel."

Tibet was just as unhappy to be pigeonholed as a folk artist as he had been to be called an industrial musician. Current 93 had worked at an incline to industrial music, and now did the same to folk. The difference, this time, was that there was no real contemporary experimental folk scene comparable to the industrial one. This led Tibet – with tongue in cheek – to create his own terminology. Asked by his distributors for a category to file *Swastikas For Noddy* under, he came up with apocalyptic folk.

"It was 'folk' as in 'guys' – almost like 'we're hipsters' or 'we're apocalyptic guys'," he says. "It was a joke, maybe slightly obscure, but it was a joke at myself, and also a joke at people's conceptions of what I was doing and what the music was." Much to Tibet's chagrin, apocalyptic folk became a genre title itself. "It's not a category for others," he says. "Because no other bands that did 'apocalyptic folk' were coming from a Christian perspective."

During the later 80s and beyond, apocalyptic folk was linked to the wider term neo-folk and splinter genres such as folk noir, industrial (and indeed post-industrial) folk, dark ambient folk, and numerous other verbose inventions. What neo-folk and its subgenres sought to describe was music that included acoustic instruments, but that did so within a tableau of other sound experimentation and controversial imagery. Use of the term seemed nebulous, to say the least: it was applied to everything from Joy Division-esque introspection to brutal industrial soundscape (and most consistently to the group Death In June, whose leader, Douglas Pearce, contributed to *Swastikas For Noddy*).

The mischievous impulse that led to the 'apocalyptic folk' tag was writ large on the cover of Current 93's next album, *Earth Covers Earth* (1988), which parodies *The Hangman's Beautiful Daughter*. Like *Swastikas For Noddy*, the album explores the relationship between Tibet's own obsessions and folk-based music. The direct influence of those folk artists whom Tibet admires peeps through at times, even if he is wary of acknowledging too much of a connection.

"I don't really like folk music at all," Tibet says. "But there are certain acts within folk that are so exquisitely truthful, like Shirley Collins. I remember talking to her once about folk music. Obviously she loves the tradition, and she squeezed my hand. 'Oh, David,' she said, 'I don't like folk very much either.'"

The late 80s were just the beginning for David Tibet. With *Swastikas For Noddy* and *Earth Covers Earth*, Current 93's music marked the first *sustained* radical folk music project since punk. As a result, it was in itself wholly distinctive, and made even more so because Current 93 carried with it a responsibility toward Tibet's own preoccupations. Tibet himself was still a long way from working through these apocalyptic fixations. He was also only in the first phase of his complex relationship to folk.

Current 93's music gained exposure and interest, even if it was largely confined to the British underground. Still, Tibet's experience of resistance to *Swastikas For Noddy* shows that a profound suspicion of folk music was still embedded in the reactions of public and press, even within the supposedly more open-minded congregation of the young post-punk avant-garde.

"If somebody knocks at the door it could be Christ," Tibet says. "We never know what's coming. It could be Christ. But it's more likely to be the postman." If Tibet, along with Michael O'Shea and Bobb Trimble, were making records that incorporated folk into a new musical topography, could there be a second coming of experimental folk music? Perhaps. We never know what's coming.

CHAPTER 14

Whither Thou Goest

MUSICIANS SELDOM offer up a term to describe their sound; journalists, of course, are obsessed with doing so. In 1984, the *New Musical Express* described Billy Bragg's music as "a fervent and earnest sort of white soul".[1] This, it might be reasonably argued, was a long-winded way of saying 'folk'. The absence of the f-word is telling. Folk had become démodé; the term was rarely invoked for artists intended to appeal to a rock audience. But the closeting of folk wasn't just down to journalists. By now, the British folk establishment had a reputation even in its own cloisters for snobbery and exclusion. As the number of folk clubs diminished, a siege mentality grew.

"Billy Bragg would naturally have come out of a folk club, but instead of that, he went to punk," says Malcolm Taylor, the Director of the Vaughan Williams Memorial Library at Cecil Sharp House. "You'd hear other stories, like [when] Elvis Costello wanted to play at Ewan MacColl's club [but] couldn't get a space." Rock and folk continued to view each other with mutual suspicion. Often, the only way bands would discuss a folk influence was to disassociate it from its 60s and 70s genus. "The folk world's become part of the heritage industry," John Jones of The Oyster Band told the *New Musical Express* in 1988. "Everyone went into their various specialisations in the '70s, getting their Morris steps right and creating this village way of doing it."[2]

There was less of a linguistic battleground in the USA. In 1986, *BAM* magazine called 10,000 Maniacs "an 80s version of Fairport Convention"[3] – but with no implicit snarky condemnation. A few years earlier, R.E.M.'s Michael Stipe had told *Alternative America* that folk-rock was the closest he and his band-mates had come to summing up their style – "and that's so indefinable in 1982 that it probably works".[4]

Meanwhile, down in the underground, a dearth of acid, psychedelic, and experimental folk music was being made. Those artists who emerged during the 80s and early 90s were not of one type: some were individual chimeras who found that an atypical take on folk somehow suited the contents of their head; others knew their history, and deliberately challenged existing musical trends. All of them bucked the dominant tendency to baulk at folk.

Formed in 1977 in Eugene, Oregon, The Tree People made particularly fragile folk music. "The main thing I go for is mood," the trio's founder, Stephen Cohen, explained in 1980. "That's why I play it, I guess. There's a certain mood I'm just trying to get."[5] *The Tree People* (1979) captures a minimal, delicate style that could have come from a decade earlier; the cover art – an infantile sketch in black and white – seems to anticipate the deliberate naïveté of some later acid-folk releases. The cassette-only follow-up, *Human Voices* (1984), sounds even more out of time. The group split soon after.

The Tree People fell just over the edge of the first generation of acid folk, but were far too early for the second. They made music in the American folk tradition, bringing to it a frail, ethereal quality that resulted in a gentle kind of neo-psychedelia. *The Tree People* does not sound like a conscious attempt at an acid-folk revival. It was a natural happenstance.

The husband-and-wife duo of Veno Dolenc and Melita Osojnik formed Sedmina in the same year, 1977, but almost a world away, in Slovenia. Although Slovenia was part of communist Yugoslavia, there was a relatively free exchange of ideas with Western Europe; French *chanson*, in particular, influenced 60s and 70s Yugoslav folk-pop.

Sedmina's first album, *Melita And Veno Dolenc* (1980), is doused in sweet harmonies and unusual instrumentation, including tamboura; the follow-up, *Il Dejanje* (1982), is truly transcendental. It's as if the progressive folk of the early 70s had carried on progressing, with elongated songs and complicated arrangements offering changes of mood and very few handles for the first-time listener to grasp. The two singers' voices pick tartly at each other, while the Max Ernst-like artwork gives a fair approximation of the constantly shifting music. The couple divorced later the same year. Veno went on to record with his new wife, Klarisa M. Jovanoviç, first as Duma and then, once again, as Sedmina.

The distinctive Basque region between Spain and France spawned two late-70s groups with similarities to Sedmina. Haizea produced *Hontz Gaua*

(1979), which looked back to the elongated jam-folk of the early 70s; Itziar made a self-titled album the same year that took its cues from progressive music, particularly in its use of operatic vocals.

The Bavarian duo Fit & Limo released their first cassette, *Haende Hoch*, in 1982. It was just the start of a torrent of sweet, lo-fi punk-pop that would continue throughout the 80s. Then, in 1993, they unveiled a new sound on the covers EP *This Moment: Fit & Limo Play Incredible String Band*. The subsequent *Angel Gopher* LP mixed the String Band influence with even headier Eastern modes and hippie wafts, but did so in the loving, endearingly handmade style of the duo's earlier work.

Fit & Limo released several more albums of updated Krautfolk on September Gurls Records, one of the few labels to offer a platform to psychedelic folk music in the 90s. They even collaborated with Bernd Witthüser (of Witthüser & Westrupp), creating a continuum between two generations of acid folk. And they were also an important influence on some of the very earliest practitioners of the new psychedelic folk in America. Both Timothy Renner of Stone Breath and Jeffrey Alexander of The Iditarod were fans; Renner included Fit & Limo on his 2002 *Hand / Eye* compilation, while Alexander found room for the duo on his label's tribute to Tom Rapp, *For The Dead In Space*.

Similar stirrings could be heard in Japan. Nagisa Ni Te, led by Shinji Shibayama and Masako Takeda, twinned delicate, psychedelic folk with post-punk valour on albums such as *On The Love Beach* (1995). "I was once trapped by the theory of improvisation," Shibayama recalled in 2001, "but as I didn't like the stiff atmosphere which is often present in so-called 'free jazz', I applied it to the folk song. In short, we recorded without practicing."[6]

Another hybrid group with acid-folk elements was Ghost, formed in 1984 by Masaki Batoh. The group enjoyed a nomadic and shape-shifting early period, passing through temple remains and abandoned subway stations. *Ghost* (1990) is rooted in psychedelia and damaged folk and was influenced by Batoh's experiences in Morocco and Europe as well as the more extreme end of Krautfolk.

Both *Ghost* and *Second Time Around* (1992) were picked up for worldwide release by Drag City in 1997. "We played a form of free improvised music," sax player Taishi 'Giant' Takizawa later recalled. "The songs were meant to be heard as requiems in the ruins of some ancient forest that had been flattened by a typhoon."[7]

At that time, Ghost lived in a large communal house in Tokyo; the band consisted of whoever was passing through. "Those 'psychedelic' years were a great time," bandleader Masaki Batoh said, "because it was so free and things were just allowed to happen naturally."[8]

Back in the USA, and taking the self-releasing, independent attitude to a conclusion that Jorge Luis Borges would be proud of, was Jandek. "I'm an inordinately private person," he told *Spin* in a rare interview. "I have declined interviews and things like that because I just put out a product and that's it. I don't want to get too involved."[9]

Jandek – or, as some would have it, Sterling Richard Smith – is a free-floating signifier, the musician who exists only in a recording or performance space. Corwood Industries is his practical front, taking care of releasing albums and handling administration. The true intent or identity behind Jandek does not matter; it is only when others interpret him that Jandek lives. Until he made the surprising move to live performance in the mid 2000s, he was known only through the blurred, ambiguous photos on his album jackets.

Jandek originally called his project The Units, but got a rude awakening when he sent out promo copies of his first album, *Ready For The House* (1978): a letter, sent by registered mail, from another group called The Units, who threatened to sue. So he needed a new name. "It was January, and I was speaking on the phone with somebody named Decker," he later recalled. "So I just combined the two."[10] He felt pretty confident that no one had thought of *that* before.

Jandek's music offers isolated chinks of remoteness. The first thing that hits is the guitar-playing: meandering, simple, harsh, grating, and expressive of some soul-slicing trauma. He uses different tunings on every album, sometimes every song. "Everyone says the guitar's out of tune," he subsequently explained, "but to me, if it's out of tune to my mind, I can tell immediately."[11] And then there's the voice: twisted with lament, as if it's reverberated through his soul until – by chance – finding an exit through his mouth. The lyrics weep and sigh.

Jandek could have been featured in many chapters of this book. But he would always have spiked out, snagging the narrative flow, a reminder that the story of music does not flow from point A to point B. It's a long way to the back of the bus.

While most mainstream music journalists had lost or shunned their collective folk vocabulary, one publication took a different approach. *Ptolemaic Terrascope* did not separate out new music from earlier eras, and it proudly covered acid and psychedelic folk. "With the *Terrascope*, we were simply writing about the stuff we happened to like, irrespective of labels or trends," says Phil McMullen, who founded the magazine in 1989 and edited it until 2005. "We covered folk music ever since our inception, but not because we were making any kind of a point or endeavouring to rekindle an interest."

Ptolemaic Terrascope favoured championing unknown and underappreciated acts over criticising those it didn't like. It preferred independently released music, since that indicated a freedom of approach. And it preferred looking for invisible threads between artists rather than following established cues. In the Terrastock Nation, Current 93 rubbed alongside Barry Dransfield, and both sat comfortably alongside The Legendary Pink Dots and The Bevis Frond. "I would frequently mix things up so that no one issue featured an overload of any one style of music," McMullen says.

The magazine was important in more that just a general horizon-expanding sense. Many of its readers were musicians, or musicians-to-be; *Ptolemaic Terrascope* introduced them, for the first time, to some of the esoteric folk music that was firmly off mainstream media's radar. Readers loved the magazine to an almost obsessive extent, and would be among the first to pick up on and perpetuate new directions in folk music. But it took the intervention of the singer from the 70s progressive-rock group Curved Air to give the term 'acid folk' a new lease of life.

As a former rock goddess, Sonja Kristina may seem like an unlikely starting point for the rebirth of acid-folk, but in fact, beneath her prog credentials, she had strong folk form. She got her first guitar at the age of 12 and soon started singing from the floor in the folk clubs of Brentwood, Essex, and Romford, on the outskirts of London. By 15, she had herself a well-connected manager, Roy Guest, and was writing her own songs as well as performing contemporary American material. Her biggest influence was Buffy Sainte-Marie. "She took things from a different place," Kristina says. "The melodies and tunes. And she had a very strident way of playing the guitar: she was raw and fiery."

By 1967, the self-starting 18-year-old was running evenings at the Troubadour, in Earl's Court, and had embraced psychedelia. "I was importing bongo players and poets, and we had a light show," she says. "Lots of people came down to that. It was a real mixed bag." After a brief stint in The

Strawbs, however, Kristina began to move away from folk. She landed a role in the stage musical *Hair* in 1968 before joining the classically inflected rock group Curved Air in 1970. The group found success right from their first album, *Air Conditioning*, which was released that November. Their six-year lifespan included numerous line-up changes, with Kristina the only constant. Her folk grounding shone through fleetingly on songs such as 'Melinda (More Or Less)' and 'Elfin Boy'.

Kristina released a self-titled punk-pop album in 1980 but then spent the remainder of the decade out of the limelight following her marriage to Stewart Copeland, who had gone on from a two-year stint in Curved Air to phenomenal success with The Police. Toward the end of the decade, however, her outlook changed. "I wanted to go out and perform again," she says, "and I wanted to get back to starting from myself, from my own songs, my own songwriting. And then I thought what I needed to do was to go out and see where there was to play, and to see what scenes there were."

What she found was a small but vibrant cluster of acoustic musicians in London. Led by the charismatic Roddie Harris and his group, Miró, these musicians would play for each other and their regular audiences at weekly club nights. The folk music that emerged was sometimes bellicose, but it could also be mellow and personal. One of Harris's sessions was based at Kristina's old stomping ground, the Troubadour. The portents were too much to ignore. "I felt this energy," she says. "They were all like little rock stars. They weren't folk singers, they were young people or crazy older people but they all had attitude." For Kristina, this truly was a successor to the original folk scene's spirit.

Roddie Harris had a sharp eye. Anyone was welcome to perform, but he would explicitly encourage and cultivate anyone he found really special. He and Kristina found a common ground, and soon she became a regular attendee. Furthermore, because of her status as a former member of Curved Air, Kristina was able to support the scene in a number of ways, not least by giving Miró access to her private studio in Buckinghamshire. "Miró was just very, very different," she says of the group's mix of frenetic violin, cello, and percussion. "I thought they were really fantastic, and [felt that] more people should see them."

While she was captivated by the grassroots spontaneity of the Troubadour scene, Kristina was also attending the trippy, kaleidoscopic clubs of the period, notably Club Dog, based at the George Robey in Finsbury Park. "It was like a psychedelic hippie club," she recalls. "They had several different stages going on at once, areas divided off by drapes, and various odd line-ups. It was very 60s but yet it was also like the traveller people, the hippies – all long hair and spiky hair, all the crazy people, and I thought: 'I like this. This is what I need.'" Among the scene's most prominent bands was The Ozric Tentacles, who spawned numerous offshoots; one was The Oroonies, who described themselves as a "pagan psychedelic folk-punk band". The folk element is particularly noticeable in their incorporation of various Eastern instruments; there are also echoes of Tyrannosaurus Rex in the lyrical woodland hypnotism.

In becoming part of these separate but complementary scenes, Kristina rediscovered her love of performance. She was also inspired to begin a new bout of songwriting. "I was writing about them, I was writing about me, about a new energy, a new time," she says. "The songs were all very truthful." To emphasise both sides of her influences, she called this body of work 'acid folk'.

Sonja Kristina's *Songs From The Acid Folk* (1991) stood slightly apart from both the acoustic and psychedelic scenes, but incorporated elements of each. 'Rollercoaster', for example, is a beefy mix of psychedelic rock and the confrontational folk style heard at the Troubadour. Kristina brought in her own folk lineage, sometimes blatantly – such as on a new version of 'Melinda (More Or Less)' – but often just in the simple joy of her voice and attitude. Backing her on the album are brothers Tym and Simon Whitaker of Ty-Lor.

Songs From The Acid Folk is not a deconstructive or an extreme album, but it was certainly a new tussle with folk music, particularly given when it was made. What is especially important about it is that Kristina brought an attitude that fused past and present in terms of both folk *and* psychedelic music. It was not a big seller, but its innovation was recognised by those who heard it. "Don't look to *Acid Folk* for links with the past – they're precious few," *Folk Roots* said. "Instead, this marks renewed commitment in fresh routes."

Kristina took the album out on the road and drew further links between contemporary and vintage folk by incorporating an original oil-wheel to project spectrums of light. "I had my rock star husband and my country mansion, but I was never happier than going off in the van and sleeping on people's floors," she says. She then formed a new band, Cloud 10, and developed another cross-genre: 'astro-folk'. The largely improvised *Harmonics Of Love* (1994) draws on ambient music rather than psychedelia, and was also ahead of the curve, prefiguring folktronica by ten years.

Sonja Kristina's experiments during this period – for which she reclaimed the word *folk* – remain underappreciated. "For me, [folk] is breaking away from templates," she says. "It's using instruments, using personalities, using voices, and improvising. Where music becomes tedious is when you've got perfectly nice little songs sitting in a rent-a-track. It might be beautifully played, and graceful, and the purists will say, well, it has to have that, but I would say that that is boring. The hardiest strands are the mongrels."

ᛗ

Club Dog hosted all manner of acts. One night a heavy, neo-psychedelic band from Detroit called Viv Akauldren played there toward the end of a European tour. Viv Akauldren date back to the early 80s. They were rocky and thrashy, but they stood out from the Detroit rock crowd. Keir McDonald's keyboards were prominent, giving the group's records a damaged yet unmistakably pop edge; Deb Agolli had not played drums before joining the band, and had a peculiarly intense style. Furthermore, there was a hint of mellow West Coast folk-rock in the group's sound, even if it was often deeply buried.

"In the 80s, folk was at its lowest point," guitarist Jeff Tarlton recalls. "We were already alienating people enough with our format as it was, without saying, all right, I'm gonna bring my 12-string. But we did that at home. A lot of the songs began on acoustic instruments."

When Viv Akauldren split up, in 1989, Tarlton felt adrift. The band had been his identity, his social life, his link to the Detroit community. "After that was all gone it was just like being thrust into a whole new reality," he says. He began to wander, literally and metaphorically. On one of his European sojourns in the mid 90s, he reconnected with Richard Allen, who was involved with the *Freak Beat* fanzine and had put out the final Viv Akauldren release – a brief, appealingly undercooked song called 'Threading The Needle' – on a flexi disc.

Allen had just started up a label, Delerium, and asked Tarlton if he had any new music. "I've got all kinds of junk under the bed," Tarlton replied. He began to think about the songs and snippets he had been fooling with since the end of the band, which dated back to when he first arrived in Europe, "fell off the map", and started busking.

"We were signing up anything that we liked that was of that psychedelic, hippie, progressive, underground ethos," Allen recalls. "I signed Jeff up because I just loved that kind of music, and he was doing it, and it was just so unusual."

Tarlton had left the louder sound of Viv Akauldren behind in Detroit. The switch from being in a band to becoming a solo acoustic performer, busking and letting his music fly on the wind, had given him serious pause. "It was a rude awakening," he says. "When you removed all the distortion and all the echo and all the keyboards, I found out I was a sloppy player. Under the microscope of acoustic playing, that's when a lot of the really beautiful things started to happen for me, and I found detail, and I found nuances." For the first time, Tarlton became a student of the guitar and learned his craft.

The resulting *Astral Years* (1997) is a strange album of reclusive, psychedelia-tinged folk. It was influenced by the music Tarlton heard "in the 60s, as a kid"; the diverse instrumentation includes bicycle wheel and teakettle alongside dulcimer and Ukrainian table harp. The pummelling lyrics trace his emotions during the demise of Viv Akauldren.

Tarlton then got further into the nitty-gritty of folk music through his friendship with Dorothy Carter, a founder member of the historical folk collective The Mediaeval Baebes. "Dorothy was the real deal," he says. "She was a big beatnik in the 50s, she'd lived life, she was very, very wise in her music." The Mediaeval Baebes' reductive name – and later reputation for sex'n'psaltery – does the musicianship and historical knowledge of their early incarnation a disservice. Carter showed Tarlton zither tunings and taught him much about British folk.

Tarlton was pleased with *Astral Years* but found it hard to promote. His booking agent told him that acoustic folk just "doesn't really fit in"; the only gigs he got were support slots alongside another Delerium act, the neo-prog group Porcupine Tree. "There was no market for what I was doing," Tarlton says. "I *hoped* to get in on the myriad folk festivals, because I played acoustic guitar. I was doing a hybrid that had elements of folk, but overall it wasn't pure enough to get in there. And, of course, I could not play as well as people that had devoted many years to the folk canon. But the fact was, I fitted in [even less] with the Porcupine Tree rock thing."

Tarlton released a second Delerium album, *draginSpring*, in 2000. "To me, they're like one record," he says; in the liner notes, *draginSpring* is subtitled *Part Two Of The Astral Years Chronicle*. In some ways, with the album's turned-up folk influence and Dorothy Carter's hammered dulcimer, zither, and hurdy-gurdy, there's a sense of continuation. But the album also has a fuller sound, rockier in parts, as if Tarlton was making peace with his musical past.

A few low-key performances and collaborations aside, Tarlton decided to withdraw from the music industry after making *draginSpring*. He still records and occasionally performs, but his subsequent body of work remains unreleased. "It's what I call the crazy old lady scenario," he says. "Where there's an old lady and she dies, and then people go into her house and clear it out, and they find this absolutely incredible interior world of things she's collected. That's sort of what I'm doing."

ᛗ

Another interior world that continued to evolve throughout the 90s was the one that belonged to David Tibet. On the Current 93 album *Crooked Crosses For The Nodding God* (1989), he reworked the *Swastikas For Noddy* material, turning creeping unease into a ramped-up, gory nightmare. The transformation of 'Panzer Rune' into 'Looney Roones' was a test case in how hymnal lore could become thrashing mantra.

The next major confrontation between Tibet and folk came on *Thunder Perfect Mind* (1992), the first Current 93 record to feature the composer Michael Cashmore. Tibet sees the album as a turning point, "The lyrics became a lot more personal," he says. They were also becoming more explicitly Christian, although some fans still assumed that Tibet was adopting a pose. "I think a lot of people really don't think I believe what I believe," he says. "But they're really wrong."

Thunder Perfect Mind offers a refined incorporation of folk and a greater sense of Tibet's conflicted feelings toward the genre. The humming pastoral beauty of 'A Song For Douglas After He's Dead' (written for Death In June's Douglas Pearce) is completely destabilised by its lyrics, in which Tibet rasps of ruined churches, swastikas carved into hands, and how "a twilight of ice / encircles his teeth". The juxtapositions are taken even further in 'Hitler As Kalki (SDM)', which explores the concept developed by Savitri Devi Mukherji that Hitler was the ultimate avatar of the Hindu god Vishnu. "I am in no doubt," Tibet wrote in 1993, in response to the controversy surrounding the song: "Hitler was Antichrist; Jesus killed Hitler – eventually … Unfortunately, since Hitler's death, all around his cruel spirit lives and multiplies, and many antichrists now surround us."[12]

Thunder Perfect Mind also features a guest vocal by Shirley Collins, on 'A Beginning'. It was her first appearance on record since 1978's *For As Many As Will*. Collins experienced emotional trauma during the late 70s, following the end of her marriage to Ashley Hutchings, and had lost all confidence in her voice. Every time she tried to sing, the psychological barrier was such that she simply could not, even when she was alone. "I got her to read the opening of

Thunder Perfect Mind," Tibet recalls. "And Shirley, she just doesn't like her voice anymore. She said: 'I don't sound like I used to.' I said: 'Well, you don't, but nobody does.'"

Tibet and Collins had become friends; he reissued some of her 60s and 70s material on his Durtro imprint. "David Tibet heard something that he liked and thought I needed rescuing, I think," she recalls. "I've always been so grateful to him for that." She remains extremely reticent about her singing voice, however – partly because she feels she can no longer do folksong justice, and partly because of her own high standards. "It's self-protection, in a way," she says. "It just embarrasses me to know that I could once sing and now I think I can't."

The poetic, drone-laced, and instinctive narrative of 1994's *Of Ruine Or Some Blazing Starre* was intended by Tibet as one piece of work rather than a collection of individual tracks. It is one of Current 93's most musically sonorous albums, but the lyrics are horrific and blood-drenched, stretching the assumed intimacy of *Thunder Perfect Mind* into a full-on fireside monologue of gut-wrenching imagery. (Many Current 93 fans cite it as their favourite album.)

It was with the *Inmostlight* trilogy of the mid 90s, however, that Current 93's sound began to dovetail with the emergent new generation of acid folk, particularly on the middle record, *All The Pretty Little Horses* (1996). From the shimmering bells and sea shanty air to the ghostly children's song and Steven Stapleton's nauseous tape loops, the album strongly anticipates the sound of those American acts whose time was soon to come. It's one of Current 93's most accessible recordings, and a profoundly moving experience. Tibet's childhood, which he spent in Malaysia, provides the album's spiritual centre.

"When I was ten or 11, I was already fascinated with Hinduism and Christianity, and I came across the works of Aleister Crowley in an airport when I was 12 or something," he recalls. "I saw this book – *Diary Of A Drug Fiend* – and I thought *wow*. I'd already read and admired Thomas de Quincy's *Confessions Of An Opium Eater*. I looked at this book, and it had this very beautiful cover and I turned it over and it said 'the wickedest man in the world'."

All The Pretty Little Horses is steeped in this sense of the young Tibet's fascination with – and fear of – knowledge. It shows how his relationship to folk music had moved on from the scratchy explorer figure of *Swastikas For Noddy*. His music, his prolificacy, and his position – none of which could ever be deemed either mainstream or static – were all far more extreme than most of the artists who would follow Current 93's decade-long folk reconnaissance. Nevertheless, the majority would be indebted – at least implicitly – to him as well as to the acid and psychedelic folk music of the 60s and 70s.

᛫

In 1991, a photograph of four youngish men submerged in the lake of a derelict Kentucky quarry, with only their bemused faces visible, announced a new phase in the American underground. It was the cover of Slint's *Spiderland*, the album that began post-rock.

Post-rock took elements of previous genres and artists – the expansiveness of The Velvet Underground circa *White Light/White Heat*-era; My Bloody Valentine's dream-pop; the erratic post-punk of Scritti Politti and Public Image Ltd; Can's Krautrock rhythms; the no-wave detachment of Ut; the belly-fire of hardcore – but did not combine them in any recognisable way. Instead, it sucked it all into that derelict quarry, stripping away clichés and comfort, and left behind a brooding abstraction derived from rock but absolutely aloof from it. When *Spiderland* came out in 1991, Slint were part of a healthy, diverse scene toying with avant-garde forms of rock in Louisville, Kentucky. The spirit of post-rock's early days had something in common with the blender of 60s psychedelic folk: taking bits of everything, with little preconception of how it would all turn out.

The arresting photograph on the front of *Spiderland* was taken by an actor currently questioning his future. Will Oldham had gained acclaim for his role as a young preacher in *Matewan* (1987), but the years since had not been kind. He had come to realise that not all roles would be so stimulating; that movie sets in general were not supportive; and that he would struggle to gain creative fulfilment from acting.

There was no obvious vocational replacement for acting, and Oldham's mental health took a nosedive. He sought solace during this difficult period with his brother Ned. "We lived in Madison, Virginia, more or less in the woods," he said in 2009. "When we were there, my daily activity was to walk through the woods to the public library and read for a couple of hours and come back."[13] One day, Ned suggested that his brother write a song to move himself along from this routine – which he did. (Oldham has alluded in some interviews to writing songs in college; in others, he has indicated that his decision to pursue music came from a mental health crisis while out on sailing lessons.)

The first fruit of Will Oldham's conversion to music was a seven-inch single, 'Ohio River Boat Song', based on the Scottish folk song 'Lach Tay Boat Song' but adapted to suit its transplantation to America. It was released on Drag City in 1993, and its bizarre beauty immediately drew attention. In a way that was analogous to Current 93, Oldham was coming from a highly unusual personal perspective, and this too resulted in a fundamentally new funnel for folk music.

An album, *There Is No-One What Will Take Care Of You*, soon followed; Oldham has since called it "very difficult" and described some of the musicians he worked with – among them three members of Slint – as "very complicated people". The album was laid down in two equally isolated locations: a freezing, flood-threatened house near the banks of the Ohio River, and a cabin in Meade County, situated on a piece of land known as Big Bend, where the river turns back on itself. This cabin was heated, but with a wood-burning stove that clogged the room, cracking and mauling Oldham's vocals.

Here, Oldham took the antique qualities of 'Ohio River Boat Song' and brewed a bubbling pot of enmity. Corrosive relationships – from incest to adultery to family dysfunction – rub alongside visions of hell and sin couched in repeated images of burning, arson, and fire. This is nerve-shredding folklore horror wrapped up in the eddy of musical discomfort that Slint pioneered on *Spiderland*.

It all sounded *very* different, and people soon became very interested in this young man who sounded like an Old Testament wanderer. This sat ill with Oldham. "Coming across [to Europe] and doing press for the first record, I was thrown off base by the level of confoundedness that I was confronted with," he said in 2009. "I didn't know how to answer any of the questions. It was all 'why, why, why'. I was just like: 'I don't know why, I just made a record.'"[14] From the very beginning, Oldham tended to be elusive in interviews, or even to sabotage them – when he wasn't able to avoid them outright.

Both *There Is No-One* and Oldham's next album were issued under the name Palace Brothers, with subsequent releases offering variations such as Palace Music and Palace Songs. He has claimed that these changes reflect different line-ups of musicians, or different sounds, but it also helped to effectively establish Oldham's knack for playing with identity and persona, undermining the well-trodden idea that singer-songwriter material should be autobiographical.

Oldham's second album, *Palace Brothers* (1994), is purely acoustic, and on first listen simpler than what came before. (It has since been reissued as *Days*

In The Wake, with Oldham reportedly so set on this change that he bought back all unsold copies of the original from Drag City.) "The second one was completely different-sounding," Oldham later recalled, "and there was a fifth of the amount of people involved. The songs to me also seemed really different."[15] They certainly were. The same distressing themes of transgression and punishment remain, but without the shroud of post-rock that had clung to his first album. And if *Palace Brothers* sounded far less complicated, that too was another false impression; the starkness belies the fact that this is an even more demanding record.

Next came the harder, rockier *Viva Last Blues*, recorded by the indie-rock icon Steve Albini. "[Oldham] doesn't rehearse," Albini recalled. "He chooses the people he's going to play with shortly before the session, so everyone is playing by the seat of their pants, and the music is at constant risk, subject to the weaknesses of whoever's in the room. But he gets absolutely spontaneous moments of greatness you couldn't rehearse."[16]

The Palace years closed with the frighteningly intense *Arise Therefore* (1996), again produced by Albini, but without the full-band sound of its predecessor. These four albums – and the numerous concurrent singles and EPs – are not easy to group together under a genre name. "Too much emphasis is put on American roots music when people try and place me," Oldham said in 2002. "You know, I grew up listening to punk: Hüsker Dü, Dinosaur Jr. I'm steeped in a lot of stuff."[17] Nevertheless, Palace was most frequently bracketed with two terms: alt.country and Americana.

For most of the 80s, country music was considered to be clean, over-produced, corporate, and conservative. The term alt.country was used to designate an alternative to this, and also to bracket its practitioners with alternative rock, the genre from which most of them arose. Americana was used more frequently to establish a genealogy with artists like Johnny Cash or Woody Guthrie, or much older country-blues. Alt.country and Americana incorporated very obviously country-influenced acts, like The Chickasaw Mudd Puppies and Freakwater, but were also commonly used to describe singer-songwriters like Oldham. If an artist gave off a sense of the American tradition, however mangled, these were the categories they found themselves ushered into.

Joining Oldham in this imposed category was his contemporary, Bill Callahan, another complicated individual fond of smokescreens and unhappy with interviews. Like Oldham, Callahan continually distanced himself from the first-person of the name he recorded as, Smog. "I don't think the 'I' that is

215

me is at all important to the song," he once said. "Besides, if you're a person, your faults are universal."[18] Callahan released a series of experimental lo-fi cassettes in the late 80s on his own label, Disaster, before moving across to Drag City. Following another home-recorded experimental splash, *Forgotten Foundation* (1992), he moved into more narrative work. Beginning with the dark and darkly humorous *Julius Caesar* (1993), Smog charred the edges of folkish darkness in its isolationist tension; along with Palace, Callahan provided an essential grounding for a new attitude to incorporating folk forms without ever being classified as folk music. Oldham would take this into his next project, for which he developed an even stronger persona; for now, it was enough that the shadows of the American woods were back.

⋈

Will Oldham had his own imprint at Drag City, the unsurprisingly named Palace Records. While its purpose was largely to release Oldham's own records, it also opened its arms to artists affiliated in sound or intent. There was Ned Oldham's group, The Anomoanon; Jason Molina's Songs: Ohia; and, most notably, Appendix Out.

Like Smog and Palace, Appendix Out was largely a pseudonym for one man. Alasdair Roberts is German by birth but grew up in Scotland, the son of folk musician Alan Roberts. "I started writing songs when I was 15 or 16," he recalls. "And then I came up with that name one day, and it stuck."

With his friend, Dave Elcock, Roberts began recording his songs on four-track and distributing them to friends and musicians he admired. "I would go to gigs in Glasgow and just give them to people," he says. "Palace was opening for Teenage Fanclub. I'd been a fan of Will Oldham, because John Peel played early Palace Brothers, and that kind of struck a nerve with me." Oldham listened to the tape, and Roberts received a postcard from Palace Records with an offer to put out a seven-inch single of the first two songs on Roberts' demo tape. 'Ice Age' / 'Pissed With You' came out in 1995.

The music that Roberts was making as Appendix Out – especially his Drag City debut, *The Rye Bears A Poison* (1997) – stood alone in the context of Britain in the late 90s. The album features mandolin and autoharp, and there are understated but undeniable elements of dark folk in its thorny, rural feel. At the time, however, folk influence was barely mentioned in the British music press; Roberts found himself aligned either with the US alt.country scene or with Scottish indie music in general.

"I don't know whether I'd truly found a voice," he says. "Before I found my voice, I think I may have sung with a little American twinge. Because a lot of the music I was listening to was coming from American bands. Alt.country is a funny term, but I did like stuff like Uncle Tupelo, bands like that."

Appendix Out released three albums, each one more layered than the last. "I think it was a conscious effort to try and do something different to that which had gone before," Roberts says. "Introduce different players and the ideas of many more people." On *Daylight Saving* (1999), Roberts brought in the beguiling harmony vocals of Kate Wright and smoothed out some of the edginess of the first album; with the third, *The Night Is Advancing* (2001), there is a clear drift toward post-rock.

Appendix Out showed only one side of Roberts's musical personality, however. Although these years were crucial in terms of reintroducing a folk influence into British independent music (even if it was barely recognised at the time), his next bold step would mark him out as a touchstone and pioneer of radical British folk.

Meanwhile, in the USA, the trend that proved ultimately most successful in reintroducing the word 'folk' was one that seemed linguistically to negate it. The term 'anti-folk' was first coined in the 80s by the singer-songwriter Lach in protest at his exclusion from the New York Folk Festival on the grounds that he was 'too punk'; he started his own 'Antifolk Festival' instead. The name – and the concept – outlasted Lach's fit of pique to become a rallying point for acoustic musicians who felt they had little in common with the folk establishment.

Anti-folk burbled along for much of the 80s with little reach beyond its own audience until the arrival in New York of a young man from Los Angeles. Beck had had only a fleeting involvement with the late 80s scene, but its impact on the 18-year-old was clear. "It was so creative," he recalled around the time of the release of his breakthrough album, *Mellow Gold*. "There was so much stuff happening, it was inspiring. To me it looked like everybody was going places."[19]

If anti-folk influenced Beck, then Beck influenced anti-folk, too, by creating a bridge between the original movement and the strain that eventually gained wider recognition: eccentric singer-songwriter material derived as much from literate indie groups like Beat Happening and early-80s DIY hip-hop as from any explicit folk or punk heritage.

This second-generation of anti-folk was playful and urban. It found poignancy in the details of everyday life, and was hardly the desecration of folk music its name suggested. Diane Cluck, The Moldy Peaches, and Jeffrey

Lewis all found critical acclaim; Lewis, in particular, demonstrated a keen love for psychedelic folk. Citing the influence of The Holy Modal Rounders, Pearls Before Swine, and Donovan on his music, he made clear that, to him, 'anti-folk' was not in any way analogous to 'against folk'. "What binds us is a mutual respect for creativity, I guess, which kind of eliminates the idea of there being a blanket 'sound'," he said in 2002. "For one reason or another, we're all kind of misfits to the wider music world."[20]

Anti-folk achieved what no other act or scene of the period did: it brought the word 'folk' back into common journalistic currency, and enabled its use as a descriptor for cutting-edge music made by and for young people. For this reason, anti-folk was a notable precursor to the renaissance of acid and psychedelic folk music. And, while anti-folk was enjoying this critical acclaim at the start of the new millennium, that renaissance was already beginning.

CHAPTER 15
Wisdom On The Moth's Wing

BEFORE THE MANY, there were the few. Three groups – In Gowan Ring, Stone Breath, and The Iditarod – predated the intense interest in modern psychedelic folk music that would blossom in the early 21st century. Each came to make the music they did through unique combinations of personalities, interests, and circumstances; none was concerned with prevailing trends or the simple revivalism of an earlier sound. The result was three near-flawless back catalogues – each of which showcases a strongly modernist take on psychedelic folk – but not much in the way of recognition. "I wish I could find those early reviews that panned us for using 'banjos and yard chimes'," says Timothy Renner of Stone Breath. "Some years later, the reviewer actually emailed me and said he was very wrong and that he just didn't 'get it' at the time."

That particular reviewer wasn't alone: few critics 'got' these bands. The conflux of conditions that brought them to the special music that they created also ensured that the music remained underground. While these three groups laid the foundations for the 'freak folk' sound to follow, they themselves saw no real benefit from its sudden popularity.

The first of these groups to appear was In Gowan Ring, founded in the early 90s by sole constant member B'eirth. He was born Bobin Jon Michael Eirth and raised in the Mormon faith; his great, great, great grandfather was Wilford Woodruff, the fourth Prophet of the Mormon Church. As a child he performed in musicals, and cites this early theatrical experience as a significant influence on his music – much more so than the few piano lessons he took. "It was getting to experience a family beyond the nuclear family," he says. "When you're involved in a theatrical troupe, it's like a tribe."

B'eirth's adolescence proved to be an unforgiving time. "I went through a pretty intense period of angst," he recalls. He stopped acting in rebellion against his childhood before being sent first to a series of psychiatrists, and then to the Mercywood Sanatorium in Ann Arbor, Michigan. "It was like a scam," he says. "The insurance would pay for it, and they'd just get all these kids that weren't going along with things and put them into the mental hospital."

On leaving Mercywood, then Mormonism, and then the family home, B'eirth began to search for "something more interesting". He devoured esoteric literature, philosophy, existentialism, and folk music. "That was the interesting section at the public library," he says. "The folk section is divided by where it was around the world. Sometimes pop music, or rock music, can seem all the same because it's all in one tradition. There are so many more unique qualities in folk." B'eirth became intrigued by the different tonalities and the variation between musical systems. "You think about the Gamelan or something – every neighbourhood, every village has got their own tuning system, their own tradition for rhythms."

Twinned with this was a growing interest in the instruments themselves: the mechanics that brought forth the sounds. "I started listening to the tones and the different hammers you get out of different instruments, whether you're playing them correctly or not correctly," he says. "It's just that curiosity of how something's made." Making instruments came next, beginning with hammered dulcimers and then bamboo flutes. The whole idea of it soon became a ritual in itself. "It's an empowering thing," he says. "You're learning about something, and you're exploring it, and testing out your skills with something. It's like you're able to make something real. I can sit with a sketchpad and imagine some crazy Dr Seuss instrument, something that doesn't exist, and I could think about how to do it and actually make something real."

Making music followed, but it didn't come easily. "It was a long incubation, really," he says. "I felt like there was something I was looking for: maybe it was an atmosphere, or a trance … it's there but it's not there." B'eirth tried to find it through tape experiments: improvising, recording to tape, and reflecting back. "You have to work to translate it. It's a lot about trying to capture these fleeting moments of inspiration when you're tapped into something like that."

B'eirth worked specifically on pinning down this 'translation' for three years, from 1990–93. "Gradually, the music became more and more structured, and less ethereal," he says. "It was a slow crystallisation of the visions and things." The eventual result was the In Gowan Ring album *Love Charms*, released on World Serpent in 1994. "I think a lot of that is very much like a painting," B'eirth says. "It was all about these visions and the tones and the atmosphere. The lyrics are like meaning paintings, they're abstract things" – a mood summed up perfectly in the opening track, 'Listen To Colors', with its echoes of hippie synaesthesia.

B'eirth knew he had got *Love Charms* right in terms of the vision in his head: "It felt like an arrival of some kind, where it had become real," he says. But the reaction elsewhere was mixed. "I remember someone saying that it sounded like Celtic music played at half speed. It was in an in-between place. It wasn't rhythmic enough to be music that you could play at bars, but it wasn't experimental enough to be John Cage music."

One piece of press proved educational – a positive review that compared the record to The Incredible String Band "when they were great". B'eirth didn't know who the String Band were, so he went to a music store and tested out a CD. "After making the record I made, and then hearing *The Hangman's Beautiful Daughter* … I just remember crying in the record store. It was like being an orphan and then realising you have a father. I don't mean that in an arrogant sense, but I thought that what I was doing with *Love Charms* was totally new, and what I was looking for didn't really have much of a reference. It was a different feeling after that."

The Incredible String Band took B'eirth on a journey of discovery. After exhausting their albums, he joined email lists and delved into the very obscure end of 60s and 70s acid folk. One thing that helped B'eirth – and that would affect subsequent acts, too – was the simultaneous emergence of file-sharing technology. In the past, many of these records would have been virtually impossible to track down. Now, for the curious and the technically capable, even the very strangest records could be rediscovered with relative ease.

B'eirth then reached back further. "I did studies of Renaissance music, which was another thing, like folk music, that I was always attracted to," he says. "The multiple parts, the harmony; being this vast mosaic, this big open space of all these interconnected relations in tone." His explorations enhanced his enthusiasm for instrument making. "With mass production, with industrialisation, something happened to make the instruments consolidate, to make them more the same. But, back then there were all these different instruments with different kinds of sympathetic strings."

B'eirth's next album, *Twin Trees* (1997), marked a significant departure from *Love Charms*. It's a record that knows its place in the world, and can be placed on a continuum, while still maintaining the compassion and strange individual eye of *Love Charms*. The In Gowan Ring sound had become more deftly psychedelic – something that would become even more pronounced on *The Glinting Spade* (1999).

Although B'eirth has since released music on CD-Rs and in other limited editions, there has to date been only one further In Gowan Ring album, *Hazel Steps Through A Weathered Home* (2002). His release schedule is unhurried, and the time it takes him to put out these albums has ensured that they sound exactly as he wants them to. "I really look at it like a thread, or a tradition of some kind," he says of psychedelic folk in general. "It's music that has that power to inspire you, to have that spark, to feel like you want to live your life in love. You want to be in that flow, or in that vibration, and you want to share it with people."

ᛉ

Stone Breath was primarily the work of one Timothy Renner, who grew up embedded in nature on a farm in Northern Maryland. He would sometimes sleep in the woods nearby and was always fascinated as a child by the beauty and brutality of the world around him. "I don't necessarily believe in faeries or dryads or Gaia *literally*," he once said, "but I do believe that divinity and perfection is found in nature."[1]

Renner has always had an equally strong reaction to music; his mother feared he was autistic because of the way the young Timothy rocked back and forth to Simon & Garfunkel. He later found strong emotional resonance in the voices of Ian Curtis and Johnny Cash, while in his teens he became involved in hardcore punk and metal before moving toward acoustic music.

"I think my ears needed a break," he says now of this switch. "One day I heard some early music being played live and I found I absolutely loved the textures of the instruments." He started listening to Coil and Current 93 before delving into The Incredible String Band, Tim Buckley, and Donovan. He also obtained an acoustic guitar. "I fumbled with that guitar for a long time," he says. "Someone would show me a chord or help me tune it. I knew that my favourite guitarists usually played fingerstyle, so I figured out a very simple way of playing with my fingers, sort of repeated patterns over changing chords."

With the encouragement of his girlfriend, Alison, Renner approached some friends in a noisy industrial band, Bondage Harvest, with an eye to a possible collaboration. From this emerged Cloud, a duo with Paul Chavez, with whom Renner created audio-collages to soundtrack his visual art. But as time went on, Renner became less interested in this 'plunder-phonic' approach. With Renner now drawn toward song-based composition, Cloud morphed into the psychedelic space-rock band Mourning Cloak.

Mourning Cloak made their first album – the heavy, layered *In Dreams You See* – in 1995. Around the same time, Renner began to develop a theory: "In very loose and simple terms, I began to think of acoustic music as 'earth' music and electronic music as 'space' music. I wanted to make music of the earth." Renner started Stone Breath as a solo and purely acoustic project, with a little help from Alison; they recorded the cassette *Of Mists And Ashes*, which he distributed to friends and associates.

Renner's theory of earth sounds – wood, bone, steel, breath, and skin – formed the basis of the first Stone Breath album, *Songs Of Moonlight And Rain* (1997). The instruments on the album include water, blackbirds, and swords alongside bowed zither, mandolin, and chimes. It was the first release by an Australian label, Camera Obscura, founded by Tony Dale. "I had been writing reviews and features for *Ptolemaic Terrascope*," he later recalled. "It opened up a whole universe of new psychedelic music to me, and I wanted to get more involved. I loved Timothy Renner's take on dark folk, and also his artwork, and ended up spending an insane amount on the packaging for that one, partly because I didn't know what I was doing. It was worth it though. There was nothing like it around at the time."

There was not. *Songs Of Moonlight And Rain* is rent with contradiction: spare and dense, melodic and inharmonious, old and new, its folk music feral, shaped by seldom-heard instruments and unusual ephemera, with Renner's aching voice bringing the songs to high-pitch intensity. There are echoes of earlier artists – Renner had covered 'Seal Of Seasons' by Tyrannosaurus Rex at the first ever Stone Breath concert – but the album resembled no one band.

Shortly after the release of *Songs Of Moonlight And Rain*, Olivardil Prydwyn joined Stone Breath. "That was one big act of serendipity on the part of the universe," he says. Prydwyn had been interested in Renaissance music from a young age, and had formally learnt the lute. "And then I discovered The Incredible String Band," he says. "Suddenly, the idea occured to me that you could just pick up an instrument and learn it, or learn it enough to make some sounds with it."

Prydwyn released his bardic debut, *At The Feet Of Mary Mooncoin*, under this principle in 1995, incorporating the sounds of the zûk, the bironne, and the gimbri. He was also part of the Celtic-tinged Green Crown, a prominent group on the Pagan music circuit, and like Renner was interested in the history of all sorts of folk music. Prydwyn had made some copies of the Incredible String Band film *Be Glad For The Song Has No Ending* in the US NTSC video format, and Renner ordered one.

"I guess we emailed a few times," Prydwyn recalls. "I remember Tim emailing me asking if I happened to know the lyrics to some Clive Palmer song. I admitted to not really hearing anything much by Clive Palmer outside of The Incredible String Band, and Tim sent me a tape of some COB stuff, and also the first Stone Breath album. I remember being intrigued by the music. It was obviously somebody else who had been listening to a lot of the same sort of things that I had been listening to." The two arranged to meet at a Pagan music festival in Pennsylvania, where Renner asked Prydwyn to contribute to the next Stone Breath album. "Prydwyn understands on so many levels," Renner says. "We tend to lockstep even when we don't realise it."

A Silver Thread To Weave The Seasons (1998) was the first album Stone Breath recorded as a *band*. Renner says that his influences at this time were love songs inspired by Eastern thought, written to people, symbols, and the seasons. The album sounds more confident, with stronger links to the first generation of psychedelic folk; a COB song, 'Evening Air', is the centrepiece. "Perhaps it's so obvious that it doesn't need to be mentioned, but it was COB, Comus, Incredible String Band, Forest, and the like that originally sent me off in the psych-folk direction," Renner said in 1998 – a year when hardly anyone was citing these bands as influences.[2]

A third Stone Breath album was planned. *The Spectral Light And Moonshine Firefly Snakeoil Jamboree* was primarily a collection of traditional folksong, but Camera Obscura was reluctant to release it as a Stone Breath album. Instead, Renner made the album title the name of the group. The record became *Scarecrow Stuffing*. The Spectral Light And Moonshine Firefly Snakeoil Jamboree existed as a more 'traditional' group alongside Stone Breath and marked the introduction of a third group member, Sarada Holt, who had previously played in Belladonna Bouquet with her friend, Jenne Micale. "One of the things that inspired me to start recording was when I first heard Stone Breath," Holt says. "I bought the first album and I think I stopped breathing for a moment because it was everything that I thought music should be. After about a year I gathered the courage to contact him and say how much it meant to me." Holt sent Renner some Belladonna Bouquet material; he then invited her to perform with Stone Breath. "Sarada is just an intuitive, empathetic, and loyal friend whose heart resonates with my own," Renner says, while Prydwyn adds: "There is no other Sarada out there. She's wonderful. It was years and years before we actually ever sang together in person. She'd record parts and a month later I'd visit and record parts, so we'd sing together, but never actually *sing* together."

Renner admits that he nearly lost himself in The Spectral Light And Moonshine Firefly Snakeoil Jamboree. He felt a deep affinity with traditional music and became increasingly skilled in clawhammer banjo. But Stone Breath returned in 2000, with Holt's haunting harmonies, to deliver their third and most lyrically ambitious album to date, *Lanterna Lucis Viriditatis*. Both Renner and Prydwyn were interested in religious history, and it is this pursuit that infuses the record: viriditas – literally 'greenness' – was used by the Christian mystic Hildegard of Bingen to express God's fecundity and power on earth.

Stone Breath worked next on an ambitious musical reinterpretation of *Sir Gawain And The Green Knight*. It was a time-consuming, complicated project, so to bridge the gap they planned a quickie stopgap album of original songs, *The Silver Skein Unwound*, which is arguably their masterpiece. Recorded swiftly and released in 2003, the album is musically malevolent and lyrically sodden with bloodied Christianity, bloodied nature, and bloodied humanity, offering little in the way of reprise or redemption. "I hesitate to discuss my thoughts and feelings about life at this time," Renner wrote in the liner notes to the 2009 reissue. "This was my *Songs Of Experience* to the innocence of *A Silver Thread*."

"In 2001 or 2002, we played the last live Stone Breath show of that era," Renner says. "I was very disenchanted with some elements of the underground music scene. I started to see *The Silver Skein Unwound* as our last album." The *Sir Gawain* project was never completed. Olivardil Prydwyn moved to the UK, where he continued to perform and record, both on his own and as part of Quickthorn. Sarada Holt turned her focus toward her art. Timothy Renner went on to various other projects – some solo, others collaborative – including the concentrated terror of Crow Tongue and the gothic ambience of Black Happy Day, and continued to run the record labels Dark Holler and Hand/Eye. But Stone Breath had – to use Renner's phrase – returned to the earth.

ᛝ

Carin Sloan (formerly Carin Wagner) first started making music at art college in the mid 90s. Her musical tastes ran slightly to the left of the general indie-rock melee of the time toward acts such as Cat Power, Helium, and The Mountain Goats. "I spent a lot of time alone," she recalls. "I just really fell into my strange little way of thinking and putting it down in words. I've never been a good guitar player, but I just kind of figured out what I wanted to do to make songs. I've always found people's flaws to be the more interesting part, so I always felt great about doing my flawed music as I personally enjoy its character."

Jeffrey Alexander was slightly older than Sloan, having graduated from the Baltimore music scene of the 80s. "A bunch of crazy stuff was happening at that time," he says. "Experimental bands were coming out of the Maryland Institute and loft parties that would literally go all night long." In Baltimore, Alexander worked at a radio station, where he ingested The Incredible String Band, The Holy Modal Rounders, and Pearls Before Swine. He started playing guitar relatively late at the age of 23.

The pair met when Alexander's band, the indie-rock Science Kit, played at a club called Memory Lane in Baltimore in 1996. Sloan had already started writing songs and recording them on a home four-track machine. After she gave a tape of them to Alexander, the two of them began working together on the material. "He went through all my tapes and just really pulled together a lot of different things, put a guitar behind it, or arranged it," Sloan recalls. "He's just fantastic at that."

Sloan had already started using the name The Iditarod; now it became the name for their shared project. The pair also began a romantic relationship and moved away from Baltimore to Providence, Rhode Island, where they felt they would find a more supportive audience. They were right: before long, the pair began to play around the local area and befriend other artists, while Alexander also organised shows further afield. "He was the brains of the act," Sloan says. "I would have gotten nowhere without him."

By the time of their first album, *The River Nektar* (1998), The Iditarod had begun to move away from Sloan's original song hoard toward material that the pair wrote together from scratch. "I always called what we were doing 'weird folk'," Sloan says, "because there's nothing really to explain it." The album is an erratic but intoxicating mix of lo-fi pop music and whispered, juddering folk. The Iditarod were a hardworking band: gigs were plentiful, as were compilation appearances and other limited releases, and it all paid off. Their mesmerising music – and Sloan's fissured voice – began to attract attention.

The Iditarod were not resting on their laurels. They issued two CD-Rs of live tracks and home recordings, both entitled *Yuletide*, over the winter seasons 2000–01 and 2001–02. These lustrous, glassy-eyed folk sets include traditional songs learnt from records by Anne Briggs and Pentangle. They also mark a time of transformation within The Iditarod.

"It evolved into Jeffrey starting to write the songs," Sloan recalls. "If I could technically add anything else, I would, but he's definitely a much better musician than I ever was, and he started becoming the main writer of the music." They were also now performing more covers and traditional songs – another of Alexander's developing interests. "Things got more layered, psychedelic, and with quite a lot of traditional folk song references," he says. "I spent a lot of time researching trad folk song lyrics, which I sometimes set to new music."

As Sloan recalls, this shift also marked the start of the group's demise. "It became more his music than my music," she says. "Whether it was my doing, whether I was becoming uninterested, or because it was becoming so much more his music that I became uninterested, I don't know." Sloan drifted away from The Iditarod, limiting her input to vocals, largely abandoning her guitar in favour of more delicate instruments, like bells. By the time of *The Ghost, The Elf, The Cat And The Angel* (2002), their music had become more verdant and less lyric-driven. "It was more Jeffrey than me," Sloan says, to which Alexander adds: "I wrote all the music and she focused on lyrics and vocals. That was when things went into more of an experimental and folkier direction."

By this stage The Iditarod had also expanded from the core of Alexander and Wagner, with regular contributors including cellist Margie Ayre (formerly Margie Wienk), who would later reach her own psych-folk maturity in Fern Knight, and violinist Matt Everett, who would go on to play with Fern Knight and Will Oldham. The group frequently invited other friends and musicians up on stage and generally gained the feel of a collective.

As it happens, Alexander's next project was also gestating, even if it wasn't a conscious move away from The Iditarod. In 2003, he was asked to provide music for the short student film, *The Butterfly Hunter*. "The filmmaker wanted the vibe of The Iditarod's music but without vocals, and he specifically asked for guitar and cello pieces," Alexander recalls. By then Margie Ayre had left the group to concentrate fully on Fern Knight, and had been replaced by Miriam Goldberg. She and Alexander spent a few weeks working on material for the soundtrack. "It went really well," he says.

Meanwhile, Carin Sloan was feeling isolated not only from The Iditarod but also from the Providence scene itself, which was now starting to gain momentum, with Alexander one of its central figures. "We were doing things with these people who were fantastic musicians who were so interested and involved in folk music and the roots of it, and things that I just I didn't get that deep into," she recalls. "I could definitely see myself as being the goof, needing to run away from the intense, quiet, serious jam sessions. Because I wasn't playing any instruments properly, either, I would never have been able to jam with any of them anyways, which left me with nothing to do."

The Iditarod didn't last much longer. Sloan and Alexander's romance ended, and the group soon followed it into history. "It ended in a bang," Sloan says. "I think we both fell in love with other people." Sloan was pregnant and left her musical career behind to start a family. Alexander continued to develop the more freeform, ruined-castle sound he had started with Goldberg on the soundtrack to *The Butterfly Hunter*. They named their new project Black Forest / Black Sea.

"We had already booked a Spring Iditarod tour with Fursaxa and Gravenhurst," Alexander recalls, "but when Carin quit we just went on the tour as Black Forest / Black Sea." Their early live sets incorporated the *Butterfly Hunter* music alongside some new material, but they were also joined by Tara Burke of Fursaxa and Nick Talbot of Gravenhurst for performances of Iditarod material – "like a strange cover band", as Alexander puts it. And, with that, The Iditarod joined Stone Breath in extinction.

M

Why is it that these artists, despite making some of the greatest acid folk since the 70s, failed to have an impact beyond a relatively small circle of fans and friends, and have since been largely written out of the 'freak folk' story? "Stone Breath and The Iditarod were two really important but completely forgotten and uncredited early psychedelic folk bands," says Greg Weeks, who played alongside both groups as a solo artist before forming Espers. "They're interesting characters, believe me. For a while we were all really close musically."

In the case of Stone Breath, it's obvious that the music is intense and the vision uncompromising. There's nothing that could ever be interpreted as kooky or arch about this band; the albums, particularly *The Silver Skein Unwound*, cover rough terrain. Their natural habitat is the copse rather than the glade, and the hardy have to make the pilgrimage out to find them. Stone Breath never seemed bothered about image or networking, and made few attempts at self-promotion. It's perhaps only natural, then, that when a less aurally acute version of psychedelic folk followed later on, it would attract a far wider audience.

"I guess I'm proud that we were there before," Timothy Renner says, "but I sometimes think we would have done better to be *on* the curve instead of ahead. In general, I think whatever wave of folk bands that came after Stone Breath, I doubt most of them ever heard us. I think our influence was probably more in the idea stages. Someone saw what we were doing, or heard about it, and liked the idea of a modern band doing this, and went from there." *Ptolemaic Terrascope* founder Phil McMullen is in no doubt about the group's importance, however. "Ask any musician and they'll all tell you: Timothy Renner is the real deal," he says. "He's the father of all this."

It seems more likely that The Iditarod might have gained wider recognition, had they continued. Their profile was higher, they played live frequently, and they had a large circle of collaborators, while Jeffrey Alexander was experienced and confident in the business side of music. Furthermore, their records chimed closely with what was just around the corner. While The Iditarod were equally as authentic as Stone Breath, their ground-level understanding of indie-rock made their music accessible in a way that Stone Breath's was not. By the time a receptive audience had emerged, however, Carin Sloan was out of the loop altogether, and Alexander's new project, Black Forest / Black Sea, had chosen to chart a far less commercial course. It was simply a case of awful timing.

As for B'eirth, the earliest of this new crop of pioneers, he too missed the wave but has continued to make music, most recently as Birch Book. Superficially, the relative obscurity of In Gowan Ring is hard to understand, particularly given the startling similarities between B'eirth and Devendra Banhart, another photogenic nomad with a compelling back-story and an interest in the history of the music he was making. But as B'eirth himself notes, "I had missed the boat. I was already out to sea too soon."

It also came down to who B'eirth was, and what he was looking for. In Gowan Ring was his own personal quest; he saw no surge in attention in the wake of the general upswing for psychedelic folk, and he didn't have the will to chase it. "I don't remember more interest, to be honest," he says. "But I might have been somewhere where I wasn't paying attention."

CHAPTER 16
A Place In Time

IN AUGUST 2003, the eclectic British music magazine *The Wire* devoted its cover to a collective with an intriguing if unusually unwieldy name, Sunburned Hand Of The Man. The photo staring out from the newsstands evoked a hazy vibe of ad-libbed creativity and organic kinship. It was captioned 'Welcome to the New Weird America'.

The Wire was reporting on the Brattleboro Free Folk Festival, a two-day event that alerted the wider world to a new experimental folk music. This loose movement of American men and women had come together in the town of Brattleboro, Vermont, on a weekend in May. They had embraced the pioneering folk music of the 60s and 70s, but they had also seized new possibilities with it. Theirs was a folk that mixed not only with psychedelia, free jazz, and various non-Western instruments and forms but also with a range of influences from hardcore noise to minimalist electronica. No point on the scale was off limits. Most significantly, free folk prioritised improvisation as an artistic approach.

The Brattleboro Free Folk Festival was started by two friends: Ron Schneiderman, who founded the independent label Spirit Of Orr, and Matt Valentine, a musician whose groups included The Tower Recordings and The MV & EE Medicine Show. Schneiderman had moved to Vermont early in 2002. Inspired by the breadth of creativity in the local area, he began to nurture the idea of organising a gathering to celebrate the shared sensibility he found among so many of the artists. One evening, over a few drinks, he and Valentine began to talk about it as a real possibility. The idea solidified when

Valentine came up with the name Free Folk Festival. They decided that Schneiderman would find the performance space and Valentine would ask the artists. And that was about it: both wanted the event to be as improvisational as possible, reflecting the nature of the music, and making the festival an artwork in itself. "It just seemed the right time and place for some sort of explosion," Valentine says.

The festival ended up being better than either Schneiderman or Valentine could have hoped. Even the weather gave its blessing. "It was simply one of the most beautiful days of the year," Schneiderman recalls. "A flatlander's dream. I was able to look around and see that people were just having a great time; you could see it in their faces. There was something going on that night that was rare. It was strongly emotional." The setting seemed to bring out the best in audiences and performers alike to celebrate both the diversity of and the commonalities in free folk. It was not their intention to coalesce a scene – "I don't know anyone who considers themself as part of a 'movement' or even a genre," Schneiderman says – but in 2003, Brattleboro became synonymous with the start of New Weird America and the free folk subgenre.

Brattleboro itself had to come from somewhere, of course. One man was introduced on stage at the festival as representing *the* history of free folk in the town, and as a vitally important link between the first wave of experimental folk and its new incarnation. That man was Dredd Foole.

Dredd Foole was the *nom de plume* of Dan Ireton, who had emerged onto the 80s hardcore noise scene in Boston with his band, The Din. "We were an *extremely* loud band," he says. "We were considered one of the loudest bands anywhere. My eardrums were just being beaten; after every show it would take me days to recover, I was just screaming, and toward the end I was getting so frustrated, I was spending a lot of time in the audience, getting hurt, and it was just a mess. I decided I didn't want to do it any more."

Not only was Ireton being pushed away from noise, he was also being pulled toward more reflective – if equally challenging – parallel worlds. In the dying days of The Din, he says, he lost interest in rock music and began to favour free jazz. He also found a resurgent love for the more outré folk of his college days. He describes Tim Buckley as "one of the greatest of all time. He was just an incredible singer. He used his voice as an instrument and that's always been my goal".

Still using the name Dredd Foole, Ireton started performing solo in venues like Boston's Rathskeller (affectionately known as the Rat), where The Din had once been a popular draw. His new sound didn't please many people at

231

all, particularly given that the name Dredd Foole was still synonymous with paint-peeling noise. "They couldn't quite figure it out," he says of these early audiences. "I was going from one of the loudest bands in town to 'folk artist', which was very uncool in those days. The bartender threw chips of ice at me. That's how much *he* liked it."

After a short period of solo shows, Ireton joined forces with Ed Yazijian, another artist in the experimental rock genre who was searching for a new direction. They began performing as an acoustic duo in 1989, thereby shattering *two* noisy reputations. "That's when we really got into trouble, because it did seem to mess with people's minds," Ireton says. A few people – Stefan Jaworzyn from Shock Records; Jimmy Johnson and Byron Coley from Forced Exposure – enjoyed Ireton's new direction, but most people just talked over (or sneered their way through) the performances. Frustrated by the negative response, Ireton dissolved the partnership with Yazijian and gave up on music completely.

"Of course, before too long I had a chance to buy a four-track and a digital reverb," he says. If New Weird America had one moment of conception, it was Dredd Foole's *In Quest Of Tense*. Recorded in two or three nights at home during 1994, it was the first Dredd Foole record to reflect the direction Ireton had steered himself toward after the dissolution of The Din. It was fully improvised, channelling Ireton's love for free jazz and Tim Buckley – and, in a wider sense, the inventive and instinctive style-skipping of Marcel Duchamp. It mirrored Ireton's own philosophy, which would be echoed by many free-folk musicians over the next few years. "There's something magical about the first time you do something," he says. "That moment of creation makes things special. And exciting."

In Quest Of Tense was released in 1996 on Forced Exposure. "I never really thought anyone would be interested in it," Ireton says. "It was pretty off-the-wall. But I was friends with Jimmy Johnson, and I just sent it to him and said: 'See what you think of it.' Within a week he called back and said: 'I really want to put this out.'" As with Buckley's *Lorca*, folk music is there as a reference point, but the music floats unfettered around its structure amid ragged instrumentation and unsettling vocal experiments, particularly on the 19-minute closer, 'Ascension: Ra And Buk (Bridge Of Cries)'. This is not pretty music – Dan Ireton's long history in noise bands leaves its legacy in the album's lack of comfort – but it is breathtaking in its originality. The ability to evoke a difficult listening experience through quiet, acoustic music was to become a hallmark of free folk. Its modern incarnation began with Dredd Foole.

Despite being pushed firmly by Forced Exposure – Ireton was now working at the label, so knew for certain that promos were sent out – *In Quest Of Tense* was barely reviewed and sold only in tiny quantities. "There was just no reaction at all from anybody, except for my friends," he says. "I just figured that nobody heard it. It made me sort of wonder: maybe this is crap. Why am I bothering? I think it's good, and I think it's interesting, but maybe it isn't."

Another key figure in Brattleboro was Joshua Burkett. Like Dan Ireton, Burkett had been obsessed with music virtually all his life. He had been in a number of bands as a teenager in the 80s, playing everything from political punk to cover versions of chart hits. He joined the group Vermonster as a saxophonist in 1990 and appeared on three of the group's hard, freaky albums, for which he also provided the artwork. At the same time, he also worked on experiments of his own, juxtaposing sounds and feelings.

"I recorded hundreds of hours of tapes, most of which I never listened to again," he says. He released some of his early-90s material in 1995 on the LP *Owleavesrustling* and the cassette *Yellowbeard*, revealing a series of volatile acoustic jams bonded together by Burkett's captivating, murmured voice.

It wasn't until *Life Less Lost* (1998) – released, like *Owleavesrustling* and *Yellowbeard*, on Burkett's own Feather One's Nest label – that the folk influence on his work became blatant. He had moved to the countryside in Western Massachusetts, and his musical tastes curved in a new direction. "I was particularly into The Incredible String Band, Clive Palmer solo, Wizz Jones, and Pentangle," he says. "No one I knew was deep into this stuff then. It was like stumbling upon some uncharted universe of unlimited beauty."

By now, Burkett was recording material every day and felt closer to the sounds he was making deep in the country. Rarely did the songs venture beyond this environment. "I think I only played out twice at that point, to five or ten people," he says. "But I was fine with that. It was more like 'painting with sound' and documenting moments than trying to be known." Folk had become a lynchpin of his earlier work, but it came filtered and mashed with shavings of Burkett's post-punk, post-sampling aesthetic.

The third major element of what would eventually bubble into the Brattleboro Free Folk Festival began with what Matt Valentine describes as "cheap loft-living, vintage guitars and amps, record store jobs, cork, and smoke". The Tower Recordings, in their initial incarnation, were three friends in New York: Valentine, Helen Rush, and Pat Gubler, who called himself PG Six.

Valentine and Gubler had played together in the hard-edged Memphis Luxure alongside Marc Wolf and Todd Margolis. "Sort of in the middle, Matt had started doing recordings with Helen Rush at the loft space he lived at," Gubler recalls. "These were stripped down, more often acoustic, lo-fi recordings. There was a lot of room for experimentation and improvisation." Gradually, Memphis Luxure mutated into The Tower Recordings. Wolf continued to play with the group, which also attracted drummer Scott Freyer and Rob Jones, who provided tape loops and effects. The Tower Recordings performed around New York with other progressive improvisation outfits, including long-standing pioneers Borbetomagus and the equally freeform Tono-Bungay.

"I had a habit of recording *everything*," Valentine recalls. "I still do. Everything went down to cassette and, when we had the resources at hand, a two-track reel-to-reel. At some point we did some local live shows, and felt that we had enough down to start 'working' on an album. We rendered beyond four-track and transferred the selects to sixteen-track half-inch, where we experimented further." The eventual result was *Rehearsals For Roseland* (1994), a 28-track collection of lo-fidelity jams and sprawling song-forms released on The Tower Recordings' own label, Superlux.

Matt Valentine's tapes continued to roll, and the unconventional spirit of The Tower Recordings – very much a collective rather than a group – was captured along with their music. Albums and singles culled from these hours of tapes came thick and fast: *Fraternity Of Moonwalkers* and *Let The Cosmos Ring* (both 1996, with the latter credited to Planet TR); a ten-inch collaboration with Tono-Bungay, *Rules Of Thumb* (1997); the full-length *Furniture Music For Evening Shuttles* (1998); and numerous limited releases and compilation appearances, including a version of 'I Saw The World' recorded for the Tom Rapp tribute album, *For The Dead In Space*.

Each Tower Recordings release represents a different aspect of free expression, from soft, sweet songs to long, atonal articulations. The songs often lean toward an obliquely rhythmic, psychedelic atmosphere, but are difficult to categorise. The album that would become The Tower Recordings' best-known work seemed – in name at least – to have one style at its centre, but *Folk Scene* was no about-turn away from their previous avant-gardism. Like its predecessors, it is a document of improvisation and sketching.

"*Folk Scene* started through some sessions we did in upstate New York, at the church where my older brother Steve worked as music director," Gubler says of the recording, which took place during the autumn of 1998. "We recorded live over the course of a long weekend." The church setting also enabled the use of piano and organ as well as a swollen Tower Recordings ensemble cast: Rush, Valentine, Pat Gubler and his brother Steve, Tim Barnes, Erika Elder, Scott Freyer, Robert Henry Jones III, Samara Lubelski, Dean Roberts, Andre Vida, and Barry Weisblatt. The church sessions were edited and fine-tuned for *Folk Scene*, which came out as a one-sided vinyl LP in 2001 on the Colorado bedroom label Shrat Field Recordings.

Folk Scene made solid a lot of the previously indistinct crossover points between recognisable folk music and the improvisational elusiveness of much of The Tower Recordings' material. In 2003, Valentine described the album as "the fulcrum of our catalogue. I wanted to make something that was really obvious to people".[1] *Folk Scene* gave a clear nod to the 60s and 70s but – like *In Quest Of Tense* or *Life Less Lost* – it also leapt far away from them.

Each member of The Tower Recordings had other, concurrent projects. As PG Six, Pat Gubler lent his music several different, complementary faces. This multiplicity had first become apparent at a young age. "I had started out improvising on piano when I was 11 or 12," he says. "Eventually, I took piano lessons, and then I took up the guitar on my own as a teenager. My brother Paul played guitar, so I had sneakily experimented around on his guitar a bit." Other instruments soon drew him in. He began to play the recorder and flute, and at the age of 17 discovered his brother Steve's small, Celtic harp.

Around 1998, Gubler started recording music of his own to four-track. He asked fellow Tower Recordings musician Tim Barnes to help him organise, tweak, and mix these home recordings, which formed the bulk of his solo debut, *Parlor Tricks And Porch Favorites*. Released on the Amish label in 2001, it remains among the most enduring records of its type. It's a work of tinctured free folk, its blobs of congealed instruments (including harp) forming little magmas of pastel sound. It is also an emotionally difficult record.

"To be honest, I was having a pretty hard time personally while I was making that record," Gubler says. "My dad had died of cancer in 1996, and my brother Paul was also sick at the time with a brain tumour, and he passed away in 1999. Dealing with those losses definitely had an effect on the music and what came across. I wouldn't say that the mood of the record is entirely sad, but there is an undercurrent of those emotions running through it."

Matt Valentine and Erika Elder also made records outside of The Tower Recordings. Depending on the combination of musicians, style, or whim, they are known variously as MV & EE, The MV & EE Medicine Show, and MV & EE With The Golden (or Bummer) Road; their discography is bewildering in its length and breadth. Like The Tower Recordings, MV & EE are impossible to pigeonhole; psychedelic folk rubs against homespun bluegrass, undulating rock, muffled, unstructured acoustics, and epic ragas. Valentine cites the influence of cinema, notably the underground experiments of George and Mike Kuchar and the work of auteur directors Satyajit Ray, Sam Peckinpah, and Monte Hellman. And then there's their surroundings. "We live deep in the woods," Valentine says. "Nature shouts back."

Meanwhile, The Tower Recordings continued with an ever-rotating cast of contributors. *The Galaxies' Sensual Transmission Field Of The Tower Recordings* (2004) contains material from the original *Folk Scene* church sessions; an extended version of *Folk Scene* itself followed. "For the *Folk Scene* addendum we worked within the embryonic framework of the tape archive and built our own anthems in miniature using the four-track idiom, with which we all felt comfortable working," Valentine says. *The Futuristic Folk Of The Tower Recordings* has a similarly semi-retro title but contains lengthier songs and sounds like a Child ballad retold by Stan Brakhage.

ᛗ

Back in their New York days, The Tower Recordings had played with Pelt, a pioneering drone-rock band from Richmond, Virginia. One of several guitarists in the group was Jack Rose, who would later end up alongside Valentine on the Brattleboro Free Folk bill.

Rose had been playing guitar since high school but only got into fingerpicking by chance after overhearing the kid next door. "I went over and asked him what he was doing," he later recalled. "He had this book [with] tunes by Mississippi John Hurt, Gary Davis, Mance Lipscomb, and I think there was a [John] Fahey tune in there as well."[2] Rose borrowed the book and bought the records it suggested.

Rose joined Pelt in 1993. Although widely considered to be a noise band, they developed a strong individual identity; by the time of *Técheöd* (2000), they were as unclassifiable as The Tower Recordings. Rose himself continued to develop as a guitarist, particularly after a period of unemployment in 1999, which gave him the time to investigate other players' styles. His first three solo albums – *Red Horse, White Mule* (2002), *Opium Musick* (2003), and *Raag Manifestos* (2004) – were all released as vinyl-only limited editions, and saw him inch toward roots-based music. He freely acknowledged the importance of the American Primitive style, even going so far as to name one track, 'Linden Ave Stomp', after the place where John Fahey made his first recordings.

"I feel more comfortable with incorporating elements of [Fahey's] style into my playing and composing now that I think I have internalised his music," he later recalled.[3] He also noted the importance of "hard work, repetition, trial, and error" in his music, but that did not mean it was not also instinctive. "Folk, American Primitive, whatever; they're just labels," he said. "I always try to play from my feelings and subconscious."[4]

If Pelt and Rose had a gritty, unruly image, *Wire* cover stars Sunburned Hand Of The Man were, as John Moloney put it, "a gang and a family in every sense of the word".[5] Moloney came from the ultra-urban environment of the projects in Everett, Massachusetts, where drug use and crime were rampant; he had been arrested six times between the ages of 17 and 21. He had tried everything from break-dancing to hardcore punk when he formed The Shit Spangled Banner in 1994 with Rich Pontius and Rob Thomas.

By 1997, the group's indie-punk had grown into an expansive but tough improvisational throng. It needed a new name. Sunburned Hand Of The Man made their debut in 1997 with *Mind Of A Brother*, a self-released album that twinned the cosmic abstraction of free folk with a steely rhythmic force, creating a kind of 'freak funk' that would later become particularly overt in the group's live performances.

It was on their third album, *Jaybird* (2000), that the Sunburned sound detonated. Evoking the persistence of dub reggae and the syncopated fire of the Washington DC go-go scene, *Jaybird* contains six long tracks that catch the Sunburned squad in perfect sonic allegiance. Sunburned were the most prolific by far of all the Brattleboro groups. They birthed enough offshoot projects to populate another Free Folk Festival, and possess a discography so enormous that even MV & EE look like slackers in comparison.

ᛗ

As the decade turned, Dredd Foole's *In Quest Of Tense* began to pick up fans. Christina Carter and Tom Carter of Charalambides, a psychedelia-sprayed improvisational duo formed in 1991, both loved it; Matt Valentine, Erika Elder, and Jack Rose were also big fans. "It honestly floored me," Dan Ireton says. "I had no idea that anybody even heard it, much less cared about it. But, apparently, there were certain people out there who thought it was, I don't know, a special record. It meant something, to them, above and beyond the typical record. That was incredibly gratifying."

Joshua Burkett, too, was beginning to realise that he wasn't alone. He had moved to a new spot in the woods, with an improved studio set up, and had met Byron Coley, a writer who ran a venue, the Yodspace, with Thurston Moore of Sonic Youth. "Byron's shows were monumental as places where everyone played and met each other, and he usually made food for everyone with no cover charge," Burkett says. "His generous nature was amazing." Burkett played shows at the Yodspace, where collaborations flowered, and began to work on his next album. "I had met some other 'similar-minded' underground acoustic folk people," he says, "and I asked them to help."

The resulting *Gold Cosmos* (2001) features PG Six, Matt Valentine, and Six Organs Of Admittance's Ben Chasny. Like *Life Less Lost*, it is a folk-oriented album, but one that speaks in an ever-more sophisticated tongue. Along with *Parlor Tricks And Porch Favorites*, *Gold Cosmos* proves free folk's capacity for profound emotional engagement – something the genre is seldom given credit for. "I really consider myself a 'bedroom' musician," Burkett says. "And I consider my solo stuff personal experiments of some kind."

By now, Ireton and Burkett had become friends, and were beginning to conceive of an event that would celebrate the musicians they felt an affinity with. Along with Byron Coley and Conrad Capistran, Ireton and Burkett organised the first Stone For festival in the small Massachusetts college town of Amherst. Although neither this nor the two subsequent Stone For events garnered the publicity of the Brattleboro Free Folk Festival of 2003, they were important precursors, featuring performances by Matt Valentine and Erika Elder, Sunburned Hand Of The Man, The No-Neck Blues Band, Ben Chasny's Six Organs Of Admittance, New York's Golden Calves, and free drummer Chris Corsano as well as by Ireton and Burkett themselves.

"At the time, I just thought it seemed like a picnic or something," Ireton says. "But they had a part in the birth of all this, much more so than I thought at the time." The local scene was now established, the musicians were all bouncing off one another, and some really special performances and records were piling up as a result. "Those were really great times," Burkett says. "Just some perfect moments, with amazing people around."

The community coalesced and artists played together in many combinations and put each other's music out on individual, artist-run labels. The improvisational approach and the tendency toward continual recording resulted in hundreds of hours' worth of material, while new technology permitted its quick, cheap transfer on to CD-R. This led to a vast output of music, often in very limited runs or with special packaging and sometimes on unusual or defunct formats.

"I like the idea of certain musics for certain audiences," says Valentine, who co-runs the Child Of Microtones and Heroine Celestial Agriculture imprints. "It gets back to that DIY approach. Some labels, like farms, can only be sustainable issuing their harvests in small numbers in order to maintain a certain standard of quality. By no means am I saying that the larger editions suffer, it is just that the larger runs contain music that is sometimes less esoteric." This approach not only resonated with the private-press folk music of previous decades – particularly the forthright approach of Perry Leopold's *Experiment In Metaphysics* – but also with the localised camaraderie of punk communities and the tradition of small-press political publications.

The mutually supportive struts within the world of free folk were reflected in the genre name itself. "I like to think of 'free folk' as something that encompasses a lot more than an acoustic guitar and a voice," Ireton says. Pat Gubler also found the term helpful after years of struggling to define The Tower Recordings. "When I would say 'folk-influenced', for many people that had the connotation of 'singer-songwriter' or 'adult contemporary'," he says. "And then, depending on what that person's experience of music was, I might cite something like a British folk band, like Pentangle or Fairport, but that would have the connotation of something much more traditional in flavour. And *then* I would have to back pedal … 'No, it's more like, uh, Pink Floyd demos played back quietly on a microcassette recorder.' Now at least these labels can give someone the idea of where you're coming from."

In *The Wire*, David Keenan introduced the Brattleboro set as "a groundswell musical movement rising out of the USA's backwoods". On the Saturday afternoon of the Free Folk Festival, Joshua Burkett, Dredd Foole, Jack Rose, and MV & EE played the stone-walled Hooker-Dunham theatre on Main Street. In the evening, the event moved to a warehouse space, the Cottonmill; the American Primitive artist Glenn Jones performed, followed by Michael Hurley, a hero to virtually everybody on the Brattleboro bill. There was a blazing collaboration between the haunting Scorces (Christina Carter and Heather Leigh Murray) and the improvisational sax-and-drums duo of Flaherty / Corsano, before the night ended with a scorching set by Sunburned Hand Of The Man. On the Sunday afternoon, the action moved to the Hampshire College Tavern at Amherst, with a line-up featuring The Tower Recordings and Charalambides. One set blurred into the next as people jumped up to play and improvise, generating a white-hot buzz of creativity.

"It *was* a very magical time," Ireton says. Following her performances with Scorces, Heather Leigh Murray described the event as "like being part of some kind of tiny utopia. All the players have this amazing, alive approach to living and making art".[6] Chris Corsano, too, was full of eulogy. "I like the political model it represents, the idea of a lot of people trying to take care of each other without any pre-written laws," he said.[7]

"It really was an amazing bunch of performances, especially Sunburned," says Joshua Burkett. "But it also signalled the beginning of the end of the great local scene around here. All of a sudden there was more competitiveness and folks started touring more. This didn't appeal to me."

Within a year of the article in *The Wire*, free folk had a solid cult following. Fans from across the world would scramble to get hold of the limited-edition releases, while most of the artists saw an increase in local, national, and international interest. The chrome-edged, harder sound of Sunburned Hand Of The Man proved particularly successful; their stage pizzazz and warrior characters appealed beyond the experimental set and reached the Sonic Youth end of the indie-rock market. The group's strenuous touring and prolific release schedules kept up this momentum throughout the 2000s.

There was a clear ceiling to free folk's success, however. A few isolated songs aside, the music was intrinsically uncommercial in its unconventional structures and dedication to experimentation. It was not an accident that it had been *The Wire* that picked up on the sound rather than a more mainstream rock or folk-based publication. By the time the article was published, bivouacs of new psychedelic and experimental folk were springing up elsewhere. Within these new clusters, gleams of free folk's contrary spirit could be heard. In some cases, the chi of improvisation was very strongly present, but in co-existence with other, more widely palatable qualities. And as these new radiant sounds and extroverted personalities began to emerge, it became obvious that this music *could* have a very broad appeal indeed.

CHAPTER 17

Sum Of All Heaven

IT IS NOT ALWAYS EASY to tell what makes communities and individuals lock together and germinate, between them, an identifiable new sound. Sometimes, seemingly distinct records and people just sound *right* together, even if there had been no real intention to make analogous records; shared interests simply blossom at the same time, bringing forth a tangible freshness, which is then maintained by a frenzy of cross-pollination and creative giddiness. The coalescence of free folk was just one example of this. As the years ticked by into the middle of the first decade of the new century, more rocks rolled into the stream, water levels rose, and interest swelled from far and wide.

Even so, there was little indication at the start of the decade that a wider audience would ever be interested in psychedelic folk music again. Many of the first wave of new acid-folk acts found the contemporary scene decidedly unwelcoming. "People would just talk through our show because we were so quiet," Carin Sloan of The Iditarod recalls. Ben Chasny of Six Organs Of Admittance faced similar problems. "When confronted with people playing as sincerely as they can, but [who] for some reason are difficult to hear, it didn't necessarily register well," he said in 1999.[1] For Greg Weeks, who was living in Manhattan at the time, there was an even more fundamental problem: "Indie rock was king. There was no way to get into any of the clubs to play."

Ptolemaic Terrascope was a virtual space for these artists to converge and find a sympathetic audience. The magazine's loyal readers had already heard of The Iditarod and would soon be introduced to Chasny and Weeks. Although these readers were geographically diffuse, *en masse* they represented quite a force. The congregation came together physically in 1997 at the first Terrastock Festival, held in Providence, Rhode Island. "I'd like to think the *Terrascope* was a catalyst, and the Terrastock festivals a crucible for the dawning of an awareness that disparate bands and artists from across the world and, vitally, from different eras, all somehow belong together like a family," founder Phil McMullen recalls. "My favourite moments at a Terrastock festival invariably happen in a completely random manner, like wandering into a room and seeing Tom Rapp backed by members of The Spacious Mind [a psychedelic folk five-piece from Sweden] and Ghost's Masaki Batoh."

The first Terrastock Festival was originally planned as little more than a release party for the *Terrascope* benefit CD, *Succour*, but once word spread, those artists who were also enthusiastic readers of the magazine clamoured to get involved. By the time of the second event, in 1998, the needle had begun to hover slightly toward psychedelic folk music, with sets by Stone Breath, Ghost, and Tom Rapp. By the fifth event, held in Boston in 2003, the bill featured those three acts plus Six Organs Of Admittance, The Iditarod, Charalambides, and Greg Weeks.

The Terrastock nation was a knowledgeable, taste-making community, and a good indicator that something was stirring. Even so, according to McMullen, there was no talk of a 'scene' back then. "It's just a disparate assortment of musicians who respect one another and happen to come together in the same place at the same moment," he says. "And it's certainly not planned."

Greg Weeks had become a firm favourite among the *Terrascope* faithful by the time of his 2003 appearance at the festival. The magazine conducted a lengthy interview with him in 2000, included his song 'For Chan' on a cover-mount compilation, and helped fund and release his mini-album *Bleecker Station*.

Weeks's music was pensive and swirling, careful but intoxicating. He had been stretching his influences over the past decade as he grew as a guitarist and songwriter in New York. He had initially tended toward math-rock before becoming acquainted with Leonard Cohen – via Pain Teens' cover of 'The Story Of Isaac' – and deciding to pick up an acoustic guitar. "From then on," he says, "it was a whole new ball game."

Around the same time, Weeks had started to immerse himself in the reissues of heavy psychedelia that were starting to emerge on CD. He was hanging around at the time in a college crowd who "wanted to listen to psychedelic rock records, but there weren't any around. You couldn't find them on vinyl unless you wanted to spend 50 or 60 dollars". One of the first CDs he got hold of was *Parable Of Arable Land* by The Red Crayola. Shortly afterward, he set up New Sonic Architecture with his friends to import those CD reissues that were available in Europe but had few outlets in the USA. "All of a sudden I was inundated with all this Krautrock and psychedelic rock and experimental rock," he says. "And then, in with those releases, you would hear something and go: 'What is this?'"

These mystery records were often by groups like Mellow Candle or Bröselmaschine who, in the mid 90s, tended to be shepherded together into the catchall 'progressive' category. Weeks soon recognised that there was something that marked these groups out from the general prog scene. "I started seeing that there was another realm that was not being paid attention to," he says, "and I got most excited by that stuff, eventually."

If Leonard Cohen had rekindled Weeks's dormant interest in the acoustic guitar, it was Nick Drake who expanded its possibilities. Weeks began to experiment with fingerpicking and different tunings, practicing for three or four hours a day. His tastes soon drifted toward the American Primitive masters. In 1997 he self-released *Fire In The Arms Of The Sun*, a record that displays his innate flair for lyrical melancholia and his meticulous guitar technique. It sold very few copies, although a re-release the following year on the Ba Da Bing! label gave it a slightly wider distribution.

Weeks found any promotional activities awkward and faintly embarrassing. He was thus grateful to Ba Da Bing! for at least undertaking the minimum required to get his music heard beyond his friends, but still the album sold only around 300 copies. (On those occasions when he was able to secure a slot at a club or performance space, he found playing live nerve-wracking.)

Weeks's next record was *Bleecker Station* (2000), a home-recorded collection of conceptual musings on a long-distance relationship that's simpler in terms of both lyrics and structure. Weeks says he was listening a lot to *The Kinks Are The Village Green Preservation Society*; the rougher guitar playing reflects the difficult emotions that arose from the relationship.

Still worse was to come. "My hands just gave out," he says. "So I actually lost the ability to play the way that I was beginning to be able to play, which was really frustrating." Weeks's exhausted, pained hands pressed down further on his general mood of despair. His tense frame of mind and these enforced technical limitations led him toward a deeper exploration of drone-laden psychedelia.

"It shifted a lot more in focus to progressive and Krautrock influences," he says, singling out Pink Floyd as a particular inspiration. Without his guitar as his muse, he found a child's organ in a junk shop and began to compose on that instead. He was working in a recording studio at the time, so had the resources at his disposal with which to experiment, but he could not shake the nagging feeling that his new songs weren't working.

Greg Weeks had seen this material as another solo project like *Fire In The Arms Of The Sun*. But, when he looked at it again, he decided he wanted other people to play on it. The resulting album, *Awake Like Sleep* (2001), became an ensemble piece. Here, Weeks's compositions are interpreted with a lighter touch, the contributions of his musician friends bringing the redemptive teasing of the truly intimate. As well as being a fine piece of work in itself, it was an early sign of his skill for collaboration.

Manhattan is an unforgiving place for those who feel in despair, particularly those cramped into tiny apartments. Realising his mood, and his records, had fallen into a black hole, Weeks wanted a change. He eventually drifted toward a new city: Philadelphia.

◽

While Greg Weeks was taking his first steps toward Philadelphia, Ben Chasny was undergoing a similar transformation in rural Colorado. "I grew up in a tiny house at the end of a place called Elk River Valley," he later recalled. "We had a gigantic redwood tree in our yard and Elk River flowed through our backyard. My childhood was spent climbing trees and playing in the forest and exploring the woods. I think my music draws a lot from those places I used to visit and hide in the woods when I was a child."[2]

Ben Chasny had been playing in bands since his mid-teens, the punk juvenilia of Smile giving way to the more refined Plague Lounge, with whom he made *The Wicker Image* in 1996. Chasny quickly tired of the group, however. "It was a real chore to keep the band from sounding like some Dead C rip-off," he later said, "since the bass player didn't have an original bone in his body and would've made us sound like a cheap imitation if he could have. The band broke up because the other members just had no passion for creation at all."[3]

More satisfying to Chasny was a concurrent experimental project, Eta Corina, a duo with violinist Aolini (formerly of the hardcore band Saké). Chasny credits Eta Corina with improving his guitar skills and spurring him to investigate traditional folk. It also led to a fixation with fingerpicking. "I just really started obsessing over it," he said in 2006. "I locked myself in my house until I learned to fingerpick things on the guitar."[4]

When The Plague Lounge split up, Chasny channelled his energy into a new project: Six Organs Of Admittance. The name came from Buddhism, wherein it describes the combination of the five senses plus the soul; the overriding concept came from Chasny's desire to explore psychedelic folk, and to work largely on his own, inspired by a whole range of obscure and challenging music by the likes of The No-Neck Blues Band, Ghost, and The Heroin Glowbugs.

In 1998, Six Organs Of Admittance released their self-titled debut, a striking bough of experimental psychedelia with limbs of folk best exemplified by its heady, lengthy centrepiece, 'Sum Of All Heaven'. Like The Iditarod's first album, *Six Organs Of Admittance* sounds prescient. Chasny followed it a year later with the more pastoral *Dust & Chimes*, which opens up his Elk Valley childhood to unsentimental rumination.

From the start, then, Chasny's music was like a bat in a cave. Its wingspan could open up and overwhelm, but could equally draw bondage-tight, eyes shut, impenetrable and intriguing. He made several other albums in the early 2000s, including the distressed *Dark Noontide* (2002) and the near-nude guitar trance of *For Octavio Paz* (2003). He was also a prolific collaborator. He had made a particularly memorable appearance on Joshua Burkett's *Gold Cosmos*, and in 1999 he formed Badgerlore with former Deerhoof guitarist Rob Fisk. Chasny's most high-profile role was as guitarist in Comets Of Fire, an explosive rock band who signed to Sub Pop and toured with the likes of Dinosaur Jr and Mudhoney.

"I think it's a myth that records have to progress a certain way," Chasny said in 2008. "I don't think there's been a step A to step B for me. It's just about how I feel at the time, which is always changing."[5]

◀

Back in Philadelphia, another musician, Tara Burke, had started to make records as Fursaxa. "Usually the way I create songs is by laying down an initial track from something that I am strumming on the guitar, or a note that I am playing on the keyboard, and then I listen back to that track and other instrumentation, and my ideas are revealed," she says. "I never have whole songs or albums composed in my head. I write in layers."

Although she had played the piano as a child and acoustic guitar as a teen, Burke didn't become an active musician until her early twenties, when she became involved with the Philadelphian art-rock scene. Playing with a group called Un, she soon became inspired to nurture her own more personal sounds, which she laid down on a borrowed four-track and performed at a few local shows. At one of these performances, Burke handed a tape to Makoto Kawabata of the Japanese psychedelic band Acid Mothers Temple. Kawabata became an early fan and released Fursaxa's opening salvo, *Mandrake*, in 2000.

Mandrake shares free folk's trends of improvisation and subliminal disclosure but has a philosophy all of its own. "Vladimir Nabokov is one of my favourite authors," Burke says, "and his poetic style of writing has influenced many of my song lyrics. I also enjoy reading about religion and mythology, and Mircea Eliade writes some of my favourite books about this subject, which I think figures into the mood of my music." Eliade, a Romanian historian and philosopher, proposed that the human experience is split into the sacred and the profane; Fursaxa's music has a similar duality in its juxtaposition between earthiness and elevated headspace.

Burke cites the influence of the cinema on her second album, *Fursaxa* (2002). "I used to work at a video store and watch a lot of films, so there are probably many that have subconsciously inspired my music," she says. "'Texas Song' is about the film *Paris, Texas*." The films of David Lynch – and his television series, *Twin Peaks* – proved similarly influential.

Fursaxa was released on Thurston Moore's Ecstatic Peace! label. It forms a twinset with *Mandrake*, since the two records were developed simultaneously. "I was going through my 'Saturn Return' years around that time," Burke says. "I felt very restless and unsure about a lot of things. I would also say my mood around that time was generally more melancholic, and I was going through some emotional turmoil."

At the same time, Philadelphia was falling into a galaxy of folk-inflected, psychedelic music, which Burke found herself a part of. "I guess it was a bit strange, since I had lived in Philadelphia since 1996 [but] I barely knew any local bands at the time," she says. "But it was a great place to be a musician, since there was lots of good local music to see and be a part of. I have always felt that people appreciate you more outside of your hometown, and that was definitely the case with Philadelphia music listeners."

In 2003, Fursaxa released a three-inch CD-R, *Harbinger Of Spring*, as part of a series called The Jewelled Antler Library. "CD burners – along with the software for making digital transfers easy – were just another iteration of the cassette and four-track phenomena which enabled a DIY approach to music-making and production," says Loren Chasse, who co-founded the Jewelled Antler collective in 1999. "Our creative impulse is aimed at breaking rules and bypassing what might be considered the 'established' music industry."

Jewelled Antler was indeed far removed from traditional notions of business and even musical expression. The umbrella name for an array of labels and musical projects, it spawned or cultivated an awe-inspiring stylistic range of collaborators and outlets, including The Knit Separates, The Franciscan Hobbies, The Skygreen Leopards, The Blithe Sons, The Birdtree, and The Child Readers. The project's centrepiece was the improvisational group Thuja, consisting of Chasse, Glenn Donaldson, Steven R. Smith, and Rob Reger. Donaldson and Smith had previously played together in the space-rock band Mirza; that group's split coincided with a desire in these musicians to explore sound in a quieter, acoustic space.

"Thuja was all about atmosphere," Chasse says. "The places where we played and recorded had everything to do with the musical choices we made. It was very much about the 'field' – a relationship of instruments and sound-making objects to plants, furniture, lighting, artwork, food. The music was mostly improvised, although certain ideas, lyrics, combinations of sounds, and locations were confronted with intention. Unlike the sort of 'free jamming' you get in a lot of improvised music, the different projects had understood frameworks and limitations that would characterise the music."

Thuja's approach meant that they stood consciously apart from the propensity for heavy noise that usually follows a dip into improvisation. For Thuja, there was no separation between rehearsal and performance; many public shows took place in the same space they used to rehearse. "Those were the most enjoyable musical experiences I've ever had," Chasse says. "Listening back to recordings was always surprising as the microphone behaved like an ear of its own, depending on where it was in the room. It heard things that none of us did."

Jewelled Antler was an early path-beater for the homemade, independent approach that would become so important to the emergent freak-folk sound. Certain of the label's releases were also sonically aligned to psychedelic folk, including Franciscan Hobbies' *Caterpillars Of The Oak Beauty* (2001), a floating delicacy created in Mount Davidson's eucalyptus forest, and The Birdtree's more overtly psychedelic *Caravans And Orchids* (2001).

Loren Chasse considers Jewelled Antler's relationship to folk carefully. "Folk music comes from a tradition of music and songs that have been passed along and more or less preserved over time," he says. "There is hardly anything improvised about folk music according to this take on it. It's a body of song that belongs not to individual artists but to an anonymous set of 'folks'. Many bands, Jewelled Antler included, have been improvising music with instruments traditionally used in folk music, namely acoustic string instruments. But the instruments themselves don't make it folk music. Certainly, the 'pastoral' vibe of Jewelled Antler – of playing outdoors and/or artificially invoking nature – has something akin to the folk ethos, although I'm not sure what that is."

M

A more mainstream take on these esoteric hives of activity came with the regeneration of Will Oldham. After recording one album, *Joya*, under his own name, Oldham metamorphosed again. While his various Palace identities gave the impression of a band constantly in flux, Bonnie 'Prince' Billy presented Oldham in a loner singer-songwriter's shawl.

Oldham's thespian past rang loudly in Bonnie 'Prince' Billy. He spoke of 'occupying' the persona, comparing the role explicitly to acting, although the role was not completely distinct from his own personality. He seemed to see the character as an authentic way to present his songs, a star both within and without its creator.

The first Bonnie 'Prince' Billy album was *I See A Darkness* (1999). Full of folk minimalism and stark chills, it contains song titles like 'Death To Everyone' and 'Another Day Full Of Dread', delivering a promiscuity of discord, demise, and dismay. "There's no pity in my music," he later said, "for myself or any other fuckhead. Most of the music I love makes me feel happy. But even unhappiness makes me happy."[6]

In 2003, Oldham happened to hear two CD EPs, *Walnut Whales* and *Yarn And Glue*. "Will Oldham contacted me after hearing those earlier EPs," their author, Joanna Newsom, later recalled. "I'm not sure how he got them, because it was back before I'd ever played any shows or sold any CDs. He told me he liked the music, and he asked me on tour."[7] (Oldham himself had mentioned "a woman named Joanna Newsom" when telling *The Wire*, in 2003, that he tends to pick support acts "that we think will be fun to travel with and that I think I can learn from".)

Joanna Newsom was from Nevada City. Her earliest childhood memories involve being drawn to the harp. At the age of three or four she pestered her parents to play it; she was told she was too young, and that the piano was a more appropriate first instrument. Nevertheless, within a few years she had her way. The harp became a phantom limb. "I wanted one for so long [that] when I finally got my hands on it, I never got over the thrill of playing," she said in 2004.[8] After spending her childhood and adolescence immersed in the instrument, she realised that she wished to compose as well as perform on it.

Newsom studied composition at Oakland's liberal Mills College but found herself distressed by the lack of melody in the curriculum. "It felt like what I was doing was so clichéd," she later explained. "Every idea I had, everything I was interested in, to everyone else seemed really passé. It was like, if I was interested in folk music and high-art music, I should have been studying in 1920 in Chicago."[9] Instead, Newsom glided sideways into a creative writing course, changing her songwriting patterns away from the epochal and toward the condensed.

During her time at Mills, Joanna Newsom heard the voice of the Appalachian folk singer Texas Gladden, an obscure artist who had accompanied Alan Lomax on field recording trips and whose work Joan Baez had championed during the 60s. Gladden has described the use of 'grace notes' in singing: unusual ways to express the song while remaining unschooled and true to folksong's rustic heritage. "I've always known I had a strange voice, because there has to be some reason I didn't use it for years and years," Newsom said in 2004. "I think it was an understanding I picked up that I didn't have a voice people wanted to listen to."[10] Now, having heard Gladden's sound and approach, Newsom felt empowered to unleash her voice.

By then she was also playing keyboards in a rousing indie group, The Pleased, alongside another Mills student, Noah Georgeson. The group gained good press locally in San Francisco, and in the UK, where they toured. Newsom worked concurrently on her own songs and small-scale shows, laying down the EPs that ended up in Will Oldham's hands. "Those CD-Rs were just things I had recorded at home as documentation," she explained in 2005. "I didn't want to forget those songs, so it was like jotting something down on a Post-It note."[11]

Oldham's interest led Newsom to Drag City, for whom she began work on a debut album. Years earlier, Alan Stivell had combined folk heritage, modernity, and the harp on his 1971 album *Renaissance Of The Celtic Harp*. Now, Joanna Newsom would become his worthy successor.

As for Oldham, he went on to deliver a series of albums that dipped in and out of folk and blues, trepidations and tremors. His work could not be called psychedelic folk, but his influence splayed in all directions and was often palpable in the introspective or brutal tinges of numerous artists. He wasn't without his critics – most of whom disliked either the portentous nature of his earlier work or the perceived populist slant in his later records – but few could deny his overall status as one of the most important cult artists of the decade.

Perhaps the best summation of Oldham and his career came in the anti-folk artist Jeffrey Lewis's 2005 song 'Williamsburg Will Oldham Horror'. Oldham, he sang, might be seen as someone who has "the world laid out before him", or even just "a rich kid, or a fascist, or a charlatan". But "if you look at indie-rock culture, you really can't ignore him".

ᛞ

Lewis's words could, with a little alteration, have been meant for the first media face of the new psychedelic folk: Devendra Banhart. Like many stars – and he certainly was one – Banhart was alternately fêted and derided. For those who like him, he's a fresh, charming, genuine talent, blessed with a gift for creating engaging music in a genre that was far from a commercial certainty; for those who don't, he's cynical and disingenuous.

Tracing Devendra Banhart's history is an imprecise science. He peppers interviews with obfuscation, contradiction, and self-mythologising, sometimes adopting the persona of the hippie child of the sun or of the *artiste* uninterested in talking to the press. He has claimed that he possesses no childhood memories, and that this is a deliberate policy. "I have this thing where I try to forget everything I've done," he said in 2005, "so then I can return to it and be objective."[12]

Banhart did have something of an unusual upbringing for an American musician. He was born in Houston, Texas, but then moved with his mother to Caracas, Venezuela. As a child he drummed with chopsticks and listened to the radio but rarely felt inspired. "And then one day 'Smells Like Teen Spirit' came out," he later recalled. "It was the first time I heard a sound that was so different. You know, *now* it sounds super-produced, but then it was the most lo-fi *soup* – just the messiest thing I'd heard in my life."[13]

Banhart returned to the USA at the age of 14, and in his late teens gained scholarship to the San Francisco Art Institute. "The only thing I got out of it was getting to meet a few people that I was friends with and who taught me a lot of things," he later said.[14] He began busking around the city, and would later claim that his first proper performance was at a gay wedding.

Further low-profile gigs followed at sushi restaurants and as part of performance art pieces. "At that time I didn't like to play guitar as much. I'd play *a cappella* and screech," he recalled.[15] He became a traveller, wandering continents and crafting songs, recording them when he could borrow a four-track machine – or, when that failed, calling friends and performing songs down the wire into their answering machines. He put together a cassette of music from these travels, wrapped it with a child's marble, and sent it in an envelope pilfered from the French Treasury to the non-profit German record label Hinah in 2002. The label released the results, completely unfettered, as *The Charles C. Leary* later the same year.

Hinah was a micro-imprint that supported adventurous music, of one with the community labels of free folk; like those labels, Hinah prioritised interesting music over unit-shifting. Similarly artist-centred, but with far greatest resources and connections, was the US-based Young God Records, founded by Michael Gira from the post-punk group Swans. Gira heard Banhart's music through Siobhan Duffy, formerly of the queercore band God Is My Co-Pilot; he and Banhart went back to the original travelling tapes, collating and organising the music but not buffing it. The resulting album, also released in 2002, was called *Oh Me Oh My ... The Way The Day Goes By The Sun Is Setting Dogs Are Dreaming Lovesongs Of The Christmas Spirit*.

While *The Charles C. Leary* had gained only a very limited release due to the nature of the Hinah operation, Gira felt he had a marketable album and personality on his hands. The press release for *Oh Me Oh My* played up the uniqueness of Banhart, laying out the carpet for his charisma to mount the world stage. In it, Gira described Banhart as a "completely unknown, preciously talented young songwriter. ... When I first heard his voice I could not believe it. His occasionally warbling falsetto is alternately bizarre, soulful, comical, gentle, and often a little frightening".

Gira continued at length to emphasise Banhart's potential as a "major talent", claiming that Banhart's music had forced him into a new way of thinking: that he had to resist the impulse to re-record the songs and instead leave them to roam free in their original form, the meandering tape loops, background noise, hiss, and static all intact. Gira created the impression that Banhart was completely without artifice (while doing so within the constraints of one of the most artificial tools of the record industry: the press release).

The full, wordy title of *Oh Me Oh My* seemed to nod to both Tyrannosaurus Rex and The Incredible String Band, and yet its deconstructionist and absurdist language felt decidedly postmodern. Its lolloping onomatopoeias also suit the album itself, the brief snippets giving a twirling, radio-dial feel befitting the music's tactile, lo-fi qualities. "People talk about that album as a collage, as cut-ups, not as a proper album," Banhart recalled. "But there's a lot less 'collaging' than people say. It's ragged, but it wasn't thrown together carelessly. It was just the way it was recorded, somebody using the most rudimentary equipment that they could get their hands on and doing the best that they could."[16]

Oh Me Oh My is not as extreme as something like The Tower Recordings but was far from commercial. Yet its warmth and character struck a chord, and it picked up press where other, more easily digestible folk-influenced albums had not.

Devendra Banhart was an extrovert and an enthusiast. Already friends with many other artists, including Joanna Newsom, he forged links with most of the emergent artists in the growing communities of psychedelic and experimental folk. He was well liked and respected, his sincerity never in doubt. As Sharron Kraus, who met Banhart early on, recalls: "He had charisma, and was very intuitive, like somebody who was completely unfamiliar with the idea of anxiety."

Back on the East Coast, the self-starting scene in Baltimore, Maryland, continued to thrive. "There weren't a lot of all-ages shows you could play if you were a band," says Brian Weitz, who would later take on the name Geologist as a member of Animal Collective. "Baltimore in the 90s became a very DIY place for teenagers."

Among Weitz's fellow teens were David Portner, Josh Dibb, and Noah Lennox, close friends who all attended liberal schools in the Baltimore County area. "I feel very much like the space I've created with these guys as friends came out of high school," Dibb said in 2005.[17] The four friends began making music, together and individually. "Looking up to bands like Pavement, like Guided By Voices, Silver Jews, or even labels like Drag City," Weitz recalls, "we realised that these people weren't that much different to ourselves when they started their projects."

These early days were a melange of influences. Watching *The Shining* one night, Weitz and Portner became interested in abstraction and aural textures. "We were at a friend's house and there was a big blizzard – we got snowed in," Weitz recalls. "And we just decided that since the guy had a copy of *The Shining* in his house, we should watch it. We were doing a lot of drugs that night, and everyone went outside afterward to play in the snow, but he and I stayed inside." The pair rewound the tape and began to scrutinise the music used to evoke the Overlook Hotel and its isolating *redrum*. "We just stayed up for a while and talked about abstract sound," Weitz says. "How you could [use] these atmospheric or abstract or completely non-musical sounds to create the same kind of emotional impact as a melody or a score. For us, at the time, it was a really important realisation."

The four friends had also begun to explore psychedelic music, with Syd Barrett a particular jumping-off point. "The tools that you would use to make a horror music soundtrack often seemed similar to what you would use if you were trying to make psychedelic rock music," Weitz says. "We got really into reading about a lot of British psychedelic music. We heard about how Syd Barrett had gotten really into that band AMM, who were just making complete noise music."

AMM were an improvisational group whose cascading musical carnage seemed extreme even by the standards of free jazz. It was their methodology, rather than their sound, that would shoot through the future records of Animal Collective. There was also The Incredible String Band, whom Weitz had first come across by way of one of his perennial favourites, Pavement. "Pavement put out a song that was different for them, and everybody said it sounded 'like Pavement have been listening to a lot of The Incredible String Band'," he says. Weitz's interest in the group solidified when a kid at school performed 'Painting Box' during a talent show.

"They were part of the Ecology Club or something, and their parents were big Incredible String Band fans," Weitz says. "They let us borrow records, and I think that's how we heard *The Hangman's Beautiful Daughter* for the first time. That was the time for us, when we were about 17 years old, when all these things we started to see had been used together in the past, and we felt that it was a way in, which we could pick up for our time period."

The first fruits of all this was a seven-inch EP made by Dibb, Weitz, and Portner with two other friends, Brendan Fowler and David Shpritz. *Padington Band* was credited to Automine and wore its love for Pavement on its sleeve. It sold only in handfuls but gave a hedonistic sense of achievement. "[Baltimore] wasn't New York or LA, where we had any chance of being signed," Weitz recalls. "And we were just kids anyway. We found it satisfying to do it ourselves."

The friends scattered across the country to attend college but made the effort to maintain their musical bond over vacations and weekends. In the summer of 2000, the four of them settled in for months of improvisation in Portner's New York apartment, exploring sounds and bringing in acoustic guitars, synths, and found objects. "We'd try to approach playing an acoustic guitar like you were making techno," Portner explained in 2005. "It wasn't a very big apartment, but we'd work with space a lot, setting up this stereo microphone and an amp on the other side of the room."[18] For Noah Lennox, that time marked the very foundation of Animal Collective. "Everything since then has been a variation of what we explored that summer," he says. "We really cracked the egg open. It seemed like we could go anywhere we wanted after that."[19]

That summer's hothouse of musical ideas was just predated by what is considered to be the first Animal Collective album, *Spirit They're Gone Spirit They've Vanished*, recorded by Portner and Lennox – aka Avey Tare and Panda Bear – in the Portner family home. The album explores the ruptures between infancy and adulthood, its themes wrapped up in feedback noise, Silver Apples-style electronic psychedelia, and moments of acoustic whimsy. Nevertheless, the accompanying insert – about two young boys, raised by "fairies and the Angels of light", who make music "deep within the Wood" – could have been pulled straight from a Tyrannosaurus Rex LP.

Next came the dense *Danse Manatee*, for which Weitz (Geologist) came on board. It's a *volte-face* into far more hysterical soundscapes that pushes the buttons of minimalist electronica, progressive rock, and even industrial music. Yet it made the collective's next work, *Campfire Songs*, even starker. This one features all four musicians (Weitz recorded it but does not play on it). It was recorded in 2001, having already gestated for a good few years in the minds of Portner and Lennox, but not released until 2003.

"They tried to record it when it was just the two of them," Weitz recalls, "[but] it didn't sound very good. We had fallen in love with these MiniDisc players, very cheap recorders with microphones, around the time. It was sort of lo-fi, but it sounded better than that. It just made portable recording anywhere really easy." MiniDiscs meant freedom to record outside on a battery-powered setup, eliminating the need to trail cables into the house; the idea grew to make *Campfire Songs* an outside project, and to incorporate the sounds of the Maryland screen porch.

"It was November, so it was fairly chilly at that point," Weitz recalls. "Everyone had on scarves, and jackets, and the guys' fingers were really cold. I think a lot of people picture it like a warm summer night or something, and a bunch of guys casually sitting around a campfire, but it was quite the opposite." *Campfire Songs* was recorded in one take, although Weitz is at pains to stress that it was meticulously planned and practiced. "Even though it's a single take, it wasn't the *first* take. It had to be played perfectly from start to finish, in an hour, with three guys playing, and me sitting outside trying not to make too much noise. There were airplanes overhead, and there was a golden retriever walking around and sometimes he got close to the mic. It took two days to get the actual take."

Like its predecessors, *Campfire Songs* was self-released. It found a fairly small yet appreciative audience. Its homemade approach was consistent with the independent and fluid approach to music that had been at the heart of all of the four-piece's music up until now. The five lengthy, swimming tracks mark the first significant intersection between the still-unnamed Animal Collective and folk music. The next would be less blatant, but would travel far, far wider.

ᛗ

In Britain, too, there was a relocating of folk music into radical terrain in the first few years of the new century. It was different in character and slower to spread, but it could be argued that the comparative lack of press attention at this stage served the music well in the long-term. The gravitas embedded in the British scene stemmed from the approach taken by the two artists present at its early rebirth: Sharron Kraus and Alasdair Roberts. Their music paralleled and intermingled with the emergent scenes in the USA while also drawing from the traditions of the British Isles.

Sharron Kraus had been engrossed in pop music as a child, and in her adolescence had leaned toward goth and rock. "I used to go to the record library when I was at school and sometimes just randomly take home records that looked like they might be good," she recalls. "I picked up The Violent Femmes' *Hallowed Ground*. The cover had this stone-carved face and a black background around it. It could have been cheesy, it could have been crap; the first song on it is kind of folky but it's really manic."

Released in 1984, *Hallowed Ground* was the Femmes' second album, written mostly when bandleader Gordon Gano was still in high school. There's nothing remotely adolescent, however, about Gano's conflicted, vicious approach to Christianity in the lyrics, or the slit-throat twitch of songs like 'Country Death Song'. "It knocked me for six," Kraus recalls. "I guess I was coming from a teenage position, thinking these bloody religions, brainwashing people, it's all a load of rubbish – and then I heard this, and I thought, *wait*. This is not a load of rubbish. This is somebody who's really going into an exploration of the depths of hell as well as the ecstasies of heaven."

During her studies at Oxford University in the 90s, Kraus joined a goth group. "Being in a band with other people writing songs just kicked me off," she says. "I thought, I can do that. I'd been writing poems and stories and it just seemed like sticking words to music was not that different." The band soon split but Kraus continued as a singer-songwriter and recorded a goth-influenced demo. "I was trying to sing very low," she says. "I thought I could be a slightly female version of Andrew Eldritch from Sisters Of Mercy or something."

When a brief flurry of interest in the demo petered out, Kraus left music in limbo to concentrate on her studies – until she chanced upon a folk session in an Irish pub. "I had that kind of 'wow, there's this other world' moment," she says. "It was almost like finding a church, or opening a door on a magical world." Kraus was already in possession of a bodhran; now she and her drum became regulars at the club. She was fascinated by the different styles of singing she found there, and how different they were from the pop and rock vocals she knew well. "I started hearing traditional singers, and the singers in the style of bands like The Watersons and The Copper Family," she says. "Spontaneous three-part harmonies, or everyone joining in on the choruses."

At the end of the decade, Kraus moved to California. Fortunately, there was an Irish pub there, too, which was where she developed the material for her debut album. "I had a quite sad break-up toward the end of my time there," she recalls, "and I ended up just writing songs. They weren't songs *about* 'I'm so sad, I've just broken up with someone', but it was coming from there. I didn't have any friends, really, I was just writing stuff." After recording the songs, Kraus realised she had an album. Not yet sure what to do with it, she returned to the UK. It was only after stumbling on a review of a band called Goblin Market that she thought of contacting their record label, Camera Obscura.

"I first heard Sharron's work when I received an unsolicited four song demo CD-R in the mail," the label's founder, Tony Dale, later recalled. "I was totally blown away by the tracks she had sent, and wondered why she wasn't signed to a much bigger label already." As it happens, one bigger label, 4AD, had expressed an interest, but Kraus opted to throw in her lot with Dale, a decision she remains extremely pleased about. "For me, it all started with Camera Obscura," she says. "Tony Dale put me in touch with a load of people, and then this whole world opened up. They're now the people that I make music with, that I go on tour with, that I hang out with, and whose music I most like."

In 2002, Kraus released her debut album, *Beautiful Twisted*, a cornucopia of her influences to date that represents both the deep impact of traditional folk and her co-existing love of cerebral goth. There was nothing gimmicky or easy to dismiss about the record, which stirs up centuries-old images while also sounding effortlessly contemporary. It also showcases Kraus's skill as a lyricist. "I've always been interested in the school of thought that embraces some of the psychedelic thinkers, people like Timothy Leary and Robert Anton Wilson, people who were writing about mind-expanding consciousness," she explains. She also found inspiration in children's literature, notably the work of Alan Garner and Susan Cooper – "writers who write about magic, noticing the things in the world that it makes sense to think of as magical, and really making the most of them".

Beautiful Twisted was largely ignored by the mainstream British music press, which still seemed reluctant to accept folk music as anything other than old hat. But it did receive some coverage in mainland Europe and the USA, where Kraus found herself swept up in the burgeoning scene. She went on tour with The Iditarod and started hanging out with the nascent Espers, Fursaxa, Jack Rose, and others. She recorded her second album, *Songs Of Love And Loss*, back in Oxford, but took it to America to mix it with Jeffrey Alexander of The Iditarod. She decided to settle in Philadelphia, where she lived for a time with Brooke Sietinsons of Espers. "For a while, there was an art and music kind of commune, but without all the shitty parts of it," she recalls. "Everyone lived in shared houses and spent time together in the back garden, and played gigs together. And there'd be lots of bands coming through on tour to visit – it was a really lovely community of people."

Although Philadelphia had become her prime base, Kraus did occasionally return to the UK. She recalls wondering, on one return visit, whether anybody was making music that might interest her. "I remember listening to John Peel and he had Alasdair Roberts in session," she recalls. "I just remember listening to that and thinking – *wow*. He's doing some really good stuff. *And* he's in the British Isles."

By now, Alasdair Roberts had retired the name Appendix Out but chose not to inhabit another pseudonym. Instead, he stepped into his own name for *The Crook Of My Arm*, a collection of 12 beautifully sparse readings of traditional folksongs with his voice their powerfully plaintive vessel.

"I was listening to a lot of unaccompanied singers," he recalls. "The song is always the thing that attracted me most." Taking a turn toward full-scale folk was not the easiest option available to Roberts at the time, with traditional music still presumed to have little artistic integrity or commercial potential. "Drag City wasn't really interested in doing a traditional record," Roberts says, "so I asked Chris [Swanson] of Secretly Canadian if he would be interested, and he said yes." *The Crook Of My Arm* was recorded cheaply in Roberts's kitchen and released on the small American label in 2001.

Through his distinctive Appendix Out back catalogue, Roberts had gained credibility within the indie scene over the preceding few years. For him then to wholly and unapologetically explore the fecundity of the distinctly unfashionable oral folk tradition was certainly a brave move, but if anyone could pull it off, it was Alastair Roberts. *The Crook Of My Arm* still stands as one of his most heartbreakingly beautiful records. Even if, as Roberts says, he hadn't truly found his voice, the songs he chose here seem to adopt him, pulling out his voice and coaxing it into maturity.

Roberts followed *The Crook of My Arm* with an album of original compositions, *Farewell Sorrow* (2003), but the same old soul and ancient rhythms are present throughout. Roberts is lucid about the influence of literature and, in particular, religious sources on his work. "I sometimes wonder whether some kind of propensity for religiosity is inherited," he says, explaining that his mother is a minister in the Church of Scotland. "Although I don't subscribe to any particular faith, I do seem to keep returning to some interest in those kinds of matters in the music."

These records by Sharron Kraus and Alasdair Roberts were released a couple of years before the wider British public was ready for overt and unapologetic folk music. But both artists would prove instrumental in recasting traditional folksong into a modern tableau, and in sounding the alarm that folk music could be radical, contemporary, and British.

ᛗ

"As time went on, it had gotten more [to the point] where we would play with a group of people who everyone knew," Carin Sloan of The Iditarod recalls. "Everyone was going to be relatively pretty quiet. Who we would hang out with changed – it was more people who were doing the same style."

Supportive scenes and venues, created by a grassroots swell and a growing buzz around these new artists, began to develop throughout the USA. The Philadelphia scene fired up around one space in particular. Brooke Sietinsons had a loft on Second Street, which from the turn of the decade served to entice those whose tastes were folkier and more experimental. She was a guitarist and vocalist, a silk-screen artist, and a great organiser.

"Every folk show that came through of this kind, it was her, at her place,"

Greg Weeks recalls. "She was putting the bills together, she was the hostess, and she provided the hospitality." Sietinsons's loft became the focal point for locals, but she would also invite similarly inclined artists to play from beyond Philadelphia. Links were formed; little by little, the entwined vines strengthened through mutual respect and returned favours.

One evening, the bill at Brooke's loft included Stone Breath, The Iditarod, The Baird Sisters, and Greg Weeks. The Baird Sisters, Meg and Laura, had recently begun to perform together. Originally from Trenton, New Jersey, they did not come from an especially folky background, although their great-great uncle, I.G. Greer, had been a traditional song collector and performer. Yet the pair had become independently interested in folk music and its surrounding culture at a relatively young age. Laura had been researching and performing traditional Appalachian music, and making home recordings; when she took her younger sister along to see Sheila Kay Adams, Meg was similarly smitten. "It literally opened up a world of possibilities of what music and performance can do," she later recalled.[20]

The Baird Sisters performed a mixture of traditional songs and Laura's original compositions, guitar and clawhammer banjo encircling their desolate, simple harmonies. Theirs was a more direct and rootsy sound than those of The Iditarod or Stone Breath, but there was still something curious about the two sisters' music that marked them apart from the mainstream folk world. They made perfect sense in Brooke Sietinsons's loft.

"I was reading *Baby Let Me Follow You Down*," Greg Weeks recalls of the night he played alongside The Baird Sisters. The book, first published in the 70s, is a history of the folk community in Cambridge, Massachusetts. When he first heard The Baird Sisters, Weeks thought: "This is something straight out of this book."

As well as performing with her sister, Meg Baird also played in a trio with Brooke Sietinsons and a third musician. When that third person left, Greg Weeks was invited to fill in. That was the beginning of Espers.

These first few years of the 21st century were a magical time for pretty much everyone involved in this music. "At this point, the New Weird America, the whole folk scene, didn't exist in the public's eye," Weeks recalls. "It only existed in the relationships between people who were all really into this music and began talking to each other." Sharron Kraus remembers Devendra Banhart and Joanna Newsom dropping by for the first time. "It seemed like it was this whole thing that we were all excited about but that was not yet public property," she says. "They were starting to get press at that point, but it was before the whole fever. It felt like there was a buzz, even if it was just *us* buzzing. We were all excited about each other's music."

Perhaps inevitably, given his boundless zeal, it was Banhart who charmed enough people to provide an early document of the scene in its widest sense, from the free folk of Matt Valentine to the hearty, port-strength sound of Iron & Wine. In 2004, Banhart assembled a CD of music he liked for *Arthur* magazine entitled *Golden Apples Of The Sun*. As he later told *Mojo*, he and *Arthur*'s Jay Babcock had been mailing mix CDs to each other for some time when Babcock suggested they put one out. "It wasn't an attempt to label a scene," Banhart said.[21]

Few musicians felt able to resist Banhart when he approached them. Ben Chasny donated the Six Organs Of Admittance song 'Hazy SF' to the project. "That particular song was kind of just a fun pop song with fairly meaningless lyrics," he later recalled, "but for some reason Devendra wanted to put it on his comp. I tried to persuade him to use something less shallow but he wouldn't have it. He's funny like that. I like him very much. How can you not? He's so hairy and filled with so much positive energy."[22]

Golden Apples was not the first document of this new community. The *Ptolemaic Terrascope* compilations illustrated the growth of a sound, while *Hand/Eye*, compiled by Timothy Renner in 2002, brought together an extraordinary selection of music. But *Golden Apples* was the one that contained the most accessible tracks by the widest range of artists. Banhart's intention may only have been to support a magazine and a selection of artists that he liked, but *Golden Apples* did more than that. It helped to forge an identifiable sound for many observers, and allowed audiences and journalists to get a sense of a previously nebulous collection of artists. All of a sudden, the planets had aligned, and the sound made sense.

CHAPTER 18
There Was Sun

IN 2004, THE *NEW YORK TIMES* asked Devendra Banhart what he thought of the term 'freak folk'. "It's cool – you have to call it something – but we didn't name it," he replied. "We've been thinking about what to call it, and we just call it The Family."[1]

The *New York Times*' profile of Banhart also mentions Joanna Newsom, Adem, and Animal Collective, including them all as part of a group, a new genre, a flowering of something. Perhaps even a Family. Soon, the music made by this set of artists would be widely known as freak folk; others too would be pulled in, even if their 'freak folk' albums were made decades before the term was first used.

Freak folk has an unclear etymology. It is likely a bastardisation of free folk; for a short time, the two terms were used somewhat interchangeably. Yet by 2006, the term 'free folk' was no longer in mainstream use. Others were bandied about – alt folk, nu folk, and Dan Ireton's favourite, avant folk – but freak folk was the name that endured for progressive or psychedelic acoustic-based music.

Devendra Banhart's patience for the term would soon evaporate. In fact, it found very little love from any of the artists it was applied to. The idea of being a 'freak' had a sneering, patronising undertone, and quickly became shorthand for haircuts and kookiness rather than anything musical. "As soon as the labels got thrown out there," Greg Weeks recalls, "everything [got] jokey. You had *Lord Of The Rings* coming out at the same time, so there was this whole contingent of press that would write about it as being about elves and magic mushrooms. That's not where any of this was coming from at all."

In a painful article in the *New Musical Express*, Banhart was dubbed both King Of The Quirkysomethings and Donnie Barko, while his music was said to "gambol freely around Planet Hatstand". The dismissive tone felt particularly awkward given than Banhart himself seemed to be in a reflective, serious mood. "Who would be affected by an ongoing massacre?" he asked, presumably about the war in Iraq, although no context is given. "This [is] the first time I've seen people being bombed on CNN."

Banhart was not the only one to experience this kind of coverage, but he certainly bore the brunt of it. This was partly because of his own smoke-and-mirrors persona and distinctive image, but mostly because he had become a celebrity and a focal point. After the ebullient tape-scramble of *Oh Me Oh My* and the similarly inclined *Black Babies* EP (2003), the expectation was that Banhart would release something equally skittering and rough-hewn. He did not. Instead, he used Michael Gira's Young God resources to move his sound on while retaining its affectionate intimacy.

Banhart worked for ten hours a day for 12 days at the home of the engineer Lynn Bridges on two new albums, *Rejoicing In The Hands (Of The Golden Empress)* and *Niño Rojo*. The first of these two was originally to be called *Rejoicing In The Hands Of The Golden Negress*; Banhart explained that The Golden Negress, his current muse, cured sick animals by "[having] sex with a cornfield".[2]

When the sessions were disrupted by a flood in the studio, Banhart saw virtue in necessity. "A studio is built to eliminate instruments," he said, "and I think in order to give the songs a sense of place, you need to include the birds and the wind and the sunrays and everything else that's happening."[3] He and other musicians recorded overdubs in New York, packing careful foam wadding around the acoustic delicacy.

The title track on *Rejoicing In The Hands* features Vashti Bunyan, with whom Banhart had been in contact for a few years. For Bunyan, Banhart and his peers "have a sensibility that was totally missing in 1969, 1970, when I made *Diamond Day*. They are really generous to each other, and have this amazing sensibility about the world and how things should be". Banhart has since said that Bunyan's encouragement helped him to feel better able to share his music with other people.

Released in April 2004, *Rejoicing In The Hands* is sweet and silly yet poignant and powerful. It's hard to disagree with *Mojo*'s description of it as a "near-flawless set of leftfield folk". The titbits of press coverage Banhart had received for *Oh Me Oh My* were duly transformed into chunky features and interviews.

Niño Rojo ('red sun') followed in September. Banhart subsequently explained that while *Rejoicing* was the 'mother' album, *Niño Rojo* was the 'son'. "The son is more excited than the mother," he said, "so the lyrics are more exuberant. *Rejoicing* is mostly observations; sonically it's very calm. *Niño Rojo* is about a child off experiencing the world, and he has a lot more instruments in his songs."[4] Banhart created one of the songs, 'Be Kind', on the spot; the whole album has the feel of impulsive frolicking in the wilderness, fallen branches cracking underfoot.

Niño Rojo is more immediate than its predecessor. It widened Banhart's fan base still further, and also brought business interest: Banhart got some flak when 'At The Hop' appeared in a commercial for cheese, but he remained unrepentant. "The definition of selling out is when you're changing what you do because people *told* you to," he told *Plan B*. He also revealed that, while he was lactose intolerant, Andy Cabic, who co-wrote the song, was a cheese fanatic. "We actually had to buy a fridge for the cheese because they gave us so much," he said.[5]

Deflecting criticism with humour was indicative of Banhart's easygoing nature at the time. He was sanguine in the face of challenge, confident that his music was hitting the mark. By now, he had made a trinity of diverse albums, but there were hints that fame did not sit too easily with him. "I wish I wasn't so exhausted," he said in 2004. "So I could probably appreciate it more."[6]

Andy Cabic also had a band of his own, Vetiver, described by Banhart, in 2003, as "the best band in the universe".[7] Cabic had played only electric guitar until he was 25; then, when the instrument was destroyed in a car accident, he was given "a guitar as a gift: a kind of crappy guitar, a really thick-necked nylon-stringed guitar". He was grateful for the thought, but found this truculent acoustic hard to play. "I taught myself to fingerpick," he says, "because that's the only thing that sounded good on that guitar, to do those cowboy chords, open chords and fingerpicking."

Cabic had grown up listening to his parents' Crosby Stills & Nash, Bread, and America records. As his own tastes developed, he veered toward solid indie-rock; as a teenager, he was a fan of the MTV alternative music show *120 Minutes*. Until the demise of his electric guitar, he had played in a band that reflected these listening habits, The Raymond Brake. Formed in 1994 in Greensboro, North Carolina, The Raymond Brake had made several records for the prestigious Simple Machines label, home to bands such as Scrawl and

Tsunami – acts that blended a pop sensibility with rock guitars in an off-balance way.

The Raymond Brake called it a day in 1998. Eventually, Cabic and his tatty acoustic guitar moved to San Francisco. "I was just working and hanging out," he says. "I would go to the Art Institute all the time, because my roommates went to school there, and I would sit in on lectures and go in movies and art openings." He spent the next few years playing in various bands and investigating songwriting away from the rock context of The Raymond Brake until something started to gel in 2003.

"It was around that time that I probably met Devendra, and I think the first Vetiver shows were Devendra and I," Cabic recalls. "And then I met Alissa [Anderson], she played cello, and then Jim [Gaylord] was living in San Francisco, and I knew him from when I lived in Greensboro. So he came in and played violin."

This line-up recorded the songs Cabic had written on his acoustic guitar, with *Vetiver* emerging in 2004. It's a modest, hushed record, the sound of planed, varnished wood. It carries within it a real sense of Cabic's surroundings and worldview without recourse to an excess of nature metaphors. "A lot of times when I'm coming up with ideas, I'm just going for a walk around the city," he says. "I walk a lot in the parks and as I'm doing those things I'm singing songs, thinking of all kinds of stuff." It was this kind of subtle seepage that made *Vetiver* so touching and understated a record.

Caught up in that first burst of Devendra mania, *Vetiver* attracted a fair bit of interest, while the other guest appearances – by Joanna Newsom (on 'Amerilie'), Mazzy Star's Hope Sandoval, and former My Bloody Valentine drummer Colm O'Ciosoig – also aroused comment. "If you look back at most of the press attention that first album got, it's mostly in conjunction with other people," Cabic says. "My music [was] framed in light of people playing on my record. Which is fair, but not that measured in terms of why the record sounds the way it does."

Banhart in particular featured heavily in the reviews; according to a review on the Pitchfork website, it's he who "ultimately infuses Cabic's soft, fraying songs with woolly layers of warmth".[8] Vetiver were occasionally, unthinkingly referred to as 'Devendra Banhart's band' in a way that was both unfair and inaccurate.

"Any attention is good, and I felt like over time people would reconsider," Cabic says. "Early on, people try to distinguish your music by pinning it to a genre. They're trying to be very apropos, but that's really naïve to think you can do that. I thought whatever characterisation I was getting given at that time would be re-examined in the long-term." Certainly, on *To Find Me Gone* (2006), Cabic moved away from the acoustic laments of his first album toward a nourishing, country-tinged psychedelia. Some reviewers, to their credit, recognised this. "Banhart has a cameo," the *Observer* wrote, "but Cabic [is] his own man now."[9]

To Find Me Gone marked the start of Cabic's trek away from overtly folk-influenced music. After recording a covers album, *Thing Of The Past* (2008), Vetiver devolved further into country-rock on *Tight Knit* (2009). Like Ian Matthews, whose song 'The Road To Ronderlin' he covered on *Thing Of The Past*, Cabic found himself tethered to the folk scene when in fact his background and interests stretched far wider. With his friend, engineer Thom Monahan, Cabic also has a remix project, Neighbors, with whom he took *To Find Me Gone*'s 'You May Be Blue' from wah-wah psychedelia to blissed-out, post-rave pop. He also played in an electroclash group, Tussle. "Vetiver and Tussle were happening at the exact same time," he says. "I was balancing both for a few years. And then touring with Devendra along with Vetiver was too much and so I stepped aside. I love Tussle.

"It's really this idiom of folk that people have used to define Vetiver, but that's never really been the focal point of my music," he continues. "That's an influence, and certainly it's a touchstone when people look at the instrumentation of that first record. But to me it was just pop songs in the folk idiom."

⋈

In the early days of Espers, Meg Baird, Brooke Sietinsons, and Greg Weeks bounced off each other well. "A lot of the first record was snippets of Brooke's that I tweaked and made into full songs, and stuff that I had written," Weeks recalls. "Meg's presence didn't really make itself felt until the second album as far as songwriting, but she came in as another instrument and added her flavour to all those songs." Espers began to record, with other stalwarts of the Philadelphia scene dropping by to help out: Laura Baird, Tara Burke, Matt Everett, Quentin Stoltzfus, and Margie Ayre.

Espers was originally released by Time-Lag Records in a limited edition of 300 vinyl copies, each housed in a luxurious, screen-printed sleeve by Sietinsons. The Maine-based label was a trusted source for modern acid, psychedelic, and free folk, having already released music by Six Organs Of Admittance, Fursaxa, and Charalambides. Time-Lag was the perfect home for

Espers, with all 300 copies selling out effortlessly. *Espers* was then picked up by Locust Music and issued on CD with much wider distribution in 2004.

The Locust edition of the album received a very strong review from the taste-making website Pitchfork. Significantly, the review was full of references to 'folk' and acts like Fairport Convention, Jackson C. Frank, Linda Perhacs, and Bert Jansch, the implication being that folk music was now an acceptable inspiration, and the Pitchfork-reading audience should have a working knowledge of the first generation of acid and psychedelic folk. The review concluded by saying that *Espers* "manages to embrace its influences while simultaneously eclipsing them".[10]

In 2005, *Espers* was given another limited vinyl release (this time without Sietinsons's opulent artwork) by the UK-based Wichita Records label. Interest in the band grew perceptibly. "With my solo stuff the press attention was close to nil," Weeks recalls, "but I can see the reason why. Espers was something really special, and I knew it was something special when we were doing it. But it still blew me away that people were paying as much attention to it as they were." By now, Espers had expanded to become a sextet, bringing in drummer Otto Hauser, cellist Helena Espvall, and bassist Chris Smith.

The group continued to explicitly acknowledge the past. Their next album, *The Weed Tree* (2005) consisted almost entirely of covers, including versions of Michael Hurley's 'Blue Mountain' and the traditional 'Black Is The Colour', here presented in an arrangement indebted to The Famous Jug Band. "We're a bunch of record nerds," Chris Smith said in 2007. "We wanted to apply the songs to our world, applying ourselves and our place and our camaraderie as a band to a set of what could be called traditionals."[11]

An intrinsic part of the Espers sound is its meticulousness, which they achieve through careful recording using analogue equipment. "It was about taking time, and making a statement by taking the time," Weeks says. "You have to do something that's musical, and you have to keep doing it until you get it close to how you really want it to sound." Unlike digital recording, there's little opportunity for chopping and changing; it's impossible to cheat in analogue. Weeks established an analogue studio, Hexham Head, initially "as a four-track with seven microphones in a bedroom". Then, as he gradually acquired more equipment and space, it became a full 24-track facility. He wasn't sure to begin with whether anyone beyond his immediate circle would want to use the studio, given how cheap and accessible digital recording equipment had become, but soon found that "there are a lot of musicians who love that music from that period. So they're willing to go to the expense".

Espers II was recorded at Hexham Head and released in 2006. It's an incredibly strong record, full of poise and razor-sharp attention to detail. Each of its tiny mosaic stones has an individual pattern. The opening 'Dead Queen' is a masterpiece of psychedelic folk that sets the scene for an album that's whittled and honed but has a backbone of pure instinct. The album brought more rhapsodic press coverage and led to increased numbers of a certain kind of admirer. "Our fans are very cerebral," Weeks says. "They know better than to embarrass themselves by going up and fawning. [But] when someone comes up and starts spewing platitudes, at least you know that they really love it."

Once the promotional activity for *Espers II* died down, however, many of the group's fans began to wonder whether they would ever make another record, particularly when news from the camp seemed focused on other projects. With Hexham Head growing in popularity, Weeks was becoming far more involved with recording other bands. Meg Baird made a solo album, *Dear Companion* (2007), before joining forces with Helena Espvall and Sharron Kraus for *Leaves From Off The Tree*. Espvall herself swerved into the avant-garde on her brilliant *Nimis & Arx* LP and subsequent collaborations with Ghost's Masaki Batoh. Otto Hauser had joined Vetiver, while the multimedia group Valerie Project was also taking up time.

The first album recorded at Hexham Head, just before *Espers II*, was *Music For Witches And Alchemists* by another Philadelphia-based group, Fern Knight. Bandleader Margie Ayre had grown up in a small dairy-farming community in upstate New York with an early penchant for soft rock. "My brother came home with the Meatloaf album one day," she recalls, "which I guess prompted me to spend my allowance on Styx's *The Grand Illusion*." Ayre was also inclined toward playing from an early age, learning first piano and then clarinet. After switching to the bass guitar, she began studying music at Ithaca College, where she formed the shoegaze band Difference Engine.

Difference Engine put out a few singles and an album, *Breadmaker* (1994), but seized up after a few years, which is when Fern Knight began. "In about 1998, I sold my amp, electric bass, and guitar to play acoustic instruments in folk-rock bands," Ayre says. After moving to Providence, Rhode Island, she contributed to two projects led by Alec K. Redfearn: the experimental free-jazz group The Amoebic Ensemble and the equally cutting-edge band The Eyesores. She also had a stint with The Iditarod.

All the while, Fern Knight was growing, having begun as a collaboration between Ayre and her former Difference Engine band-mate Michael Corcoran. "My idea was for Fern Knight to be mostly acoustic folk-rock, achieved on whatever instruments we had lying around my living room," Ayre says. "From germs of song ideas to fully-formed ones, we homed in on a sound for about three years." The first Fern Knight album, *Seven Years Of Severed Limbs*, emerged in 2003. It's a promising and intriguing collection that seems as indebted to Ayre's classical training as it does to folk.

Fern Knight had developed an entirely bolder sound by the time of *Music For Witches And Alchemists* (2006), which Ayre calls "my first foray as a solo songwriter for an entire album". Ayre was still based in Providence at this point but had recruited a new band under the Fern Knight name that included her old buddy Alec K. Redfearn. "There were issues with the tape machine," Ayre says of her first attempt at recording the songs in 2003. "I knew Greg Weeks was setting up Hexham Head, so I decided to shelve the album until he was ready to record it in 2005."

Ayre's 2003 demos have since been made available as part of the *Winter Solstice* boxed set. They reveal a flecked ingenuity at times but can't compare with the striking final version. "I had started working with Jesse Sparhawk," Ayre recalls. "He graced a handful of the *Witches* songs with his beautiful harp-playing. I think it ended up being a better album [than the 2003 version], with my songs and arrangements leading to a more fully developed sound." Released on VHF, *Music For Witches And Alchemists* is one of the most textured and complicated albums of its time, its torch-song sorrow melting into creaks and crinkles of folk.

In 2007, Fern Knight returned to Hexham Head to make a third, self-titled album. "I wrote most of the songs in Ireland in early 2006, drunk on the sea, and landscapes, and the love of my life, whom I was about to marry," Ayre recalls. That love was Jim Ayre, who was now also playing in Fern Knight; also new on board was violinist James Wolf. The album ends with the three-part 'Magpie Suite'. "The spirit conveyed in the song cycle is that of a beautiful green age in an apocalyptic landscape about to be laid to dust and its struggle to escape this end," Ayre says. "My hope was that the album's overall musical effect is a lush and pastoral ode to all things living, a running theme that winds through the album."

Fern Knight passed through the heyday of freak folk on nodding terms with the bigger names while forging something more progressive and classically hued. In this, they had much in common with the other artists who followed them into Hexham Head and sometimes ended up on Greg Weeks's own label, Language Of Stone.

"I was recording a lot of bands that were making really great records," he says. "And at the end they would ask, do you know anyone who would put this out?" Weeks set up Language Of Stone during the summer of 2007 as an outlet for these records and a showcase for the distinctive analogue recording process at Hexham Head.

Although its output was not entirely limited to folk-related music, Language Of Stone did unleash a number of interesting albums during the second wave of new psychedelic folk. There was the self-titled LP by Lights, a fiery mix of Runaways-style rock and wandering modern folk; *Come, Arrow, Come!* by Festival, all psychedelic discomfort and howling, rhythmic rings; and *Because I Was In Love* by Sharon Van Etten, who made modern folk of another hue entirely.

"I lived in Tennessee from right after high school to try to go to college," Van Etten recalls. "And I fell in love with a boy as soon as I moved to Tennessee and gave up everything I had in my life to be with this person. But he wasn't exactly supportive, musically." She had been singing, playing a variety of instruments, and writing songs from a young age, but made no music for the six years the couple were together.

When the relationship ended, Van Etten moved back home. "My parents got me a computer with GarageBand [recording software] on it and told me to start recording," she says. "I recorded all these songs that I [hadn't] played for anyone for six years." She put out a CD-R, *Home Recordings*, in 2008, and subsequently handed a copy to Weeks after a chance meeting in Glasgow, Scotland.

Impressed by the unflinching honesty of the songs, Weeks invited Van Etten to Hexham Head. "Then, after we recorded the album, he wanted to release it," she laughs shyly. "Very awesome. Way more than I could have thought, you know?" The resulting *Because I Was In Love* won praise for its open-handed confessional style and fresh approach to the singer-songwriter genre. "I want it to be cool to be sad," Van Etten says, "and I want to let it be known that it's OK to be in love and to get your heart broken."

By the time *Because I Was In Love* was released, three years had passed since the last Espers record. As fans had feared, the band had indeed spent very little time together during the intervening period. "Most everything for [*Espers III*] came out of one jam session of ideas that we had," Weeks recalls. "After that, almost another year went by, and then it was like: 'OK, we've got to really start doing something here, it's just ridiculous to wait this long.'"

Espers III didn't surface until late 2009. The fractured approach to its creation is clearly audible. It's a less measured album than *Espers II* and, notwithstanding moments of incandescence (like 'Another Moon Song'), feels slightly undercooked. "It came out of a period where everybody involved was having difficulties in life, and there was a lot of stress present and a lot of anxiety, fatigue, and there were a lot of changes going on in the band," Weeks says. "I guess it triggers those feelings for me, and maybe it'll take a while before I've got enough distance to actually listen to it as a record on its own."

Espers brought gravitas to the new psychedelic folk. Their music is grounded in the past but of the moment and not blinded by unquestioning reverence to history. For many of the overt psychedelic-folk bands that followed, the quiet influence of Espers loomed as large as had that of The Incredible String Band after *The Hangman's Beautiful Daughter*.

◄

Like Greg Weeks, Devendra Banhart and Andy Cabic also decided to form their own label, Gnomonsong, with much the same ethos as Language Of Stone. "It was an idea between Gary Held, who runs Revolver, and Devendra and me," Cabic says. "It's sort of an in-house label at Revolver. Initially it was friends' albums that didn't have an outlet for release, but we just try to put out things we really like."

The first Gnomonsong release was Jana Hunter's *Blank Unstaring Heirs Of Doom* (2005). Hunter had already put out a split LP with Banhart on the Troubleman Unlimited label; her hypnotic, lo-fidelity music was an immediate indication that Cabic and Banhart didn't intend the label to be only (or even primarily) about psychedelic folk.

Nevertheless, the label did put out some albums that fit squarely in the genre. The second Gnomonsong release was a reissue of *Feathers* (2006), the self-titled album by a Vermont group who had originally issued the album themselves a year earlier. If the promotional photographs of the band-members daubed in face-paint seemed to echo the Amon Düül freak-scene, the music resembled a chaotic version of *Espers*. *The Bride Of Dynamite* (2007) by Rio En Medio, the solo project of vocalist and ukulele player Danielle Stech Homsy, was another carefully selected release: a hairline fracture of home-recorded folk that Homsy had not planned to make public at all until persuaded to do so by Banhart. He then helped her re-record and organise the material, while keeping its graceful poesy intact.

Banhart himself embarked on a new label journey by switching from Young God to XL Recordings, which had begun in 1989 as a dance label but expanded its remit over the years to take in a wide range of alternative but still commercially viable acts. "I don't think any music lover only listens to one type of music," founder Richard Russell said in 2008.[12] Devendra Banhart, too, was a music lover; appropriately, his diversity of interests became more apparent on his XL debut, *Cripple Crow* (2005).

Banhart spoke at length during this period about the influence of Tropicália on his music. "It's about being open, and it's about exploring," he said in 2005.[13] *Cripple Crow* is about Devendra Banhart zealously bringing in other influences while reducing, very slightly, his folkishness. His vocals have lost something of their Bolan-esque extremity; the quiet acoustic surrealism has been superseded by a Technicolor Dada; and there's an unmistakably soaring, soulful quality to the record. It's still far from slick, but it is a move away from the bobbled harmony of what came before. It was also the first Banhart album not to feature his own artwork on the cover. Instead, it shows a gathering of friends and collaborators, with Banhart himself crouching at the front under a carnival-esque wingspan.

Aside from some mild consternation over the lusty 'Little Boys', which Banhart said was intended as a way to guarantee the album wouldn't be played in Starbucks, the album was well received. Several reviewers noted that Banhart was growing up. It was a fair observation. He had lost something of the sweet purity of the Young God years, but that was, on balance, probably a good thing. Another album of wayward acoustics might have started to grate. Despite overstaying its welcome at 22 tracks (or a whopping 30 on the vinyl version), *Cripple Crow* was a refreshing plunge into new territory.

Banhart recorded the follow-up, *Smokey Rolls Down Thunder Canyon* (2007), over a period of six months at his house in Los Angeles. "It was a trip and a challenge," he recalled.[14] Perhaps due to the extended gestation time and homely atmosphere, the album gravitates toward languid siestas. This may have been a natural outgrowth on the expansiveness of *Cripple Crow*, but for some it proved that Banhart was now heading in the wrong direction. *The Wire* had been among Banhart's earliest supporters, but was particularly scathing about this latest album, complaining: "Only after wading through the swamp to the final three tracks do we get anything approaching sincerity, albeit of a cloying kind."[15]

Others found this 'sincerity' intriguing, since it was widely interpreted as stemming from Banhart's split from his girlfriend, Bianca Casady. "Love is a difficult thing to hold on to," he later recalled. "It's a slippery little beast. It's not always the most sunny day, or the most sunny experience; there's thunder too. But that's just how we all ride through life. It's hard not to have the things in your life leave an indelible mark on your perspective, your vision, and your dreams, although I try to be very careful about my inner space all the time."[16]

It may be that Banhart, too, had come to recognise the problems inherent in *Smokey Rolls Down Thunder Canyon*. "I think this record, compared to the last, is a lot more focused," Banhart said about the follow-up, *What Will We Be* (2009). "Often, I feel that things are coming apart at the seams, that the tectonic plates are moving too fast to make sense, but with this record I felt as close as I have done to real control."[17]

Banhart recorded *What Will We Be* in the Northern Californian town of Bolinas, which held special meaning as the place where one of his favourite authors, Richard Brautigan, lived out his final years. The town also has a reputation for secrecy; any attempts at putting up road signs have always been swiftly dismantled by local residents. Banhart did his best to uphold this spirit, although those curious enough were able to work out the setting from the Brautigan-themed hints he dropped in interviews.

More folk-rock than folk, *What Will We Be* sounds pegged and hemmed, but perhaps this wasn't a bad thing, given the misfires of *Smokey*. One big change was Banhart's decision to bring in an outside producer, Paul Butler of the British band The Bees (or A Band Of Bees, as they are known in the USA). "Having an outside perspective brought just that: perspective," Banhart later revealed.[18] Butler imposed discipline, insisting that Banhart warm up vocally for an hour before each session.

Like *Smokey*, *What Will We Be* received mixed reviews. For some, there wasn't *enough* Banhart this time. The fact that the album was released on Warner Bros also drew criticism, although Banhart himself insisted that he had recorded the album without knowing who was to release it, and claimed to have made no concessions to the label. "Majors have changed," he said. "It's no different from being on a very, very small indie."[19] Indeed, he had had to compromise when making his first records for Young God: he didn't like the label's house style for album artwork, and was unhappy that music videos were released without his final agreement.

Back in 2003, Banhart had admitted to feeling "kind of naïve about all this. All the press stuff, and all this – I don't feel like it changes anything, and it doesn't change me".[20] But it *did* affect him, at least a little. He began to bristle at interviewers' questions, particularly if they were about 'freak folk' or 'selling out'. He was clearly tired of going over similar ground. As the decade drew to a close, however, there were signs that the sparky, surreal Devendra Banhart of old was returning. "As I get older, there's this new realisation …

that I can never be who I once was, but only who I want to become," he said. "And who is it he wants to become?" the interviewer wondered. "A nice old lady," he said, a smile spreading once again across his bewitching features.[21]

Another act that briefly approached Banhartian levels of press interest was CocoRosie, formed by sisters Bianca and Sierra Casady in 2003. Like Banhart, the Casadys had an unconventional childhood. Their mother was an artist, keen on upping sticks and getting rid of all her possessions every now and then; their father was involved in The Peyote Way Church of God, a Native American religion known for its ingestion of mescaline. "We always felt pretty much like freaks," Bianca recalled in 2004.[22]

For many years, the sisters did not speak to each other. "We would go to family gatherings and not even make eye contact," Bianca later recalled. "We even lived in the same apartment building in New York for a while – and that was when we were the furthest apart. We would cross each other in the hall like total strangers."[23]

The sisters lost touch completely when Sierra moved to Paris to study opera. Bianca has professed to being completely uninterested in music prior to CocoRosie, but Sierra was long fascinated by it. She had been attracted to medieval music in high school, but had been shepherded into opera, which was felt to be more suitable for her voice. It was all fine for a while, but Sierra developed a mistrust of the operatic hierarchy. "In the society of classical music and opera there is a really narrow and particular audience – upper class elitist," she said in 2004. "That community has such a narrow mind about the creator, the composer."[24] She had expressed an interest in writing as well as singing, which was frowned on by her institution and further contributed to her estrangement.

Then, unexpectedly, Bianca turned up on Sierra's doorstep in Paris. The sisters found each other again and soon began to dress up, drink champagne, and make music in the bathtub. Experimenting with acoustic guitar, found objects, and a range of vocal styles, they recorded a set of songs that eventually became *La Maison De Mon Rêve* (2004). The sisters have since said that they never intended these recordings to be heard by anyone except their own friends – until the hip Touch & Go label found out about them and released them into the wider world.

La Maison De Mon Rêve was unburdened with expectation. It was an experiment, an expression of the Casadys' newfound closeness, and perhaps a rebellion against Sierra's classical training. But when it was released, and especially when it picked up a fair amount of interest, the weight of anticipation grew quickly. "We tried to do something that wasn't a huge jump from what we were doing, something really earthy and basic, but people just wanted to put it in the computer and equalise the voices," Bianca later recalled of the duo's initial attempts at making another album.[25]

These experiences told CocoRosie that they would have to do things themselves again. And they did – almost literally. *Noah's Ark* (2005) was shaped on tour and recorded in fields, barns, and studios in various geographical locations. It contains a similarly objective mix of what had made *La Maison De Mon Rêve* so fresh and attractive, albeit with a soupçon more gloss than before. But whereas *Maison* seemed genuinely ditzy, *Noah's Ark* sounds uncomfortably studied.

The sisters chose wisely to regroup before returning with *The Adventures Of Ghosthorse And Stillborn* (2007) and *Grey Oceans* (2010), on which they move away from the *Maison* template toward a postmodern, art-pop sound with barely any reference to folk. They rejected both the 'freak folk' tag and also the very notion that they formed part of a wider group. For the Casadys, any association with people like Banhart – who makes a guest appearance on *Noah's Ark* – came from friendship rather than shared musical sensibility. "We grew up thinking of ourselves as outsiders," Bianca recalled. "We still do, although maybe not as much."[26]

◩

While Bianca and Sierra Casady were making their first bathtub recordings, the four Baltimore musicians who called themselves Geologist, Avey Tare, Panda Bear, and Deakin were slowly coming around to the idea that they needed a unifying name to avoid confusing or frustrating potential listeners. And so they became Animal Collective, although there was no shift in their general perspective: the 'Collective' part of the name meant that as many or as few of them could appear on each project as they saw fit.

Having established that principle, however, all four of them *did* appear on the first Animal Collective album proper. Like *Campfire Songs*, *Here Comes The Indian* (2003) was recorded live but marked a return to the electronic-based experimentation of the musicians' earliest recordings. The sense of frenzied abandon came about as a result of the way the album evolved. Not only was this the first time that all four musicians had played on a recording, they were in a cramped studio, having just returned from an intense tour,

274

while Noah Lennox and David Portner were sharing both a day job at the same record store *and* an apartment. Cabin fever became the group's fifth member. "That's why the album's so hectic and chaotic," Brian Weitz said in 2005. "It was trying to shove all this weird energy into one recording."[27]

In late 2003, Animal Collective signed to Fat Cat Records. After the chest-tightening anxiety of *Here Comes The Indian* came the exultant *Sung Tongs* (2004), which featured only Portner and Lennox. The pair approached things differently from the start, developing songs with a focus on open-tuned acoustics and voice, with few sound effects and minimal drumming.

Animal Collective had not arrived at *Sung Tongs* through listening to folk music. According to Portner, the album was primarily inspired by electronica, including the Kranky label's annual *Pop Ambient* compilations. "Just like a wall of hums," he said. "We wanted that feeling but with acoustic guitars."[28]

Sung Tongs was recorded at a house owned by Portner's parents in Lamar, Colorado. Like *Campfire Songs*, it has the warmth of a field recording; the patron of a local deli even makes an appearance on 'Who Could Win A Rabbit'. But while *Campfire Songs* sounded like a home-cooked jam session, the pop aesthetic of *Sung Tongs* brought Animal Collective into new and more accessible territory. That, combined with the clout and kudos of Fat Cat, resulted in more widespread press coverage, with some journalists all but fainting with joy. Released slap-bang in the middle of freak folk's first feeding frenzy, *Sung Tongs* fell effortlessly if unintentionally in step with the emergent genre.

"We certainly don't consider ourselves as part of a folk lineage," Brian Weitz says now. Nor did they at the time. "Devendra's the only new-folk guy," Noah Lennox said in 2005. "He's the sole member of that group. It's always been his thing. He's what it is."[29]

One subsequent collaboration aside, Animal Collective have increasingly distanced themselves in word and deed from folk music in the years since. "We listen to folk," Josh Dibb said in 2007, "but there's no way we're folk artists in any sense, and this whole notion that we improvise stuff is just bullshit."[30]

In the years between her first album, *The Milk-Eyed Mender*, and her third, *Have One On Me*, Joanna Newsom changed in the public perception from folkish pixie-girl to roaring auteur – someone spoken of in the same breath as Joni Mitchell, Robert Wyatt, and Kate Bush.

She recorded *The Milk-Eyed Mender* in her apartment, with Noah

Georgeson, in exactly the same fashion as her previous EPs. The only differences were in terms of care, time, and the use of multi-tracking, whereby Newsom would record her harp first and the vocals afterward. "I hadn't done it that way before," she said in 2005. "I had to teach myself how."[31] The songs on the album are a mix of new tracks with re-recordings from *Walnut Whales* and *Yarn And Glue*.

Even from this first record, Newsom's creative process was scrupulous. The songs went through many guises and changes before being recorded. She has said that her lyrics often begin as gibberish, the actual words only coming later. That too was a push-pull process. "I do choose words very deliberately," she said at the time. "Sometimes it's because I like to play with syllabic emphases, and where they intersect with the downbeats. Or maybe I like to think of the sung part as a contrapuntal line, so sometimes it'll syncopate with the music and other times it'll be parallel to it."[32]

When Drag City released *The Milk-Eyed Mender* in March 2004, few would have heard Newsom's self-released EPs or experienced her live performances. All people had to go on were the testimonies of her friends and supporters, notably Will Oldham and the ever-munificent Devendra Banhart, who both promised the world that she was something special. Yet, even without any foundation stones at all, *The Milk-Eyed Mender* would likely have grabbed attention.

Hearing Joanna Newsom for the first time is an arresting experience. "This thing that's been hammered into my head [is] that you either love my music or hate it," she said.[33] Fortunately, most critics loved it, even if they were unprepared either for an album built around a harp or for Newsom's unique vocals. Some found her voice perplexing, dismissing it as 'childlike' even while acknowledging that her lyrics held considerable intellectual cachet and emotional colour.

Like the words, the album's cover art crowds meaning into every space. It shows a piece of embroidery stitched together by Newsom's friend, Emily Prince, from dresses and other found objects. "I was specifically thinking of the alchemy of closeness, of all these things bumping up at the edges, crammed together in this sort of airless, lush, dense collection," Newsom later said. "I wanted there to be a sense equally of something a child would make for a Mother's Day present, but also of a shrine to someone who's died."[34]

Newsom made her feelings about 'freak folk' clear early on. "There is as much of a connection between my music and some of the people I'm being grouped with as there is between it and music that has been made for the last

30 years," she said.[35] It was the only hook readily available to hang her on, however, and hung she was. *The Milk-Eyed Mender* was acknowledged as a high-water mark of freak folk by critics who placed it comfortably within the genre. This association only strengthened when she toured with Devendra Banhart and Vetiver in 2004, a summer adventure since documented on film in *The Family Jams*.

With Newsom's second album, *Ys* (2006), the shock factor of her voice was gone. But if audiences thought they knew what to expect, Newsom managed to flummox them once again. *The Milk-Eyed Mender* is bite-size, cropped, and tart compared to the sprawl of *Ys*'s five long, intense pieces. And where her first album was a relatively simple, home-recorded piece, *Ys* took a vast leap away from comfortable surroundings.

Newsom had been listening to ambitious albums. She has acknowledged the influence of *Stormcock* by Roy Harper, *Anthems In Eden* by Shirley & Dolly Collins, and *Song Cycle* by Van Dyke Parks; it seems likely that Alan Stivell's *Renaissance Of The Celtic Harp* was an inspiration, too, given that its first track is called 'Ys'. (Newsom says the two letters came to her in a dream.)

"I'd say it's a pastoral record," Newsom told *Mojo* around the time of the album's release. "And I really feel like that pastorality is an almost unbearable, trembling sense of your own mortality, and the beauty of life." She has also cited the influence of pre-Christian mythology and the chasm between it and post-Christian morality. "The subject matter and the things I was thinking about and feeling demanded a longer song form," she said.[36] The language of *Ys* is arcane and impenetrable yet graceful and fluid. The lyrics deal with the big questions: love, loss, death, life, and how responses to these things can crucify or liberate.

Newsom maintains that every single line of *Ys* holds significance. In a frank conversation with *Arthur* magazine in 2006, she went into specifics that she previously evaded elsewhere. She revealed that three things underpinned *Ys*: the death of her best friend, her family, and the recent break-up of a relationship. All three combine on the album, particularly on 'Only Skin', their fibres interweaving like the wheat and flowers in her hair on the cover. The centre of the family story, meanwhile, can be found on 'Emily', written about and named after Newsom's sister, who also sings on it. "In some ways this song is a tribute to her," she said, "and in other ways it was like a plea, a letter to her about some stuff that's happening close to home, and a reference to the fact that a lot of the little structures and kingdoms and plans we built when we were younger are just falling to fucking pieces."[37]

Newsom has been particularly voluble on the influence of West African kora music on her harp playing, and her own individual take on its rhythms. "That disorientation is really effective for creating something that you actually have to listen to," she said. "When any element in the musical environment is tweaked in such a way that you don't feel like you know what's coming next, it can cause less of a passive listening experience across the board."[38] Another factor that contributed to the sound of Ys, in a roundabout way, was Newsom's heavy touring schedule. Constantly using her voice didn't only help the world get used to it: it also make it easier to control. Vocalist and listener met in the middle.

Newsom started work on Ys in December 2005, when she laid down harp and vocals with Steve Albini. She and Van Dyke Parks then hammered out the sumptuous arrangements, which were recorded to analogue tape in May 2006. Then, in July, Jim O'Rourke mixed the record. It was a massive task – even the cover art, a richly allegorical portrait by Benjamin Vierling, took six months to complete – but Newsom was fully satisfied with the results, telling journalists that there was nothing she would change about the record. Ys is a singular achievement, and one that guillotined any connection between Joanna Newsom and freak folk.

Following a one-off EP, *Joanna Newsom And The Ys Street Band* (2007), all was quiet on the Joanna Newsom front. For Newsom herself, things fell silent in a different way. She developed nodules on her vocal cords, leaving her voice "like the hiss on opening a Coke can".[39] She could not sing, speak, or even cry for two months; the resulting operation altered her voice, although Newsom has since admitted that she also made a deliberate attempt to modify her singing style.

Newsom's label, Drag City, announced her third album, *Have One On Me*, with a cryptic cartoon only a month before its release date. The album's muse, and the subject of the title track, was Lola Montez, a royal mistress and dancer notorious in 19th century Bavaria. "I found there was a parallel between what I do as a profession and what it meant to be a female artist at that time," she said. "I was noting the intersections between being a courtesan or a whore, and these professions that were socially looked down upon, the sort of professions that were basically creative."[40]

No credible review sought to tie *Have One On Me* to freak folk. This was not only because the term itself was no longer a buzzword, but was also because the album simply *isn't* freak folk. Any genre tie placed around Joanna Newsom from Ys onward would prove as easy to break as saffron thread.

On the surface, 'freak folk' was an easily identifiable phenomenon, but the label hid more than it illuminated. "The idea that 'folk' came back was a very self-congratulating idea for the indie media," Ben Chasny said in 2009, "because they got to pretend like they discovered something."[41] It's a reasonable point. Most of these artists were thoroughly knowledgeable about musical history; those who accepted the folk tag tended to qualify it, or pointed to a far longer history than the freak-folk bubble.

Psychedelic-folk artists multiplied in number throughout the second half of the decade. Some would use freak folk as a starting point for digging back into the past, judiciously mixing old and new influences; some would hear the structures of psychedelic folk and go off wildly into reverie, creating music direct from an awakened muse; others, inevitably, would simply produce counterfeit versions of 'Dead Queen' or 'The Body Breaks'.

Perhaps the last word on the freak-folk phenomenon should go to B'eirth, who carried on throughout the period as he had done before: making instruments, playing beguiling psychedelic folk, working through the ideas in his head for a small, loyal audience. Somewhere around the middle of the decade, B'eirth was asked what kind of music he made.

"Err, I play psychedelic folk," he said, with a self-effacing shrug.

"Oh come *on*," his inquisitor replied, clearly unimpressed. "*Everybody* plays psychedelic folk!"

"Wow," B'eirth replied. "I didn't notice."

CHAPTER 19

Reality's A Fantasy

"WE WERE AWARE, as a group, that there was this undercurrent of something happening in America," says Ben Phillipson, who formed The Eighteenth Day Of May in 2003. "The Americana thing had happened a few years before that. Americans were seemingly a lot less neglectful of their heritage and their roots."

At the start of the new millennium, the image of psychedelic folk in Britain was as stodgily unfashionable as ever. The 90s Britpop craze had eulogised a certain type of 60s music – short, sharp, intellectual pop – while shoving away anything with the stain of hippies or folk (or both) as a perpetual embarrassment. Britain in the 60s came to be associated with swingin' Carnaby Street; The Incredible String Band languished far from rehabilitation.

The early 2000s hadn't really helped either. "You had all this indie-rock, and indie-rock had become the default sound of pop music, which I find ironic and almost slightly disturbing," says musician and journalist David Sheppard, whose many musical projects include Ellis Island Sound. Stephen Cracknell of The Memory Band found the live circuit particularly lacklustre. "It was pretty unexciting," he says. "Also, at that time, people weren't putting bands on. If they did, it was a very narrow world."

There were a few spangles of activity, but they felt unconnected to any wider national trend. Alasdair Roberts and Sharron Kraus had released solo albums, but both did so as exceptions that proved Britain was *not* especially interested in any radical overhaul of folk music. Kraus had found her community in Philadelphia rather than her native Oxford, while Roberts also continued to be associated with the American scene. This was partially historical, following the Appendix Out years and the Drag City connection, but the relationships were ongoing, and manifested again in the 2002 project Amalgamated Sons Of Rest, which featured Roberts, Will Oldham, and Jason Molina of Songs: Ohia. While Kraus and Roberts cared far more about making interesting music than consciously spearheading any kind of specifically British movement, the ease with which both found kindred spirits in America rather than in Britain surely spoke volumes.

Ptolemaic Terrascope was a British magazine, but editor Phil McMullen's attempt to recreate in London the successful Terrastock festivals that had played out in America brought financial catastrophe. "The London Terrastock was simply much too early," he says of the event, which took place in 1999. "I totally and completely misjudged the level of interest over here. Just because we completely sold out Terrastock 2 in San Francisco within a couple of weeks of going on sale back in 1998, I assumed that putting a lot of the same bands on here in England a year later would generate similar levels of interest. It didn't. We struggled to sell 200 tickets."

There were a few bands that had been quietly practising psychedelic folk music, on a similar scale to acts of two decades earlier, like Caedmon or Stone Angel. One of the most consistent among them was Mary Jane, formed in Southampton in 1993 by Paul Taylor, who had previously played in the very 60s-influenced group The Magic Cat. Taylor found a kindred spirit in Jo Quinn, whose mother was a folk singer. As Mary Jane, they carved a small niche for themselves during the 90s, but not without a struggle.

"We will never think fondly of our years playing working men's clubs or restaurant pubs, where we vied with the condiments for attention," Quinn says. They also tried playing at what Taylor calls "hardcore folk clubs" but soon realised "we were indeed miles away from that, too". They found more open-minded audiences on the psychedelic scene, at student-oriented venues and summer festivals, but still stuck out. There was so little *general* interest in psychedelic folk that attendances were modest at best. Spread across the world, however, there *was* a small, record-collector interest in psychedelic folk, and to these listeners the Mary Jane sound was authentic and appealing. Thanks largely to mail order and the internet, the albums *Hazy Days* (1995), *The Gates Of Silent Memory* (1997), *Tacit* (1999), and *To The Prettiest One* (2000) sold in small but respectable quantities.

In the early 2000s, Mary Jane noticed an increase in gig attendances – particularly when more appropriate venues began to open – and general interest in their music. "There has been a surge of interest, and much more open-mindedness among the younger audiences to give folk a chance," Quinn says. This also coincided with a new approach from within Mary Jane, their music now drawn, to a greater extent, from the well of improvisation. Younger people, more familiar with Devendra Banhart than Trees, could identify better with this approach, and this too helped Mary Jane find a new audience.

Another of those British spangles was Circulus. Michael Tyack had loved garage rock and psychedelia since his teenage years, and had duly played in a series of bands influenced by these sounds: The Mad Hatters, Margin Of Sanity, The Jackals. Even then, however, he was just as attracted to Pentangle's *Sweet Child*. "It's got tracks like 'The Earle Of Salisbury', which is an Elizabethan piece," he says. "And those particular tracks really interested me."

Tyack moved to the USA in 1988; in New York, on a whim, he bought a cassette of Renaissance lute music. "That was it," he says. "It was like, now I know what the missing ingredient is in the music that I need to make. I've never looked back." He began to study the lute and, in doing so, drew himself away from contemporary music. He moved back to Britain in 1991, experimented further with lute and guitar, and recorded his first solo album in 1996. Sadly, he was paralysed by a crisis of confidence and shelved the project.

A year later, however, Tyack decided the time was right to "do what I've always wanted to do, which was create a medieval rock band". He met Emma Steele, who seemed to share his rare vision, and the two of them formed a core around which other members have since rotated. Circulus was born. The *Giantism* EP (1999) garnered the attention of *Ptolemaic Terrascope*, but Tyack had a nagging feeling that Circulus wasn't really the band of his dreams. *Giantism* was more conventionally and cosily rock-oriented than he wanted. "The years that we were together in the band, and that line-up, had about a five-year span – it was never really a medieval rock band," he says. "It wasn't until Emma left that I said: 'Right! We'll make it a medieval rock band!'"

ᛝ

One of the recurring touchstones for musicians of the new British psychedelic folk is the soundtrack to *The Wicker Man*. "There's a bit of a *thing* with men of roughly my age, who discovered *The Wicker Man* at round about the same time," says Steven Collins of The Owl Service. "That was my first exposure to folk music. And I'll forever make the connection between certain British horror films from that period and folk music."

In 1998, 25 years after the film was first in cinemas, the soundtrack finally gained an official release. The label responsible was a small independent, Trunk Records, founded by Jonathan Benton-Hughes (known colloquially as Jonny Trunk) and three friends – all men of roughly Stephen Collins's age – in 1995. It was a label of love, an outlet for obscure film and television soundtrack obsessions and library music geekery; they released *The Wicker Man* purely because they wanted to.

Jonny Trunk first saw the film as a teenager. "We used to watch it as a comedy film," he says. "It is seriously funny. Christopher Lee is extraordinarily camp, and there are some really funny lines in there." Trunk had been interested in film music from a young age, however, and recognised the importance of *The Wicker Man* in this regard. There were rumours that the soundtrack had made it to vinyl, which Trunk tried in vain to track down. ("I'd ask people in the know," he says, "and they'd say: 'Oh, yes, we've seen one of those, it's got a blue cover, I think.'")

After finally accepting that *The Wicker Man* had *not* been released as a soundtrack album, Trunk Records set about correcting the oversight. It was not a simple process. The composer, Paul Giovanni, had died in 1990; the rights to his soundtrack were held in a labyrinth of anecdote, myth, and buck-passing. But with a flurry of faxes, phone calls, and sheer bloody-mindedness, Trunk Records eventually yielded results, and permission was gained to release a limited run of albums.

The source for the Trunk release was a stash of original music and effects reels archived in Pinewood Studios. Jonny Trunk went down to supervise the process. "They put these enormous reels on this giant tape machine, and pushed play on reel one," he says. "It immediately started with the noise of the aeroplane at the beginning, as the film started. It was one of those moments you never forget."

The upshot of obtaining *The Wicker Man* from these reels was that the soundtrack LP became more than just the music. "It has this acid thing to it because it's got those sound effects in it," Trunk says. "It's got *thunks* and *whooshes* and *clunks* – it has this other atmosphere. The whole album's like this weird trip, almost like a bit of sound design."

Under the terms of the contract, Trunk's release of *The Wicker Man* was strictly limited. The initial vinyl release sold out immediately; the subsequent vinyl and CD editions didn't hang around for long either, although a healthy bootlegging industry started up. The soundtrack wasn't made available officially again until 2002, when Silva Screen released a new version – minus sound effects – sourced from tapes owned by the film's Associate Music Producer, Gary Carpenter.

Trunk's 1998 release had all sorts of consequences that the label couldn't have anticipated. Firstly, it was a factor in *The Wicker Man's* entry into the canon of landmark British films, increasing awareness of it beyond the existing small community of fans and cinema buffs. Secondly, it established Trunk as a creditable label with strong cult appeal. Thirdly, and most unexpectedly of all, it helped many to see that folk music could be creepy and dark and *brilliant* – and that it couldn't be typecast in comfortable cardigans or ludicrous kaftans.

"*The Wicker Man* soundtrack was one of those things that happened just before the new folk boom," says Sam Genders, formerly of Tunng. "Did I really just say 'the new folk boom'? Anyway, it was an influence on a lot of people. Certainly on me and [Tunng band-mate] Mike [Lindsay]."

Jonny Trunk, too, is aware of the impact the record had. "Without a shadow of a doubt it was a little bit of a fuse to this whole thing," he says. "The record came out and it was after that when it all went off. People started getting into spooky folk."

One of the friends involved with Jonny Trunk in the label's earliest releases was Stephen Cracknell. "I've known Jonny since we were teenagers," he says. "I'm very proud of being involved with Trunk and I think it's a fantastic record label. But, after a while, you don't need four people to run a record label. I was getting more and more busy with recording, and The Memory Band was starting to come together."

Cracknell had been in bands for years. "What interested me right from the beginning was doing things that were production-based, and that involved computers," he says. "And also I would do acoustic stuff with different people. It's always been a mixture." Cracknell was open-handed in his approach to genre. Dissatisfied with the expectations and limitations of guitar-based indie music, he widened his world by taking lessons from musician Alan Weekes, a member of the hugely influential British group The Jazz Warriors. "I went in thinking I'd like to become a guitarist, and actually he taught me how to be a musician," Cracknell says. "It did improve my guitar playing a lot but he also got me interested in arrangements more, and all the things I could do. I began to see how drum machines, messing around with samplers, playing different instruments, could all fit together however I wanted. I think this is actually what Alan intended – he probably understood what I could do better than I could myself."

As Gorodisch, Cracknell started exploring the pathways between acoustic and electronic music, notably on the mini-album *Thurn & Taxis* (2001). It was also around this time that he was asked on tour with Manchester singer-songwriter Badly Drawn Boy who was then using a band called Fridge as his touring group. (Fridge – Adem Ilhan, Kieran Hebden, and Sam Jeffers – were at the forefront of British post-rock. Ilhan would soon become known by his first name only, while Hebden had already adopted the moniker Four Tet, mangling folk and electronics on his 2001 album *Pause*.)

The tour was both validating and inspiring for Cracknell. "I hadn't played live for a long time," he says, "and I really enjoyed it. Particularly meeting the guys involved with Fridge, whose music I was a fan of anyway. I once again saw how easy it was to be both a live band and to make music on computers."

After the tour, Cracknell briefly revisited his plans for a new Gorodisch album but soon scrapped it. "I just realised that something else was coming in some of the material," he says. "It suddenly clicked in my head." He had the idea to form a group instead, but was clear from the start that it would not be a traditional unit. "I wanted it to be influenced by people coming in, and then going, and coming back. I wanted it to be about bringing people together, and them reacting together. We started putting out EPs, doing the odd show. It was all very small scale and disorganised, but it seemed to work."

After making two seven-inch singles, The Memory Band released a self-titled album in 2004. It features Cracknell at its centre alongside a gyroscope of guests: Nancy Wallace, Adem, Polly Paulusma, Sam Jeffers, Rob Spriggs. "I would just get in touch with people and say: 'I need double bass, Adem you play the double bass' – and then he'd do it. I never really stopped to think too much about what that record was."

The Memory Band grasps at many different reeds. There's the folk electronica of Gorodisch; the hum of psychedelia; a dusky jamming quality; and the delicate hue of British tradition, as channelled by Nancy Wallace's pure voice. Embedded in The Memory Band's construction was a safety valve against stagnation. "The whole point of us was to carry on, because the narrative is in the people, and the narrative is in what we do, the experiences," Cracknell says. This revealed itself on the next album, the more structured *Apron Strings* (2006), the result of touring with a more regular band. The response was particularly strong in the USA, where the album was issued by DiCristina, home to Vetiver.

Stephen Cracknell did not evoke shallow graves or bronze-streaked leaves in the manner of an Alasdair Roberts or a Sharron Kraus. He didn't have the studied folk-rock history of Mary Jane or the eccentricities of Circulus. But what he did have was a lightness of touch, a wide interest in music, and a collaborative spirit. This made The Memory Band stand out, and sound unforced in both approach and effect. "We live in the world of the 15-second pitch," Cracknell says. "Right from the beginning, I wanted to do something that couldn't be pitched in 15 seconds. People have to take a little bit of time to learn about it."

From the outset, however, Cracknell found that people attempted to define The Memory Band. "That was quite alien to what we were doing," he says. "We set out our stall and we do it, and we don't worry about chasing people." The term most often used was folktronica. "It has always struck me as a very ugly-sounding word," Cracknell says. "It's not so much the ideas of these phrases. I'm quite into the sound of words, and they just never sound comfortable."

Folktronica – also known as electro-folk or laptop folk – became a densely populated hamlet in Britain during the early 21st century. Fridge alumni Four Tet and Adem were among the earliest and most innovative of its practitioners; Tunng came slightly later, but ultimately went furthest in incorporating pastoral grace and lysergic purrs with electronic modernity.

Singer-songwriter Sam Genders had been working the Derbyshire scene for a good few years following the breakup of his teenage bands, Smoke and Three Quarters To Dust. "I used to work in a pub in Matlock Bath, my home village," he says. One day a guy named John Tams, formerly of Muckram Wakes and The Albion Band, came in for a drink. "I gave John a demo tape. He helped me out with some advice, and I took an interest in some of the music he'd made."

Genders was in thrall to English folk when he met Mike Lindsay, then a freelance musician and producer. One of Lindsay's assignments was for The Fantasy Channel. "It wasn't actually making music for porn films," Genders says. "It was those things in between." Genders ended up singing on another of Lindsay's gun-for-hire commissions: "one of those *Daily Mail* free CDs, *Late Night Chill* or something. The track didn't get on. But then Mike worked on it some more, and we thought, oh, it's quite good, why don't we do some more stuff?"

The pair continued to record, influenced, as Genders recalls, by The Memory Band, *The Wicker Man*, Four Tet's *Rounds*, and early Fairport Convention. Genders was struck by the way Lindsay treated the electronic sounds he made with the delicate touch of a troubadour playing an acoustic guitar. Their daily sessions soon yielded an album's worth of material, although they hadn't really thought of releasing any of it until they discovered the Static Caravan label.

Geoff Dolman founded Static Caravan in 1999, inspired by other small but identifiable labels like Wurlitzer Jukebox, Earworm, and the Stereolab-run Duophonic imprint. He loved Genders and Lindsay's submission. The label released *Mother's Daughter And Other Songs* in 2005, with Genders and Lindsay adopting the name Tunng. "We couldn't really have released that record at a better time, for it to sound fresh, and for people to take an interest in it," Genders says. *Mother's Daughter* received a *lot* of coverage. "It did feel, quite quickly, like there was a kind of scene there. People understood what it was, so that was really good."

Tunng accepted invitations to play at both folk and dance music festivals, and found themselves dragged into press arguments about 'folk music'. The debates were telling – and an indication that the British music press was finally willing to discuss the subject. "I'm fascinated by why people get so wound up about it," Genders says. "I never had a problem with people labelling us. Actually, as a record buyer, it's slightly helpful. I probably wouldn't buy an album labelled death metal, even if the band don't consider *themselves* to be death metal."

For their next album, *Comments Of The Inner Chorus* (2006), Tunng expanded beyond Genders and Lindsey. Becky Jacobs, who appears as a featured vocalist on *Mother's Daughter*, became a full-time member; gradually, since "everyone knew someone", Tunng became a six-piece. "As a group of people, we grew in understanding as to what each other could do," Genders says. "It sounds more like a band as you go through. I do think on the first album you can hear the join a bit more – you can hear the songs and guitar, and then there's the electronics. On the second album it's less obvious, and on the third album you can't really tell the difference at all."

Genders left Tunng after 2007's *Good Arrows*. In 2008, he made the one-off album *There Were Wolves* in collaboration with The Memory Band's Stephen Cracknell, the idea for which came from a mutual friend, Paul Lambden, founder of the reissue label Spinney (most notable for reviving Vashti Bunyan's *Just Another Diamond Day*) and another of the initial Trunk records foursome.

"It was a bit like me and Mike with the first Tunng record, actually," Genders says of the project, which took the name The Accidental. "We wrote a few songs without any real plan to do anything with them." Cracknell found the process exciting. "Sam and I never sat down in a room and tried to write a song together," he recalls. "We very much worked on the basis that someone would send an idea and the other would go away and write on it. I think it was very liberating. For me, it was getting back to something where I didn't really know what was going to happen." *There Were Wolves* also features Hannah Caughlin of The Bicycle Thieves and singer-songwriter Liam Bailey.

Tunng, meanwhile, carried on without Genders. They were unusual among folk-tinged acts in that they put out a number of singles alongside their albums. One of these was a limited edition remix project whereby Tunng and the lesser-known Dollboy tackled each other's songs. As Oliver Cherer, the musician behind Dollboy, recalls: "Folk was the enemy. I'm just about the post-punk generation. I was in sort of punky bands and things in that period. So I came away from that with a real sort of closed attitude to all sorts of things." In the 90s, Cherer turned to dance music; then, after making some "horribly noisy records", he moved into minimalist ambient territory as Dollboy on *Plans For A Modern City* (2004) and *Casual Nudism* (2007).

Collaborating with Tunng gave Cherer pause. "They would be singing proper songs, but doing it with the same kit that I was using," he says. "That would have been a significant moment." Cherer had already been working on songs of his own, but had kept them hidden. Now, at last, he began to display them in public.

"Most of what I have done in the last couple of years has been just old fashioned tunesmithing," he says, "where you fiddle with the guitar and suddenly there's something there." It all came together on the song-based folktronica album *A Beard Of Bees* (2009). "I'm much more interested in making something that is in danger of falling down the cracks between things," he says of his combinations of electronics and folk. "But I hope that it doesn't."

Tunng continued to receive very favourable coverage from the indie media, dance magazines, and more serious muso publications. But there was also a parallel development, one that received, initially, less coverage. This was a return to the bucolic *and* the psychedelic, with fewer buzzing concessions to the here and now. The contradictory experiences of The Eighteenth Day Of May and The Owl Service show how much difference a couple of years could make in the fortunes of folk-influenced music in Britain, and serve also as a microcosm of the rapid changes taking place within the music industry.

The Eighteenth Day Of May began as a trio of Ben Phillipson, Richard Olson, and Alison Brice. For someone of his generation, Phillipson had quite an unusual background: he had played in folk clubs around Oxfordshire from the age of 11, and was used to being around fiddles, melodeons, and Morris dancers. "Seeing things like that, I suppose, as a kid, I didn't have the same prejudices I would have done if I was a little bit older," he says. He soon learned those prejudices, however. "I started listening to The Smiths and The Cocteau Twins, which just seemed far more appropriate music for a 16-year-old. And I remember going to see My Bloody Valentine playing, and just thinking, wow, this isn't like watching Martin Carthy or The Albions."

Phillipson consciously and decisively pushed his guitar style toward indie music and joined a series of bands during the 90s. "I was trying really hard to find my niche, and just failing miserably at it," he says. His father's death, in 1997, led to a period of re-evaluation and introspection. "Music sounded a lot different after that," he says. "I went back to a lot of the things I'd liked as a child. Because I'd disowned them so thoroughly, I couldn't believe the depth of what I was hearing." He cites Steeleye Span's *Please To See The King* as having had a particularly big impact.

By the time Phillipson met Olson and Brice in 2003, he was once again fully acquainted with folk music. Once they realised they all knew who Barry Dransfield was, they decided to form a group. "We thought that no one's really doing this, at this point, in Britain," he says. After adding Mark Nicholas, Karl Sabino, and Alison Cotton to the line-up, The Eighteenth Day Of May recorded demos, started gigging, and put out a seven-inch single on the small Transistor label.

"We got a phone call from someone at RykoDisc saying that they'd really like to do an album," Phillipson recalls. "Those original demo recordings actually ended up on the LP. We didn't realise that we were making an album when we were doing [them] … the first five songs on the album are from before we'd even done any shows." Pleased to be taken up by a label with some financial and promotional weight, the group celebrated the release of their gentle, intelligent debut in 2005. Issued at the height of the freak-folk boom, *The Eighteenth Day Of May* offered a nice balance to that trend: a fresh, young, British take on psychedelic folk.

Within a year, however, everything had turned sour. Although there were personality differences within the band, Phillipson is clear that it was a mismatch between their music and a marketing strategy that felt resolutely out of tune with it that caused most of the stress. "I didn't realise how the music industry worked," he says. "Well, maybe I did know, but I just didn't realise that it would ever affect a group like us."

RykoDisc allocated The Eighteenth Day Of May a press agent, who would periodically ring up the initially enthusiastic – then increasingly cautious – group. "The press people and the TV people were really keen to get as many column inches as they could," Phillipson says. "They would call us up and ask if we'd like to be photographed with stuffed animals. We found it very strange, quite disorientating, the whole process of it."

Bigger problems arose as a direct result of the vast structural changes taking place within the music industry at the time. When Warner Bros bought out RykoDisc, The Eighteenth Day Of May became minnows within an enormous conglomerate. Warners had initially expressed interest in a second album by the group, but soon all went quiet. Phillipson took the hint. "In a lot of ways we succeeded beyond our initial intentions by some distance," he says. "I think we would have all liked to make a second record, but I don't think we wanted to go knocking on people's doors. So basically we decided to call it a day."

The trajectory followed by The Eighteenth Day Of May – play live, make demos, get signed, release an album, and then split up, with a side order of bureaucratic clashes – was long-established. It reflected the experience of thousands of groups: Comus, Mellow Candle, Synanthesia, and numerous others had followed similar paths 35 years earlier. But The Eighteenth Day Of May were part of the final wheeze of this system. Their quick route from acceptable sales of around 10,000 records within the RykoDisc environment to insignificance under Warner Bros was symptomatic of a panicked industry focusing on the bottom-line. The Eighteenth Day Of May splintered into several different psychedelia-tinged folk outfits – The See See, The Left Outsides, The Silver Abduction, and The Trimdon Grange Explosion – and released their records on independent concerns.

The Owl Service did things differently from the start. A MySpace page existed even before the band did. Unlike Ben Phillipson, Steven Collins had grown up with hip-hop and metal, and had only discovered folk music in his late teens. Like Phillipson, however, he had circled the music world for about a decade with little direction. "I just played in bands, never particularly taking it seriously," he says. "I had never been much of a songwriter. I was always in someone else's band, never the leader."

By the turn of the millennium, Collins was in his late twenties and had pretty much given up on music. He would remain in this musical slump until June 2006, when he became excited by the possibilities of home recording, social networking, and folk music. "I was over at Conway Hall, the Homefires Festival that Adem organised," he recalls. "Vashti was playing. A friend of mine just leaned over and said 'you could do that'. I'd never really thought that I could. My mind just started going into overdrive. Two days later, I set up a MySpace profile for The Owl Service."

Inspired both by 60s and 70s folk music and by The Memory Band, Six Organs Of Admittance, and Espers, Collins had in mind the concept of the perfect Homefires band. "I thought this is what they would be called, and this would be their visual aesthetic," he says. "For band-members, I took names of characters from British horror films. It was like a dream band for a while. And what amazed me was that, within days, I was getting friend requests and messages from people, all asking when I was going to post up some songs."

Collins's perfect concept had stirred up interest; now he started on some home recordings. He didn't know any musicians back then, he says, so he decided to do everything itself. He could play bass, guitar, and keyboards already; software filled in most of the gaps. Only one problem remained. "When I came to do the vocals, I just wasn't really comfortable singing, even though I'd intended to," he says. "So I gave in."

Eventually, he found Dom Cooper of The Straw Bear Band and two female vocalists, Jo Lepine and Diana Collier. After putting out two EPs, *Wake The Vaulted Echo* and *Cine* on Hobby Horse Records – "really just me knocking up CD-Rs" – he decided to embark on an Owl Service album.

"People were drawn to the project," Collins says. "But it was still me doing all the music, really, with just odd people singing and sending me files." The exceptions were Collins's ongoing relationships with Cooper and another important new collaborator. After playing bass in The Memory Band for six months, he had become friends with Nancy Wallace. "I was giving her work-in-progress stuff," he says. "She really liked it, and said she wanted to be on the album. So she did a song for The Owl Service."

A Garland Of Song came out in July 2007, once again on Hobby Horse. But the buzz around The Owl Service, built up through social networking, soon meant that a label came to them. *A Garland Of Song* was reissued in 2008 by Southern Records, which also offered Collins the opportunity to head up a more formal imprint. And so, in 2008 Midwich began. In a mirror of labels such as Polydor Folk Mill, Midwich had only a mayfly lifespan. There were many limited CD-Rs in the Hobby Horse tradition, but only three full CD releases. Each offered an artistically strong and diverse take on the new British folk music.

The first Midwich release was *Old Stories* by Nancy Wallace. Wallace had previously released a solo EP, *Young Hearts* (2005), featuring folkified covers of disco songs by Chic, Candi Staton, and Elton John; *Old Stories* was a far more introspective proposition. The vocals are vitrious, the music spartan, the effect chilling.

Next came *The Crescent Sun*, the debut album by Ellen Mary McGee. Although it was her first album under her own name, McGee was no stranger to psychedelic folk. She had started out at open-mic nights as a teenager during the 90s, soaking up a few traditional songs, learning about performance, and was an avid reader of *Ptolemaic Terrascope*. She formed a group, Saint Joan, inspired equally by the contemporary post-rock scene and recordings by Shirley Collins, Steeleye Span, Pentangle, and Vashti Bunyan.

Saint Joan released a single, 'The Ice House' / 'All Things Melt' (2005) on McGee's own Dakota imprint, and made a well-received album, *The Wreckers Lantern* (2007), for Camera Obscura, but split soon afterward, partly as a result of the difficulty of "juggling five people's schedules". McGee became a solo performer, recording *The Crescent Sun* in 2007 at a friend's studio in Nottingham. "I wrote some of the album when I was living in Brooklyn in 2007," she says, although some of the themes had been gestating for a long time. "'Upon Death And Dying' is mainly about my dad, who died suddenly when I was 20. Other songs confront things I've experienced within my family, a general city sickness and a disillusionment with romantic love – which fortunately I have since become more positive about."

McGee got in touch with Collins through MySpace. "I was a fan of The Owl Service," she says, "and so was in touch with Steven. I mentioned that I'd recorded this album, and did he have any ideas as to where I should send it." For Collins, *The Crescent Sun* "fitted in perfectly with the loose vibe of the label". It was released in 2009, the most psychedelic of the Midwich albums.

The third and final Midwich release was *Lofoten Calling* by The Kittiwakes, the closest of the three acts to the world of mainstream folk. Kate Denny had played briefly in an early live incarnation of The Owl Service and had shared early Kittiwakes demos with Collins. "I said to Kate all along that if she could nail a whole album that sounded as good as her demos, I'd have no problem putting it out," he recalls.

Denny had visited Norway's Lofoten Islands, located within the Arctic

Circle and known for their mountainous terrain and rich mythology, during the autumn of 2006. "There are resonances between the Lofoten Islands and Britain, specifically Scotland, because of the Viking link, and the musical link as a result," she says. "I decided that I was going to write a folk album about this place, and thought, well, I need a folk line-up. I hadn't grown up through folk music in the slightest. In fact, I would say that my background is based on anything but."

Denny was classically trained and had already released an experimental new age record, *Runa Megin* (2005), under her maiden name, Kate Waterfield. For *Lofoten Calling*, she recruited Jill Cumberbatch, the violinist in a Pogues tribute band, and Chris Harrison, a music teacher who had run a folk club in the 70s, to help bring the project together.

Denny's lyrics merge mythology and history, fantasy and reality. Harrison and Cumberbatch helped hammer out the arrangements. "We do a lot of improvising," Cumberbatch says. "Kate would initially play the melody to us, then we would spend an hour or something going over the same melody, and we'd improvise." The result is an amalgamation of Norwegian subject and English folk structure. "It's not a Norwegian folk album, by any stretch of the imagination," Harrison says. "We imprinted our own musical backgrounds, and that's all you could do."

In another illustration of the difficulty of maintaining a specialist label imprint on a larger label, Midwich folded shortly after releasing *Lofoten Calling*. Collins has since established a new label, Rif Mountain, which has a similar ethos but exists as a completely independent label.

ᛗ

Another artist-run label to grow in popularity during the second half of the 2000s was Bird, run by Jane Weaver. "Bird started off with a really bad outsider-art-style doodle of a penguin," she says. "I had an idea to start a label for my own stuff, but also other female musicians, as a platform to put out limited releases." Weaver had been in the Britpop band Kill Laura during the 90s but had since turned to folk. "It was a nice change," she says. "I didn't have a band, and I had to do solo gigs acoustically. At the time, I was listening to stuff like Karen Dalton, Anne Briggs, Pentangle, Vashti Bunyan, Linda Perhacs, and Wendy & Bonnie." She was part of the girl group Misty Dixon but also released the solo soul-folk albums *Like An Aspen Leaf* (2002), *Seven Day Smile* (2006), and *Cherlokolate* (2007).

"I hate the imbalance," Weaver says. "I hate to see talented women floundering and running out of energy through the lack of opportunities presented to them, and I wanted a group of inspiring fellow sisters." Bird released the mini-fairytales of Magpahi, the neon anti-folk of Beth Jeans Houghton, and the lonely acoustics of Emma Tricca's album *Minor White* (2008).

Weaver had first seen Tricca at the Green Man festival. "She was striking not only because of her songs, but because she was wearing white stilettos in the mud," she recalls. Tricca grew up in a strict Italian Catholic household. She was brought up largely by her grandparents, and started playing the guitar at 16. She soon became affiliated with the prestigious Folkstudio in Rome. "The owner, he wanted me to get better and better," she recalls. "Any time that anyone, like John Renbourn or Davy Graham, was in town, I was invited along for the soundcheck, and the dinner after the event."

Tricca went through her first heartbreak around the same time. "He's a musician, an amazing songwriter, a brilliant poet," she says. "And we split up. He went his way. I stayed in Rome for a few months, but nothing was making sense." Deciding to leave Italy, she travelled to London and New York and wrote songs about her experiences.

After an aborted attempt at recording in New York, Tricca signed a publishing deal back in London and started work afresh. It proved to be another dispiriting experience. "I was reminded every day how they were the producers, and they knew what was right, and I didn't," she says. "It was an amazing piece of work made by great musicians but they were just showing off their skills. And they used to tell me 'your songs are crap' as well." The material remained unreleased and Tricca lost all confidence in her work.

Jane Weaver's support was a major factor in pulling her back. When it came to recording *Minor White*, Tricca did things differently. "I really insisted on wanting to play the songs live," she says. "We went into the room, played the song three times, and chose the best take. We kind of just made the arrangements up on the spot."

ᛞ

While all these mini-scenes were springing up, Circulus became their own ecosystem. In 2003, when he reshuffled the line-up, Michael Tyack had set about transforming the group from a slightly peculiar rock band into Britain's most immediately recognisable Technicolor psychedelic-folk troupe. The revolution in sound was matched with an overhaul of the group's visual impact. They now dressed in medieval-style garments and made performance a part of their live shows. "I wasn't allowed to do that in the first line-up, because people in the band were too scared," Tyack says. "But I think we're in the entertainment business. It makes the thing what it has to be. You don't go and see an opera and they're all wearing their jeans."

Circulus unleashed *The Lick On The Tip Of An Envelope Yet To Be Sent* in 2005. It's a far more folkish affair than *Giantism*, with early music foundations and an unselfconscious, fantastical whimsy soaring over its top. Then came *Clocks Are Like People* (2006). "Each Circulus album, for some strange reason, tags on to the next one," Tyack says. "On the first album, the last track is 'Power To The Pixies', which is another way of saying power to the unseen. The next album started with 'Dragon's Dance' and ended with 'Reality's A Fantasy', where reality is an illusion."

On *Thought Becomes Reality* (2009), Tyack structures his songs around a central concept: that of the earth being struck by a giant tsunami of consciousness. The previous two albums had been released by Rise Above, the label founded by ex-Napalm Death singer Lee Dorian; this one came out on Tyack's own Mythical Cake imprint and was partly funded by contributions from fans.

"Everything moved very, very slowly," he says. "But having released two albums with Rise Above, I kind of understood how the music industry works. Releasing this album myself was my way of trying to take control of things. Rise Above did us a great service by raising our profile; now, hopefully, I can scrape by with Mythical Cake, put out music, and live in the countryside."

The rise of Circulus coincided with a renewed interest in folk music, yet Tyack and his band-mates opted to construct a parallel reality rather than piggybacking on an existing one. "You're just trying to make a perfect world around you," he says. "When I put on a Circulus show I just want to show the people that you *can* make your perfect world. And anyone can do it."

These scenes were supported by a new live circuit, with specific modern folk events growing in number. There were large events, like the Moseley Folk Festival and Adem's Homefires, alongside innumerable local folk nights that welcomed the new psychedelic and experimental acts. The biggest of them all was the Green Man festival, based in Wales and founded by Jo Bartlett and Danny Hagan in 2003 as a one-day affair at the small Craig Y Nos castle in the Brecon Beacons.

At the time, Bartlett and Hagan were performing and recording together as It's Jo & Danny. Their debut album, the self-released *Lank-Haired Girl To Bearded Boy* (2000), was well received and led to a deal with RCA for *Thug's*

Lounge (2001), but the jump to a major label proved to be a brief, unhappy experience. "We got dropped," Bartlett recalls, "so we were wondering what to do." She and Hagan had recently moved away from the hubbub of London to the Brecon Beacons in Wales. "We were living in such a beautiful, awe-inspiring area that Danny, one night, had the idea – why don't we start a festival?"

The pair decided to name the event Green Man after the folk legend of rebirth and re-growth. It seemed to fit well with their post-London, post-RCA outlook. The event was billed explicitly as a folk festival. "We actually thought it would shock [people]," Bartlett says. "We thought it was like calling something a punk festival in 1976."

Strongly represented at the first Green Man was Glasgow's growing Fence Collective, with both King Creosote and James Yorkston playing. By the time of the second year, interest had grown enough for the festival to relocate to a larger site at Baskerville Hall. This was the year that established Green Man as a central part of what was now seen as a 'folk revival' in the UK. The event's two very different headline acts, Alasdair Roberts and Four Tet, represented the breadth of the modern folk scene in the UK at that time.

"That year was possibly the most magical," Bartlett says. It was also notable for the buzz created during a Saturday lunchtime set by a young harpist, Joanna Newsom. "She was astounding, just jaw-droppingly good," Bartlett recalls. "The otherworldly, wonderful music that the Americans were bringing into it was just a whole other dimension." (Newsom appeared again the following year, this time as a main-stage headliner.)

With the resurgence of interest in folk music gathering pace, Green Man needed to change location again, while Bartlett and Hagan found that they could no longer do everything themselves. "It nearly killed Danny and myself," Bartlett says. "We had 2,200 ticket sales, then with the journalists, the bands, the stallholders, guest list, and so on we had about 3,000 people on site. You become aware that you've got to feed people, let people go to the loo, *and* entertain them. I don't think we slept a wink the whole weekend."

To make matters worse, most of the stewards the pair had hired left their posts. Bartlett and Hagan had to undertake refuse collection duties themselves, while Bonnie 'Prince' Billy's headline set was interrupted by a power cut. "Somebody made a film of the festival that year and they interviewed us on the Thursday, and we're all healthy, and we look really optimistic about the weekend ahead," Bartlett recalls. "Then they interviewed us again on Sunday, and we were totally emaciated and wired. I'm sitting there fiddling with my fingers the whole time, talking like some nutcase."

Green Man moved to the Glanusk Park Estate in 2006, when it was attended by 6,500 people. By 2009, the capacity had grown to 10,000. In the intervening years, the event has moved gradually away from billing itself explicitly as a folk festival. "It's a very tricky thing," Bartlett says. "The general public are a little bit scared of the word folk. And it's more than just a folk festival, which is why I'm a bit nervous of being labelled."

All of this seems to indicate that folk had become mainstream again by the close of the decade, particularly with the rise of indie-folk acts like Mumford & Sons, Laura Marling, and Noah & The Whale, all of whom have found considerable success by combining acoustic music with a populist sensibility. It would certainly have been much harder for these acts to break through without the important groundwork laid by Trunk's *Wicker Man* release, The Memory Band, and The Owl Service, not to mention Alasdair Roberts and Sharron Kraus.

But what this also indicates is that post-millennial British psychedelic folk was not a cohesive beast in itself. It was only a small part of a much wider rejuvenation for young British folk-influenced musicians during the first decade of the 21st century, and one likely to mix with other forms of music. As such it was less identifiable, and less tightly knit, than the US 'freak folk' boom had been. It caused a smaller media firestorm and spawned fewer derivative artists. What happened now, in Britain and elsewhere, was a splay. The experimental flourished, and the individuals spoke up.

CHAPTER 20
Hellical Rising

"MY OWN VERSION of folk music didn't have marks of diplomacy," says the Finnish singer Islaja. "It was purely from one person, and could not be performed by anyone else but me." Just as was the case during the first wave of psychedelic and experimental folk, once the form had re-emerged as a creative power, all bets were off. Folk music was malleable and maverick once more. Psychedelic, acid, weird, *wyrd*, freak, experimental, avant: inspired.

In 2004, Eclipse Records put out an album by a disarming yet unassuming new talent. "I am painfully shy," says Marissa Nadler. "I can't even look people in the eye when I pass them on the street. I used to shake when I had to speak to a teacher. I order coffee black so I don't have to talk much to strangers. Perhaps there was a part of me that was pushing myself into this to see if I could cure myself of my own trappings."

In her childhood, Marissa Nadler listened to classic blues and folk artists. Her teenage years saw the incursion of grunge and shoegazing, "but the songwriters and solo singers always reached me the deepest". Nadler began to play guitar in her mid-teens. Her older brother played in bands; she was more introverted, and tended to stay in her bedroom. "No boyfriends in those days to distract me, and a quiet town where I didn't fit in," she says. "Learning to play the guitar was difficult for me because I am a lefty at painting, drawing, and everything else. There was only a righty guitar in the house, and it did not occur to me to flip it over. So, I learned as a righty. I had a hard time getting a basic strum down because it seemed foreign on my right hand." She found fingerpicking much easier.

Nadler was an artist, too, with an interest in unusual and archaic techniques such as encaustic painting (with hot wax), making books, and carving wood. She enrolled at the Rhode Island School of Design to develop her art, which seemed to co-exist with her music. "When I drew portraits and watercolours, there was a softness and subtlety very similar to the colours of my music," she says. "I covered everything in wax by the time I was nearing the end of my early painting career. It was similar to shrouding my voice in reverb. If the emotions are too strong, I have always felt the need to suppress them just a bit."

With a growing disillusionment for the fine art establishment, Nadler concentrated more on her music, attracted to its directness. As soon as she had to play to anyone other than herself, however, stage fright took over. Recording always seemed a lot more appealing. "I like being alone in a room and spending time layering harmonies and putting soul and life into a recording," she says. "Then, I like to be able to connect and share with other people, as a way of 'talking' to them."

Nadler began to craft homemade CD-Rs with intricate artwork. Her compelling music found an audience at Eclipse Records, which released her debut album, *Ballads Of Living And Dying*, in 2004. It is indeed a balladeer's lament, an inner sanctum populated by the lonely and the strange, with Edgar Allen Poe's 'Annabelle Lee' in among Nadler's own characters.

"I think any time you talk about death in a song, it seems to come across [as] Gothic," she says. "I suppose I think a lot about the cycles of life, and have always been drawn to tragic tales that have some kind of moral lesson." The narrative peaks and pulls only intensify on *The Saga Of Mayflower May* (2005). "I definitely am interested in telling a story in my songs," she says, revealing that her characters are usually based on real people. Mayflower May herself is almost Nadler's id, acting in ways her creator wishes she could.

"There is a black and a white," she says, "and I tend to see the world like that as well. It's life or death, love or hate. I am trying to see more of the grey." The grey became apparent on Nadler's third and fourth records, *Songs III: Bird On The Water* (2007), which she recorded at Greg Weeks's Hexham Head, and *Little Hells* (2009). *Songs III* remains her most spine-tingling release to date, her honeyed voice and pouring guitar slowly unveiling songs of brutal candour.

"It's OK to be naked in your songs," she says. "So, I am not using so many cryptic poetic devices any more." This nakedness is even more brightly lit on *Little Hells*, with Nadler's singing voice crisper than ever before.

Playing live, Nadler says she still worries that something will go wrong, or that she will not live up to expectations. For a while she needed alcohol to stop her legs and hands shaking with nerves for long enough to walk on stage; now she straddles the fine line between being tough enough to take on the pressures of touring and maintaining the sensitive approach that allows her songs to grow.

"In my songs there is an idealised sense of serenity and place and time," she says, looking back on her work to date, "and a peace that I have certainly not found in my own life. In reality, the mind never stops spinning."

><

Another unconventional and eclectic storyteller who sees few stylistic limits is Josephine Foster. Hers is among the most eclectic back-catalogues in modern music, stretching from psychedelic folk-rock to reinterpretations of German *lieder*. That gluttony for variety has been present since her childhood in Colorado.

"I liked it all, really," she says. "In the school choir, we would do songs from around the world. Italian songs, spirituals ... Sometimes Benjamin Britten, or Henry Purcell. And I just loved the radio. I liked The Platters, I liked those expressive songs, and the wide-ranging vocals. It was popular song, but stretched to the limit." One thing the young Foster found particularly striking was opera. Her family attended the Methodist church, where she would hear operatic singers in full voice. "Sometimes they would just bellow," she says, "and sometimes they would take me on a complete feeling of them channelling something very strong. Their bodies were delivering this *thing* and I wanted to have that ability."

Foster began training as an opera singer, first with a local teacher, who encouraged her wayward explorations, and then at Chicago's Northwestern University, where the tone of the teaching was very different. "I felt like there was this obsession with perfection," she says. "It started right from the beginning. And I almost quit music." Foster's voice was not always a reliable vessel. These rocky rivulets would later become something to treasure in her subsequent recording career, but left her feeling that she could not truly perform opera. "Nobody knew what to think of my voice, or of me," she says. "I kept at it for a while, and I learned a lot, but it's kind of like [being] a ballerina. You can't be a ballerina if one day you're riding high and the next day you're tripping over all the stage props."

Foster stayed on in Chicago and did bits of theatre, taught music, played the harp and ukulele, and hung around with free-jazz musicians. "I was trying to do everything that wasn't opera, basically," she says. "I feel that this was to work out who I was outside of opera. Kind of a metamorphosis, like an adolescent or something."

Three projects began more-or-less at once. The first was a "pop band" in collaboration with Andy Bar, The Children's Hour, with whom she recorded the album *SOS JFK* (2003). The group's accessible sound found a mainstream indie-rock audience as the opening act on the 2003 tour by Zwan, the ill-fated group led by Billy Corgan of The Smashing Pumpkins and Slint's Dave Pajo.

The second project was Born Heller, a duo with bassist Jason Ajemian. Ajemian came from a jazz background, and his rhythmic skitter seemed a good match for Foster's more mannered style. He was also far savvier about the music industry than she was and encouraged the idea of making a record, *Born Heller* (2004), that sounds totally different to The Children's Hour and is full of acoustic clots and thorns.

In the meantime, Foster had been writing songs for herself on harp and ukulele. Encouraged by her then boyfriend, Matthew Masada, she began self-releasing material on CD-Rs, starting with *There Are Eyes Above* (2000) and the childhood-themed *Little Life* (2001). "He said: 'Well, why don't you record your songs, and we'll copy the CDs?'" she recalls. "And that was a whole revolution in my mind."

As Foster's 'official' recording career took off, she maintained her CD-R regime as a vehicle for ideas. "The home recordings were sometimes more relaxed," she says. "I think the nice thing about CD-Rs is that there's always the feeling that 'this is mine'. It doesn't belong to a label; I can do whatever I want. Also, I think you can find beautiful things in very raw material. I'm not afraid of showing that side to the songs."

It wasn't only recording and the machinery of popular music that Foster was getting used to. Playing live at Chicago's open-mic nights and dive bars felt totally different to operatic performance. "The thing that I struggled with, more than anything, was the microphones, because everything we're trained in opera is not for microphones, it's the opposite. It was a whole learning process of how to work with and use the microphone as a friend instead of an interloper."

In 2004, Foster made *All The Leaves Are Gone* with the group The Supposed (Brian Goodman and Rusty Peterson). "Brian, who was a musicology student, is a brilliant guy," she says. "He's a wicked musician, but at the same time he's really fearless." Foster had started playing the guitar as well as the ukulele, and her compositions became rockier. The result was an extraordinarily, epically psychedelic album that channels West Coast rock with gut-level blues and intensely pessimistic lyrics. It was a towering achievement, and one that drew notice.

Following her inclusion on Devendra Banhart's *Golden Apples Of The Sun* compilation, Foster found herself tagged as a freak-folk artist. It bemused rather than annoyed her. "I had all these ideas that I hadn't even done, so I knew that that was just somebody's idea," she says. "Some of what I've done connects with what other people have done. The mind tries to draw connections and make a rational whole, and put a meaning toward it, but sometimes there is no meaning."

Foster's next album, *Hazel Eyes, I Will Lead You* (2005), could but for the distinctive vocals have been the product of a completely different artist. It's a solo acoustic work of heartbreak and longing, its rack of emotions set out for harp, bells, sitar, and flute. "I wanted to go back and try and work alone a little bit," Foster says. The recurrent images of trees are rooted in the death of her birth father when she was a baby. "I was quite obsessed with his death growing up," she said in 2005, "and made up all manner of explanations for this. I was very preoccupied with his mystery and determined at one point that he could be discovered residing in apple trees."[1]

Foster followed *Hazel Eyes* with *A Wolf In Sheep's Clothing* (2006), an album of reinterpretations of German *Lieder*, some of which were recorded in a church. "I didn't want to stop doing classical music, but I wanted to do it in a way that wasn't constrained by the rules of the score and the music," she explains. "I just wanted to play them in a simple way, and also open them up to new dimensions. They're so filled with potential to go on to many directions, other than the way they're consistently done over and over."

It wasn't long before another set of original songs surfaced: *This Coming Gladness* (2008), which Foster says "started off as wanting to write a song about erotic love". Then came another high-concept project, *Graphic As A Star* (2009), for which she set Emily Dickenson's poems to music, having first read them after moving to Spain with her husband, the guitarist Victor Herrero, in 2006.

"I brought a book of her poems along and I ended up reading the whole book, and just being really, totally blown away by her genius," she recalls. "I started to speak through the ones that I really liked, looking for a lyrical clarity or some immediacy. The ones that turned into a melody in my recitations [were] the ones that I recorded."

Josephine Foster remains as unpredictable as ever. "I think that I wanted to be an actress, and that's what an opera singer is," she says. "The idea is not to cultivate your own cult of personality, which is so boring. It's to explore."

⋈

"I had been staying with Marissa Nadler in Brooklyn and working with her on some material for her new record," says Nick Castro. "At the last second, Marissa decided to join Josephine [Foster] and me on our tour, and although she only played a few of the shows, she travelled with us for the duration."

Nick Castro had made his recorded debut with the solo work *A Spy In The House Of God* (2004), which channels Syd Barrett and Simon Finn via ancient folk minstrelsy. He was living in Hollywood at the time and described it as "an easy place to hate if you don't understand or know it well, but it is still a magical place in a lot of ways: great weather and a beautiful history".[2]

In 2005, Castro assembled The Poison Tree and released *Further From Grace*, which features Chris Smith, Meg Baird, Otto Hauser, and Helena Espvall of Espers. "We played a show at the Espers house," he says. "I camped out at Chris Smith's house while I recorded at Miner Street studios. I introduced Brian [McTear] from Miner Street to Marissa, and she did her record [*The Saga Of Mayflower May*] there as well."

Unlike a lot of albums that try to squash too much talent into too small a space, *Further From Grace* is coherent and spellbinding. It careers through dexterous psychedelia and looser improvisation, and is structured enough while also remaining open to harnessing the talents of sympathetic and intuitive fellow travellers. There's even a musical duel, on 'Music for Mijwiz', between Otto Hauser's doumbek (a Middle Eastern drum) and Castro's mijwiz (a Syrian dual-reed pipe) – quite possibly a first for two American musicians. Castro then went on to form The Young Elders for *Come Into Our House* (2006), which features B'eirth and members of Current 93 and successfully expands his juxtaposition of unusual instrumentation with modernist drone.

For some of the Espers crew, meanwhile, there was a new undertaking on the horizon. Greg Weeks recalls being "haunted" by the 1970 Czech film *Valerie And Her Week Of Wonders*, which he thought would be perfect for Espers to soundtrack, but not everyone agreed. Unfazed, Weeks assembled a group of musicians from Philadelphia; he and Fern Knight's Margie Ayre acted as musical directors. "I really was inspired by *Once Upon A Time In The West*, how each character had their own instrument theme song," he recalls. "I thought, that's the perfect way to approach this movie: to take the main

Seasons They Change

characters, source them out, give them a theme, take those themes, and then fill in the blanks."

By coincidence, Philadelphia-based cinema buff Joseph Gervasi had been thinking for some time about collaborating with Espers on a soundtrack project, and even happened to have a 16mm print of *Valerie And Her Week Of Wonders*. The project premiered at the 2006 Philadelphia Fringe arts festival. "It was a great collision-collage of bands and solo projects and their respective sounds," Margie Ayre recalls. The reception was very encouraging, with all involved enjoying the experience and determined that it shouldn't just be a one-off. Successful follow-up shows took place at New York's Museum Of Modern Art and London's Meltdown Festival in 2007, but it was far from plain sailing elsewhere.

"We couldn't get a booking agent to put it on," Greg Weeks recalls. "So we booked six or seven shows ourselves on the West Coast, in Middle America. It was really financially stressful. Ten people travelling around, and then renting a 35mm print." A handful of better-attended shows followed on the East Coast, galvanising the musicians. One of the performers was Tara Burke, who loved the experience. "I thought that I might get tired of seeing that film all the time," she says, "but the 35mm print is just so gorgeous that I never tired of it. Sometimes it was a bit difficult having ten people on stage and making sure that everyone could hear each other, but generally I think it all worked out rather well."

The new soundtrack was recorded and released as *The Valerie Project* (2007) by Drag City and the British label Finders Keepers, but several other attempts at getting funding for further live engagements fell through. "And that was pretty much it," Weeks says. "You can only smash your head against the wall so much."

For other established artists – many of them still unhappily lumped in with freak folk – the experimentation grew. Fursaxa continued to offer an always-intriguing panorama, with Tara Burke increasingly listening to non-Western music from Africa, South America, and Bulgaria. "I guess you could consider some of the instruments I play 'folk' instruments," she says, "but I don't play them in a very traditional way. I think my music is free and psychedelic, but I don't feel my music is folk."

A sense of place is vital to the music of Fursaxa, and no more so than on *Alone In The Dark Wood* (2007). "Through both nature and music I am able

304

to retreat from the stress and anxiety of everyday life and enter into other realms," Burke says. "There are sounds in nature I try to replicate, such as the drone of spring peepers or the repetitive call of birds."

Elsewhere, as the decade progressed, Jeffrey Alexander and Miriam Goldberg settled into their Black Forest / Black Sea project. From *Black Forest / Black Sea* (2003) onward, they proved much trickier to grasp than The Iditarod had been. "What I'm doing now would probably be considered less folk really, but I guess it still is 'folky'," Alexander says. "I love experimental music and psychedelic rock and traditional stuff and acoustic sounds and things that are heavy and things that are mellow and things that are both. I love improvisation and jazz and country and blues. It's all folky to me, in a way."

Alexander is one of the busiest men in experimental folk. Alongside Black Forest / Black Sea, he is involved in an improvised noise-rock band with a rotating cast of players ("face-melting folk", he calls it). He also runs the Secret Eye label, a performance space in Pittsburgh, and was the festival director for the 2006 Terrastock Six. "Oh yeah, that was something!" he says. He had worked tirelessly on the project for over a year, heading off the threat of personal debt to assemble an event of great panache. "When the performances finally all went down, it was an extremely cathartic weekend for me," he says. "I think the only sleep I got during those four days was a short nap on stage when I should have been playing guitar."

Dredd Foole, too, was a consistent touchstone. In 2003, Dan Ireton released *The Whys Of Fire*, reviving the name The Din but with new personnel. "The Din was Pelt, Thurston Moore, and Chris Corsano," he says. "The album was just improvised vocals and instruments. There's no songs or anything on that. It's a pretty whacked-out record." The challenging, intriguingly illogical *Daze On The Mounts* and *Kissing The Contemporary Bliss* (both 2004) and the hand-stroking closeness of *A Long, Losing Battle With Eloquence And Intimance* (2005) provided the counterpoint. Then, toward the end of the decade, Ireton revived his partnership with Ed Yazijian for *That Lonesome Road Between Hurt And Soul* (2009).

"Ed travelled up here from where he lives in South Carolina," Ireton says. "It was a winter week. It snowed three or four times, and we just stayed in the house, got up, played music, recorded music, and that's pretty much all we did the whole time he was here." The record found a home on Bo'Weavil. "After the first five minutes I knew that it was totally a record I wanted to put out," says Mark Morris, the label's founder. "Dan sounds like a cross between Tim Buckley and Nick Cave, and Ed's guitar playing is wonderful."

Also resurgent in 2009 were Stone Breath. On *The Shepherdess And The Bone-White Bird*, the group's music is as cracked, weathered, and uncompromising as ever. The album's opening lines – "I heard the fingers of the dead / Clawing from inside my head" – lead into an oratorio on mortality, salvation, terror, and mercy. Stone Breath had risen from the earth.

Back in Britain, Sharron Kraus embarked upon a journey into her personal heritage. Although she had been a keen collaborator throughout her career, her 2007 album *Right Wantonly A-Mumming* was different. Firstly, it sounded particularly English, and locally focused. Secondly, it was a planned project rather than a spontaneous outgrowth of friendship.

"I specifically asked some Oxford singers to be involved, the ones that I was first inspired by," Kraus says. "As far as traditional singing goes, they're my mentors. There are two of them in particular, both with large beards, a gruff Yorkshireman and an equally gruff Suffolk boatman."

Right Wantonly A-Mumming is an important Sharron Kraus album. It reminded the UK of how lithe and grounded her music was, and that to see her simply as a hue of the freak-folk scene was to miss a large part of what made her unique. "I wanted to write something that folkies would relate to, but also pagans or nature lovers," she says. "It was for the kind of people that would think: 'I'll go for a walk tonight, because it's a full moon.'"

The album was released in the UK on the Bo'Weavil label. "I wanted to work with Sharron Kraus because for me she's very much in the lineage of traditional folk music," founder Mark Morris says. "The way she writes and sings songs, for me, sounds like they could have come out of the folk revival of the 50s and 60s. *Right Wantonly A-Mumming* has traditionals on it. The rest were songs that she wrote, [but] to me, they very much felt like traditionals."

During the second half of the decade, Alasdair Roberts's music also became more intricate in its incorporation of mythological and religious history. He explores these ancient and modern, personal and universal conundrums in a number of typically intelligent, individualist ways on *Spoils* (2009). 'The Book Of Doves', for example, is rooted in his interest in early Christianity and Russian folklore. "The last verse about Derry and Stirling, and Sicily and Anglesey, has to do with the collapse of ancient Bardic and druidic seats of learning with the encroachment of the Roman Empire," he says.

"'Hazel Forks' is all about 'coll', the hazel tree in the Celtic tree alphabet, associated with the month of August, and with me, being a McCall by clan. 'Under No Enchantment (But My Own)' is about a visit I made to a friend of mine who is a herbalist. It was at a time of particular psychic and emotional turmoil, when I wasn't thinking so straight, and so this song emerged. There are some other even crazier songs, which never made the record. There's one about Theodor Adorno coming to me in the guise of Orion the Hunter and saving me from entanglement in a hawthorn hedge into which I've strayed to steal a red ruby.

"At times national identity has seemed important to me," he continues. "There are times when I've believed that what I'm involved in is making Scottish or British music, that what I'm doing has importance for the furtherance of my national culture. But there are other times where I've reacted against that notion as jingoistic, narrow-minded bullshit. Times where I've felt that what I'm doing is of national worth and importance, and other times where it, and I, have felt very insignificant. But I think I've come to accept that my work will always be in some way connected with Scotland and Britain. It's also complicated by the fact that I'm not really Scottish. I'm half-German, and some of what I do reflects that, I think."

ᛞ

On his 2007 tour, Alasdair Roberts was supported by a newcomer from Brighton, Mary Hampton. "He's a very fine musician as well as a lovely performer," Hampton says of Roberts. "And he's really very devoted to the roots of the music." Hampton herself had studied for a degree in 20th century music but felt disheartened by "having to write pastiches" of composers like Stockhausen and Schoenberg.

It was only after completing her degree that Hampton heard English folk music for the first time. "I just thought it was a crime actually, that I'd done all this musical education and I was so interested in all forms of music and, but for my school lessons, I'd never heard English folk music," she says.

Something else Hampton had not yet experienced was singing, but she soon set about recording often-unaccompanied settings of poems and traditional songs. Two CD-Rs arose from this period: *Book One* (2005) and *Book Two* (2007). By the time of the second, Hampton had started writing original songs, too. "It wasn't even that much of a conscious thing, really," she says. "All of those themes in the old songs are really templates from nature, of how things grow and survive, and deal with what's coming at them, and are still totally relevant. I just got interested in trying to find some new ways of putting those ideas."

Hampton was asked to make an album by the Drift label and used this opportunity to expand her songwriting. *My Mother's Children* was released in

2007. "I'd never really written poems or songs before, just the same as I hadn't sung," she recalls. "But I think, as you get older, you start to realise what things are interesting to you in the world, what things are archetypal, and that you can relate to other people with, and make them relate to you with. Things just become clearer, even if just momentarily." The songs on *My Mother's Children* were all sparked off by personal and cultural experiences. 'The Bell That They Gave You' had the most unusual germination. "I was watching *Big Brother*, the live final, and Davina McCall was heavily pregnant," Hampton recalls. "I connected her pregnancy with the people who were being evicted from the *Big Brother* house, and the new lives they would have to face. Then, at the same time, I bought this basil plant, and it had a cocoon on it. It was about new life."

Someone with a unique perspective on both the British and international scenes at this time was David Sheppard, for he was both a musician and a music journalist. He formed his first significant band, Balloon, in the early 90s. "It was all looking very hopeful," he says. "We did have a lot of things on paper that looked quite good, but somehow it didn't translate." Balloon popped after about two-and-a-half years, having released one album and recorded a second (later shelved by the record company). "You do feel a bit burned by the music industry," Sheppard says. "It's happened a million times, but when it happens to you it does rather take the wind out of your sails."

After that, Sheppard concentrated mainly on writing. Among his many interests, he was a close observer of post-rock, the creaked Americana of Will Oldham and Smog, and freak folk. "I liked the idea that you had people doing the process of folk music, which went back to this thing of a community," he says. "They were trying to do things which were not hidebound by ideas of making a good hit single."

Like most musicians who take a hiatus, Sheppard couldn't stay away for too long. Triggered by an interest in electronic music, he formed a partnership with an old school friend, Kieron Phelan, in the early 2000s. The pair recorded as Phelan Sheppard and State River Widening. Sheppard also hooked up with Pete Astor, a former member of The Loft and of The Weather Prophets. Astor and Sheppard formed two groups: the song-based Wisdom Of Harry and the abstracted Ellis Island Sound, the second of which incorporated folk influences.

"Even though Ellis Island Sound had beats and lots of programming, it always had that element of acoustic guitar, and I guess some kind of rural element," Sheppard says. "I was buying a load of John Fahey records, and a few other Takoma things like Leo Kottke's *Six And Twelve String Guitar* and Peter Walker's *Rainy Day Raga*. I really *listened* to those records, and that got me back into the idea of acoustic guitar experimentation."

This concept reached its zenith on *The Good Seed* (2007). "We had done a Wisdom Of Harry record that was much more guitar, and Pete was getting into folk music, in a serious way, and going to Cecil Sharp House," Sheppard says. "So we had the idea to do an Ellis Island Sound record where we brought this folky element back into it." Having previously recorded mainly in gritty London basements, Astor and Sheppard decided to go for the *Liege And Lief* experience and retreat to the country – in this case East Anglia.

"We found this really great place called Mendham, which is right on the Norfolk-Suffolk border," Sheppard says. "It's a tiny hamlet. We stayed in a converted chapel, with a big garden, miles from anywhere." They had packed Astor's Volvo with an eight-track, guitars, dulcimers, and ukulele, but also took a drum machine, a Stylophone, and a basic Casio keyboard. Over the course of a week, in between trips to the pub and cycle rides, they created 20 short, impulsive tracks.

The Good Seed also had a nice coda, whereby Ellis Island Sound supported the East Anglian community that had provided the album's setting. The album came out to good reviews, and people started agitating for a live performance. Since Astor and Sheppard played numerous instruments each on the record, this seemed like an impossible task. But then Astor hit on an idea. "Pete had started teaching writing courses, and he had all these kids in his class, great musicians, and they were all from Norfolk," Sheppard says. "So he recruited the band from these people from the same area that we'd recorded *The Good Seed*. That was a real journey back. Full circle."

Ellis Island Sound's records were linked to folktronica, although as Sheppard admits, they were "more folk than tronica". The sub-genre retained its popularity in Britain, with Static Caravan its spiritual home. In 2007, the label released a spare, classically tinged, pop-folk album called *Cheap Demo Bad Science* by a young London harpist.

Harp wasn't Serafina Steer's first instrument, but she had felt an attraction to it from a young age. "I do really love harp," she says, "but it's such a strange instrument because, certainly in classical terms, you can almost feel ornamental. You're often not really part of the body of sound in an orchestra. I think that's also why I was guided into doing songs, and other people's songs, because it's a bit of a conundrum to play an instrument you love [when] you don't really enjoy half the repertoire."

Steer had studied musicology at Trinity College of Music in London and shared a squat with Tunng's Mike Lindsay. "He had a studio set up there, so it meant I was just financially a bit more free," she says. "We just had loads of time to try stuff out." The songs on *Cheap Demo Bad Science* took about a year to come together. The album filters Steer's mini-drama lyrics through tactile electronica and beautiful harp. It was one of the most memorable Static Caravan releases to date.

Unfortunately for Steer, however, her career was dogged by the prominence of another 21st century harpist. "I was already pretty fully formed when I found out about Joanna Newsom," she says. "I'd like to think they were comparing me to the fact that she's very special, but they're probably just comparing us on the basis that she plays the harp, and in that case I feel quite inadequate. My boyfriend at the time bought me the album, which I thought was very sensitive of him."

In fact, Steer's influences are far more wide ranging. They include Brian Eno, Zeena Parkins, and Julian Cope; musicians who "just have a breadth of manic inspiration and are not too bogged down with wanting to be a personality".

In February 2009, Steer's harp was stolen. "It's a big deal to not play for so long when you've always played," she says. She had already started recording her second album, *Change Is Good Change Is Good* (2010), before the theft, and felt reluctant to lose the momentum. Taking over the harp's role were vintage synthesizers, while Steer found herself moving closer to a pop sound inspired by the work of Arthur Russell. "Some of his songs are looping cellos, and he's got such a lovely voice," she says. "He's all over disco and house, and a really experimental guy."

A few years earlier, Serafina Steer played a gig on a boat in Lyon, France, with a band called Spires That In The Sunset Rise. "It was a very low-budget tour," she says. "Their train was late. There was no heating – it was fucking freezing. They were very nice. They were very tired!"

Spires That In The Sunset Rise are one of the thorniest of all modern acoustic groups. Comus-like in their ability to create distress, they also draw on everything from the modern avant-garde to the multi-headed post-punk of The Raincoats and Young Marble Giants. Originally a collaborative project, they eventually settled on a trio of Kathleen Baird, Georgia Vallas, and Taralie Peterson, three childhood friends from Decatur, Illinois. They took their name from a translation of Baudelaire's 'The Voyage'. "It's a mouthful," Baird said in 2005. "Very few people can remember it the first time they say it." She went on to explain that the name evokes "this melodrama that runs through some of the songs. And also it hints at some kind of spirituality that's gone totally fantastic and surreal".[3] *Spires That In The Sunset Rise* (2003) is a very distinctive, if difficult, listen. The bare, lo-fidelity sound and seasick structure was one thing; it was the voices, shrill and icy enough to chill Hades to its core, that caused mouths to gape.

Taralie Peterson's sister, Tracy, joined the group for *Four Winds The Walker* (2004). She may only have been one extra person, but the project seemed to increase disproportionately; their instruments, tuned to nauseous disharmony, chased one another around tight, locked rhythms. The drums became more prominent, the overall sound less mud-flecked. If the first album sounded like a one-off, it's clear from the second that the Spires sound was no accident of extemporisation.

"There's very rarely one person who comes with a solid body or a structure," Baird explained, adding that, while the songwriting process might sometimes begin in a spontaneous fashion, the songs themselves are very precise constructs.[4] *This Is Fire* (2006) is an even tighter affair that marks a conscious shift from the malcontent of *Four Winds*. The ritual dance element is still there, but the horror story lurking beneath has been tamed.

Tracy Peterson left the group after *This Is Fire*; Georgia Vallas played on *Curse The Traced Bird* (2008), but then she too departed. Taralie Peterson and Kathleen Baird have carried on as a duo, while Baird maintains a more traditional solo career under her own name and as Traveling Bell. *Curse The Traced Bird* is Spires' most accessible album, the dissonance fluttering and mercurial rather than brutal. It was engineered by Greg Weeks and gives a more pronounced sense of the worldwide folk traditions touched upon in their earlier work. "I don't think we're folky, really," Taralie Peterson said in 2005. "We're a little unhinged for that."[5]

Like the members of Spires, drummer Alex Neilson was fascinated by how music and sound – rather than just clearly set-out lyrics – could run the emotional gauntlet. "I don't really have much formal training," he says. "I was just drumming and smoking marijuana, and jamming, but heavily interested in music as human expression."

While his initial motivation to learn drums was to get out of a school physics lesson, Neilson found he was a natural at the instrument and soon became a zealot. "It was a real vocation, to play the drums," he says. "I moved to Glasgow, to university, and I dropped out after the first year because all I could really think about was doing music."

In Glasgow, Neilson formed his first band, Scatter, with Chris Hladowski. "We were trying to incorporate a lot of superficially disparate things that I was interested in, like free jazz and traditional music, and psychedelic music," he recalls. "There seemed to be a commonality between those things – in my mind, anyway." Scatter shared some members with the larger Glasgow Improvisers Orchestra and both were part of a vibrant local improv scene.

Meanwhile, across town, The Pendulums, founded by Lavinia Blackwall and Mike Hastings, were making music in a more song-based and explicitly psychedelic way, helped by Blackwall's stunningly powerful and flexible vocals. "From a young age I had a good singing voice," she says. "I was in training from about the age of seven. I was doing classical stuff, I was in opera school, I was doing arias and all sorts. If I'd wanted to, I could have done that, and it probably would have worked out. But the fact is, I didn't really want to."

Blackwall retained and nurtured one aspect of musicology in particular. "My real passion was early music," she says. "I think there is a real crossover between a lot of folky music and early music. The themes are the same, pretty much."

"There were a lot of great musicians involved in The Pendulums," Mike Hastings adds. "Martin Beer's a fantastic bass player. He was playing with Scatter as well." The Pendulums had a well-considered sound and were studied in image, too. Blackwall created Fillmore-inspired posters to give the group a strong visual identity. "It worked for a while," she says. "But then, for various reasons, we all had to go off and do different things. I wanted to go and do my Masters course."

By then, having released a couple of strong free-folk records, Scatter too had come to an end. Alex Neilson was now in demand as a drummer, working with an awe-inspiring list of collaborators that includes the legendary folk outsider Jandek. One day, Neilson was meant to be recording with Bonnie 'Prince' Billy. "They cancelled at the last minute, and so we still had the free studio time," he recalls. "I invited Vinnie [Blackwall], who was my girlfriend at the time, along. We just improvised drums and voice."

The result was Directing Hand. "Alex is always pushing me to do things that I feel uncomfortable with," Blackwall says. "I think a lot of the Directing Hand stuff was a bit like that. I just thought: 'What the fuck am I doing?' But at the same time, once you commit to it, you really give yourself to it. And that really counts for something." They released their first album together, *What Put The Blood*, in 2008. "It's very direct and very primal," Neilson says. "The only thing I've ever really heard like that, with the voice, was Max Roach and Abbey Lincoln on a record from 1960 called *The Freedom Now Suite*."

At the same time, Neilson says, he had also been "toying with the idea of writing songs. I wanted to try in some small way to re-imagine the places that I came from, those that meant a lot to me, like Yorkshire particularly, areas of Scotland, Cornwall, and Sussex". These songs fed into Trembling Bells, the most personal of Neilson's various projects. "I think the catalyst for it was Vinnie and I breaking up," he says. "I started to write abandoned love songs. It was a channel for my angst at the time."

Blackwall and Neilson remained close friends and musical kindred spirits. She helped shape the Trembling Bells songs; he would hum them to her, and she would interpret them. "She can translate the ideas really easily, from abstract hums to what comes out in her voice," Neilson says. Blackwall played chords, and between them she and Neilson would work out which ones chimed best with the original sketch. "I'm much more of an arranger," she says. "I'm the opposite, really," Neilson adds. "I don't know how to implement anything, but I have a lot of ideas."

In 2008, Neilson and Blackwall were invited to appear on the radio show *Soundwave*. It was presented by John Cavanagh, who had been one half of Electroscope in the 90s, recorded solo under the name Phosphene, and had produced artists like the French minimalist composer Colleen. "I was expecting their free-form voice and drums sound," he recalls of Blackwall and Neilson. "They wanted to bring more people to the session, which was fine by me, but I was very surprised when they turned up playing a much mellower, song-based set than I had envisaged."

This session formed the basis of the Trembling Bells album *Carbeth* (2009), which Cavanagh co-produced. "At the outset we discussed different styles of production," he says. "We talked about Joe Boyd, whose recordings we all admired, and how his style had more to do with encouraging a good atmosphere and getting people to play together, rather than aiming for clinical studio separation and tracking all the instruments at different times." The sessions lasted only three days but were intensive and fruitful. Among the contributors were Simon Shaw and Ben Reynolds, while Mike Hastings contributed guitar and vocals and became a full-time member of Trembling Bells shortly afterward.

Carbeth came out on the Honest Jon's label, with a painting by Susan

Neilson, Alex's mother, on the front cover. "It was really important to me, from a personal point of view, that my mum did some artwork," he says. "I wanted to cash in, doing that music, on a lot of personal experience. She used to paint before I was born and then abandoned it, and had just picked it up again." *Carbeth* received some of the strongest reviews of all the new British psychedelic folk records; *Mojo* called it a "deeply affecting ode to lost love [that] resonates with the ancient spirit of Britain".

The second Trembling Bells album, *Abandoned Love* (2010), proved the sustainability of Neilson's songwriting, laying bare more emotional turmoil and establishing the Bells as both accessible and thought provoking. It was a testament to Neilson and Blackwall's adaptability that such approachable music could come from two people who had previously improvised with psaltery and wine glasses on *What Put The Blood*. Neilson is well aware of this dichotomy. "When we did Directing Hand it was more intense, noisy improvised music," he says. "It's gone from one extreme to the other, really."

ᛞ

Alex Neilson and Lavinia Blackwall weren't alone in their ability to whoosh between clattering improvisation and deeply affecting songcraft. Formed in 2001, Ireland's United Bible Studies also started life as a duo. "Dave Colohan and I started the band in an attempt to sound like the Incredible String Band or those other folkies we were listening to at the time," James Rider recalls. Rider's interest in acoustic music had swelled from Britpop to Nick Drake, and then taken in 60s and 70s folk-rock, Takoma, and Irish folk, while Colohan had a long and thoughtful relationship with different types of music.

"When I was 11 or 12, as the school day came to a close, we would gather around the master's desk to learn the tin whistle," he recalls. "I always preferred the slow airs to the jigs and reels, which I found much more difficult to play." What came later was a love of Neil Young, The Doors, Pink Floyd, Julian Cope, Fairport Convention, the improvised music of Pago Libre and Sergey Kuryokhin, and the early-90s Riot Grrrl movement. The last of these proved particularly important in that it triggered Colohan's own creativity. He began his own tape label and fanzine in a spirit that, he says, "is very much alive in me ... I still occasionally have nightmares involving photocopiers".

Gavin Prior joined in 2002. He had been playing guitar since he was 12, writing songs since 15, and was equipped with a Masters in Music Technology. He too had an interest in folk, psychedelia, and experimental music, and was trying to make it as a sound engineer when he met Rider and

Colohan. "I joined through playing improvisation with Dave," he says. "It changed my life I guess." From this point on, United Bible Studies became a tornado; intrepid musicians of all hues and abilities were drawn into its whirling eye. "I think everyone who likes our band actually joins the band," Prior says. "There's no one left to buy the records, that's the problem."

The potential for innovation was immense. United Bible Studies' early releases were CD-Rs: *Huntly Town* (2004), *Airs Of Sun And Stone* (2005), and the 'Observatory' series, which began with *The Lunar Observatory* (2004). The release dates were often fairly arbitrary; according to Prior, they did not always correspond to when the music was actually recorded, and much less to any trajectory of development. Instead, the CD-Rs represent a series of vignettes, involving a wide variety of musicians, often recorded in ambient space or unusual landscapes: the Scottish Highlands; Dublin's North Circular Road; H. P. Lovecraft's grave. "Music that means the most to me almost always carries some feeling of the land within it," Colohan says. "I feel a strong affinity with Robert Holdstock's liminal landscapes, where myth and reality collide and overlap. Sound seems to pour through the cracks between where you are and what you're feeling."

The first 'official' United Bible Studies album was *The Shore That Fears The Sea*, which was recorded sporadically between 2001 and 2004 but not released until 2006. No two songs use the same combination of people. The earliest track completed for the album, 'Hellical Rising', dates back to when the band was just Rider and Colohan. Apart from the live track, 'Watching The Rain Reshape Galway', the songs were all recorded in people's houses.

"I love the tension of recording live to open mics," Prior says of 'Watching The Rain Reshape Galway'. "This was recorded upstairs in the Galway Arts Centre. The windows were wide open. You can hear gulls and car horns echoing off the buildings outside. You can just about hear my mother laughing at Dave's self-deprecating introduction to the song in the very first second of the recording." The album's title track provides its arresting core. "No other United Bible Studies song has shape-shifted so often," Prior says, "or taken us to so many different places when we play it live. There was a phase when our entire set consisted solely of an extemporised version of this one song. In every way this felt like the last track on the album, which is exactly why Shane [Cullinane, another early group member] thought it shouldn't be." *Shore* closes instead with the murmuring 'Captain William Coey'.

By the time *Shore* was released, United Bible Studies had already started work on their next full album, *The Jonah*. "For a couple of years it was called

The Prog Album," Prior says. "We just kind of threw everything in there, and that's the title track." The musicians – particularly Colohan and Cullinane – were listening a lot to Richard Youngs's prog-rock band, Ilk, and planned a group get-together in the countryside. The result, released by Camera Obscura in 2009, is an epic journey through acoustic heart, progressive rock pastiche, and traditional music.

As well as playing in United Bible Studies, the band-members have numerous side projects. The most popular of them was all-acoustic Magickal Folk Of The Faraway Tree, led by Shane Cullinane and Dave Colohan. "I lived with Shane at that time," Prior recalls. "I came home one day and they played me this song that they'd recorded, 'Le Bon Marian', a French ballad." Colohan had found the song in a library book, but the pair had come up with their own music. Also involved in the Faraway Tree was Caroline Coffey, whose fluency in Irish added to the authenticity.

Colohan, meanwhile, was increasingly finding inspiration in unaccompanied singing. "I have fond memories of us huddled around a mic trying to find our harmonies," he says. "We had a lot of fun getting our bearings with that project." Two CD-Rs were released, followed by a compilation, *The Soup And The Shilling* (2010).

United Bible Studies have two 'house' labels: Deserted Village, headed by Gavin Prior, and deadslackstring, run by James Rider. Between them, they've put out much of the Bible Studies and Magickal Folk material, along with the pre-UBS, free improv group Murmansk; Colohan's recordings as Agitated Radio Pilot; and a number of innovative releases by other rotating band-members, including Richard Moult's *Ethe* (2010), a work of haunting piano vistas inspired by the Welsh Marches, and Plinth's *Albatross* (2010), which deconstructs Fleetwood Mac's hit song in five iridescent movements.

Plinth, an alias for the Dorset-based composer Michael Tanner, had been recording music since the late 90s. "The first thing I did was called *Wintersongs*, when I was 18," he says. "It was a soundtrack to *The Children Of Green Knowe*. It got me laughed at by all my friends, who were into grunge bands." Tanner began playing with United Bible Studies in 2008; he also performs with The A. Lords, Directorsound, and The Rural Tradition. He has played live and on record with Sharron Kraus and accompanied Pantaleimon on *Tall Trees*.

There's rarely anything approaching six degrees of separation between experimental folk artists. Needless to say, for the United Bible Studies throng, the connections didn't take long to reach outside of Ireland and Britain. "The biggest thing on Deserted Village is Thinguma*jigSaw," Prior says. "We sold out of that twice. They really make an impression."

Describing the origins of Thinguma*jigSaw, the Norwegian duo of Martha Redivivus and Seth Horatio Buncombe recall: "Once upon a time there were these two bewildered souls and they met up and felt they could create music together. But they were scared. So they brought their flute, banjo, and saw, moved to Ireland for a while, and for some reason felt a bit more at ease there." The first Thinguma*jigSaw album was *Awakeinwhitechapel* (2007). "We were deeply influenced by horror movies, and also the literature of Edgar Allan Poe, Roald Dahl, and Stephen King," they say. "We loved the soundtracks, especially the work of Goblin and John Carpenter, but we also knew we were aiming for a folk sound and instrumentation."

This visceral, horrific influence is matched by something more philosophically creepy, and influenced too by their interest in absurdist and modernist literature. They use the term 'splatter-folk' to convey their mixture of fear and acoustic music. "We wanted to come close to the audience," Redivivus and Buncombe reveal. "We wanted to intimidate, but to somehow have a comforting quality at the same time. We aim for a certain emotional instability, which means that we consciously arm the songs with an almost schizophrenic ambiguity. For instance, in the midst of a dark, grim lyric, we like to insert a few lines of subtle wit and clumsy light-heartedness. And visa versa."

Over the course of the past decade, acid, psychedelic, and experimental folk has continued to spring forth from a wide variety of pools. The Finnish singer Islaja made her recorded debut in 2004 on Fonal, a tiny, homegrown imprint that has seen its international reputation rocket in recent years as a home for experimental music. The label's original motto was "warm and small"; the one unifying factor, beside the consistent high quality of its releases, has been founder Sami Sänpäkkilä's good taste.

Islaja met Sänpäkkilä when they were both enrolled on a songwriting course at art school. "As we presented our homework sketches, he said he liked what I do," she recalls. "That gave me a push to record more." Islaja had begun writing songs at the age of five. "I was a really sad child," she says. "To be able to survive, I locked myself in to my music. But the problem was, the music I made was so whiny, it made me even sadder."

Islaja's debut, *Meritie* (2004), drew on a core of what she called "secret and sacred songs", many of them written in her teens, while her mother was ill. She composed them on piano or with a "strangely tuned" acoustic guitar. "They all sounded like demos," she says, "but the time was right for that kind of aesthetic. It was right around the time of Devendra Banhart's first album, and that lo-fi world was new and exciting."

Islaja also became friends with Kemialliset Ystävät, a psychedelic-folk group led by Jan Anderzén, whose approach inspired her to delve yet further into her music. "For me, the years 2003–06 were just one long art-school project," she says. "Life was just about expressing yourself."

After making another similarly experimental album, *Palaa Aurinkoon* (2005), Islaja decided to turn her hand to something closer to pop music. "When I recorded my first album I had no gear, really," she says. "That is what you hear: cheap instruments recorded with a four-track." *Blaze Mountain Recordings* (2008) is a cleaner, more polished production. "I'm in the gap between mainstream and underground," Islaja says. "Wherever I play its a bit uncomfortable."

As well as playing in Kemialliset Ystävät, Jan Anderzén was also the co-founder of the well-regarded fanzine *Hindupyöräilijä*. One of its regular contributors was Laura Naukkarinen, who began playing in DIY improv bands in her teens. Her first album as Lau Nau, *Kuutarha* (2005), is a response to the experience of playing with a wide range of musicians in various expermental and inspirational outfits.

"Playing in and travelling with bands is great," she says, "but I wanted for once to be the dictator and make my own decisions about the music. Some of the most important inspirational ideas were my love for many instruments as well as the improvisational and instant songwriting sessions that I had had with the other bands I was in."

Lau Nau's second album, the transcendent *Nukkuu* (2008), came about after she moved to rural Western Finland and gave birth to her first child. Further from the realm of traditional instrumentation, it's a work of abstract art with a still-beating heart. "I still appreciate warm sounds that smell and have a soul," Naukkarinen says. "For me, recording is more like making good food than working in a laboratory."

Despite its name, The Abaton Book Company also released music, some of which was flecked with folksiness, including *From St Petersburg With Love* (2004) by Julia Vorontsova and *Tall Trees* (2008) by Pantaleimon, aka Andria Degens, who had previously worked with Current 93. But the imprint's strongest example of experimental folk came from Marianne Nowottny, a New Jersey teenager with a cavalier, carnival-esque approach to music.

Nowottny credits her grandparents with introducing her to a wide range of music – everything from "Germany University songs" to "belly-dancing records". She was also taken with Indian pop and Bollywood soundtracks, and obtained her first keyboard at the age of five. "It was a tiny Casio with a built-in, rudimentary sampler," she says. "I made music in my room to stay occupied."

At 15, Nowottny formed Shell, a "dark electro-keyboard girl group", with her friend Donna Bailey. "We were having fun and living in a fantasy world," she says. "We were not watched children, we ran wild and free." Their experiments piqued the interest of The Abaton Book Company, which put out a Shell cassette in 1998, quickly followed by Nowottny's solo debut, *Afraid Of Me*, recorded when she was still only 16. The album's detuned, clashing glissandos led to a promising review in the *New York Press* and a first solo gig at Maxwell's in Hoboken.

Afraid Of Me was certainly a remarkable record, but it was on *Illusions Of The Sun* (2002) that Nowottny really matured. Recorded for the Camera Obscura label, the album captures the sound of unhappiness harshly illuminated by the colourful lights of the fairground. "I had just graduated high school at that time," she says, "and I thought that I fell in love with someone from afar. I was working next to the ocean in Avalon, New Jersey, and adapting to a new stepfather and a new place to live. All I remember was not feeling excited for the future but lost and scared. Being a young woman can be frightful with uncertainty."

A couple of years later, the Camera Obscura label put out yet another barrier-blowing folk album, this time by The Satyrswitch, a one-off project led by Jason Kesselring of the space-metal group Skye Klad. "Skye Klad initially started as a reaction against 'rock music' as I saw it," he says. "I was inspired by Can, Fripp, Eno, Eastern music, industrial, 20th century classical music. It initially sounded nothing like it later turned into."

Skye Klad released a clutch of cultish albums during the late 90s and early 2000s. The last of these, *Skye Klad Plays The Musick Of Cupid's Orkustra Asleep In The Magick Powerhouse Of Oz* (2004), was released on Timothy Renner's Hand/Eye label and gave an indication of what was to follow with The Satyrswitch. Travelling in Bavaria, Kesselring says he was struck by its medieval ambience; he found links in the *Süddeutschland* landscape to Appalachian folk music, particularly the work of Roscoe Holcomb.

"I wanted to make an album that was all acoustic," he says, noting the inspiration of The Vortex Navigation Company, whose work combines Americana, paranormal folk, and psychedelic improvisation. *The High Lonesome Sound Of The Satyrswitch* (2004) features several traditional songs, including a dense reading of 'Nottamun Town'. "What a spooky old song that is," Kesselring says. "I think I read somewhere that it was rumoured to be a magic spell. There is something about playing some of these old songs that is magical. It's like communicating with a ghost."

The Satyrswitch album was an only child but its 'space folk' sound lived on in other groups, among them The Ghost And Swift Moths, led by Jason Zenmoth. "When I play, I try to tap into some kind of collective subconscious," Zenmoth says. "I believe 'folk' to be nothing more than something that has been passed to you, whether around a campfire, singing, or through dreams and the subconscious." As with most micro-genres, the borders of space folk are fuzzy, with collaboration common. Zenmoth has played with Kris Thompson, who was a member both of the hugely psychedelic Abunai! and Bobb Trimble's band, The Flying Spiders, while Kesselring subsequently joined up with Roger Williamson, a later member of Dando Shaft.

Perhaps the most unexpected journey into experimental folk came from the German duo Cobra Killer. Having previously made several albums for the self-describing Digital Hardcore label, the duo then decided to reinterpret their own back catalogue in collaboration with the group Kapajkos on their 2005 LP *Das Mandolinenorchester*. The album turns driving electroclash songs like 'Heavy Rotation' and 'Mund Auf Augen Zu' into frenetic, Eastern-flavoured folk framed by mandolin, singing saw, and cajón.

Not far behind in the unlikely folk conversion stakes was Kelli Ali. Born Kelli Dayton in Birmingham, England, Ali had listened to her mother's folk records as a child but was drawn toward grunge and rock as a teenager. Then, after meeting Rick Lennox from the One Little Indian label, she was invited to audition for an electronic group soon to be known as Sneaker Pimps. The group's unique mixture of trip-hop and Britpop was fresh and widely liked. They hit the US and UK singles charts with '6 Underground'; *Becoming X* (1996) was also a critical and commercial success.

"I completely loved it," Ali says of the band's whirlwind success. "It just seemed like everything was happening the way it should be." Then, on the eve of recording a second album, her band-mates decided they wanted to carry on as a duo. "They asked me to go. I was really, totally devastated by it." Ali left the band and dropped out of view. She made two pop-oriented solo albums but was plagued by record company maladministration and media hostility. "I was getting more and more frustrated, I was struggling with alcohol dependency, I was broke, and it was probably one of the darkest times of my life," she recalls. "I was really at a loss what to do."

In 2005, Kelli Ali and her partner sold all their possessions and went to Mexico. "We just discovered life again, something fresh and beautiful," she says. "I very naturally found that, while we were backpacking, camping, and sleeping on beaches, I was writing on the guitar. I found that that changed my voice because, in order to hear myself, I had to sing in a higher pitch. And that's when a lot of my earlier folk influences started to come back."

Ali was now writing ballads, and started to meet others who were also on similar voyages. "I was introduced to the music of Devendra Banhart, Marissa Nadler, and Vashti Bunyan, and that changed everything. I knew Joan Baez and Nick Drake and all the legends, but I didn't know all these new young people. And they were making this really innovative but really delicate and beautiful music. They just hit a nerve. Something real, something organic, and it doesn't depend on production as much as it does on the song behind it."

By the time she returned to the UK, Ali wanted to record her new songs, but not in the ways she had before. "I didn't want to go into a studio with some producer who's just going to think about what's current, or what his vision is for the album," she says. Instead, she sought out Max Richter, known for his instrumental album *The Blue Notebooks* (2004) and his work with Vashti Bunyan, among others. The resulting *Rocking Horse* (2008) was recorded in a vintage studio and stands among the most poignant of all British gossamer-folk records.

⋈

Notwithstanding the many musical changes that occurred between the first and second waves of psychedelic and experimental folk, huge structural changes have also taken place. The idea that a modern artist analogous to Jan Dukes De Grey, Forest, or even Tim Buckley would get an opportunity to release an album on a major label seems fanciful at best. Virtually all of the musically important records of the second psychedelic folk generation have been issued by independent labels or by the artists themselves. This, combined with the democratisation of the recording process brought about by digital technology, has led to a torrent of albums in every genre, but perhaps none so much as folk.

"It's a really, really confusing time to be a musician," says Greg Weeks. "There are a lot more bands, and there are a lot more *great* bands. And when you are one band doing one type of music, and there's only a couple of other people close to you, that's one thing psychologically. But if there are 400 other bands that you think are great doing the same thing, then all of a sudden you think, what is it that I'm really doing here? Am I making any impact culturally? Is this really all that important if so many other people can do what I'm doing equally as well? Those are the times when you just turn out the light and go to bed."

CHAPTER 21

Here Before

IN THE AUTUMN OF 2008, Wembley Stadium listened to Vashti Bunyan. She may not quite have reached stadium rock-level superstardom, but her voice was heard by tens of thousands of sports fans at a special NFL game, held in London, between the San Diego Chargers and the New Orleans Saints. 'Train Song' – that gem of a single that flopped dismally on its release in 1966 – was now being used to soundtrack an advert for Reebok's new Speedwick Tee (a T-shirt that, through some convoluted technology, minimises the inconvenience of sweating). The advert, entitled 'Join The Migration', was shown on the stadium's mammoth screens, with Bunyan's voice seeping from the giant speakers.

"I lost contact with Peter Snell," Bunyan says of the man who produced the song 42 years earlier. "He's the one person in the music world I haven't been able to trace. I would love to be able to tell him that, actually, 'Train Song' did fantastically well. It worked in the end." 'Join The Migration' was an extreme example of how the second wave of acid, psychedelic, and experimental folk was accompanied by a wide-ranging re-evaluation of the first. (Another of Bunyan's songs, 'Diamond Day', appeared in an advert for T-Mobile.) This in turn led to the renewal and resurgence of some of the musicians from that first wave, frequently in collaboration with younger artists. It was a fine partnership, resulting in a crop of interesting records and inspiring performances.

"None of us have a lot of money hanging around from record labels," says Alison O'Donnell, who likewise found a new lease of life in the mid 2000s.

"We've found ways and means of working with each other economically, and I think it's led to some great music."

"I hadn't been able to play guitar or listen to my own voice for all of those years, ever since *Diamond Day*," Vashti Bunyan recalls. "But after the reissue came out – it was a complete shock that it actually did anything, or anybody listened to it at all – with the first royalties, I bought a Mac and a little keyboard and a mixer and I started playing my guitar again."

The reissue came at a strange time. Bunyan had recently moved back to a city – this time Edinburgh – after 25 years of living in the country. "I thought, coming back into the city, that all of those pastoral ideas would go," she says. "But they didn't, and that was the imagery I drew on, without thinking really." Emotionally, too, it was a difficult period. Her brother had recently passed away.

Bunyan made some demos on her new computer and planned to record the songs with Simon Raymonde, formerly of Cocteau Twins. "I told him that I wanted it to be as unlike *Diamond Day* as possible," she says, "because I was still kind of embarrassed by it. I wanted lots and lots of percussion, lots of bass, lots of everything else except no choirboy vocals and no acoustic guitar. Which is what he did. But it didn't work. It really didn't work."

Bunyan withdrew from the project and carried on writing songs in the little room just off the lounge in her Edinburgh townhouse. Then Raymonde asked her to perform at the Royal Festival Hall, in April 2003, as part of an event curated by Stephen Malkmus. "It was just to do three songs in a collective thing," she recalls. "Simon said that he would come and play piano for me, and that he would find other musicians. It was only going to be for ten minutes. I was absolutely petrified."

When Raymonde found out that he could no longer attend the concert, he arranged for Fiona Brice, Adem, and Kieran Hebden – Four Tet – to accompany Bunyan instead. It all proved to be rather serendipitous: not only did the event go well, Bunyan kept the connections alive. When Hebdon was touring, he dropped in to see Bunyan in Edinburgh and brought with him his support act, Animal Collective. They had all been big *Diamond Day* fans ever since David Portner and Noah Lennox (who were then working at New York's Other Music record store) introduced the rest of the group to the record. "They just brought it home and started playing it," Brian Weitz recalls. "Immediately, on first listen, we all were quite taken in by it."

After the meeting, Dave Howell of FatCat Records put forward the idea of a collaboration. "Everyone was super excited," Weitz says. The result was the

2005 EP *Prospect Hummer*: four eerie, fluid tracks that partnered Bunyan's wisp with Animal Collective's sensitive sonic explorations.

The EP marked the start of a lasting relationship. Howell heard Bunyan's recent demos and offered to release her new material. He also introduced her to Max Richter. "As soon as I heard his recordings, I knew that that was what was missing really – that classical background," Bunyan says. "We immediately hit it off and started working together in his studio in his house." Bunyan had six songs ready; the rest soon flowed out. "There was a lot to come up with," she says. "There were all of those years, and the children, and the life, the life that I had had in between. I had an awful lot to draw on for the songs, because an awful lot had happened."

Bunyan's new songs told of the joys and knots of human relationships, of how innermost feelings are revealed by the tiniest actions. "Max wanted to do all the songs with real instruments and real musicians," Bunyan says. She wasn't so sure about that; she liked the demos she'd already recorded, on her own, with "every note in the right place". So they compromised. "There are a lot of electronic sounds on there that you might think are real instruments, but actually they're not," she says.

Those musicians who do appear on the record include some of the leading lights of the new generation: Adem, Devendra Banhart, Vetiver, and Joanna Newsom. There was also a reunion with Robert Kirby, with whom Bunyan had originally worked on *Diamond Day*, and who came in to play French horn and trumpet. "That whole day was totally extraordinary," she says. "Adem was able to come with his extraordinary array of instruments. Devendra was in town with Andy [Cabic], Otto [Hauser], and Kevin [Barker]. And Robert Kirby had agreed to come in the evening. To hear Max's string players playing an arrangement that I'd done, and to have Robert Kirby there – I hadn't *seen* him since that *Diamond Day* session and there he was. All of those people there, just a wonderful, wonderful day. I'll never forget it. And it's something that you couldn't ever arrange, it was totally organic."

Bunyan named the album *Lookaftering* – a word used in her family. "Three days later, I woke up in the middle of the night and thought, what have I done?" she recalls. "That is the most stupid word, nobody's going to take me seriously now. And I'm going to put a rabbit on the cover! What am I thinking?" She needn't have worried: released in 2005, *Lookaftering* received the critical plaudits that *Diamond Day* had not.

"I think the thing about *Lookaftering* is that it was the bookend to *Diamond Day*," Bunyan says. "*Diamond Day* was really looking forward and dreaming of this fantastic pastoral future. And *Lookaftering* was having done all of that, survived it, come through it. It's as if those two looked at each other across the years." 'Wayward Hum', the closing track, says as much. The liner notes reveal that Bunyan's performance was taken from a rehearsal, and that she was unaware that she was being recorded. Its spontaneity evoked afterglows of her creations of 35 years earlier, while her wordless voice, so gentle and so strong, offered wise solace to the deepest hurts.

┲

Devendra Banhart and Andy Cabic had already gone on record with their love for Vashti Bunyan's *Just Another Diamond Day* before they had the opportunity to play with her. Similarly, Olivardil Prydwyn of Stone Breath had been a very big Pearls Before Swine fan for years before meeting his hero, Tom Rapp. "That was at the time when nobody knew where Tom Rapp was," he recalls. "There were stories that he'd become a gravedigger in Amsterdam and all these wonderful tales."

What had actually happened was that Tom Rapp had been working as a civil rights lawyer. *Ptolemaic Terrascope* had run the first retrospective feature about him in 1993. Four years later, Phil McMullen pestered Rapp to perform at the inaugural Terrastock festival. Rapp agreed in part because his son, who plays in the band Shy Camp, was already on the bill.

"I had not performed in 22 years," Rapp recalls, "and seldom played the guitar, even at home. So I relearned the words and chords, re-established the calluses on my fingers – some bleeding was involved – and played a half-dozen songs. The other musicians, half my age, beautifully sat in on some. I was so surprised that 'kids' even knew my songs, let alone liked them!" Rapp also found out that Jeffrey Alexander's Secret Eye label was due to put out a tribute to him, *For The Dead In Space* (1997), which includes versions of his songs recorded by acts such as The Tower Recordings, Fit & Limo, and Flying Saucer Attack. It all served to reinvigorate Rapp, who promptly recorded *A Journal Of The Plague Year* (1999), which features contributions from Damon & Naomi and The Beavis Frond's Nick Saloman.

Rapp only realised the full extent of how much his music meant to people when he played at the London Terrastock in 1999. "A man with cancer, his face all wrapped in bandages, asked me if he could use one of my songs at his funeral," he recalls. "I hugged him and said 'sure'. He died two months later."

By then Prydwyn had met, played with, and become friends with Rapp. Their first encounter came in 1997. "I was visiting Tim and Alison [Renner]," he recalls, "and they were going to see the Japanese group Ghost play in Philadelphia. I remember before the show started, one of them said: 'There's Tom Rapp.' So here's me, in a very small room, suddenly across from one of my very biggest musical icons in the world! Tom and Lynn [Tom's wife], Ghost, Tim, Alison, and I went to have dinner between the soundcheck and the show.

"It turned out that the restaurant we'd gone to didn't take credit cards, which meant that Tom had to go and find a cash machine, at night, in a fairly rough section of Philadelphia. I got the job of accompanying Tom Rapp to the cash machine so he wouldn't be assaulted by the undesirables of Philadelphia, because I was apparently the fiercest looking person in the company. That probably tells you something about the fierceness of psychedelic folk musicians."

⋈

Most of the original swell of psychedelic folk from the 60s and 70s has been reissued, often by sensitive, specialist labels like Sunbeam. "You just have to wait a bit," says David Costa of Trees, "and *then* people go: 'Hang on, actually this is really quite something.'" Or as Clive Palmer puts it, paraphrasing Renoir: "You can always afford the best steak when you've got no teeth."

For some more obscure artists, finding out that a decades-old album was suddenly in demand came as quite a surprise. "We had a registered letter arrive here from a chap called Steve Smith who was the originator of the Kissing Spell label," says Ken Saul of Norfolk's Stone Angel. Smith's friend had picked up a copy of the LP at a car boot sale and played it to him. "He was saying, did we have any copies left of the original LP? So Joan and I sent him one – there you go, have that, thank you for your interest."

The Sauls received another registered letter by return of post asking if they had any more copies of the record. It seemed Smith was interested in buying all of them. "We thought, the man's a nutcase," Ken says. "We wrote back and said: 'Are you serious? Because if so we've got a box of 90 here and you can have 'em for three quid each.'" They promptly received a cheque and duly discharged the box of LPs, pleased that they had finally recouped the initial outlay for the project.

A few months later, Ken Saul was at the Waveney Folk Club, where he met his friend Richard, who had been an avid fan of Stone Angel from the early days. "Bloody good news about your LP, isn't it?" Richard said.

Ken was puzzled. "Richard, what are you talking about?" he asked.

"That article in *Record Collector* – didn't they tell you about it?"

"What *are* you talking about?"

"There's an article in *Record Collector* about your LP and there's a picture of it. And they reckon they're worth 250 quid!"

"Don't be daft, Richard," Ken replied. "You mean £2.50."

"It bloody isn't! It's 250 quid! I told my wife and said that you gave me a copy, and she said I better give it back to you. I told her not bloody likely!"

Ken Saul's friend was right: *Record Collector* had run a feature on privately pressed albums in May 1992, and there, sure enough, was the now prohibitively expensive *Stone Angel*. "It describes us as being one of the most interesting examples of acid folk," Saul says. "That was the first time we'd come across the term."

The Sauls aren't bitter about letting the LPs go at cost price. "If Steve Smith hadn't got in touch, they'd still be sitting under the bed," Ken says. Furthermore, reissues by Kissing Spell of *Stone Angel*, the Midwinter material, the later Filby Church session, and new material recorded in the 2000s ensured that the group reached a far wider audience than the original LP ever could have.

"A lot of people clearly think we're something much more than we are," Ken Saul says with a chuckle. "A lady in America sent me an email wanting to know when we're going to be touring the States. Well, we've done the Far East – or Lowestoft, as we call it."

Others too have been rejuvenated upon finding out that albums they had considered dead and buried were in fact still very much loved. "A few years ago, I googled my name for something about my paintings," says Mark Fry. "All of a sudden, all this stuff about *Dreaming With Alice* came up, reams and reams of it." Fry had been living in France and working as an artist for the past 20 years, and had almost forgotten the album he made as a teenager in Italy. "Then I started getting emails from someone called Richard Morton Jack, who runs Sunbeam," Fry continues. "I kept turning his emails down because I thought, God, no, I can't face this. But I got *Alice* out and had a listen, and thought it sounded pretty good. So it all took off from there."

Fry was duly inspired to start recording again. "I'd never stopped playing to friends in the evenings," he says. "But then I started to build a little recording studio next to my painting studio in the barn opposite the house, so I could get on with recording." *Shooting The Moon* (2008) is Fry's understated, reflective follow-up to *Alice*. Like *Diamond Day* and

Lookaftering, the two albums run a tightrope between the decades. It's as if the teenage and mature Mark Frys are offering each other words of advice and support across the chasm.

Another fan of Mark Fry's was Michael Tanner. "I was completely consumed with *Alice* for weeks after first hearing it," he says. The two men started corresponding through MySpace. Fry was impressed by the music Tanner made as Plinth and his work in the experimental folk duo The A.Lords with Nicholas Palmer. "I was listening to his stuff for ages before they suggested doing something together," Fry says. "I think they're amazing."

Mark Fry and The A.Lords have since performed together, playing new material alongside reinterpretations of the songs from *Dreaming With Alice*. "They just translated immediately," Fry says. "They sound *more* like I wanted them to sound when I wrote them all those years ago."

Interest also swelled in the work of Bill Fay. After 27 years, his two Decca albums were reissued alongside a previously unreleased late-70s studio album, *Tomorrow Tomorrow And Tomorrow*, which was put out in 2005 by David Tibet on his Durtro label. Around the same time, Caedmon reunited for live gigs and recording. "It's been rewarding, because we have discovered a chemistry there that just works," says Ken Patterson. Elsewhere, David and Angie McNiven of Bread Love And Dreams have taken tentative steps toward a revival, performing under the old name in 2008 at the request of an old friend on the occasion of her 60th birthday.

"It was just lovely to do it all again," Angie McNiven says. "We thought to ourselves, why haven't we done this a lot sooner?" The fires were stoked once again when Espers were in Edinburgh for a gig and turned up at the McNivens' house with backstage passes. "It's so reassuring to think that a younger generation have been listening to your music and are really inspired by it," Angie says.

⋈

The members of Comus had largely disowned their former group long before the dawn of the 21st century. "For years and years after the band split up I couldn't even listen to the album," Glenn Goring says. Bobbie Watson says that she "never, ever told anybody what I'd done. Comus was so strange, it didn't seem to have any relation to any other kind of music at all".

In 2005, Sanctuary Records released a compilation album, *Song To Comus*, which prompted rumours of a Comus reformation. Yet still the band remained unmoved. "I'd built another life, completely outside of that, playing

329

different kinds of music," Goring says. "For me, it just seemed like a mission impossible."

It took one persistent fan to break the deadlock. "I got forwarded an email from Sanctuary Records from this guy Stefan," Goring recalls. This was Swedish concert promoter Stefan Dimle, who was keen for a reunited Comus to play at his Melloboat Festival. "I replied to this guy at Sanctuary and I said this guy has got more chance of seeing God than Comus back together," Goring says.

Eventually, however, the band decided to accept Dimle's offer. Founding member Rob Young had been part of the original discussions, but in the end decided not to participate. His place was taken by Bobbie Watson's husband, Jon Seagroatt, who played flute and percussion and also provided technical support. The show was a success and led to further offers to perform. More than 35 years after they first split up, Comus had become a band again. They even returned to writing, with a new song, 'Out Of The Coma', taking up where 'The Prisoner' bowed out.

Jon Seagroatt has an objective perspective on the Comus reunion and the band dynamic. "Comus is an interesting mix of very complex individuals," he says. "I have gradually realised how committed they all were to Comus the first time round, and how wounded they were by the band's collapse. It took them a long time to agree to the reformation, but they did it, perhaps in part because they felt they owed it to their younger selves."

Since the turn of the millennium, there has been a huge and renewed swell of appreciation for The Incredible String Band. It's not something that has always been chased by the original members, however. "I've done something like 58 albums, 45 of them after The Incredible String Band," Robin Williamson says. "That's a lot of stuff, and it covers a lot of different areas." He made a triptych of albums for the avant-garde German label ECM – *Seed-At-Zero* (2000), *Skirting The River Road* (2002), and *The Iron Stone* (2006) – and has explored folk and Bardic tradition as part of a duo with his wife, Bina Williamson.

Mike Heron too continues to perform, often with his daughter, Georgia Seddon. "We do a double-act," he says. "We do the String Band stuff together and a few other songs of mine, and then she does her songs separately." Clive Palmer has also continued to release albums, albeit very much when he wants to. "I don't want to be a star; I'm not interested," he says. "All that happens is you just get a bigger house and a bigger telly and bigger problems. And when you decide to pack it in, everybody rings you up."

There have been sporadic String Band reunions over the years. In 1997, Williamson and Heron played two concerts together; Palmer and Williamson then collaborated on the album *At The Pure Fountain* (1999). "It was more or less traditional," Palmer says. "I remember Joe Boyd saying he liked that record. So we did that, and then I went home, and then Robin said: 'Would you like to do some gigs?'"

That same year, there was a reunion of all three members. "It was in Edinburgh, to celebrate the String Band," Palmer says. "So we got Mike in. Billy Connolly came and did a bit, and Archie Fisher was there. It was a real success." The performance set off a series of occasional concert appearances, including one at the 2005 Green Man Festival. "We were honoured to have them," says organiser Jo Bartlett. "It showed what we were trying to do, pick out the iconic 60s folk heroes from our version of folk and mix them in with the new, young breed of folk." Further shows followed in the USA, with support from a wide range of new artists, including Josephine Foster and Spires That In The Sunset Rise.

The most high-profile event was one organised by Joe Boyd at London's Barbican in 2009 under the name Very Cellular Songs: The Music Of The Incredible String Band. The band, on this occasion, was Heron and Palmer, who performed with a number of other artists, including Trembling Bells and Alasdair Roberts. "It was such an honour to be asked to be involved," says Roberts. "It was pretty hard to memorise 'Maya', and I'm not sure I pulled it off, but I felt more comfortable with 'My Name Is Death'. Everybody was friendly and easy to work with."

"A lot of the stuff has mileage," says Heron. "It does translate across the years quite well. One of my favourites, and I think it's a brilliant song, is Robin's 'Seasons They Change'. It's also called 'The Circle Is Unbroken', that's what it's called on the record label. I did that at The Barbican with my daughter. It's a lovely song."

Of course, not everything came to a happy ending. Alexander 'Skip' Spence's *Oar* was one of the first acid-folk albums to be rediscovered. A tribute album entitled *More Oar* was released in 1999, while *Oar* itself was reissued the same year and hailed as an essential album not just in acid folk or folk-rock but in the whole of rock history. Sadly, the acclaim came a little too late for Spence. He had been living with a number of physical and mental health problems ever since recording the album and passed away in April 1999.

In December 2009, Jack Rose died of a heart attack. Phil McMullen set up a tribute on the *Ptolemaic Terrascope* website, and those within the magazine's community shared their memories. Phil himself wrote that "Jack was like an uncle to the whole extended Terrascopic family; always there for us to talk to, always the first to encourage us when we needed it, and, bless him, usually the first one drunk at any family gathering. Larger than life and twice as natural. To say we'll miss him is a massive understatement".[1]

The posthumous *Luck In The Valley* (2010) is a recording by Rose and his band The Black Twig Pickers, and followed on from a self-titled release a year earlier. Rose and his band had embraced a rollicking, joyful approach to the American tradition and the art of the guitar. These later records are full of Rose's usual sincerity, intelligence, and respect but are laced at the same time with humour and impudence. Never one to fall into the trap of simple revivalism or iconoclasm, Rose had continued to stand as one of the most innovative figures in roots music.

For *Jack Rose & The Black Twig Pickers*, Rose and the band recast 'Kensington Blues', the title track from his 2005 album. "*Kensington Blues* is a really hard record to live up to," Rose said in 2007.[2] It was indeed a career-defining work: the point where his past ken and modern edge come together in perfect elegance. Most of Rose's records were released in limited editions; *Kensington Blues* was in such demand that it was kept on VHF Records' catalogue indefinitely.

The introspection and heart of Jack Rose's guitar was a compelling and necessary spike in the ground for the many of the musicians whose own work tended toward the psychedelic and the avant-garde. His guitar's intense, ragged beauty continues to bend, slide, and reverberate.

ᛝ

The cross-generational linkages continue. The Story is a collaboration between Martin Welham, formerly of Forest, and his son, Tom Welham. "Tom and I had always shared a love for the same things in music," Martin says. "We began, co-incidentally, to sing together in very much the same way as Adrian, Dez, and I had done when we were Tom's age, by unaccompanied harmony singing, but making up melodies as we went along." The Story's first release was a split LP with the Santa Cruz psychedelic-folk group Whysp, who were themselves partially inspired to make music together when they first heard *Forest* and *Full Circle*.

Marianne Segal admits that she had "not been doing very much music" when Jade's *Fly On Strangewings* was reissued in 2003. She began to re-explore her old music and set up a Jade website, but was still dumbfounded when Michael Tyack got in touch to ask her to appear on the first Circulus album. They recorded a version of Segal's 'Swallow' together in 2005. "I was really happy," Segal says, "and a little bit nervous because I wasn't really sure that working with Circulus was the way I should go. But in the same breath we had such fun together and I loved the medieval instruments, the lutes and the cittern." The collaboration was so successful that Tyack and Segal went on to collaborate again on her 2007 album *The Gathering*.

Jane Weaver's Bird record label has explicitly forged bonds between artists across the generations. The label's 2007 *Bearded Ladies* compilation album mixed up 60s and 70s recordings by female psychedelic-folk singers with new tracks by contemporary voices. In 2010, Weaver made *The Fallen By Watch Bird*, which she credited to Jane Weaver & Septiéme Soeur, an umbrella name for seven female artists of all hues and ages: Weaver, Susan Christie, Wendy Flower, Lisa Jen, two members of Misty Dixon, and the Bosnian singer Behar.

The most ambitious and glorious outpouring of Bird's cross-generational sisterhood came with the Lost Ladies Of Folk event, which formed part of the Jarvis Cocker-curated Meltdown festival of 2007. Perhaps the most surprising attendee was Bonnie Dobson. "I stopped performing in 1989," she says. "I had a concert in Chicago, for the Canadian Club … it was absolutely wonderful, and I thought, OK, let's just go out." Dobson had not released an album since *Morning Dew* (1976). She had been working full-time at Birkbeck College, part of the University of London, since the mid 80s, and "never talked a lot about my singing days. But although I hadn't done any performing at all, I had still been singing, and the voice was still there".

Dobson was pleased to accept the invitation to perform at the event. Susan Christie did so with a creeping terror. "I thought, gee, I don't know if I can do it anymore," she recalls. "I practiced every day – I practiced while walking the dog, I practiced everywhere you could. I was very nervous." Dobson, too, was "pretty scared. But once I got on stage it just felt 'OK, you're here' and it was lovely". The third 'lost lady' on the bill was Wendy Flower. "The night was like a dream come true, quite surrealistic, actually," she said in 2008. "I had never met [Dobson and Christie], but I was a great admirer of their music. They're extraordinary women [and] tremendous artists."[3] Christie, Dobson, and Flower followed support sets by Cate Le Bon, Jane Weaver, and Emma Tricca. "I don't think it really occurred to me that something like this could happen," Christie says.

Perhaps the most energetic collaborator of all is Alison O'Donnell. "I've written something like 25 songs in the last 18 months," she says, "more than in my whole life up until then. It just poured out of me, and I think that ten years that I didn't do anything stifled me." After Mellow Candle, she had played in the bands Flibbertigibbet and Earthling, but her musical career was sidelined by a high-profile public sector job in London. She returned to Ireland in 2001 and made tentative steps toward reigniting her musical muse. "When I first started back it was *so* hard," she says. "I was so frustrated and downcast, because I couldn't find anybody decent to work with."

Undeterred, O'Donnell took a new approach by appearing on other people's projects, including *The Jonah* by United Bible Studies and *The Fabric Of Folk* by The Owl Service. She was stimulated by both acts' approach. "Steven [Collins] has got the whole picture I think, in terms of being contemporary and the understanding of the past," she says. "I've been involved with United Bible Studies since I started doing stuff with Dave [Colohan] in Agitated Radio Pilot. It's very experimental and always different, nothing's ever the same." Members of both groups appear on O'Donnell's album *Hey Hey Hippy Witch* (2009) alongside Head South By Weaving, Mr Pine, Richard Moult, Fern Knight, and Circulus. "It's cohesive, but the angles are different," O'Donnell says. "They're bringing something else to it. Whatever they're doing, it's made me write a different type of song than I would with someone else."

In 2006, Current 93 released *Black Ships Ate The Sky*. "I think of *Black Ships* as my *Jesus Christ Superstar,* with star guests, and angels skating and humans dating, whilst in the skies above, AntiChrist's Black Ships pour in and Christ sharpens His sword and prepares His white horse." Tibet makes clear that the lyrics are a literal vision of black ships devouring the sky at the apocalypse. "People say: 'I think we must have misunderstood. You're talking about a metaphorical Second Coming of Christ, aren't you?'" he says. "I say: 'No, I'm not.' Of course I might be wrong, but that's what I believe will happen. If you're standing next to me, looking at the sky, you'll perhaps see something different. What I'm doing is trying to find out, or come as close as I can to the truth that waits for me."

Black Ships is a powerfully affecting work; listening to it is akin to examining a disturbing mural on a crumbing basilica wall. It was widely considered to be Current 93's most 'apocalyptic folk' album in years – except by Tibet himself. "I don't like folk in any case, and especially not genres that I created," he says. The album features appearances by a number of other artists with their own complex relationship to folk music: Ben Chasny, Bonnie 'Prince' Billy, Clodagh Simonds of Mellow Candle, and Shirley Collins. "I'm a fan, I love these people," Tibet says. "I've never become jaded. I've met nearly all the people whose work I really admire and love. Except I haven't met Cyndi Lauper."

Amorphous Androgynous is a psychedelic project begun by Future Sound Of London's Garry Cobain and Brian Dougans. In 2008, they released *A Monstrous Psychedelic Bubble (Exploding In Your Mind)*, a compilation album that mixes Espers and Devendra Banhart with Donovan and Tim Buckley, as well as heavier progressive and psychedelic material. The CD also includes 'The Phoenix' by Magic Carpet, which led to Amorphous Androgynous forging a connection with the group's singer, Alisha Sufit. "Gaz Cobain is a great encourager and inspirer, never detracting, always full of creative energy and ideas," Sufit says. "It's given me a new boost – I've been writing songs and singing solo again." Sufit also appeared as guest vocalist on Amorphous Androdgynous's remix of 'Falling Down', a UK Number Ten hit by the megastar rock group Oasis.

Hip-hop and dance music's enormous popularity since the 80s created household names akin to those found in rock. Moreover, it brought about the mainstreaming of sampling. Things have changed a great deal since DJ Kool Herc started looping funk beats in the Bronx in the 70s. By the start of the 21st century, its very ubiquity in the modern pop song had made it harder for musicians to stand out with a sample-based track. Like band names, all the good ones have been used before. Anyone interested in sampling as *art* or *innovation* has to dig deeper in the crates or use samples in a fundamentally different way. Folk or folk-rock samples hadn't been overused, however, so still offered the potential for forging interesting affiliations.

David Sheppard and Kieron Phelan formed State River Widening with a broad musical knowledge and a human approach to electronic music. As Sheppard recalls, they were working at one point on what he calls "a drifting track. Kieron had the idea that it would be really nice to have some sort of vocal in it. It just so happened that in my bag I had various CDs. One of them was an Anne Briggs compilation, and a lot of it was unaccompanied". Sheppard and Phelan overlaid Briggs's 'Lowlands'. It worked perfectly.

"We sent it to Anne, thinking she's not going to be into this – there's synths, it's a very processed piece of music," Sheppard recalls. "And she wrote a lovely long letter saying 'it works really well'." 'Lowlands' was a highlight on the duo's *Cottonwood* (2004) and even fooled many into thinking it was a new Briggs vocal. "That isn't the case," Sheppard says. "But the fact that she approved it is, to me, just as significant."

A more high-profile case of folk sampling came with the title track to the American neo-soul duo Gnarls Barkley's *St Elsewhere* (2006), which came about after producer Danger Mouse heard 'Geordie' from Trees' *On The Shore*. "I loved it," says David Costa. "The sample is the backbone of that entire track. It's wonderful to hear it." Given that Trees had seen so little monetary benefit from their albums, the financial rewards were nice, too. "They'd left it late to clear it," Costa recalls, "so I was able to negotiate something that was, ironically, exploitative."

⋈

Inevitably, the modern incarnation of acid and psychedelic folk will fade, just as the first wave did in the 70s. Sounds swell and break on the shore. It's a natural cycle, and one that ensures growth, energy, and future renewal. Sands shift and seasons change. Yet left behind among the shells and seaweed is the music of the human heart. Music that will continue to offer wonderment, fear, and beauty to anyone curious enough to pick it up.

And what of those two young people, Peter Stampfel and Shirley Collins, whose talent and inquisitiveness helped set up this whole story? Peter Stampfel was reunited once again with Steve Weber when Weber returned to New York in 1996. They enjoyed playing together at the Bottom Line that year, and made another album together, *Too Much Fun*, in 1999. The partnership ended yet again, however, during attempts to stage a 40th anniversary Rounders concert in 2004, a saga documented in the 2006 film *The Holy Modal Rounders ... Bound To Lose*.

Stampfel continues to perform locally, often with younger musicians. "Right now I'm playing with a whole shit-load of people, basically," he says. "I keep finding new people to play with, and the group is getting bigger and bigger. I finally decided to stop trying to limit the size of the group because I keep running into people and I think, oh, I'll play with him too! I'll play with her too!"

Stampfel's super-enthusiasm hasn't diminished since his days as a young man haunting coffee shops in New York. "Playing music that sounds good gets me really high and really exuberant and really happy and in an elevated state of consciousness that enhances my life and, I believe, lives in general," he says. "I'm constantly aware of how far I have to go in terms of what I would like to achieve. So I've *never* been ready to say, OK, I'm good enough, I'll stop right here."

Shirley Collins was awarded an MBE for services to music in 2006. She wrote a memoir of her time collecting songs with Alan Lomax, *America Over The Water* (2004), and is the president of the English Folk Dance & Song Society (EFDSS). "What a president to have, eh?" says Malcolm Taylor, the Director of the Vaughan Williams Memorial Library at Cecil Sharp House. "She's done a lot of talks here. She's got a whole young audience following her. *Love, Death And The Lady* – she's got a young goth audience following that." Collins still lives in Sussex, where she was born, and works tirelessly to promote knowledge of and respect for traditional folksong.

Her refusal to sing continues, however, despite many requests for her to perform or record. That's why it was a surprise to many when the retrospective boxed set *Within Sound* (2002) featured one track, 'Lost In A Wood', with a new vocal. "I rewrote it from the Copper Family one ['Babes In The Wood']," she says. "I'd found it in a nursery-rhyme book in this slightly different form, so I reset the tune slightly. I do think it's lovely, but it just sort of scares me to listen to it." Her face breaks into a smile. "It took a whole day to record that song as well. I'm used to making two *albums* in a day."

Endnotes

All quotes taken from author's interviews unless otherwise stated.

Chapter 1

1 Pat Thomas, *Ptolemaic Terrascope* (2007)
2 Pat Thomas, *Ptolemaic Terrascope* (2007)
3 Graeme Thompson, *Record Collector* (October 2007)
4 Alexis Petridis, *Guardian* (August 3 2007)
5 Graeme Thompson, *Record Collector* (October 2007)
6 Will Hodgkinson, *Independent* (May 5 2006)
7 T.J. McGrath, *Dirty Linen* (April/May 1995)
8 T.J. McGrath, *Dirty Linen* (April/May 1995)
9 Alan Robinson, *Jackson C. Frank* liner notes (2001)
10 T.J. McGrath, *Dirty Linen* (April/May 1995)
11 Alan Robinson, *Jackson C. Frank* liner notes (2001)
12 Joe Boyd, *White Bicycles*

Chapter 2

1 Stefan Grossman, guitarvideos.com
2 Stefan Grossman, guitarvideos.com
3 *Blue Navigator* (November 2006)
4 *Blue Navigator* (November 2006)
5 Frederic Ramsey Jr, *First Songs* liner notes (1965)
6 Nick Jaina, *Local Cut* (October 7 2009)

7 Iker Spozio, *Morning* (2010)
8 Izzy Young, *Tim Buckley Live At The Folklore Center, NYC, March 6 1967* liner notes (2009)
9 David Browne, *Dream Brother*
10 Andy Childs, *ZigZag* (September 1974)
11 Chris Nickson, *Folk Roots* (November 1998)

Chapter 3

1 Donovan, *The Hurdy-Gurdy Man*
2 Donovan, *The Hurdy-Gurdy Man*
3 Stuart Grundy, John Tobler, *The Record Producers*
4 Joe Boyd, *White Bicycles*
5 Ken Hunt, *Swing 51* (August 1979)
6 Andy Farquarson, *Guardian* (October 22 1999)
7 Pat Gilbert (ed), *The Mojo Collection*
8 Pat Gilbert (ed), *The Mojo Collection*
9 Andy Farquarson, *Guardian* (May 14 1999)
10 John Ingham, *Rolling Stone* (December 7 1972)

Chapter 4

1 Franz A. Matzner, allaboutjazz.com (January 6 2009)
2 Franz A. Matzner, allaboutjazz.com (January 6 2009)
3 Franz A. Matzner, allaboutjazz.com (January 6 2009)
4 Mike Jahn, *New York Times* (December 4 1968)
5 Jason Weiss, *Always In Trouble*
6 *The Holy Modal Rounders ... Bound To Loose* (Badbird Films 2006)

7   Franz A. Matzner, allaboutjazz.com
     (January 6 2009)
8   thefugs.com
9   Jason Weiss, *Always In Trouble*
10 Jason Weiss, *Always In Trouble*

Chapter 5
1   Andy Childs, *ZigZag* (September
     1974)
2   Richie Unterberger, *Eight Miles High*
3   Richie Unterberger, *Eight Miles High*
4   Richie Unterberger, *Urban Spacemen
     And Wayfaring Strangers*
5   Richie Unterberger, *Urban Spacemen
     And Wayfaring Strangers*
6   Ben Fong Torres, *Rolling Stone*
     (February 1 1969)
7   Richie Unterberger, *Urban Spacemen
     And Wayfaring Strangers*
8   Mike Fornatale, *Shindig!* (December
     2007)
9   Jeff Tamarkin, *Got A Revolution!*
10 Jud Cost, *Oar* liner notes (1999)
11 Lester Bangs, *Creem* (December
     1971)
12 Mike Jahn, *New York Times*
     (December 4 1968)
13 Lahri Bond, *Dirty Linen*
     (February/March 1994)
14 Kees Van Der Lely, rockmusic.com
     (1997)
15 Jeanette Leech, *Shindig!* (May/June
     2009)

Chapter 6
1   Simon Nicol, fairportconvention.com
2   Karl Dallas, *Melody Maker* (April
     1968)
3   Stuart Grundy, John Tobler, *The
     Record Producers*
4   Barney Hoskins, *Uncut* (February
     2010)

5   *Strangely Strange And Oddly Normal*
     (2007 documentary)
6   *Strangely Strange And Oddly Normal*
     (2007 documentary)
7   John Peel, Sheila Ravenscroft,
     Margrave Of The Marshes
8   Patrick Dean, *Yorkshire Evening Post*
     (January 1970)
9   Nigel Cross, *Ask Me No Questions*
     liner notes (2005)
10 Richard Morton Jack, *Record
     Collector* (August 2007)
11 Richard Morton Jack, *Record
     Collector* (August 2007)
12 Richard Morton Jack, *Record
     Collector* (August 2007)

Chapter 7
1   Grahame Hood, *Empty Pocket Blues*
2   Phil McMullen, *Ptolemaic Terrascope*
     (1990)
3   Richard Morton Jack, *Record
     Collector* (April 2005)

Chapter 8
1   Allan Brown, *Inside The Wicker Man*
2   Phil Milstein, *Ugly Things* (2001)
3   Phil Milstein, *Ugly Things* (2001)
4   Michaela Williams, *New York Times*
     (April 6 1969)
5   David Buckley, *Dream Brother*

Chapter 9
1   Michael Moll, folkworld.de (June
     2000)
2   Jason Gross, furious.com/perfect
     (August 2008)
3   Jean-Pierre Lantin, *Actuel* (January
     1973)
4   Nina Johansen, Rune Walle,
     Dedicated To The Bird We Love liner
     notes (2006)

5   Nina Johansen, Rune Walle,
    Dedicated To The Bird We Love liner
    notes (2006)

Chapter 10
1   Richard Morton Jack, *Record
    Collector* (April 2005)
2   Richard Morton Jack, *Record
    Collector* (April 2005)

Chapter 11
1   Richie Unterberger, *Record Collector*
    (August 2005)
2   Richie Unterberger, *Record Collector*
    (August 2005)

Chapter 12
1   *Melody Maker* (March 28 1970)
2   Steve Turner, *Beat Instrumental*
    (February 1971)
3   Steve Turner, *Beat Instrumental*
    (February 1971)
4   Harry Doherty, *Melody Maker*
    (November 1975)
5   Lester Bangs, *Who Put The Bomp*
    (Summer 1971)
6   Richard Cromelin, *Rolling Stone*
    (February 1972)

Chapter 13
1   John Robb, *Punk Rock: An Oral
    History*
2   John Robb, *Punk Rock: An Oral
    History*

Chapter 14
1   Gavin Martin, *New Musical Express*
    (January 14 1984)
2   Len Brown, *New Musical Express*
    (July 1988)
3   Dave Zimmer, *BAM* (February 1986)
4   Blake Gumprecht, *Alternative*

America (Winter 1983)
5   Peter Leibik, *Eugene Magazine* (May
    1980)
6   David Keenan, *The Wire* (November
    2001)
7   Edwin Pouncey, *The Wire* (April
    2004)
8   Edwin Pouncey, *The Wire* (April
    2004)
9   John Trubee, *Spin* (September 1985)
10 John Trubee, *Spin* (September 1985)
11 John Trubee, *Spin* (September 1985)
12 brainwashed.com (undated)
13 Derek Walmsley, *The Wire* (March
    2009)
14 Derek Walmsley, *The Wire* (March
    2009)
15 Matt Ashare, *Boston Phoenix*
    (January 30 2003)
16 Greg Kot, *Rolling Stone* (May 30
    1996)
17 Sean O'Hagan, *Observer* (November
    17 2002)
18 Ben Thompson, *Independent* (May
    11 1997)
19 Mark Kemp, *Option* (March 1994)
20 Rob Hughes, *Uncut* (January 2002)

Chapter 15
1   Phil McMullen, *Ptolemaic Terrascope*
    (1999)
2   Phil McMullen, *Ptolemaic Terrascope*
    (1999)

Chapter 16
1   David Keenan, *The Wire* (August
    2003)
2   Brian Rademaekers, *Arthur* (July 2009)
3   Stewart Gardiner, *Plan B*
    (September/October 2004)
4   Ned Raggett, *Loose Lips Sink Ships*
    (Autumn 2005)

5 David Keenan, *The Wire* (August 2003)
6 David Keenan, *The Wire* (August 2003)
7 David Keenan, *The Wire* (August 2003)

Chapter 17

1 Tony Dale, *Ptolemaic Terrascope* (September 1999)
2 Tony Dale, *Ptolemaic Terrascope* (September 1999)
3 Tony Dale, *Ptolemaic Terrascope* (September 1999)
4 Jennifer Kelly, popmatters.com (August 9 2006)
5 Cian Traynor, seewhatyouhear.com (May 31 2008)
6 Pat Gilbert (ed), *The Mojo Collection*
7 tinymixtapes.com (January 2006)
8 Sophie Harris, *Loose Lips Sink Ships* (Summer 2004)
9 Alexis Swerdloff, *Papermag* (March 2008)
10 Francis May Morgan, *Plan B* (September/October 2004)
11 Marc Masters, *The Wire* (January 2005)
12 Francis May Morgan, *Plan B* (September/October 2004)
13 Sophie Harris, *Loose Lips Sink Ships* (Summer 2004)
14 Sophie Harris, *Loose Lips Sink Ships* (Summer 2004)
15 Brian M. Palmer, *Thrasher* (April 2006)
16 Andrew Male, *Mojo* (December 2006)
17 Simon Reynolds, *The Wire* (July 2005)
18 Simon Reynolds, *The Wire* (July 2005)
19 Simon Reynolds, *The Wire* (July 2005)
20 Tyler Wilcox, junkmedia.com (April 26 2007)
21 Andrew Male, *Mojo* (December 2006)
22 Tyler Wilcox, junkmedia.com (February 21 2005)

Chapter 18

1 Alec Hanley Bemis, *New York Times* (December 12 2004)
2 Imran Ahmed, *New Musical Express* (November 8 2003)
3 Marc Masters, *The Wire* (July 2004)
4 Marc Masters, *The Wire* (July 2004)
5 Sophie Heawood, *Plan B* (November 2005)
6 Sophie Harris, *Loose Lips Sink Ships* (Summer 2004)
7 George Zahora, splendidzine.com (2003)
8 Amanda Petrusich, pitchfork.com (April 15 2004)
9 Neil Spencer, *Observer* (December 31 2006)
10 Hartley Goldstein, pitchfork.com (February 12 2004)
11 Frances May Morgan, *Plan B* (June 2007)
12 hitquarters.com (September 15 2008)
13 Sophie Heawood, *Plan B* (November 2005)
14 Pat Thomas, Nat Russell, *Ptolemaic Terrascope* (2007)
15 *The Wire* (October 2007)
16 Michael Bonner, *Uncut* (February 2007)
17 John Robinson, *Uncut* (September 2009)
18 Craig Jenkins, *Prefix* (November 2009)
19 Hermione Hoby, *Observer* (October 18 2009)

20 Jennifer Kelly, splendidzine.com (2003)
21 Hermione Hoby, *Observer* (October 18 2009)
22 Alexis Petridis, *Guardian* (November 12 2004)
23 Frances May Organ, *Loose Lips Sink Ships* (Summer 2004)
24 Anne Hilde Neset, *The Wire* (April 2004)
25 Frances May Organ, *Loose Lips Sink Ships* (Summer 2004)
26 Everett True, *Plan B* (April 2007)
27 Simon Reynolds, *The Wire* (July 2005)
28 Simon Reynolds, *The Wire* (July 2005)
29 Daniel Spicer, *Plan B* (December 2005)
30 Neil Kulkarni, *Plan B* (September 2007)
31 Marc Masters, *The Wire* (January 2005)
32 Frances May Morgan, *Plan B* (September/October 2004)
33 Sophie Harris, *Loose Lips Sink Ships* (Summer 2004)
34 Frances May Morgan, *Plan B* (September/October 2004)
35 Rob Young, *The Wire* (November 2006)
36 Rob Young, *The Wire* (November 2006)
37 Erik Davis, *Arthur* (Winter 2006)
38 Erik Davis, *Arthur* (Winter 2006)
39 Sophie Heawood, *Times* (February 20 2010)
40 Jude Rogers, *Guardian* (May 10 2010)
41 naturalismo.wordpress.com (July 22 2009)

Chapter 20

1 David Keenan, *The Wire* (May 2005)
2 Brad Rose, foxydigitalis.com (June 2005)
3 Jennifer Kelly, splendidzine.com (2005)
4 Jennifer Kelly, splendidzine.com (2005)
5 Jennifer Kelly, splendidzine.com (2005)

Chapter 21

1 Cory Card, foxydigitalis.com (April 2007)
2 Phil McMullen, terrascope.co.uk (December 2009)
3 Jeanette Leech, *Shindig!* (January/February 2008)

Bibliography

Boyd, Joe *White Bicycles: Making Music In The 1960s* (Serpent's Tail 2007)

Brocken, Michael *The English Folk Revival 1944-2002* (Ashgate 2003)

Brown, Allan *Inside The Wicker Man* (Sidgwick & Jackson 2000)

Browne, David *Dream Brother: The Lives And Music Of Jeff & Tim Buckley* (Fourth Estate 2001)

Charters, Ann (ed) *The Portable Beat Reader* (Penguin 2006)

Collins, Shirley *America Over The Water* (SAF Publishing 2004)

Cope, Julian *Krautrocksampler* (Head Heritage 1995)

Dukoff, Lauren *Family* (Chronicle 2009)

English Folk Dance And Song Society *The Folk Handbook* (Backbeat 2007)

Gilbert, Pat (ed) *The MOJO Collection: The Ultimate Music Companion* (Canongate 2007)

Grundy, Stuart, and John Tobler, *The Record Producers* (BBC 1982)

Harper, Colin *Dazzling Stranger: Bert Jansch And The British Folk And Blues Revival* (Bloomsbury 2006)

Harper, Colin, and Trevor Hodgett *Irish Folk, Trad And Blues: A Secret History* (Cherry Red 2005)

Heylin, Clinton *No More Sad Refrains: The Life And Times Of Sandy Denny* (Helter Skelter 2000)

Hodgkinson, Will *The Ballad Of Britain* (Portico 2009)

Hood, Grahame *Empty Pocket Blues: The Life And Music Of Clive Palmer* (Helter Skelter 2008)

Jones, Mark *Bristol Folk: A Discographical History Of Bristol Folk Music In The 1960s And 1970s* (Bristol Folk Publications 2009)

Joynson, Vernon *Fuzz Acid And Flowers Revisited* (Borderline 2005)

Joynson, Vernon *The Tapestry Of Delights Revisited* (Borderline 2006)

Kotsopoulos, Nikos (ed) *Krautrock: Cosmic Rock And Its Legacy* (Black Dog 2009)

Laing, Dave, Karl Dallas, Robin Denselow, and Robert Shelton *The Electric Muse: The Story Of Folk Into Rock* (Eyre Methuen 1975)

Larkin, Colin (ed) *The Guinness Who's Who Of Folk Music* (Square One 1993)

Leitch, Donovan *The Hurdy-Gurdy Man* (Century 2005)

Loog Oldham, Andrew *Stoned* (Vintage 2001)

Lundborg, Patrick (ed) *The Acid Archives* (Lysergia 2006)

McDevitt, Chas *Skiffle: The Definitive Inside Story* (Robson 1997)

Morton Jack, Richard (ed) *Galactic Ramble* (Foxcote 2009)

Napier-Bell, Simon *Black Vinyl, White Powder* (Ebury 2007)

Paytress, Mark *Bolan: The Rise And Fall Of A 20th Century Superstar* (Omnibus 2006)

Reynolds, Simon *Rip It Up And Start Again: Postpunk 1978–1984* (Faber 2006)

Robb, John *Punk Rock: An Oral History* (Ebury 2006)

Roberts, Andy *Albion Dreaming: A Popular History Of LSD In Britain* (Marshall Cavendish 2008)

Rotolo, Suze *A Freewheelin' Time: A Memoir Of Greenwich Village In The Sixties* (Aurum 2009)

Savage, Jon *England's Dreaming: The Sex Pistols And Punk Rock* (Faber 2005)

Stringfellow, Tony *The Wizard's Gown – Rewoven: Beneath The Glitter Of Marc Bolan* (Breeze Hayward 2007)

Sweers, Britta *Electric Folk: The Changing Face Of English Traditional Music* (OUP 2005)

Tamarkin, Jeff *Got A Revoluton!: The Turbulent Flight Of Jefferson Airplane* (Atria 2003) Underwood, Lee *Tim Buckley Remembered* (Backbeat 2006)

Unterberger, Richie *Eight Miles High: Folk-rock's Flight From Haight-Ashbury To Woodstock* (Backbeat 2003)

Unterberger, Richie *Turn! Turn! Turn! The 60s Folk-rock Revolution* (Backbeat 2002)

Unterberger, Richie *Urban Spacemen And Wayfaring Strangers: Overlooked Innovators And Eccentric Visionaries Of 1960s Rock* (Backbeat 2000)

Weiss, Jason *Always in Trouble: An Oral History of ESP-Disk', the Most Outrageous Record Label in America* (TBA 2011)

Welch, Chris & Napier-Bell, Simon *Bolan: Born To Boogie* (Plexus 2008)

Whittaker, Adrian (ed) *Be Glad: An Incredible String Band Compendium* (Helter Skelter 2008)

Index

Acknowledgements

Jawbone Press have been brilliant to deal with and extremely patient. Thomas Jerome Seabrook, my editor, was a huge source of support throughout the process and it's safe to say I couldn't have done it without him. Jon Mills, Mark Brend, Nigel Osborne, and Kevin Becketti should also be singled out for their belief in the project and hard work on its behalf.

Hearty thanks go to each of my interviewees. The time I spent conducting the interviews was one of the most fantastic periods of my life; everyone was so honest and warm, generous both in spirit and the time they took to share their experiences.

Some went even further. It's always an especial privilege to be invited into someone's home, and for that I thank Ian A. Anderson, Vashti Bunyan, Shirley Collins, David Costa, Bonnie Dobson, Sonja Kristina, Clive Palmer, Serafina Steer, and David Tibet. Moreover, Bonnie gave me some scrumptious homemade jam and David generously filled in the empty spots in my Current 93 collection; my continued friendship with both of them has been a joy. Jennifer Lewis and Angela Strange insisted on buying lunch for me in Oxford; Sam Genders wouldn't let me pick up the tab in a South London café. Andy Cabic, Alasdair Roberts, and The Kittiwakes were not only kind enough to take the time at a gig to speak to me, but so thoughtful that each put me on a guest list too. David John Sheppard offered me sage words of advice, not least "this will take over your life, you know". Steven Collins cheered me up after I found out I'd been pick-pocketed and lent me £20 to get home. Sharron Kraus, Ellen Mary McGee, Phil McMullen, Michael Tanner, Emma Tricca, and Jane Weaver all gave their amazing warmth and friendship to me as well as enormous practical assistance.

I was beyond thrilled when Greg Weeks, whose music I had admired for years, agreed to write the foreword for this book. Moreover, his ongoing support for the project, right from the first time we made contact, was an early motivating factor for me.

I have not yet met some of my interviewees in person, having spoken via the wonders of modern technology, but I feel as if I have thanks to their unwavering and continued enthusiasm. To Kelli Ali, Margaret Ayre, Joshua Burkett, Judy Dyble, Mark Fry, Dan Ireton, Alison O'Donnell, Prydwyn, Timothy Renner, Clodagh Simonds, Jeff Tarlton, and all the fine members of United Bible Studies: your encouragement has meant the world and I really hope, one day, we shall chinwag in person.

I also wish to pay tribute to three people who sadly passed away during the writing of this book. Mike Evans of Mighty Baby, an early interviewee; Jack Rose, who I did not get to interview before his passing, to my eternal regret; and Tony Dale of Camera Obscura records. Tony offered moral support, humour and friendship as well as his considerable insight and knowledge, and I miss our chats more than I can say.

So much support came in to me. The staff at Research In Practice in Sheffield; the diligent posters of the Very Good Plus message board; *Shindig!* magazine, especially Andy Morten, Marco Rossi, and Richard S Jones; the Abaton Book Company; and Jeffrey Lewis, for kindly agreeing the use of his lyrics in this book. Others passed on knowledge and contacts: Richard Allen, Alissa Anderson, Lauren Barley, John Byrne, Mike Cole, Geoff Dolman, Brendan Foreman, Will Hodgkinson, Mark Jones, Douglas McGowan, Mark Morris, Richard Morton Jack, Walter Nowicki, Ernesto De Pascale, Raül of Wah Wah Records, David Shook, Maximillian Spiegal, Malcolm Taylor, Pat Thomas, Kris Thompson, Martin Val Baker, Gerald Van Waes, Andy Votel, Jason Weiss, David Wells, Roger Williamson – thanks for being so accommodating and just all-around good eggs.

My family have been a rock for me throughout the years. I give thanks to all my aunts and uncles, to all my cousins, and especially to my Aunt Sheila, my Aunt Gladys, and my cousin Paul, who have seen me through some very difficult (and some very happy) times.

To friends: there's my Sheffield posse who bore the brunt of my tortured author *shtick* but never stopped believing that I could do it (and had a unnerving instinct about when I needed to go to the pub). Thank you Keith Archer, Katherine Bishop, Matthew Clark, Ian Cracknell, Andy George, Anita Hollinshead, Naomi Lewis, Barry and Kris McKeown, Debbie Rawlings, Gary Whittles – and especially Tim Hollinshead, Niklas Thoren, and Noshee Zameer, three of the most marvellous and supportive people anyone could hope to call friend.

Nearest and dearest, far and wide, offered sofas to sleep on, an ear to be bent and just their wonderful companionship: Suzanne Bird (and my Godsons Elliot and Gabriel), Rupert Cook, Stephen Drennan, Tracey England, Stuart Evers, Alex and Helen Farebrother-Naylor, George Julian, Lizzie Lidster, Craig Mills, Alix and Malcolm McKenzie, Jude Rogers, Oliver Shepherd, the Tucker family, and, above all, my soul sister, Kathryn Cook.

To Simon Tucker: thanks for everything.

I dedicate this book to my mum and my dad, whom I miss every day.

Jeanette Leech
September 2010

Picture Credits

The pictures used in this come from the following people, and we are grateful for their help. We have tried to contact all copyright holders, but if you feel there has been a mistaken attribution, please contact the publisher. Where there is more than one picture on a page, credits are listed clockwise from top left. **2** Alissa Anderson; **6** Brian Shuel/Redferns; Michael Ochs Archives/Getty Images; **7** Keith Morris Estate/Redferns; **8** Jan Persson/Redferns; **9** Vashti Bunyan; Tom Rapp; Christopher Beaver; **10** Jay Myrdal; Ian A. Anderson; Tony Kite; **11** Giorgio Cipriani; Alison O'Donnell; Collie Ryan; **12** Bobb Trimble; Simon Ferguson; Ruth Bayer; **13** Carin Sloan; pi; Erika Elder; **14** Barron Bixler; Alissa Anderson; **15** Howie Reeve; Daniel Daskivich; Alissa Anderson; **16** Alissa Anderson; **jacket back** Philip Ryalls/Redferns.

"Somewhere deep inside that mountain is the music of angels." MICHAEL TYACK.

Other books in this series:

MILLION DOLLAR
BASH: BOB DYLAN,
THE BAND, AND THE
BASEMENT TAPES
by Sid Griffin

HOT BURRITOS:
THH TRUE STORY OF
THE FLYING BURRITO
BROTHERS
by John Einarson with
Chris Hillman

BOWIE IN BERLIN:
A NEW CAREER IN A
NEW TOWN
by Thomas Jerome
Seabrook

BILL BRUFORD THE
AUTOBIOGRAPHY:
YES, KING CRIMSON,
EARTHWORKS, AND
MORE
by Bill Bruford

BEATLES FOR SALE:
HOW EVERYTHING
THEY TOUCHED
TURNED TO GOLD
by John Blaney

TO LIVE IS TO DIE:
THE LIFE AND DEATH
OF METALLICA'S CLIFF
BURTON
by Joel McIver

MILLION DOLLAR
LES PAUL: IN SEARCH
OF THE MOST
VALUABLE GUITAR IN
THE WORLD
by Tony Bacon

THE IMPOSSIBLE
DREAM: THE STORY
OF SCOTT WALKER
AND THE WALKER
BROTHERS
by Anthony Reynolds

JACK BRUCE:
COMPOSING
HIMSELF: THE
AUTHORISED
BIOGRAPHY
by Harry Shapiro

FOREVER CHANGES:
ARTHUR LEE AND THE
BOOK OF LOVE
by John Einarson

RETURN OF THE
KING: ELVIS PRESLEY'S
GREAT COMEBACK
by Gillian G. Gaar

A WIZARD, A TRUE
STAR: TODD
RUNDGREN IN THE
STUDIO
by Paul Myers

SHELTER FROM THE
STORM: BOB DYLAN'S
ROLLING THUNDER
YEARS
by Sid Griffin

Spring 2011:

WON'T GET FOOLED
AGAIN: THE WHO
FROM LIFEHOUSE TO
QUADROPHENIA
by Richie Unterberger

THE
RESURRECTION OF
JOHNNY CASH:
HURT, REDEMPTION,
AND AMERICAN
RECORDINGS
by Graeme Thomson

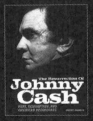